BABY BLUES **16** SCRAPBOOK

Dad to the Bone

Other Baby Blues® books from Andrews McMeel Publishing

Guess Who Didn't Take a Nap?
I Thought Labor Ended When the Baby Was Born
We Are Experiencing Parental Difficulties. . . Please Stand By
Night of the Living Dad
I Saw Elvis in My Ultrasound
One More and We're Outnumbered!
Check, Please. . .
threats, bribes & videotape
If I'm a Stay-At-Home Mom, Why Am I Always in the Car
Lift and Separate
I Shouldn't Have to Scream More Than Once!
Motherhood Is Not For Wimps
Baby Blues®: Unplugged

Treasuries

The Super-Absorbent Biodegradable Family-Size Baby Blues®
Baby Blues®: Ten Years and Still in Diapers
Butt-Naked Baby Blues®

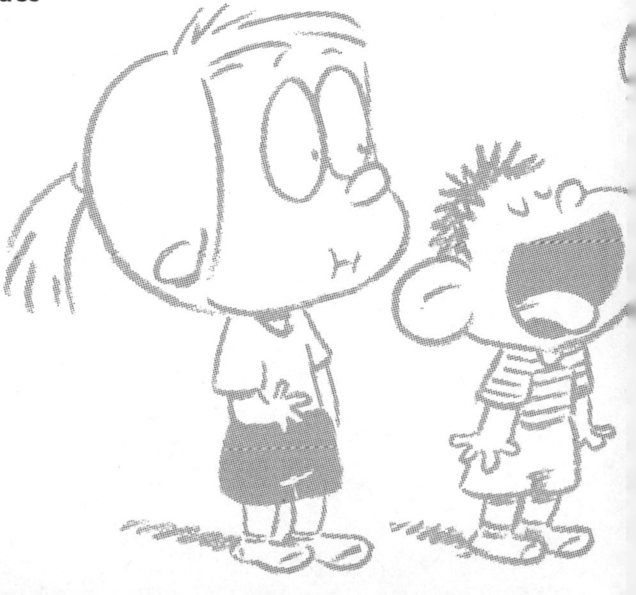

BABY BLUES 16 SCRAPBOOK

Dad to the Bone

by Rick Kirkman & Jerry Scott

Andrews McMeel
Publishing

Kansas City

Baby Blues® is syndicated internationally by King Features Syndicate, Inc. For information, write King Features Syndicate, Inc., 888 Seventh Avenue, New York, New York 10019.

Dad to the Bone copyright © 2002 by Baby Blues Partnership. All rights reserved. Printed in the United States of America. No part of this book may be used or reproduced in any manner whatsoever without written permission except in the case of reprints in the context of reviews. For information, write Andrews McMeel Publishing, an Andrews McMeel Universal company, 4520 Main Street, Kansas City, Missouri 64111.

02 03 04 05 06 BAH 10 9 8 7 6 5 4 3 2 1

ISBN: 0-7407-2670-6

Library of Congress Control Number: 2002103765

Find *Baby Blues* on the Web at
www.babyblues.com

──────── **ATTENTION: SCHOOLS AND BUSINESSES** ────────

Andrews McMeel books are available at quantity discounts with bulk purchase for educational, business, or sales promotional use. For information, please write to: Special Sales Department, Andrews McMeel Publishing, 4520 Main Street, Kansas City, Missouri 64111.

To Dick and Dolly, with love and laughter.
—J.S.

For Taylor, our first to leave the nest.
With love,
Your very proud dad
—R.K.

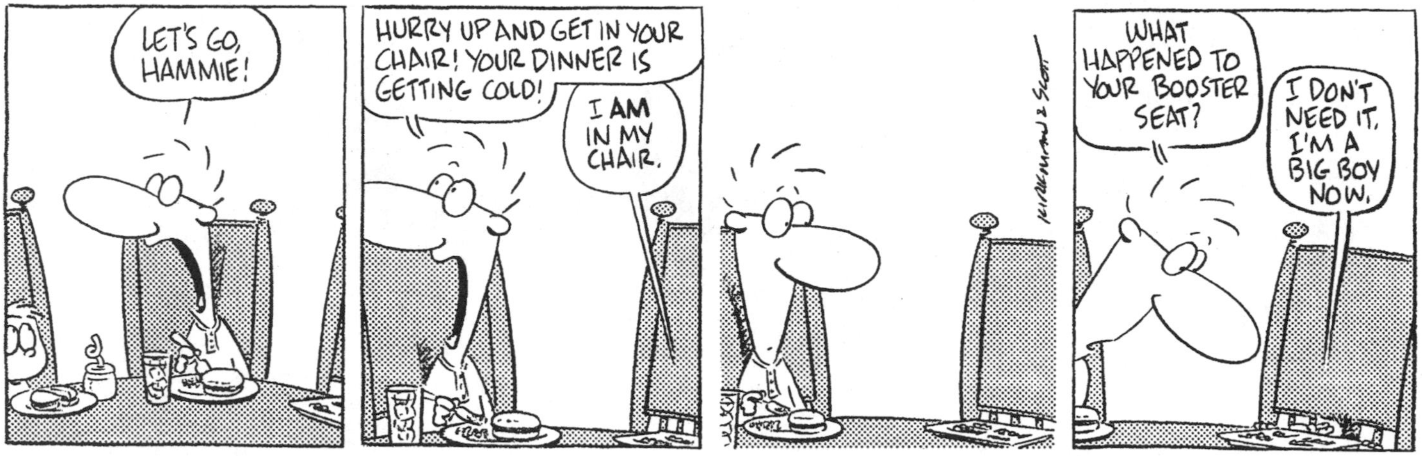
LET'S GO, HAMMIE!
HURRY UP AND GET IN YOUR CHAIR! YOUR DINNER IS GETTING COLD!
I AM IN MY CHAIR.
WHAT HAPPENED TO YOUR BOOSTER SEAT?
I DON'T NEED IT. I'M A BIG BOY NOW.

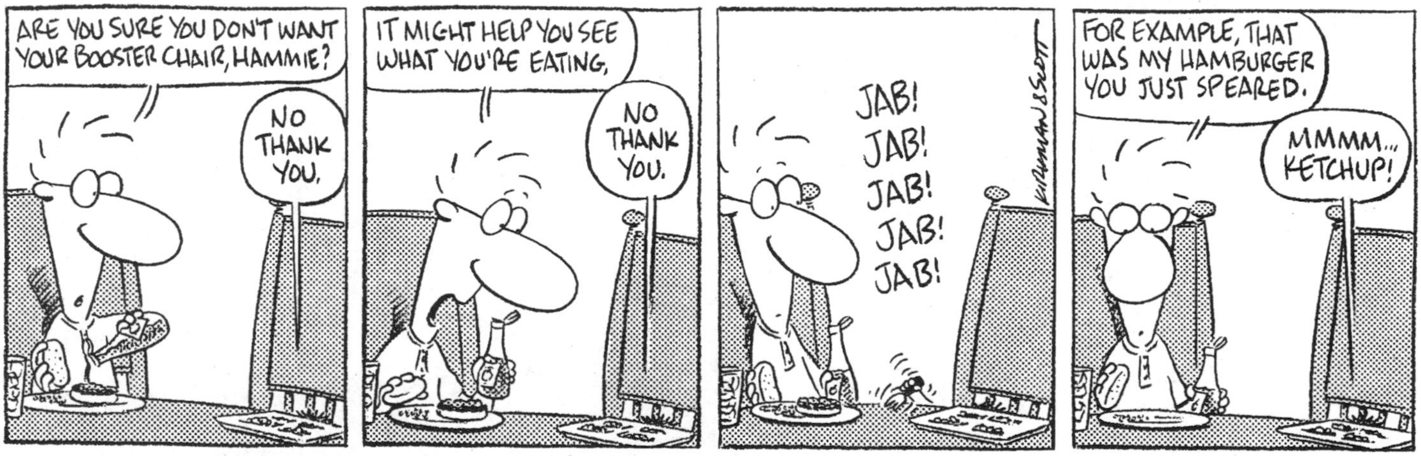
ARE YOU SURE YOU DON'T WANT YOUR BOOSTER CHAIR, HAMMIE?
NO THANK YOU.
IT MIGHT HELP YOU SEE WHAT YOU'RE EATING.
NO THANK YOU.
JAB! JAB! JAB! JAB! JAB!
FOR EXAMPLE, THAT WAS MY HAMBURGER YOU JUST SPEARED.
MMMM... KETCHUP!

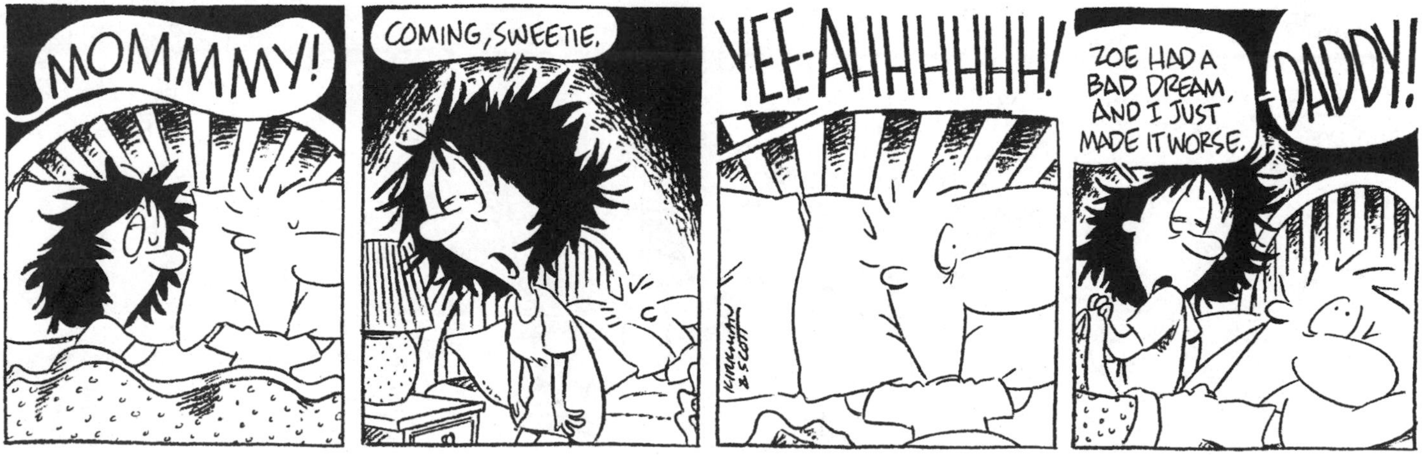
MOMMMY!
COMING, SWEETIE.
YEE-AHHHHHH!
ZOE HAD A BAD DREAM, AND I JUST MADE IT WORSE.
DADDY!

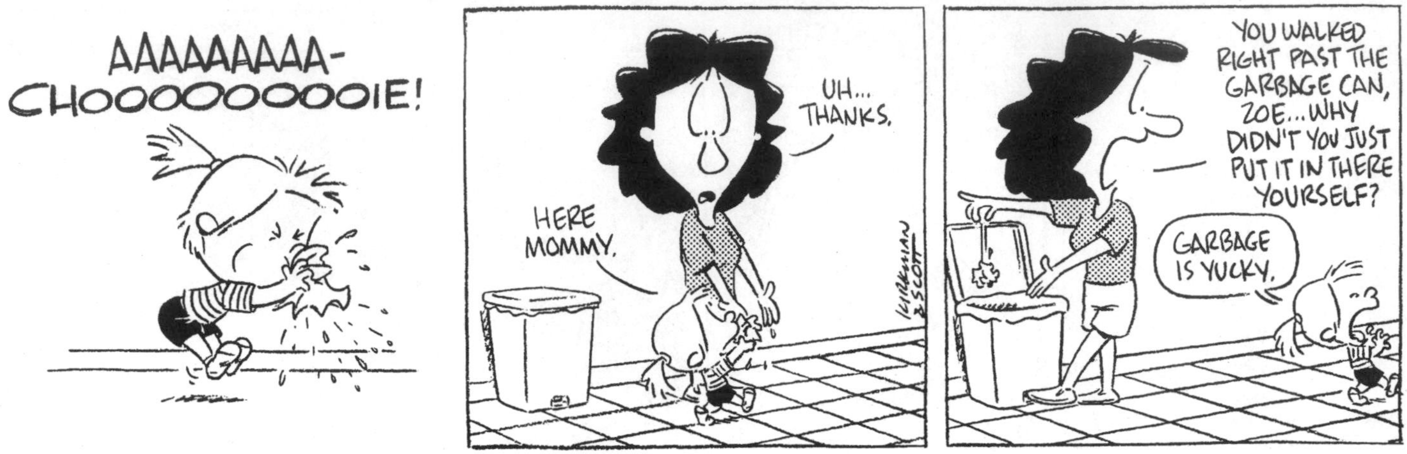
AAAAAAAAA-CHOOOOOOOOIE!
HERE MOMMY.
UH... THANKS.
KIRKMAN & SCOTT
YOU WALKED RIGHT PAST THE GARBAGE CAN, ZOE...WHY DIDN'T YOU JUST PUT IT IN THERE YOURSELF?
GARBAGE IS YUCKY.

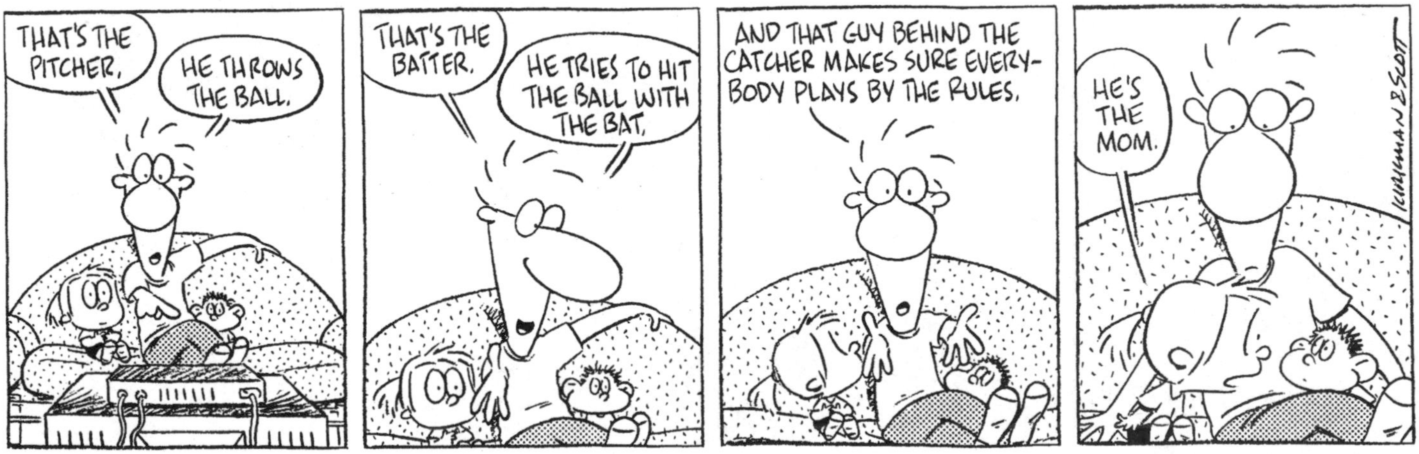
THAT'S THE PITCHER.
HE THROWS THE BALL.
THAT'S THE BATTER.
HE TRIES TO HIT THE BALL WITH THE BAT.
AND THAT GUY BEHIND THE CATCHER MAKES SURE EVERYBODY PLAYS BY THE RULES.
HE'S THE MOM.
KIRKMAN & SCOTT

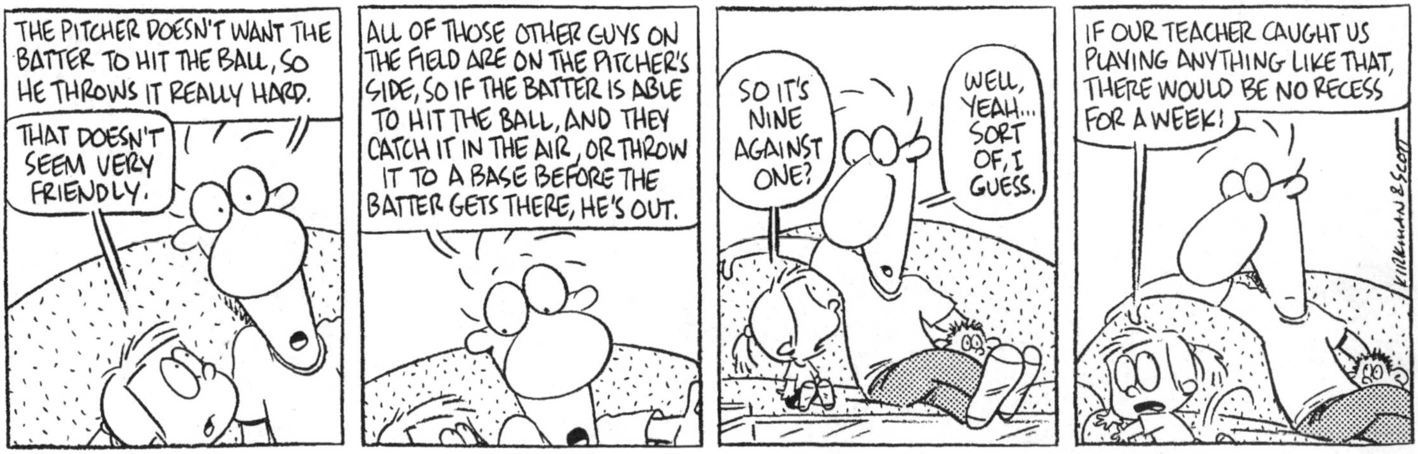
THE PITCHER DOESN'T WANT THE BATTER TO HIT THE BALL, SO HE THROWS IT REALLY HARD.
THAT DOESN'T SEEM VERY FRIENDLY.
ALL OF THOSE OTHER GUYS ON THE FIELD ARE ON THE PITCHER'S SIDE, SO IF THE BATTER IS ABLE TO HIT THE BALL, AND THEY CATCH IT IN THE AIR, OR THROW IT TO A BASE BEFORE THE BATTER GETS THERE, HE'S OUT.
SO IT'S NINE AGAINST ONE?
WELL, YEAH... SORT OF, I GUESS.
IF OUR TEACHER CAUGHT US PLAYING ANYTHING LIKE THAT, THERE WOULD BE NO RECESS FOR A WEEK!
KIRKMAN & SCOTT

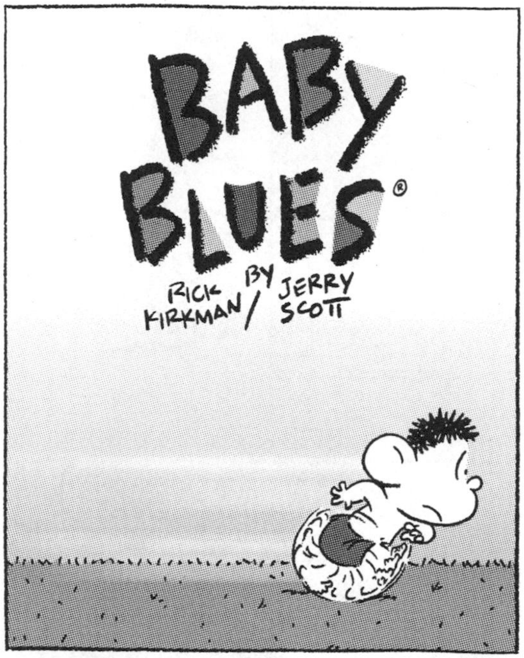
BABY BLUES®
BY RICK KIRKMAN / JERRY SCOTT

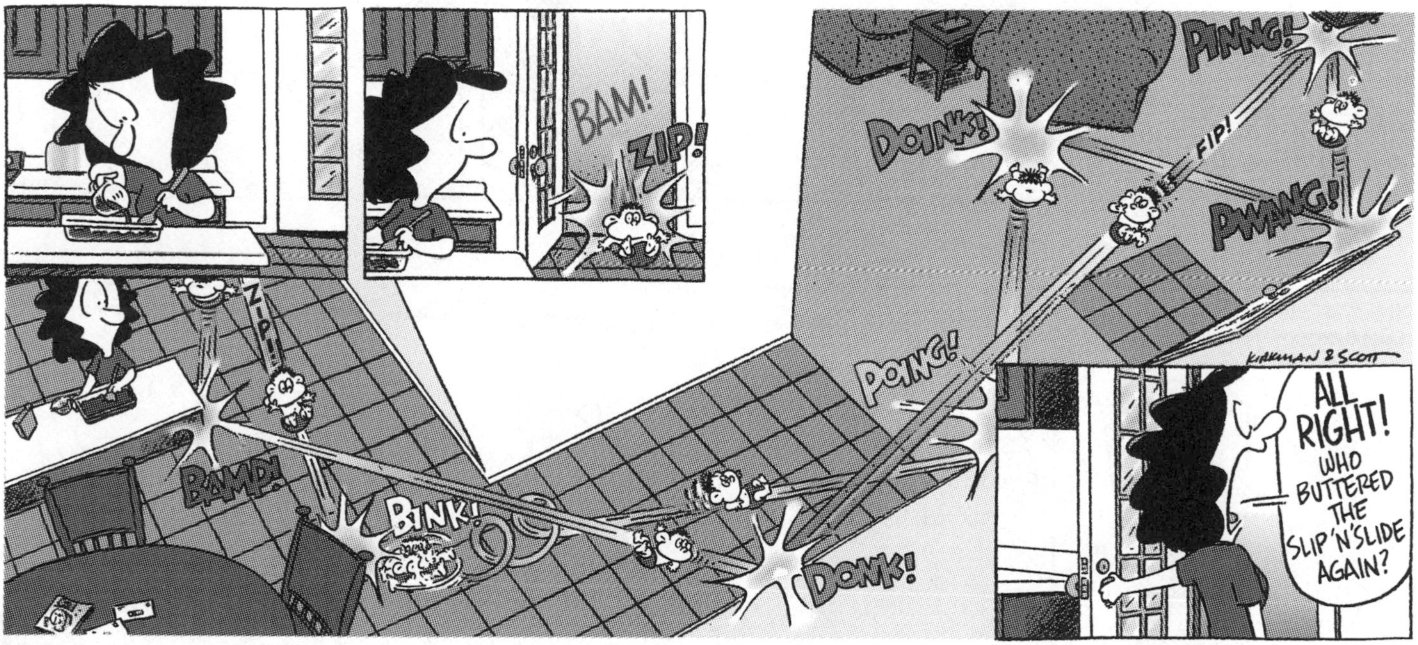
BAM!
ZIP!
ZIP!
BINK!
DONK!
POING!
DOINK!
FIP!
PINNG!
PWANG!
KIRKMAN & SCOTT
ALL RIGHT! WHO BUTTERED THE SLIP'N'SLIDE AGAIN?

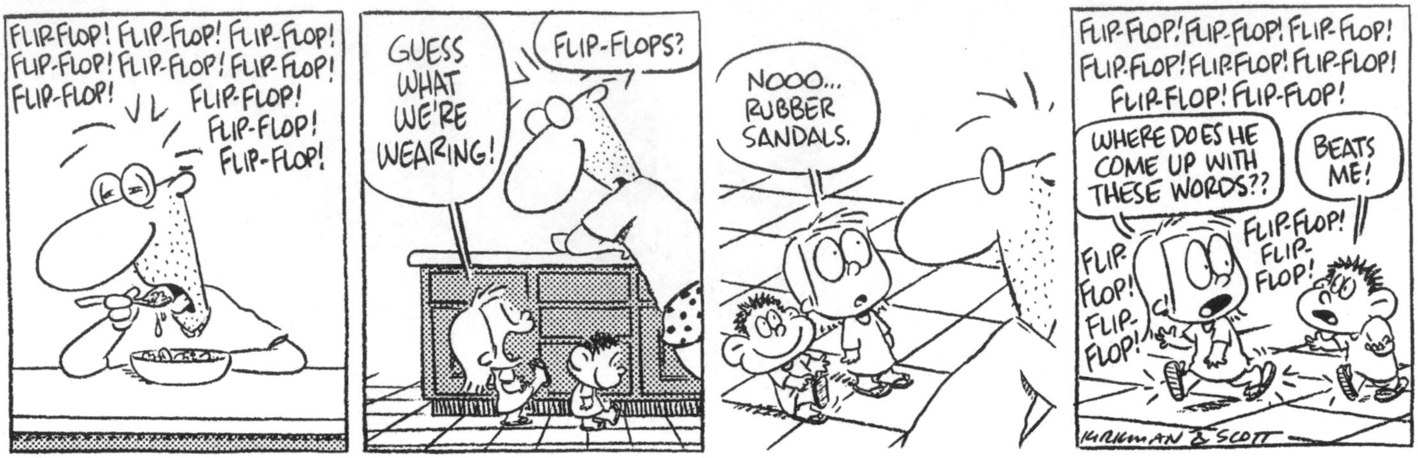
FLIP-FLOP! FLIP-FLOP! FLIP-FLOP! FLIP-FLOP! FLIP-FLOP! FLIP-FLOP! FLIP-FLOP! FLIP-FLOP! FLIP-FLOP! FLIP-FLOP!
GUESS WHAT WE'RE WEARING!
FLIP-FLOPS?
NOOO... RUBBER SANDALS.
FLIP-FLOP! FLIP-FLOP! FLIP-FLOP! FLIP-FLOP! FLIP-FLOP! FLIP-FLOP! FLIP-FLOP! FLIP-FLOP!
WHERE DOES HE COME UP WITH THESE WORDS??
BEATS ME!
FLIP-FLOP! FLIP-FLOP!
FLIP-FLOP! FLIP-FLOP!
KIRKMAN & SCOTT

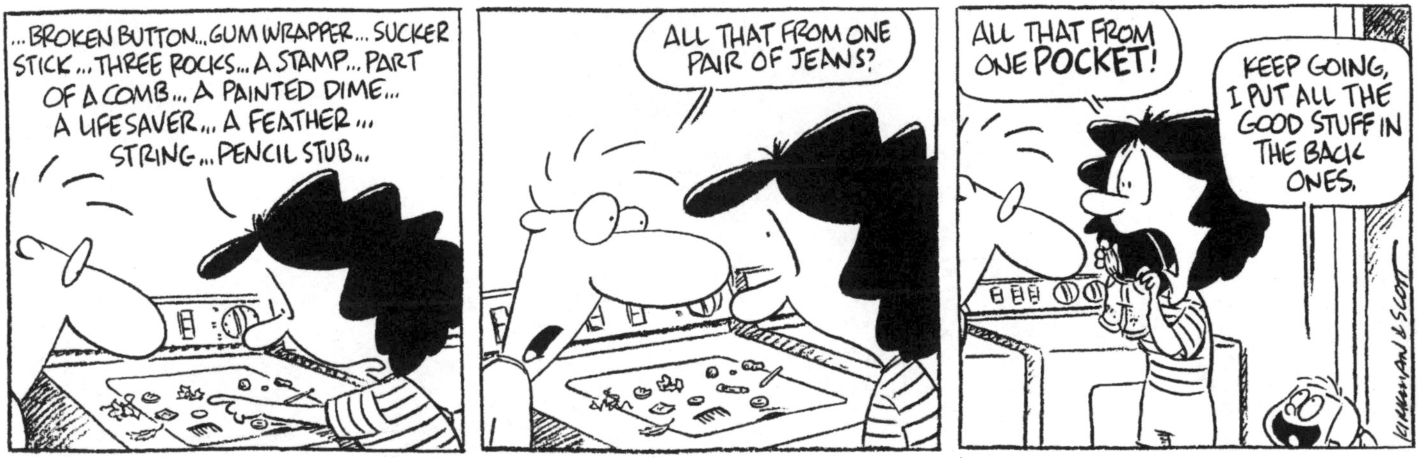
...BROKEN BUTTON...GUM WRAPPER... SUCKER STICK... THREE ROCKS... A STAMP... PART OF A COMB... A PAINTED DIME... A LIFESAVER... A FEATHER... STRING... PENCIL STUB...
ALL THAT FROM ONE PAIR OF JEANS?
ALL THAT FROM ONE **POCKET**!
KEEP GOING, I PUT ALL THE GOOD STUFF IN THE BACK ONES.
KIRKMAN & SCOTT

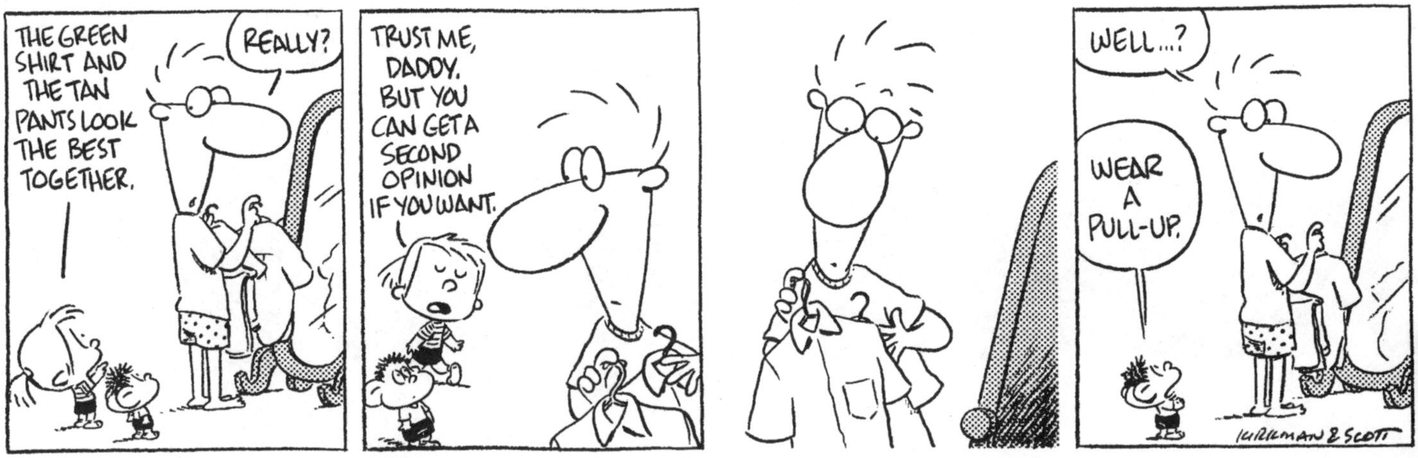
THE GREEN SHIRT AND THE TAN PANTS LOOK THE BEST TOGETHER.
REALLY?
TRUST ME, DADDY. BUT YOU CAN GET A SECOND OPINION IF YOU WANT.
WELL...?
WEAR A PULL-UP.
KIRKMAN & SCOTT

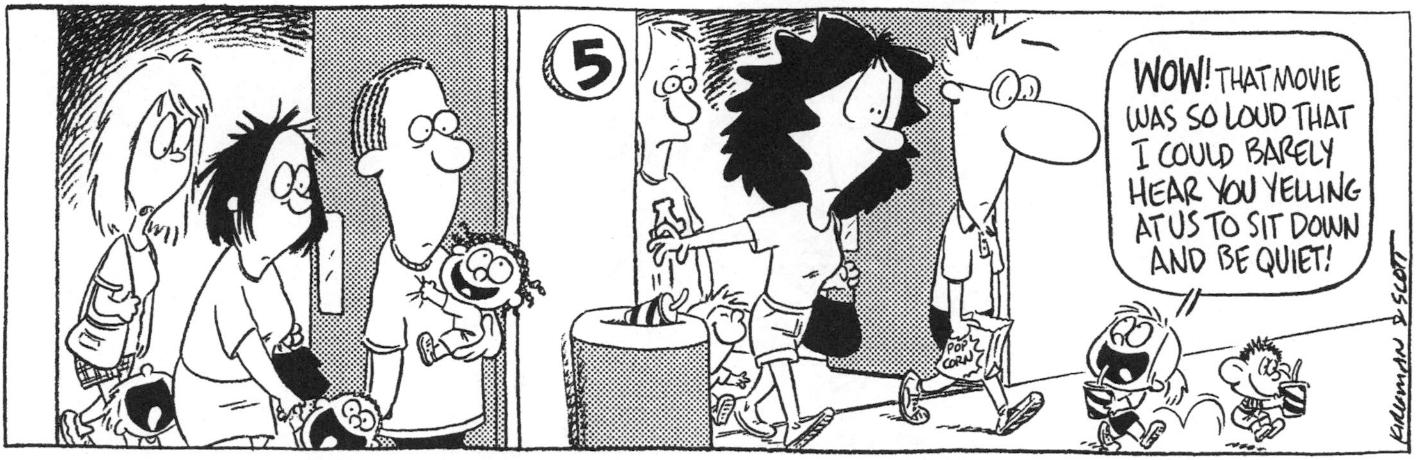
5
WOW! THAT MOVIE WAS SO LOUD THAT I COULD BARELY HEAR YOU YELLING AT US TO SIT DOWN AND BE QUIET!
POP CORN
KIRKMAN & SCOTT

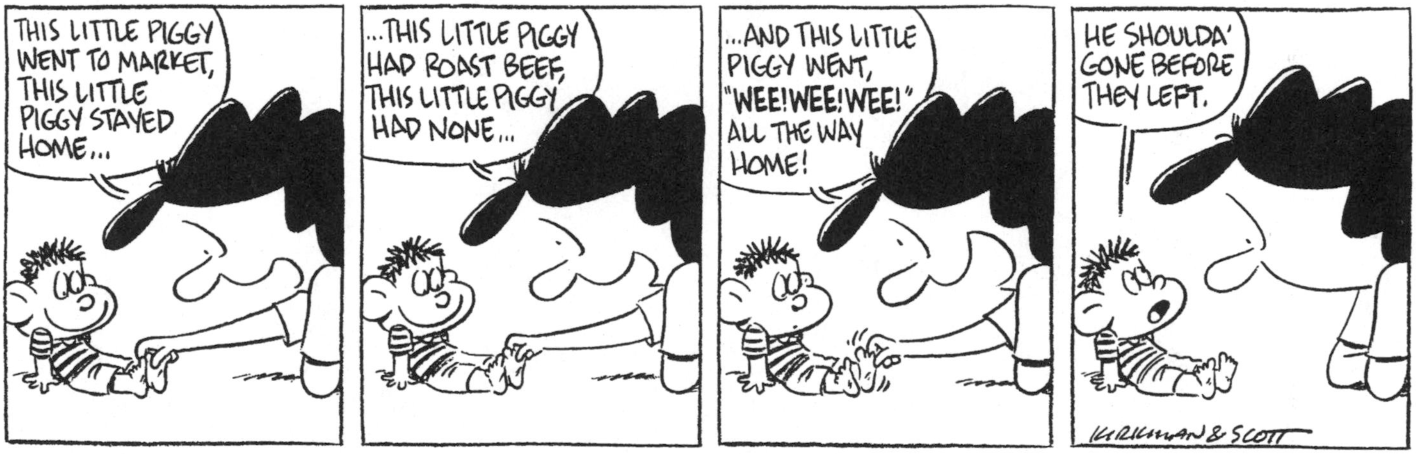
THIS LITTLE PIGGY WENT TO MARKET, THIS LITTLE PIGGY STAYED HOME...
...THIS LITTLE PIGGY HAD ROAST BEEF, THIS LITTLE PIGGY HAD NONE...
...AND THIS LITTLE PIGGY WENT, "WEE! WEE! WEE!" ALL THE WAY HOME!
HE SHOULDA' GONE BEFORE THEY LEFT.
KIRKMAN & SCOTT

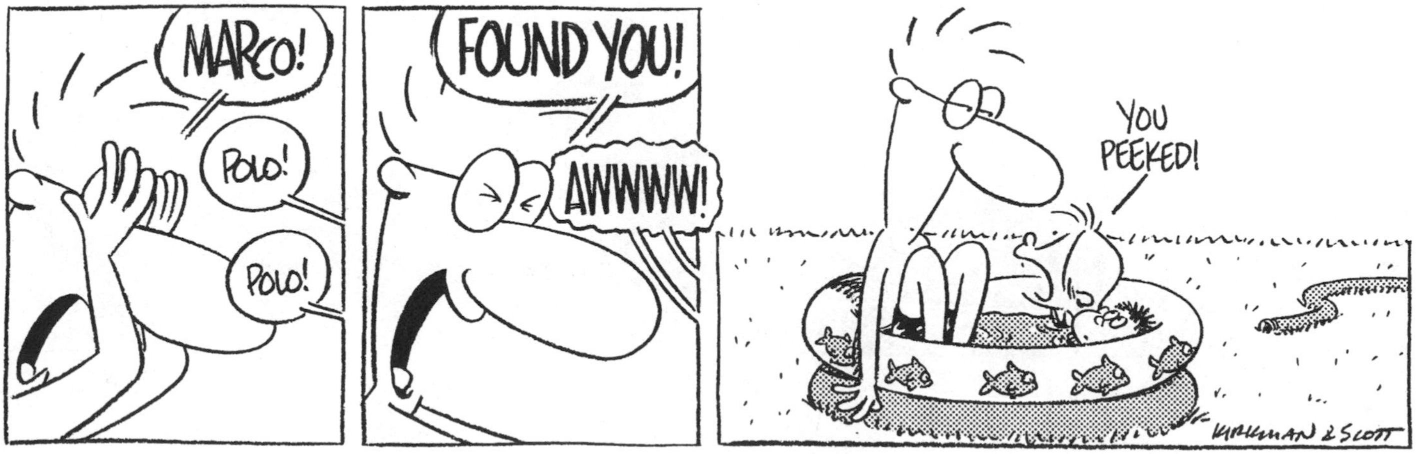
MARCO!
POLO!
POLO!
FOUND YOU!
AWWWW!
YOU PEEKED!
KIRKMAN & SCOTT

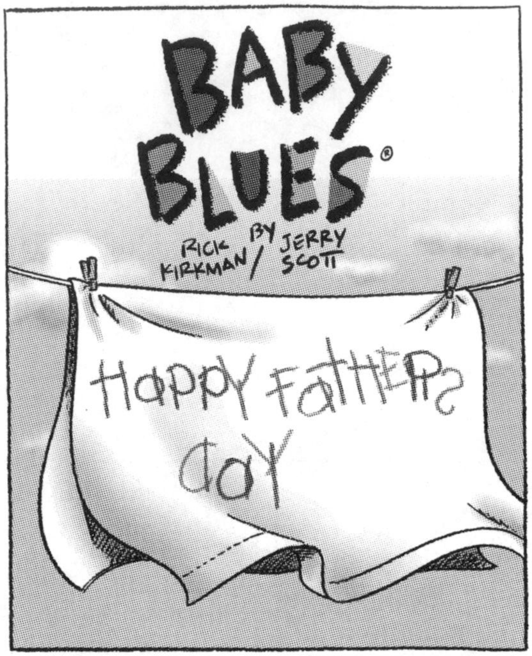
BABY BLUES®
BY RICK KIRKMAN / JERRY SCOTT
Happy Fatters day

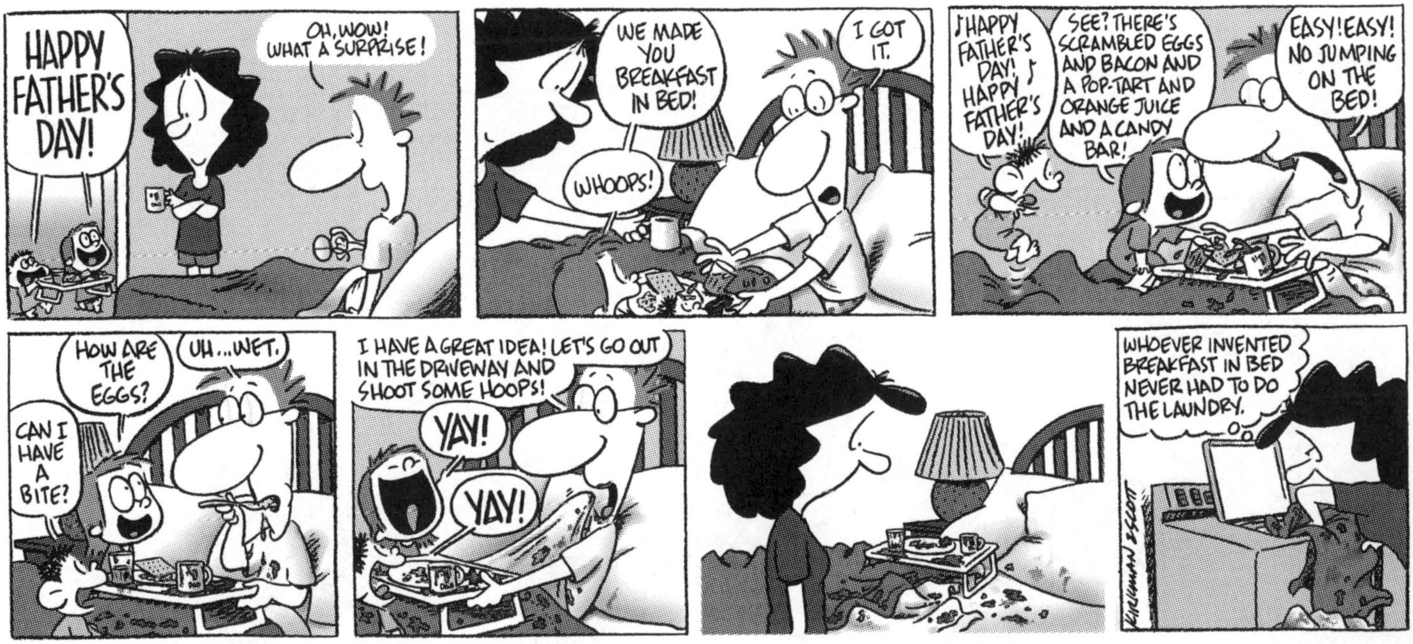
HAPPY FATHER'S DAY!
OH, WOW! WHAT A SURPRISE!
WE MADE YOU BREAKFAST IN BED!
WHOOPS!
I GOT IT.
♪HAPPY FATHER'S DAY! HAPPY FATHER'S DAY!♪
SEE? THERE'S SCRAMBLED EGGS AND BACON AND A POP-TART AND ORANGE JUICE AND A CANDY BAR!
EASY! EASY! NO JUMPING ON THE BED!
HOW ARE THE EGGS?
UH...WET.
CAN I HAVE A BITE?
I HAVE A GREAT IDEA! LET'S GO OUT IN THE DRIVEWAY AND SHOOT SOME HOOPS!
YAY!
YAY!
WHOEVER INVENTED BREAKFAST IN BED NEVER HAD TO DO THE LAUNDRY.
KIRKMAN & SCOTT

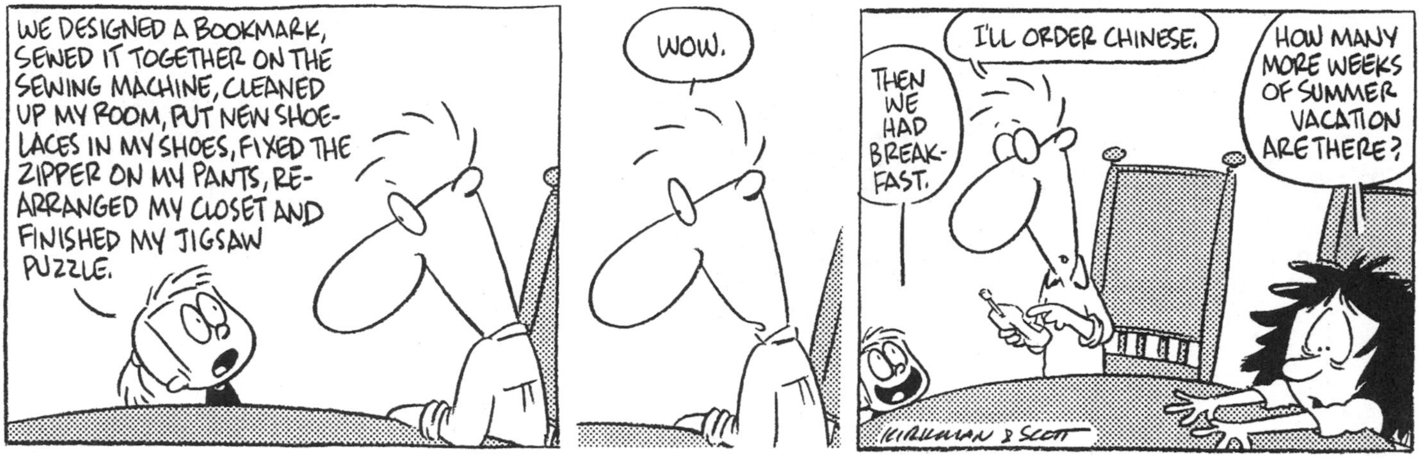
WE DESIGNED A BOOKMARK, SEWED IT TOGETHER ON THE SEWING MACHINE, CLEANED UP MY ROOM, PUT NEW SHOE-LACES IN MY SHOES, FIXED THE ZIPPER ON MY PANTS, RE-ARRANGED MY CLOSET AND FINISHED MY JIGSAW PUZZLE.
WOW.
THEN WE HAD BREAK-FAST.
I'LL ORDER CHINESE.
HOW MANY MORE WEEKS OF SUMMER VACATION ARE THERE?
KIRKMAN & SCOTT

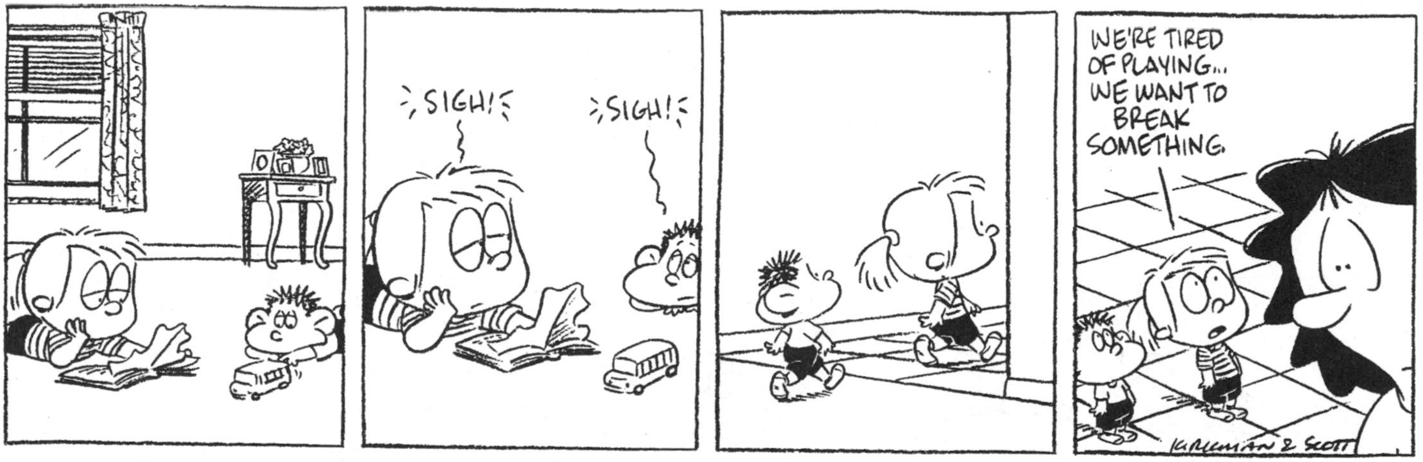
SIGH!
SIGH!
WE'RE TIRED OF PLAYING... WE WANT TO BREAK SOMETHING.
KIRKMAN & SCOTT

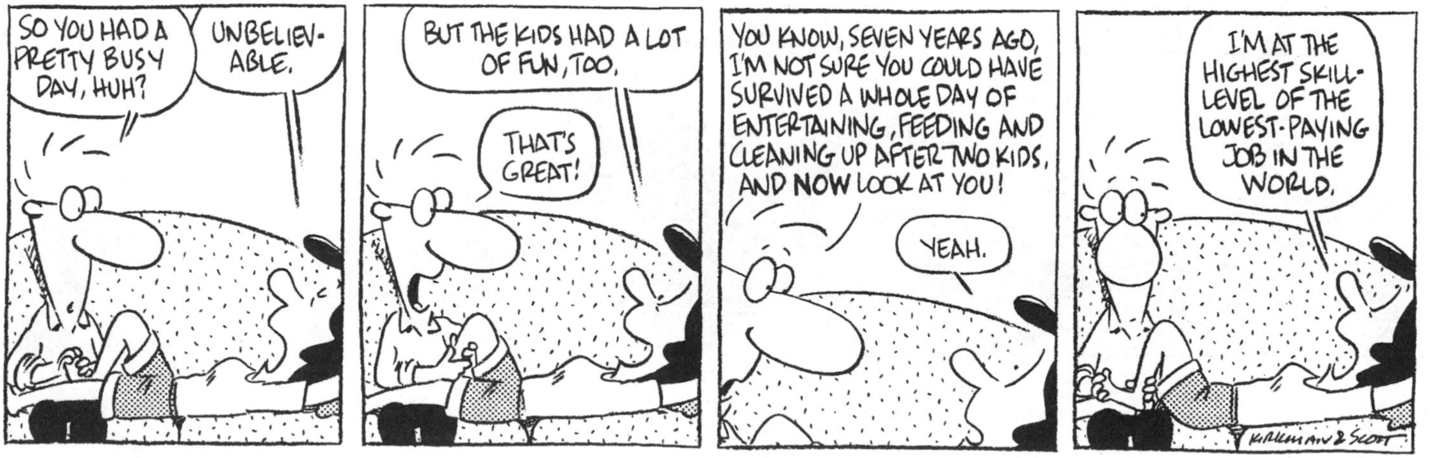
SO YOU HAD A PRETTY BUSY DAY, HUH?
UNBELIEV-ABLE.
BUT THE KIDS HAD A LOT OF FUN, TOO.
THAT'S GREAT!
YOU KNOW, SEVEN YEARS AGO, I'M NOT SURE YOU COULD HAVE SURVIVED A WHOLE DAY OF ENTERTAINING, FEEDING AND CLEANING UP AFTER TWO KIDS, AND NOW LOOK AT YOU!
YEAH.
I'M AT THE HIGHEST SKILL-LEVEL OF THE LOWEST-PAYING JOB IN THE WORLD.
KIRKMAN & SCOTT

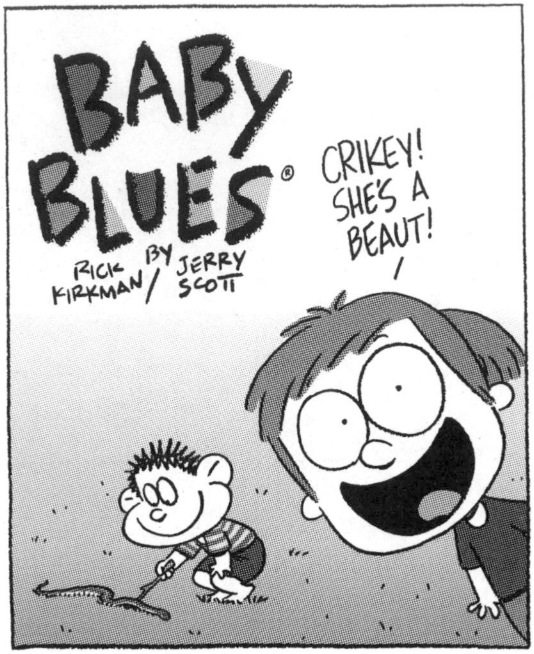
BABY BLUES®
BY RICK KIRKMAN / JERRY SCOTT
CRIKEY! SHE'S A BEAUT!

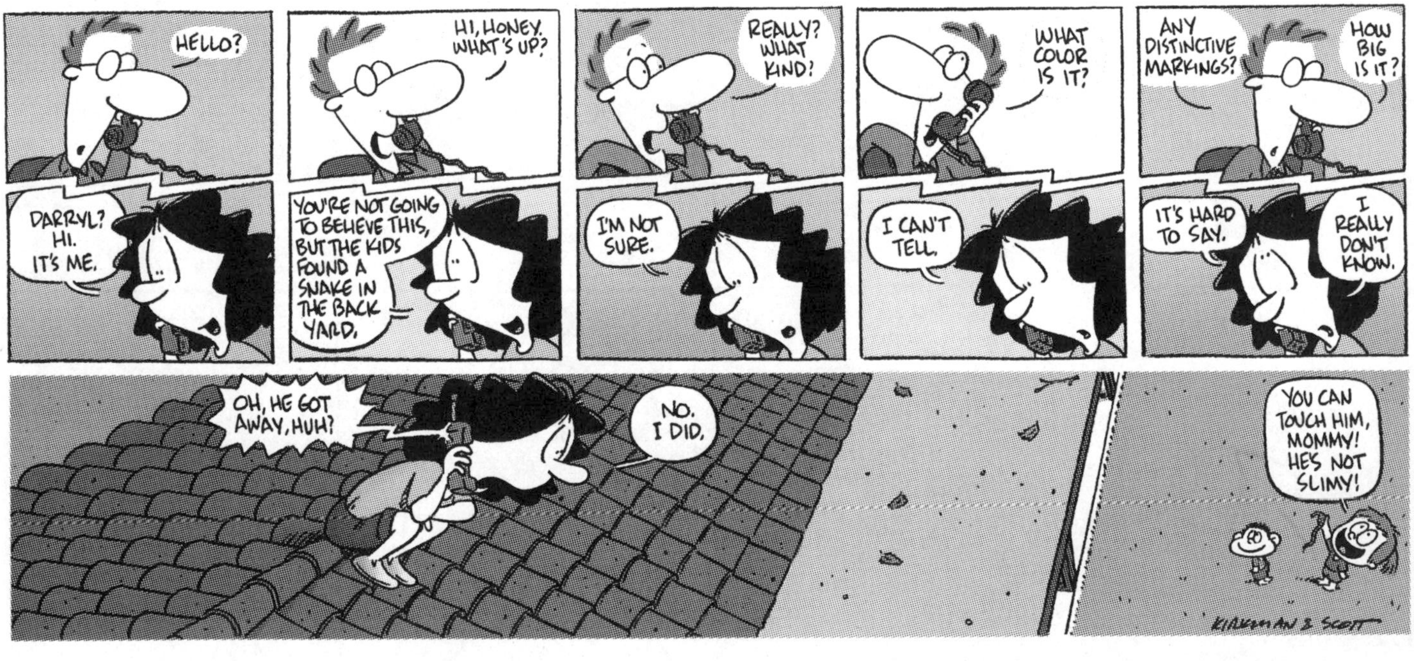
HELLO?
DARRYL? HI. IT'S ME.
HI, HONEY. WHAT'S UP?
YOU'RE NOT GOING TO BELIEVE THIS, BUT THE KIDS FOUND A SNAKE IN THE BACK YARD.
REALLY? WHAT KIND?
I'M NOT SURE.
WHAT COLOR IS IT?
I CAN'T TELL.
ANY DISTINCTIVE MARKINGS?
IT'S HARD TO SAY.
HOW BIG IS IT?
I REALLY DON'T KNOW.
OH, HE GOT AWAY, HUH?
NO. I DID.
YOU CAN TOUCH HIM, MOMMY! HE'S NOT SLIMY!
KIRKMAN & SCOTT

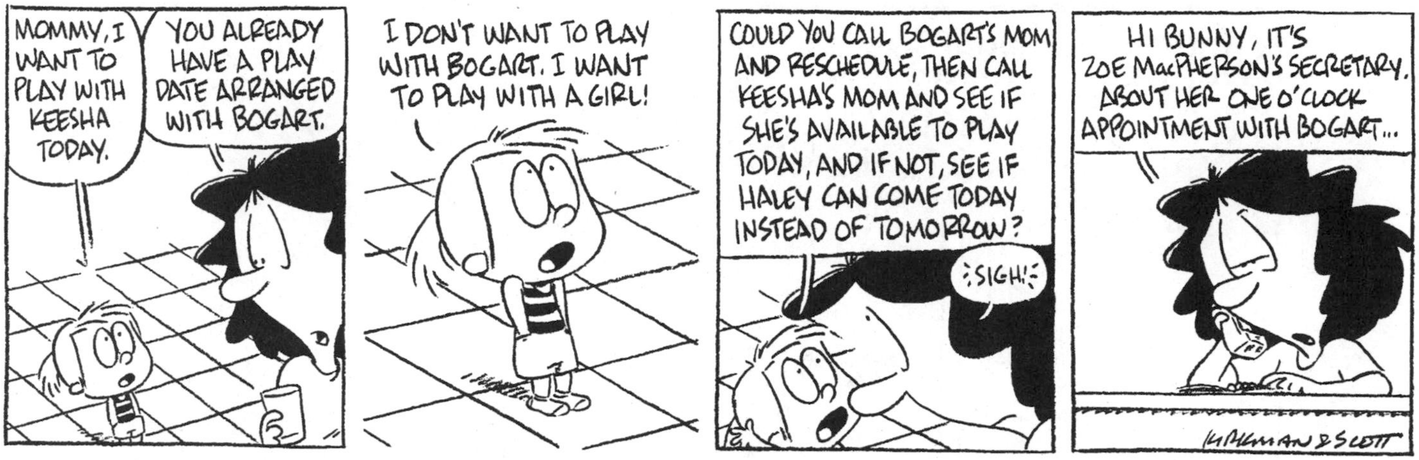
MOMMY, I WANT TO PLAY WITH KEESHA TODAY.
YOU ALREADY HAVE A PLAY DATE ARRANGED WITH BOGART.
I DON'T WANT TO PLAY WITH BOGART. I WANT TO PLAY WITH A GIRL!
COULD YOU CALL BOGART'S MOM AND RESCHEDULE, THEN CALL KEESHA'S MOM AND SEE IF SHE'S AVAILABLE TO PLAY TODAY, AND IF NOT, SEE IF HALEY CAN COME TODAY INSTEAD OF TOMORROW?
SIGH!
HI BUNNY, IT'S ZOE MacPHERSON'S SECRETARY. ABOUT HER ONE O'CLOCK APPOINTMENT WITH BOGART...
KIRKMAN & SCOTT

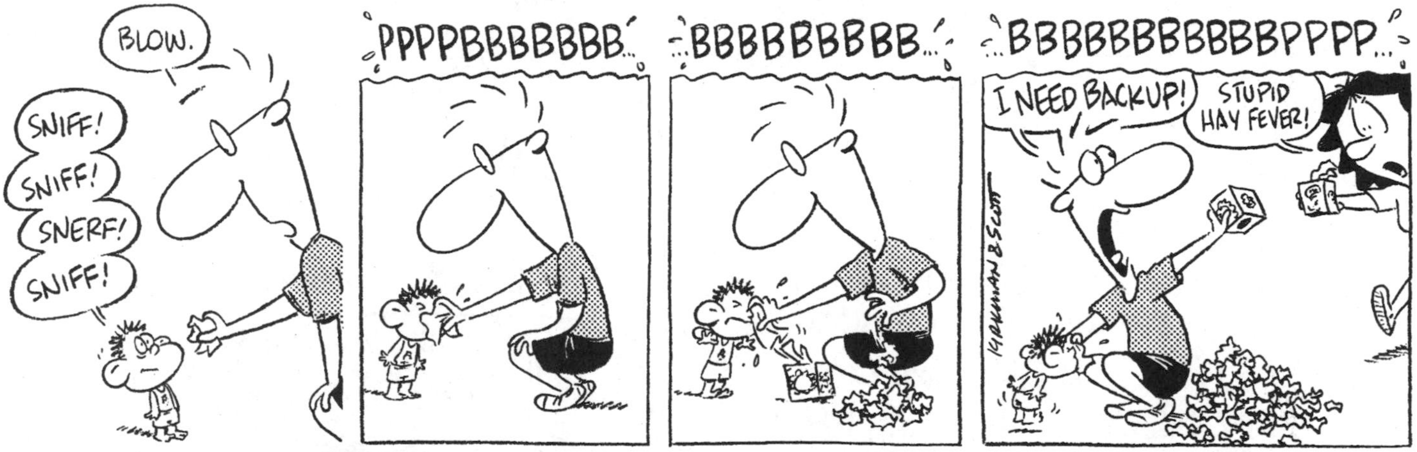
BLOW.
SNIFF!
SNIFF!
SNERF!
SNIFF!
PPPPBBBBBBB...
BBBBBBBBB...
BBBBBBBBBBBPPPP...
I NEED BACKUP!
STUPID HAY FEVER!
KIRKMAN & SCOTT

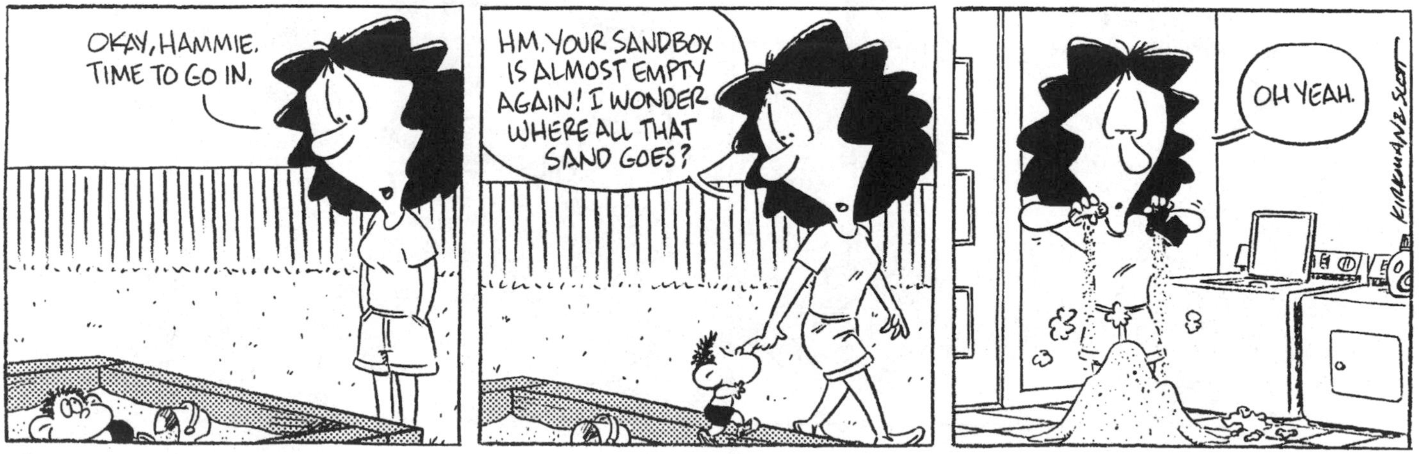
OKAY, HAMMIE. TIME TO GO IN.
HM. YOUR SANDBOX IS ALMOST EMPTY AGAIN! I WONDER WHERE ALL THAT SAND GOES?
OH YEAH.
KIRKMAN & SCOTT

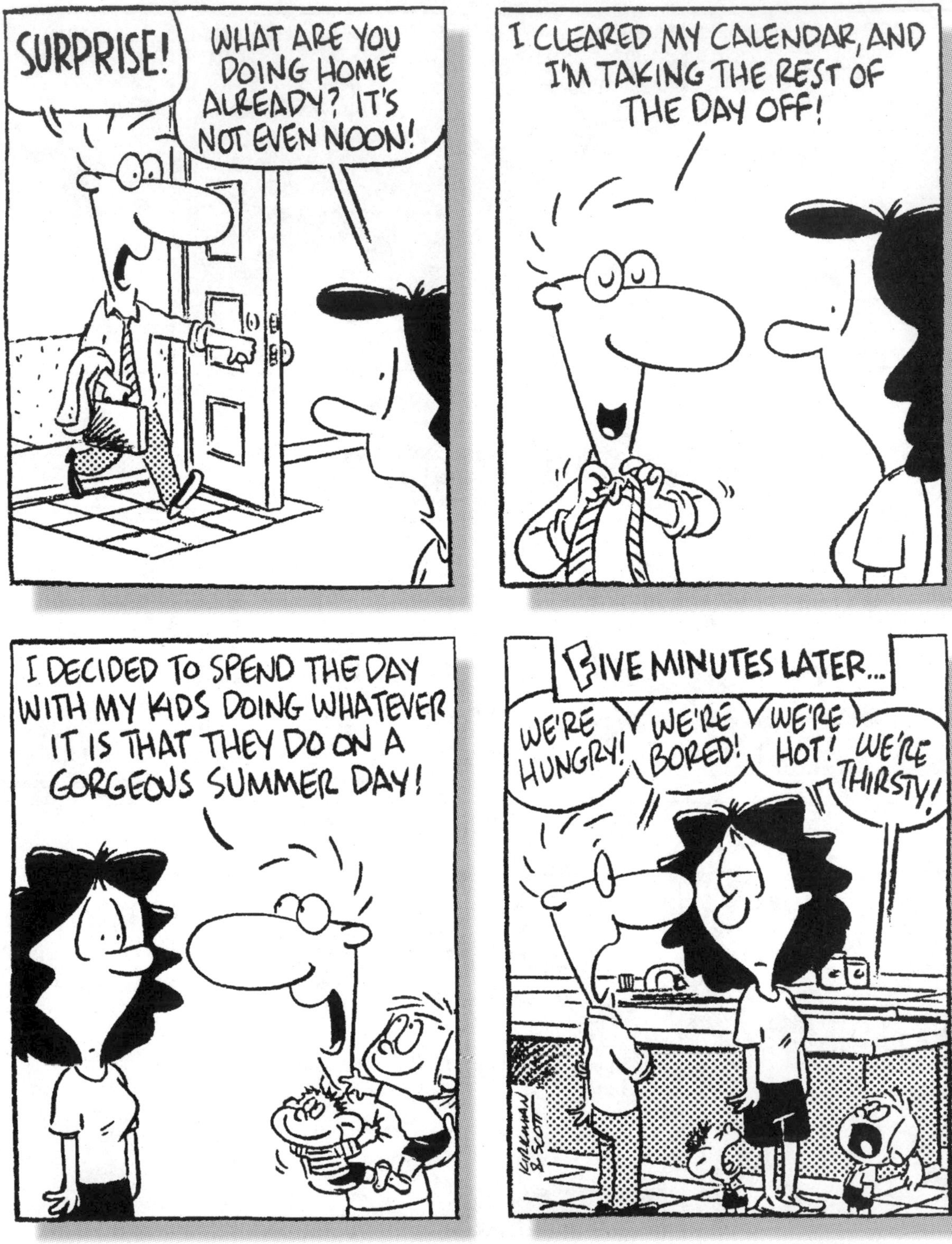
SURPRISE!
WHAT ARE YOU DOING HOME ALREADY? IT'S NOT EVEN NOON!
I CLEARED MY CALENDAR, AND I'M TAKING THE REST OF THE DAY OFF!
I DECIDED TO SPEND THE DAY WITH MY KIDS DOING WHATEVER IT IS THAT THEY DO ON A GORGEOUS SUMMER DAY!
FIVE MINUTES LATER...
WE'RE HUNGRY!
WE'RE BORED!
WE'RE HOT!
WE'RE THIRSTY!
KIRKMAN & SCOTT

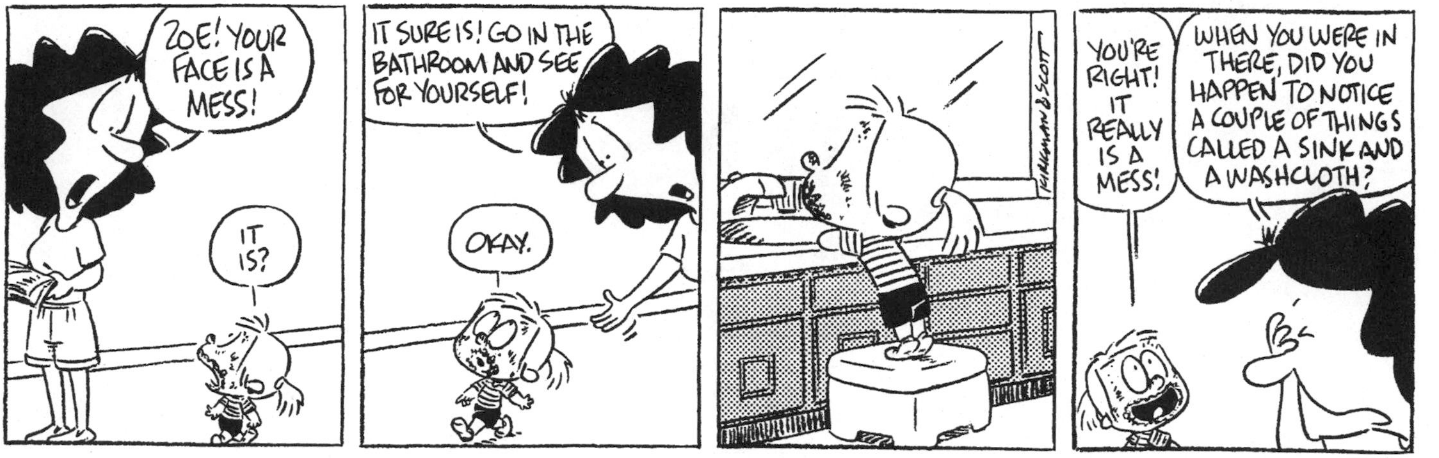
ZOE! YOUR FACE IS A MESS!
IT IS?
IT SURE IS! GO IN THE BATHROOM AND SEE FOR YOURSELF!
OKAY.
KIRKMAN & SCOTT
YOU'RE RIGHT! IT REALLY IS A MESS!
WHEN YOU WERE IN THERE, DID YOU HAPPEN TO NOTICE A COUPLE OF THINGS CALLED A SINK AND A WASHCLOTH?

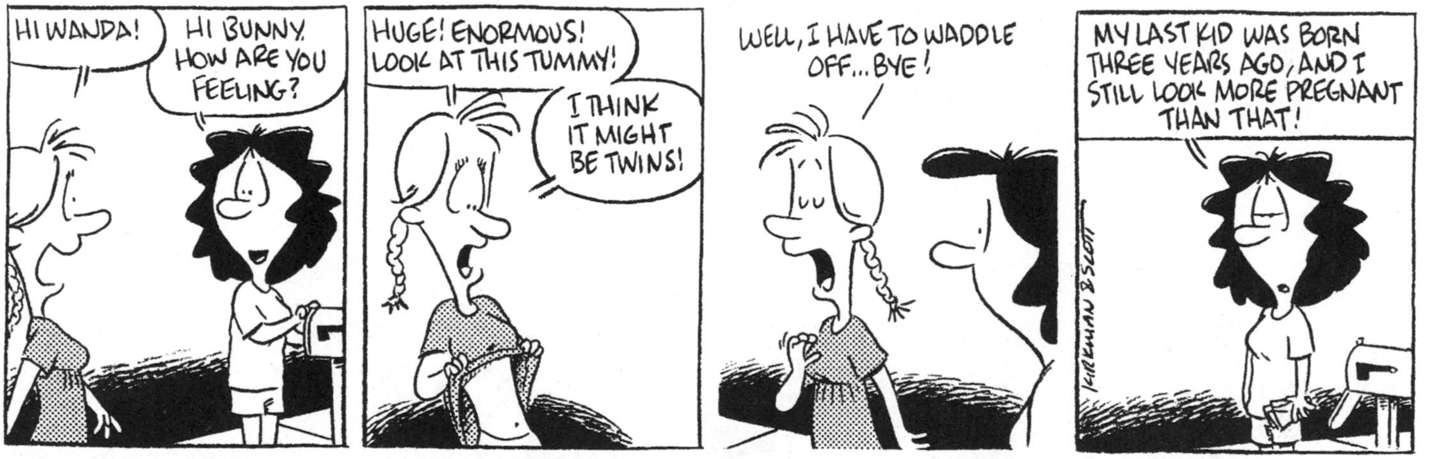
HI WANDA!
HI BUNNY. HOW ARE YOU FEELING?
HUGE! ENORMOUS! LOOK AT THIS TUMMY!
I THINK IT MIGHT BE TWINS!
WELL, I HAVE TO WADDLE OFF... BYE!
KIRKMAN & SCOTT
MY LAST KID WAS BORN THREE YEARS AGO, AND I STILL LOOK MORE PREGNANT THAN THAT!

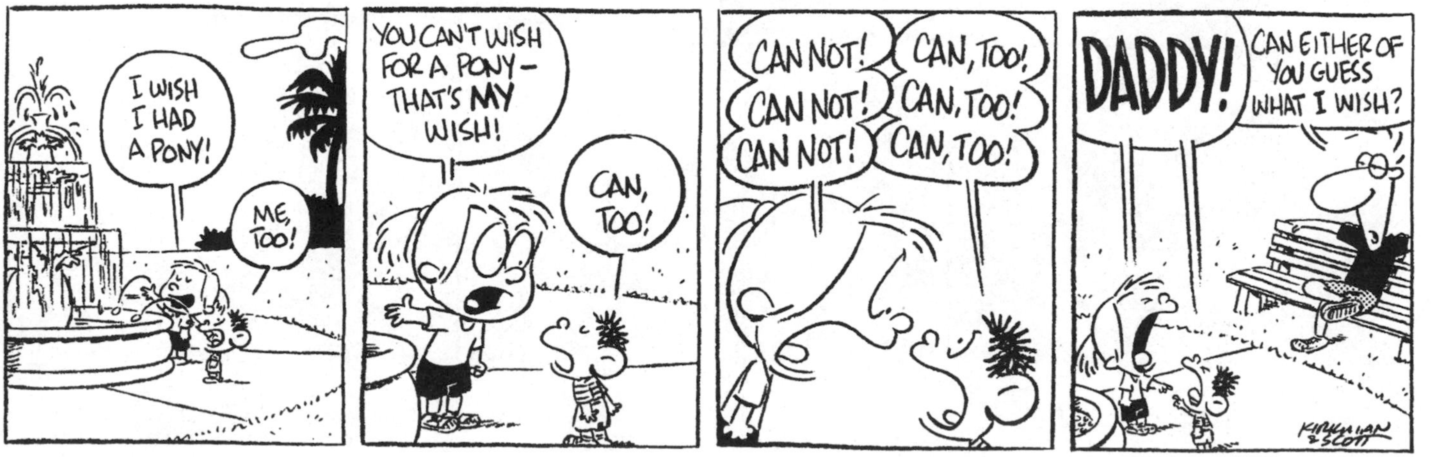
I WISH I HAD A PONY!
ME, TOO!
YOU CAN'T WISH FOR A PONY— THAT'S MY WISH!
CAN, TOO!
CAN NOT!
CAN, TOO!
CAN NOT!
CAN, TOO!
CAN NOT!
CAN, TOO!
DADDY!
CAN EITHER OF YOU GUESS WHAT I WISH?
KIRKMAN & SCOTT

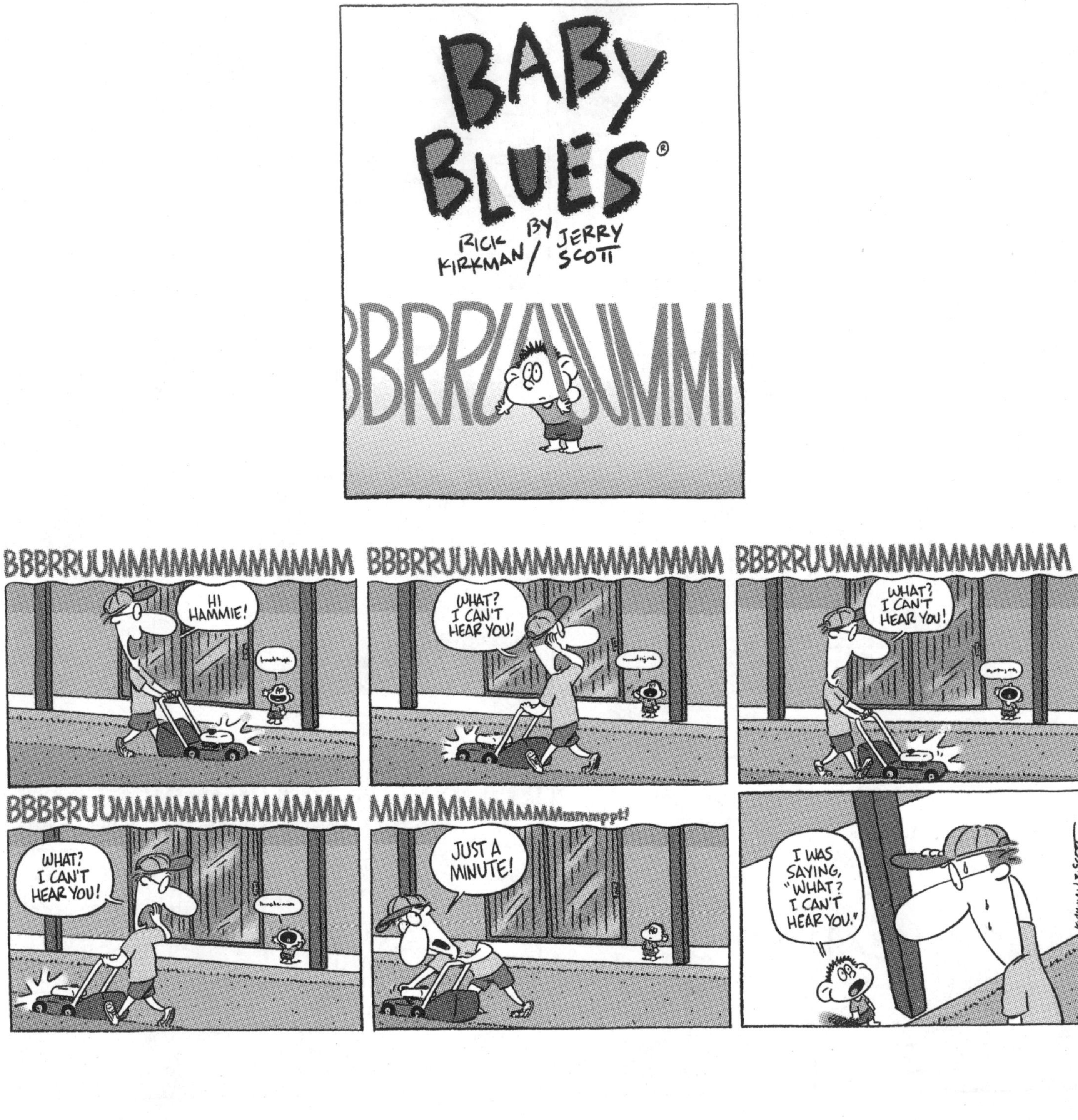
BABY BLUES®
BY RICK KIRKMAN / JERRY SCOTT
BBRRAUMMM
BBBRRUUMMMMMMMMMMMM
HI HAMMIE!
BBBRRUUMMMMMMMMMMMMM
WHAT? I CAN'T HEAR YOU!
BBBRRUUMMMMMMMMMMMM
WHAT? I CAN'T HEAR YOU!
BBBRRUUMMMMMMMMMMMMM
WHAT? I CAN'T HEAR YOU!
MMMMMMMMMmmmppt!
JUST A MINUTE!
I WAS SAYING, "WHAT? I CAN'T HEAR YOU."
KIRKMAN & SCOTT

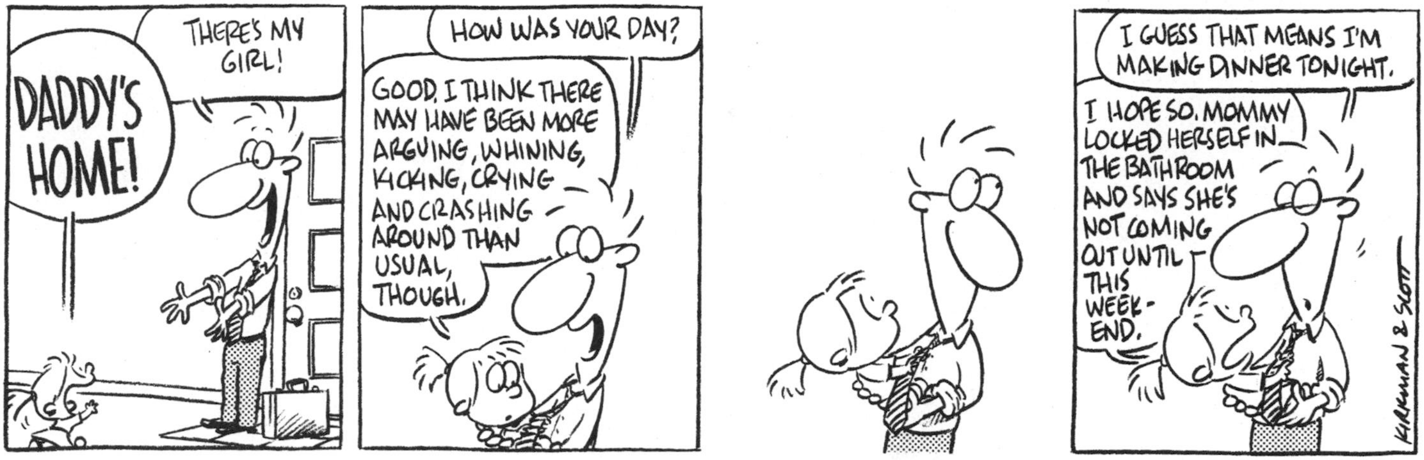
DADDY'S HOME!
THERE'S MY GIRL!
HOW WAS YOUR DAY?
GOOD. I THINK THERE MAY HAVE BEEN MORE ARGUING, WHINING, KICKING, CRYING AND CRASHING AROUND THAN USUAL, THOUGH.
I GUESS THAT MEANS I'M MAKING DINNER TONIGHT.
I HOPE SO. MOMMY LOCKED HERSELF IN THE BATHROOM AND SAYS SHE'S NOT COMING OUT UNTIL THIS WEEK-END.
KIRKMAN & SCOTT

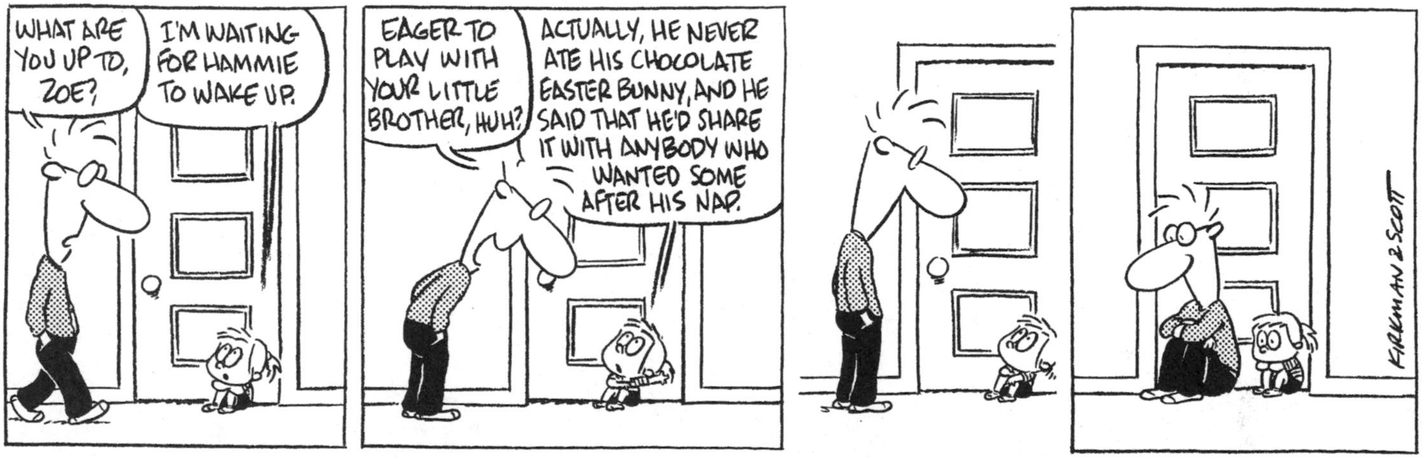
WHAT ARE YOU UP TO, ZOE?
I'M WAITING FOR HAMMIE TO WAKE UP.
EAGER TO PLAY WITH YOUR LITTLE BROTHER, HUH?
ACTUALLY, HE NEVER ATE HIS CHOCOLATE EASTER BUNNY, AND HE SAID THAT HE'D SHARE IT WITH ANYBODY WHO WANTED SOME AFTER HIS NAP.
KIRKMAN & SCOTT

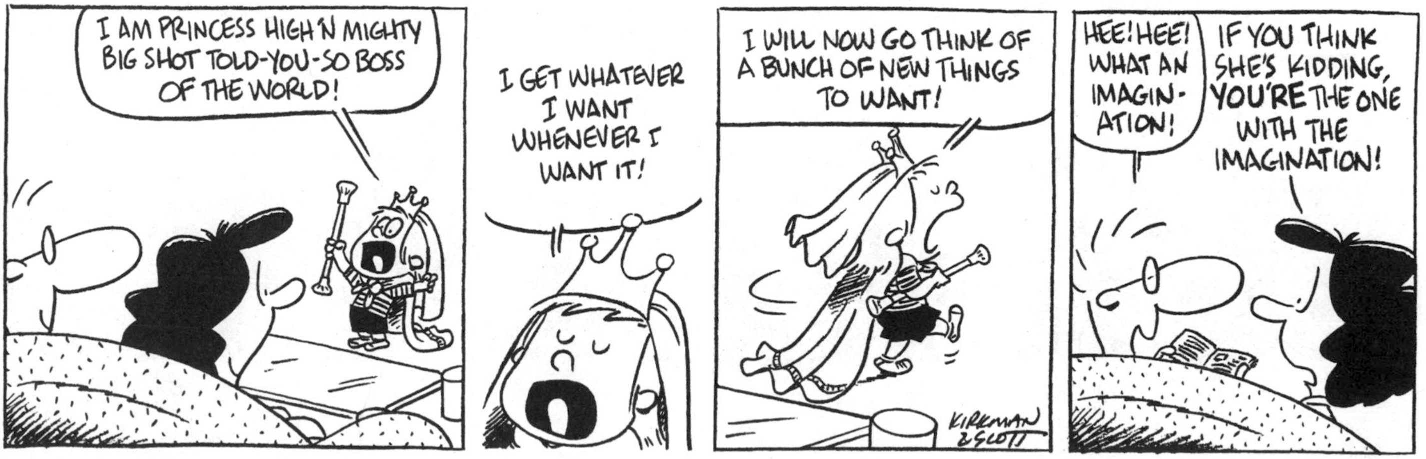
I AM PRINCESS HIGH 'N MIGHTY BIG SHOT TOLD-YOU-SO BOSS OF THE WORLD!
I GET WHATEVER I WANT WHENEVER I WANT IT!
I WILL NOW GO THINK OF A BUNCH OF NEW THINGS TO WANT!
KIRKMAN & SCOTT
HEE! HEE! WHAT AN IMAGIN-ATION!
IF YOU THINK SHE'S KIDDING, YOU'RE THE ONE WITH THE IMAGINATION!

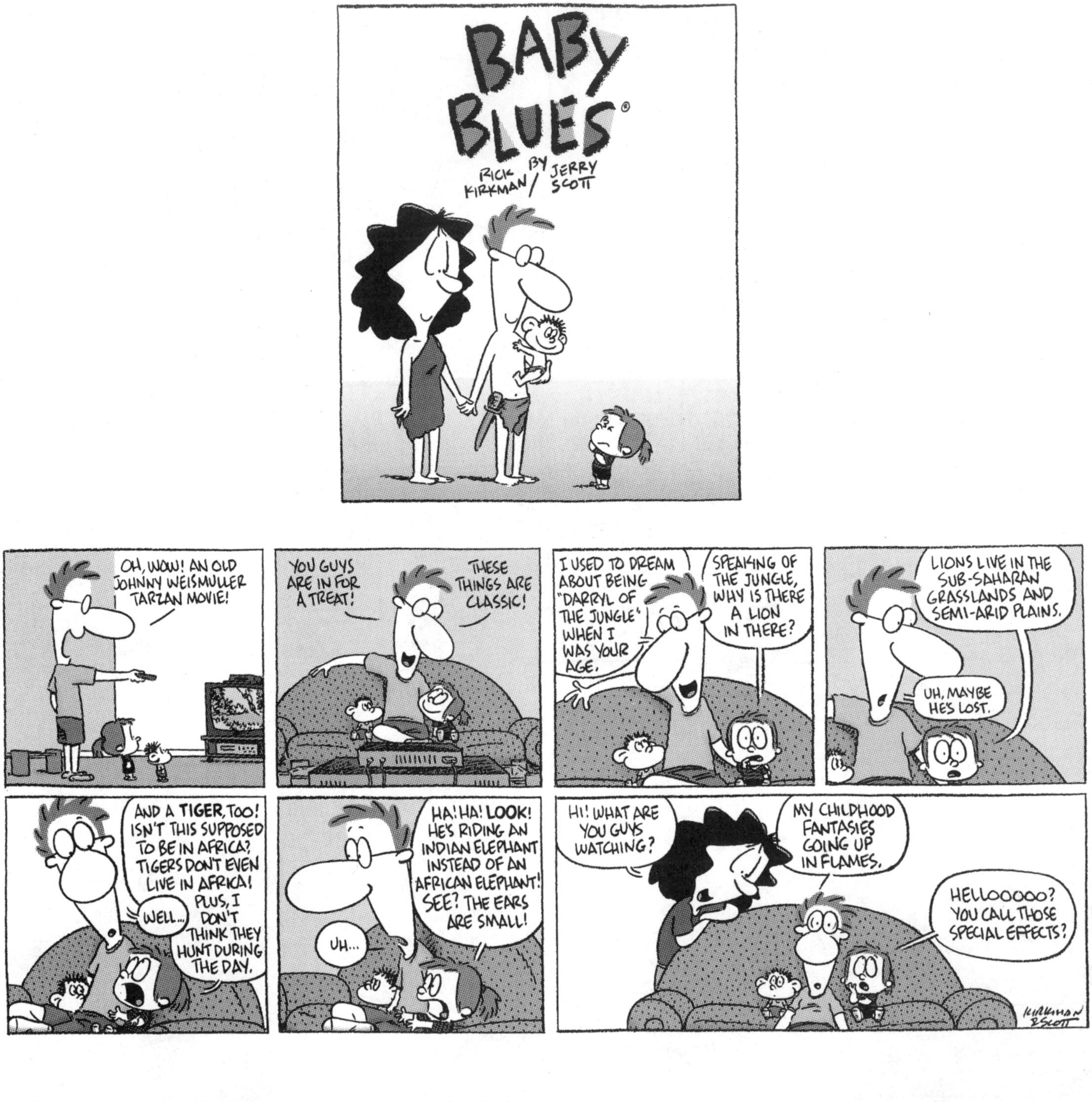

BABY BLUES®
BY RICK KIRKMAN / JERRY SCOTT
OH, WOW! AN OLD JOHNNY WEISMULLER TARZAN MOVIE!
YOU GUYS ARE IN FOR A TREAT!
THESE THINGS ARE CLASSIC!
I USED TO DREAM ABOUT BEING "DARRYL OF THE JUNGLE" WHEN I WAS YOUR AGE.
SPEAKING OF THE JUNGLE, WHY IS THERE A LION IN THERE?
LIONS LIVE IN THE SUB-SAHARAN GRASSLANDS AND SEMI-ARID PLAINS.
UH, MAYBE HE'S LOST.
AND A TIGER, TOO! ISN'T THIS SUPPOSED TO BE IN AFRICA? TIGERS DON'T EVEN LIVE IN AFRICA!
WELL...
PLUS, I DON'T THINK THEY HUNT DURING THE DAY.
HA! HA! LOOK! HE'S RIDING AN INDIAN ELEPHANT INSTEAD OF AN AFRICAN ELEPHANT! SEE? THE EARS ARE SMALL!
UH...
HI! WHAT ARE YOU GUYS WATCHING?
MY CHILDHOOD FANTASIES GOING UP IN FLAMES.
HELLOOOOO? YOU CALL THOSE SPECIAL EFFECTS?
KIRKMAN & SCOTT

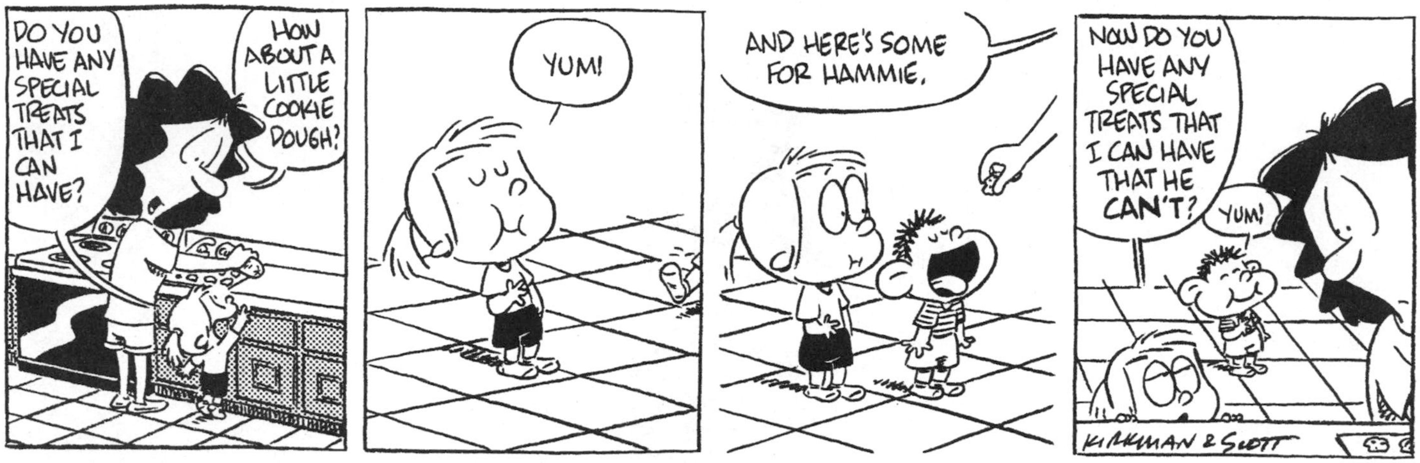
DO YOU HAVE ANY SPECIAL TREATS THAT I CAN HAVE?
HOW ABOUT A LITTLE COOKIE DOUGH?
YUM!
AND HERE'S SOME FOR HAMMIE.
NOW DO YOU HAVE ANY SPECIAL TREATS THAT I CAN HAVE THAT HE **CAN'T**?
YUM!
KIRKMAN & SCOTT

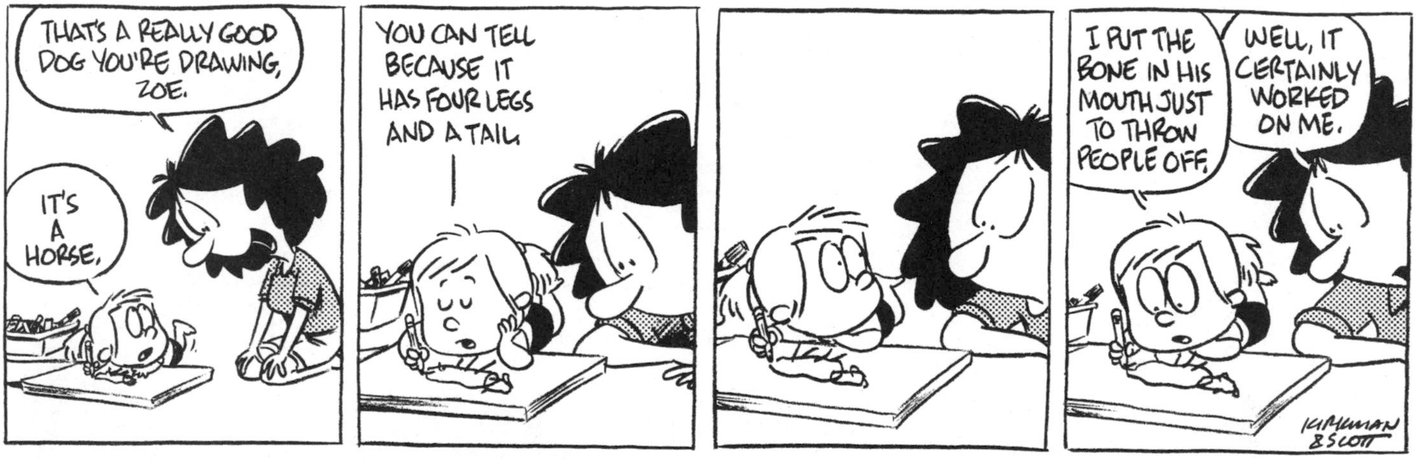
THAT'S A REALLY GOOD DOG YOU'RE DRAWING, ZOE.
IT'S A HORSE.
YOU CAN TELL BECAUSE IT HAS FOUR LEGS AND A TAIL.
I PUT THE BONE IN HIS MOUTH JUST TO THROW PEOPLE OFF.
WELL, IT CERTAINLY WORKED ON ME.
KIRKMAN & SCOTT

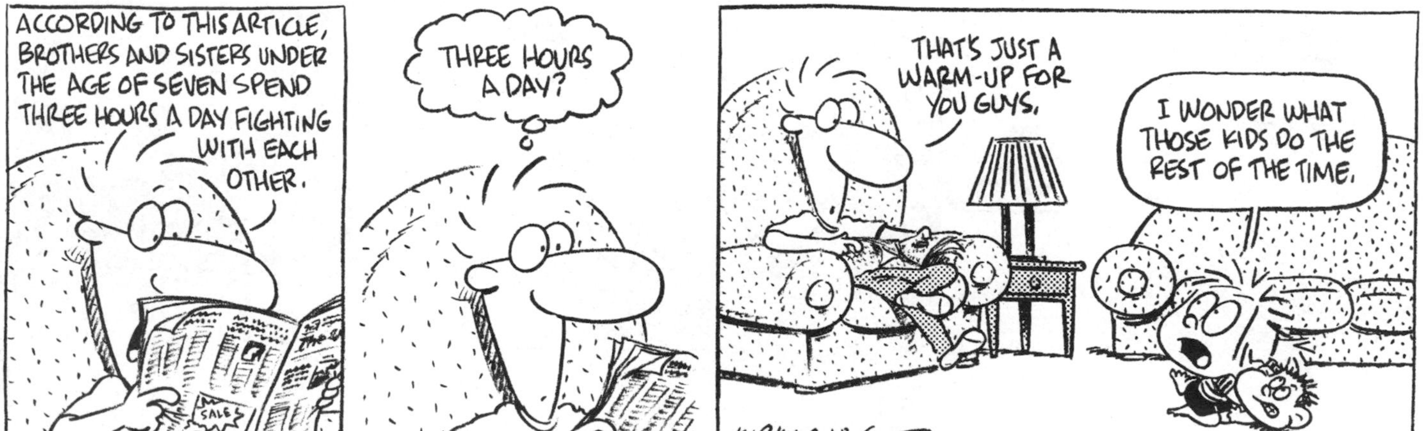
ACCORDING TO THIS ARTICLE, BROTHERS AND SISTERS UNDER THE AGE OF SEVEN SPEND THREE HOURS A DAY FIGHTING WITH EACH OTHER.
SALE
THREE HOURS A DAY?
THAT'S JUST A WARM-UP FOR YOU GUYS.
I WONDER WHAT THOSE KIDS DO THE REST OF THE TIME.
KIRKMAN & SCOTT

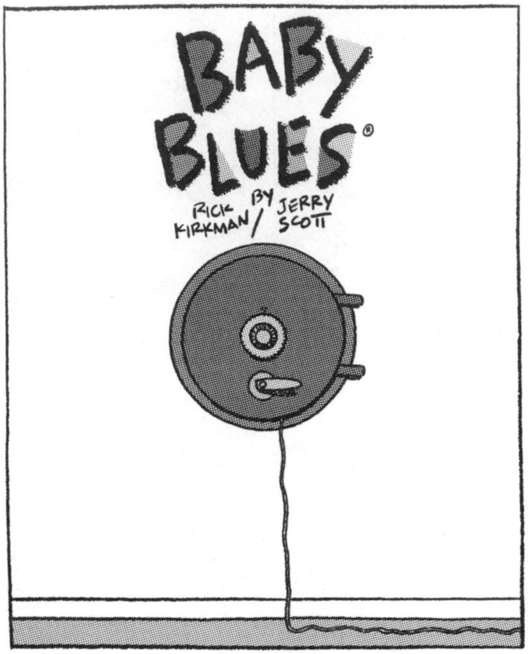
BABY BLUES®
BY RICK KIRKMAN / JERRY SCOTT

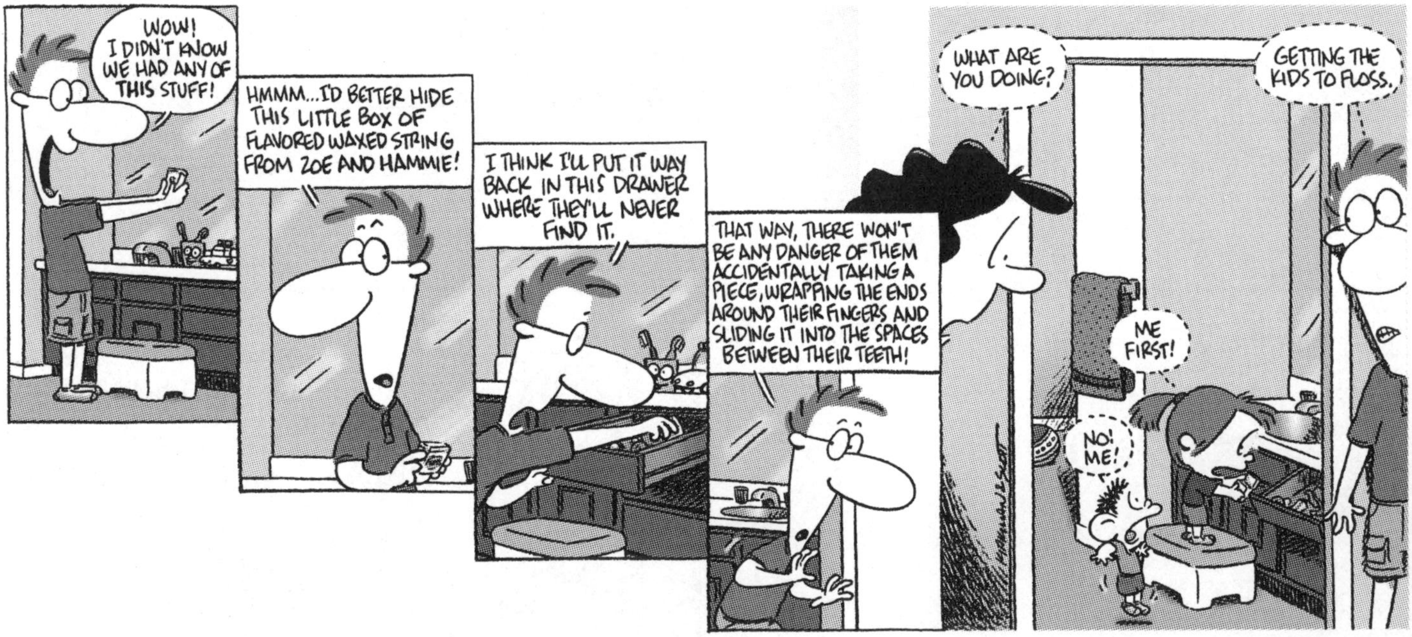
WOW! I DIDN'T KNOW WE HAD ANY OF THIS STUFF!
HMMM...I'D BETTER HIDE THIS LITTLE BOX OF FLAVORED WAXED STRING FROM ZOE AND HAMMIE!
I THINK I'LL PUT IT WAY BACK IN THIS DRAWER WHERE THEY'LL NEVER FIND IT.
THAT WAY, THERE WON'T BE ANY DANGER OF THEM ACCIDENTALLY TAKING A PIECE, WRAPPING THE ENDS AROUND THEIR FINGERS AND SLIDING IT INTO THE SPACES BETWEEN THEIR TEETH!
WHAT ARE YOU DOING?
GETTING THE KIDS TO FLOSS.
ME FIRST!
NO! ME!

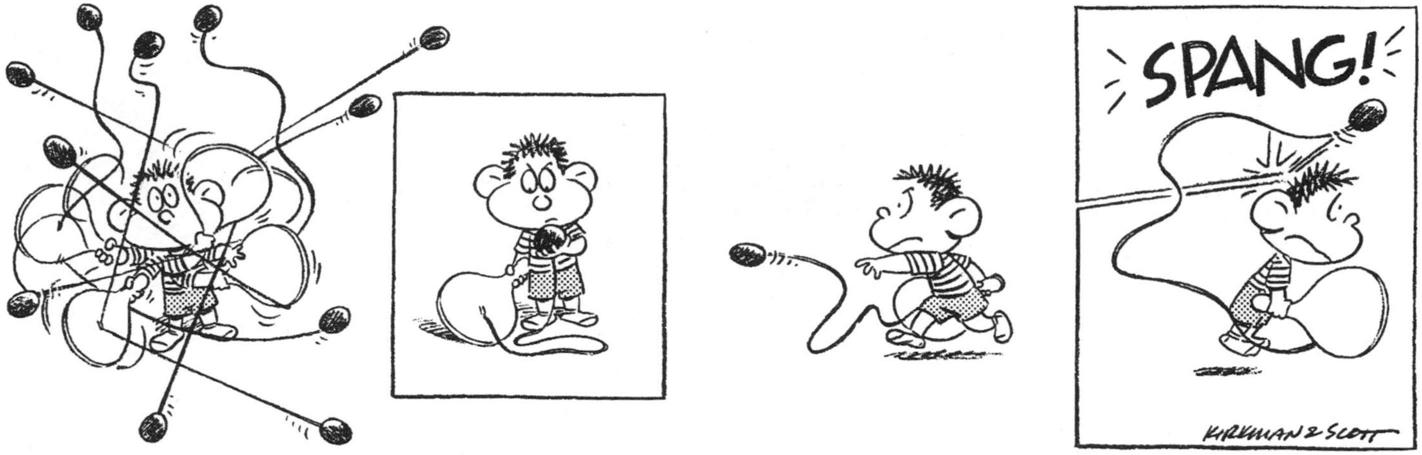
SPANG!
KIRKMAN & SCOTT

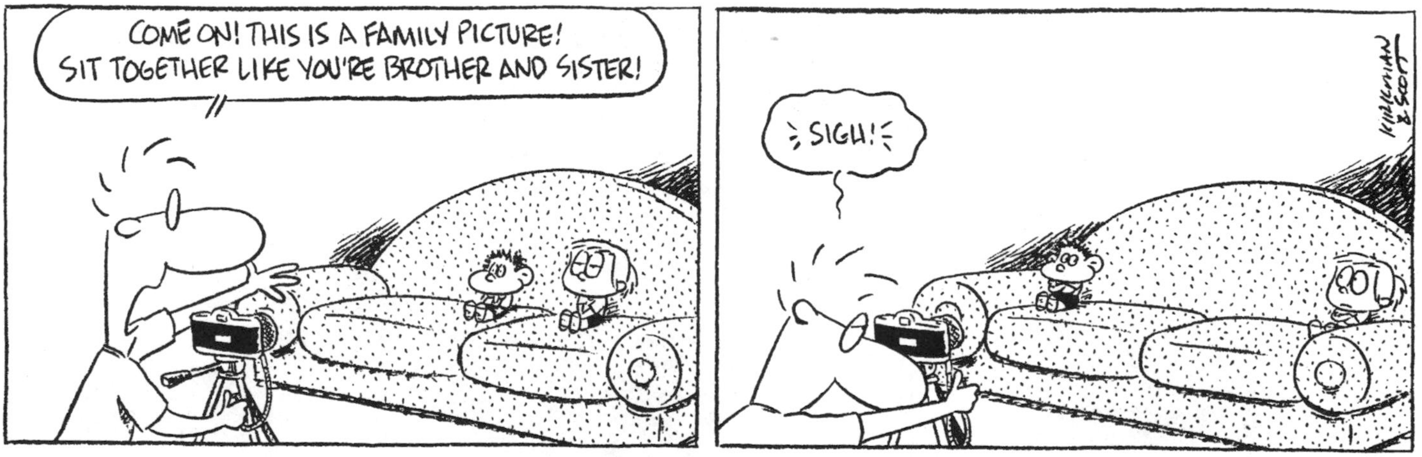
COME ON! THIS IS A FAMILY PICTURE! SIT TOGETHER LIKE YOU'RE BROTHER AND SISTER!
SIGH!
KIRKMAN & SCOTT

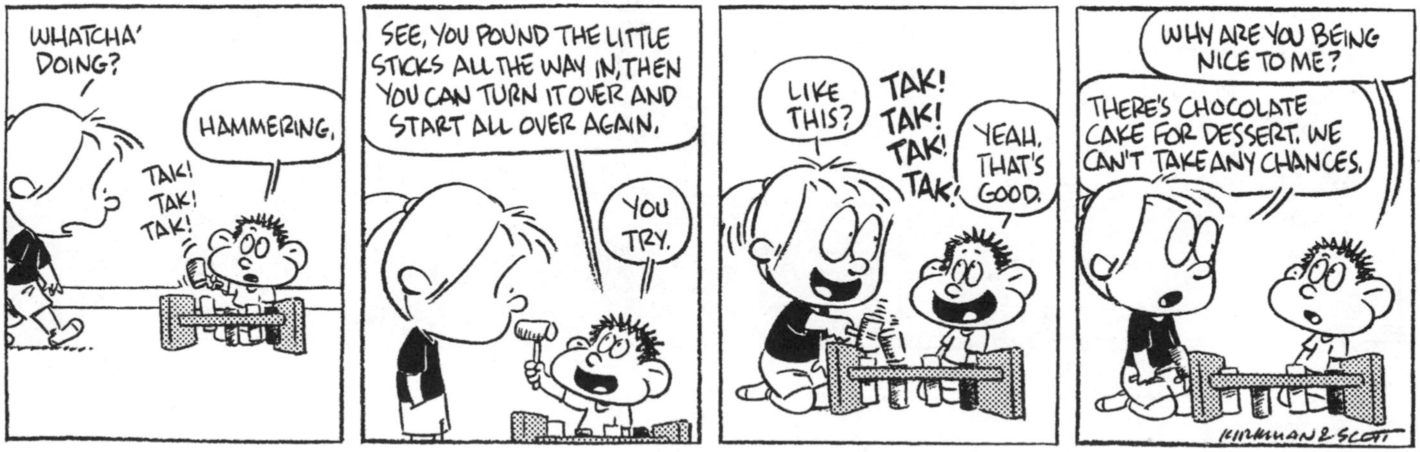
WHATCHA' DOING?
HAMMERING.
TAK! TAK! TAK!
SEE, YOU POUND THE LITTLE STICKS ALL THE WAY IN, THEN YOU CAN TURN IT OVER AND START ALL OVER AGAIN.
YOU TRY.
LIKE THIS?
TAK! TAK! TAK! TAK!
YEAH, THAT'S GOOD.
WHY ARE YOU BEING NICE TO ME?
THERE'S CHOCOLATE CAKE FOR DESSERT. WE CAN'T TAKE ANY CHANCES.
KIRKMAN & SCOTT

BABY BLUES®
BY RICK KIRKMAN / JERRY SCOTT
RXXL
PATIENT
MEDICATION

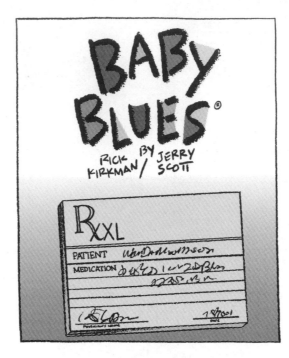

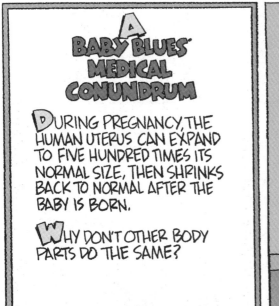

A BABY BLUES® MEDICAL CONUNDRUM
DURING PREGNANCY, THE HUMAN UTERUS CAN EXPAND TO FIVE HUNDRED TIMES ITS NORMAL SIZE, THEN SHRINKS BACK TO NORMAL AFTER THE BABY IS BORN.
WHY DON'T OTHER BODY PARTS DO THE SAME?
WHY CAN'T YOU BE MORE LIKE MY UTERUS?
KIRKMAN & SCOTT

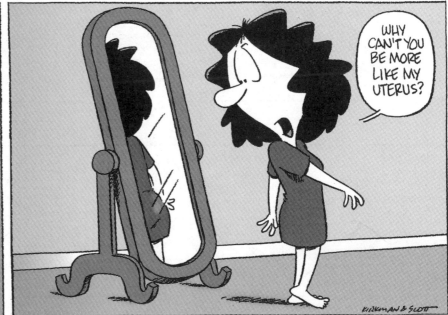

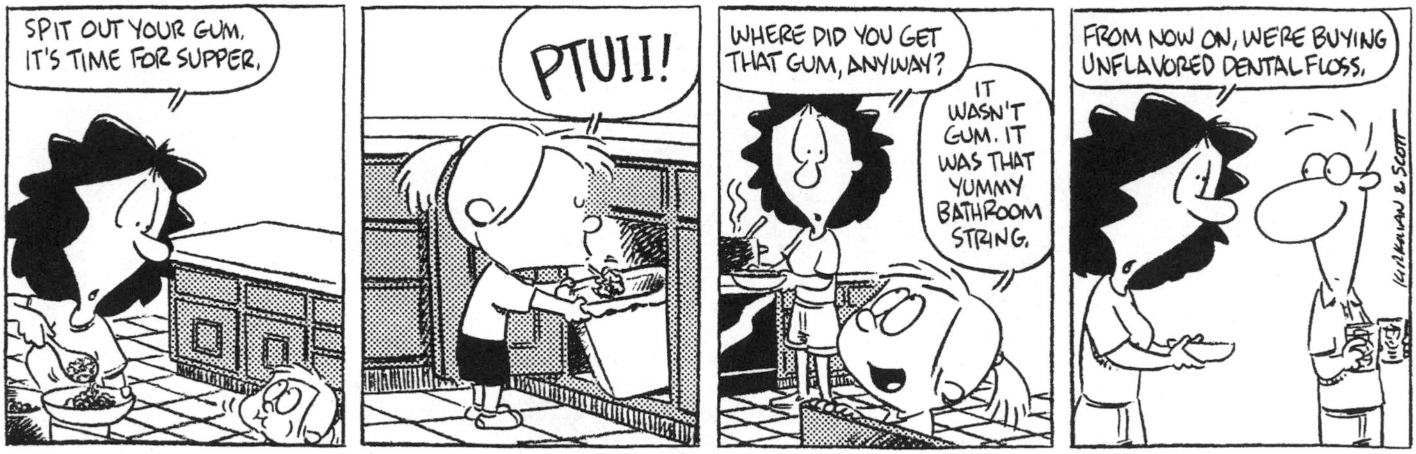
SPIT OUT YOUR GUM. IT'S TIME FOR SUPPER.
PTUII!
WHERE DID YOU GET THAT GUM, ANYWAY?
IT WASN'T GUM. IT WAS THAT YUMMY BATHROOM STRING.
FROM NOW ON, WE'RE BUYING UNFLAVORED DENTAL FLOSS.
KIRKMAN & SCOTT

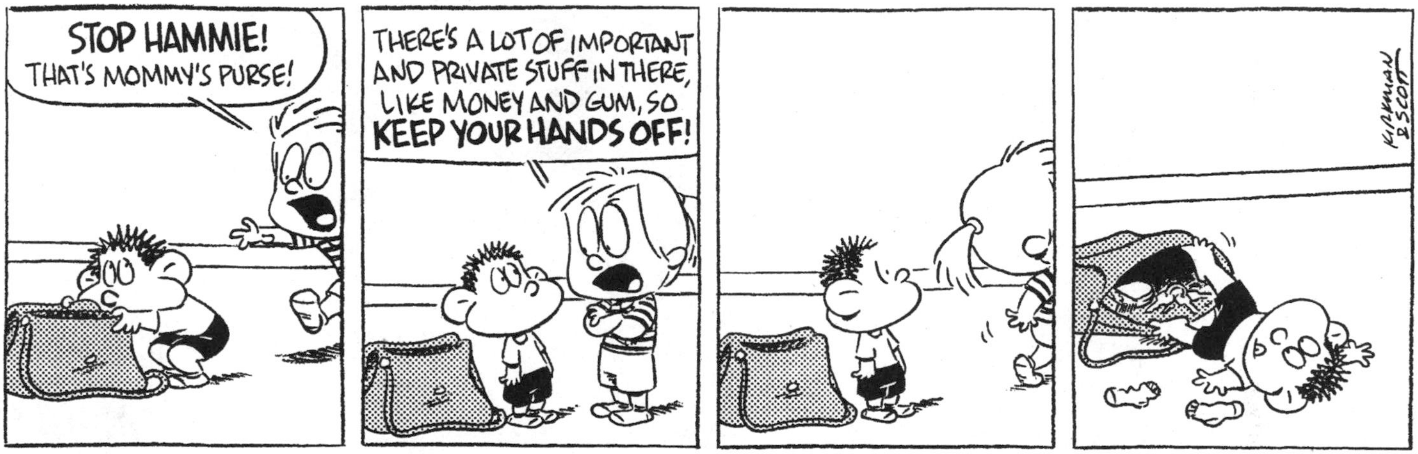
STOP HAMMIE! THAT'S MOMMY'S PURSE!
THERE'S A LOT OF IMPORTANT AND PRIVATE STUFF IN THERE, LIKE MONEY AND GUM, SO KEEP YOUR HANDS OFF!
KIRKMAN & SCOTT

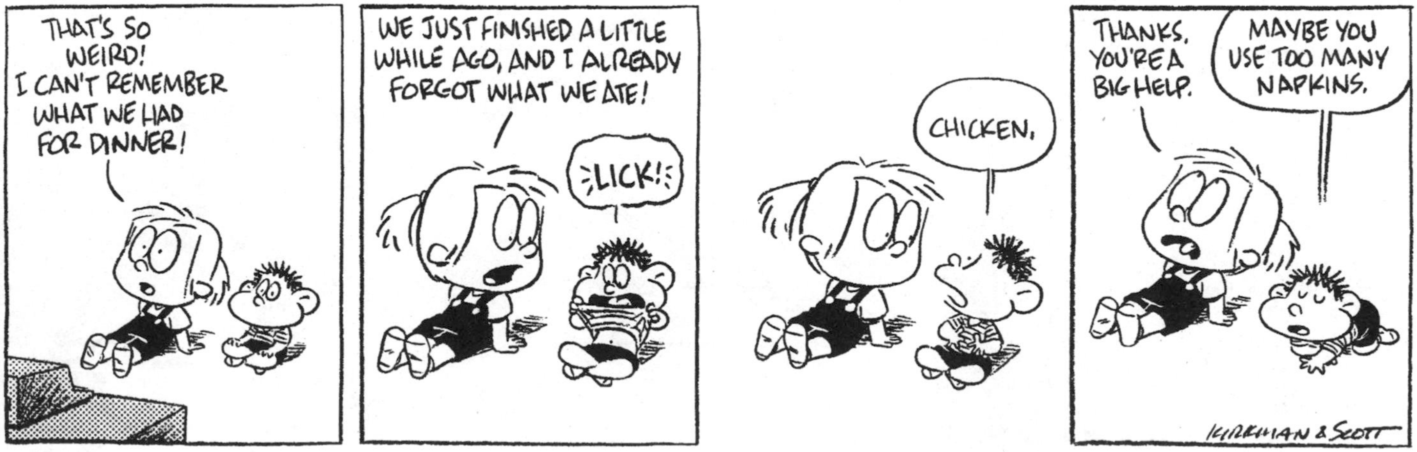
THAT'S SO WEIRD! I CAN'T REMEMBER WHAT WE HAD FOR DINNER!
WE JUST FINISHED A LITTLE WHILE AGO, AND I ALREADY FORGOT WHAT WE ATE!
LICK!
CHICKEN.
THANKS. YOU'RE A BIG HELP.
MAYBE YOU USE TOO MANY NAPKINS.
KIRKMAN & SCOTT

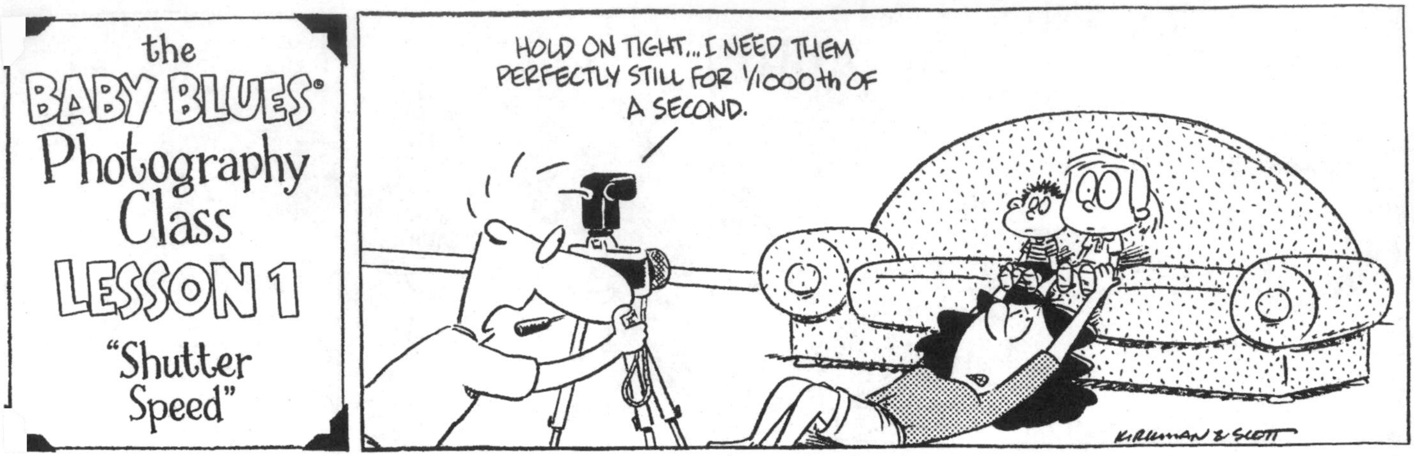
the
BABY BLUES®
Photography Class
LESSON 1
"Shutter Speed"
HOLD ON TIGHT... I NEED THEM PERFECTLY STILL FOR 1/1000th OF A SECOND.
KIRKMAN & SCOTT

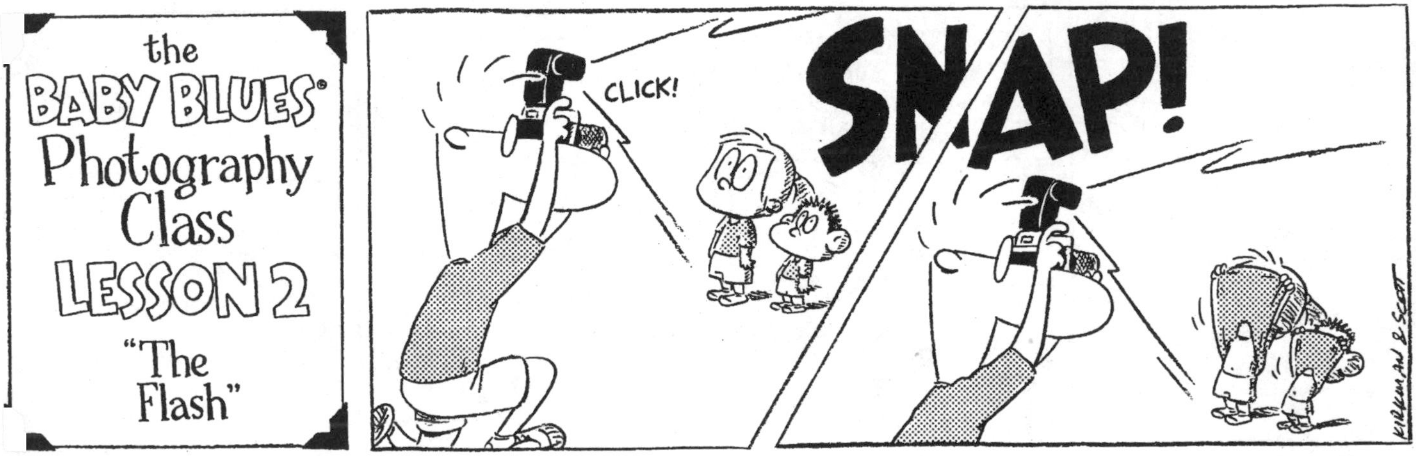
the
BABY BLUES®
Photography Class
LESSON 2
"The Flash"
CLICK!
SNAP!
KIRKMAN & SCOTT

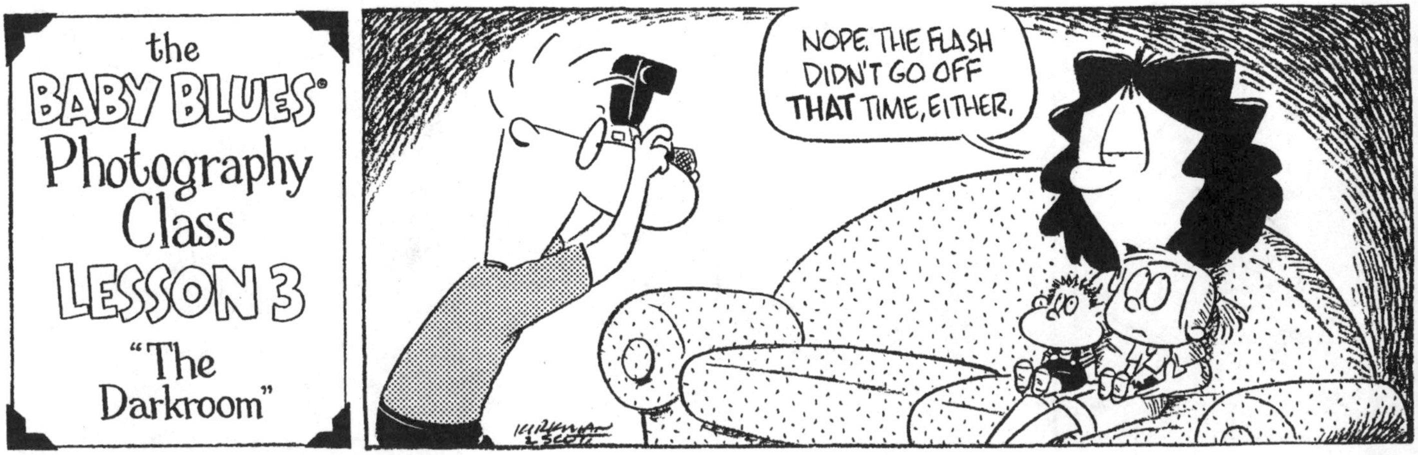
the
BABY BLUES®
Photography Class
LESSON 3
"The Darkroom"
NOPE. THE FLASH DIDN'T GO OFF **THAT** TIME, EITHER.
KIRKMAN & SCOTT

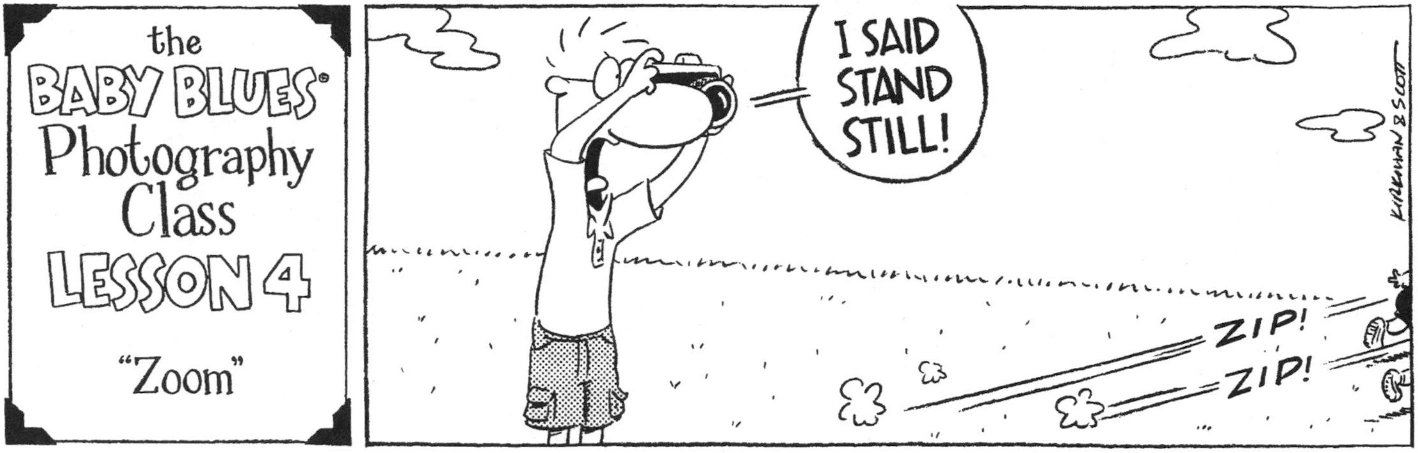
the
BABY BLUES®
Photography Class
LESSON 4
"Zoom"
I SAID STAND STILL!
ZIP!
ZIP!
KIRKMAN & SCOTT

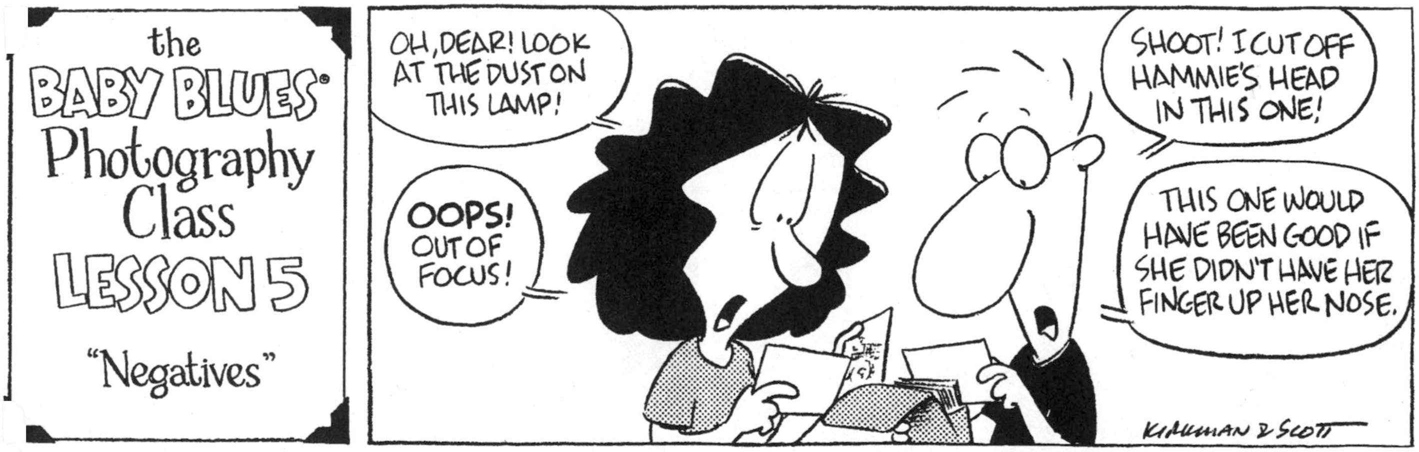
the
BABY BLUES®
Photography Class
LESSON 5
"Negatives"
OH, DEAR! LOOK AT THE DUST ON THIS LAMP!
SHOOT! I CUT OFF HAMMIE'S HEAD IN THIS ONE!
OOPS! OUT OF FOCUS!
THIS ONE WOULD HAVE BEEN GOOD IF SHE DIDN'T HAVE HER FINGER UP HER NOSE.
KIRKMAN & SCOTT

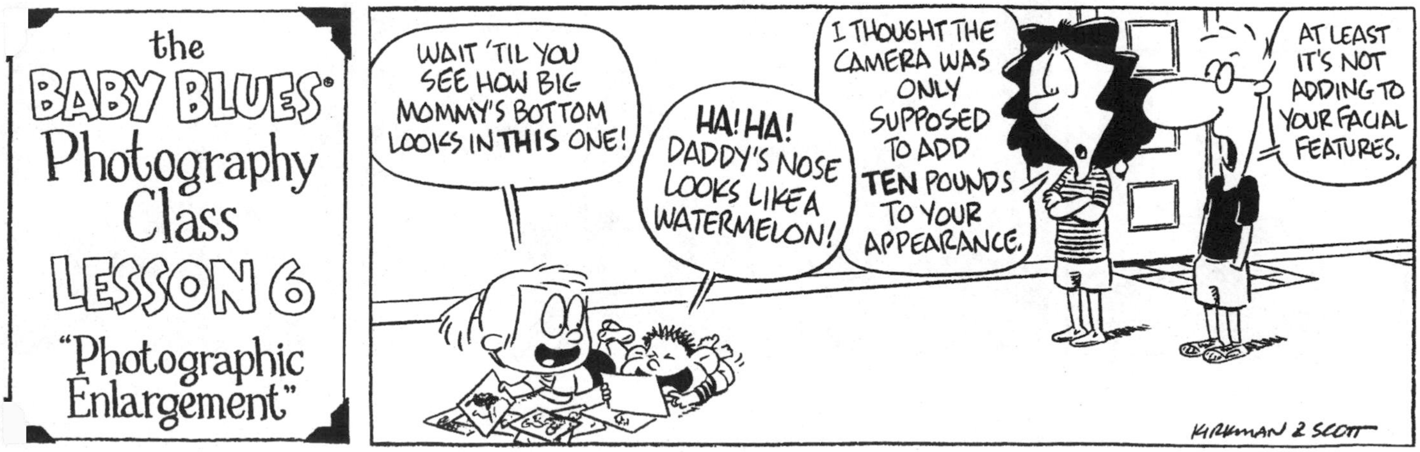
the
BABY BLUES®
Photography Class
LESSON 6
"Photographic Enlargement"
WAIT 'TIL YOU SEE HOW BIG MOMMY'S BOTTOM LOOKS IN THIS ONE!
HA! HA! DADDY'S NOSE LOOKS LIKE A WATERMELON!
I THOUGHT THE CAMERA WAS ONLY SUPPOSED TO ADD TEN POUNDS TO YOUR APPEARANCE.
AT LEAST IT'S NOT ADDING TO YOUR FACIAL FEATURES.
KIRKMAN & SCOTT

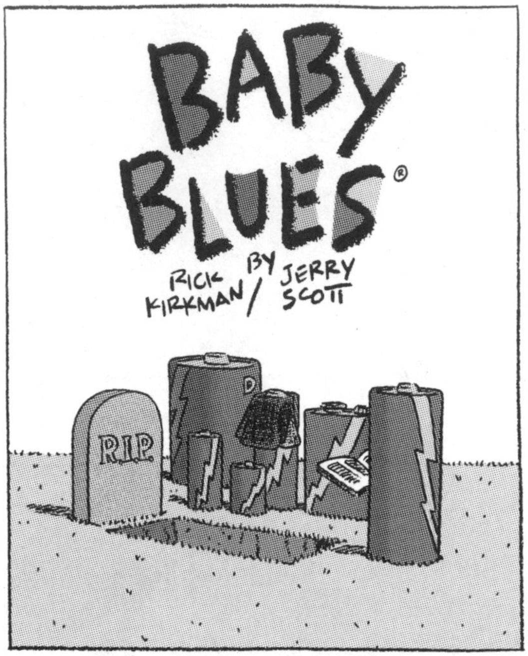
BABY BLUES®
RICK KIRKMAN / BY JERRY SCOTT
R.I.P.

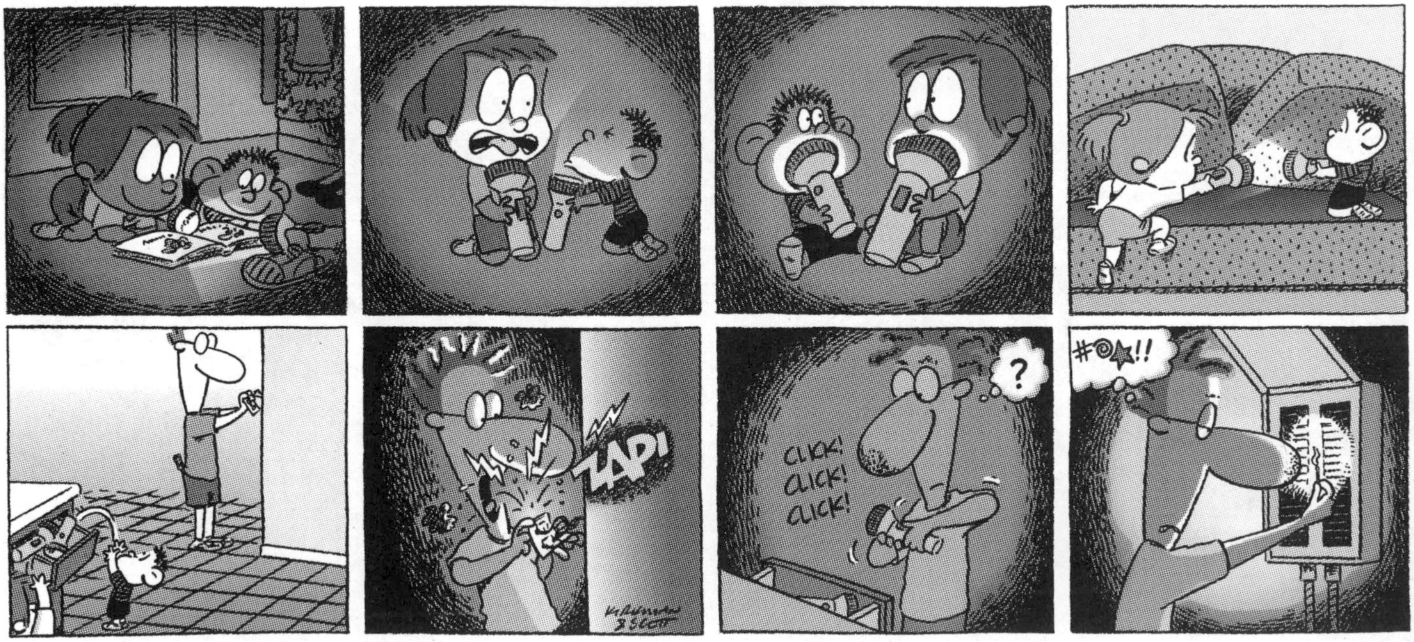
ZAP!
CLICK!
CLICK!
CLICK!
?
#@★!!

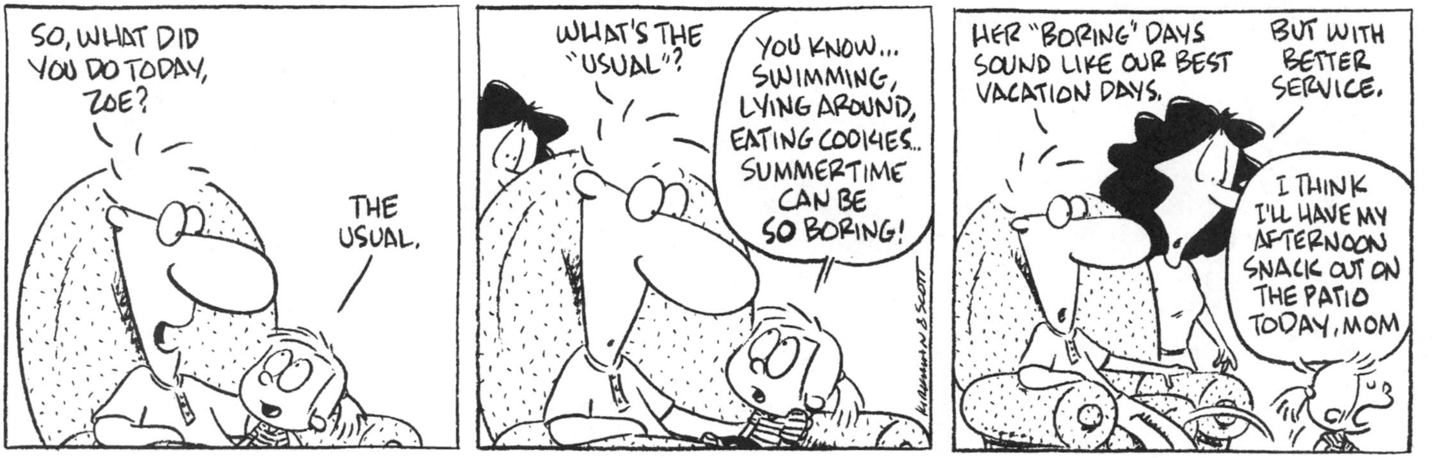
SO, WHAT DID YOU DO TODAY, ZOE?
THE USUAL.
WHAT'S THE "USUAL"?
YOU KNOW... SWIMMING, LYING AROUND, EATING COOKIES... SUMMERTIME CAN BE SO BORING!
KIRKMAN & SCOTT
HER "BORING" DAYS SOUND LIKE OUR BEST VACATION DAYS.
BUT WITH BETTER SERVICE.
I THINK I'LL HAVE MY AFTERNOON SNACK OUT ON THE PATIO TODAY, MOM

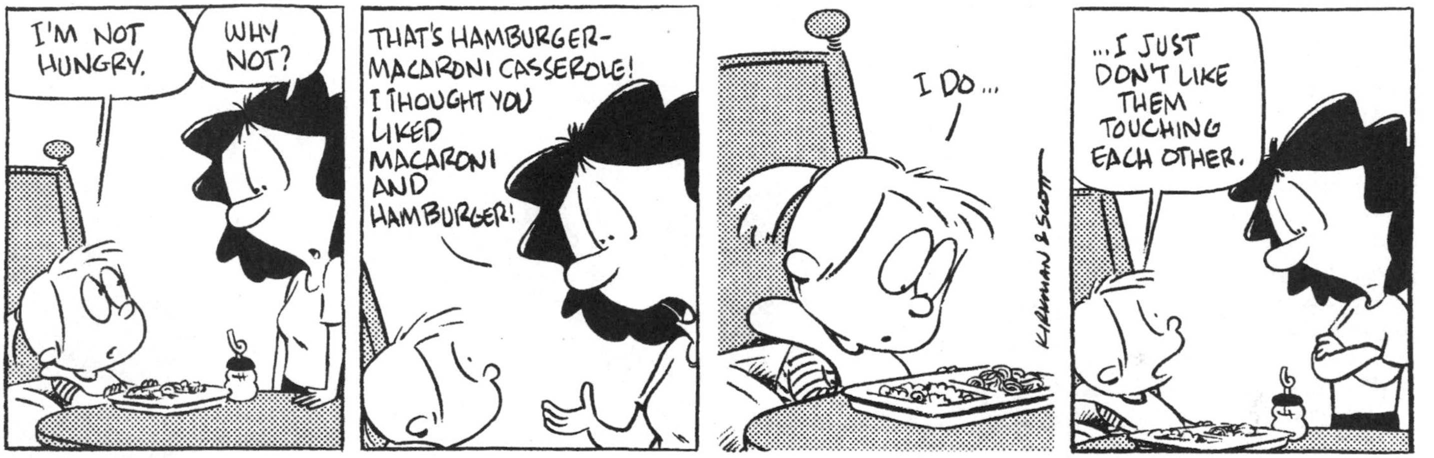
I'M NOT HUNGRY.
WHY NOT?
THAT'S HAMBURGER-MACARONI CASSEROLE! I THOUGHT YOU LIKED MACARONI AND HAMBURGER!
I DO...
KIRKMAN & SCOTT
...I JUST DON'T LIKE THEM TOUCHING EACH OTHER.

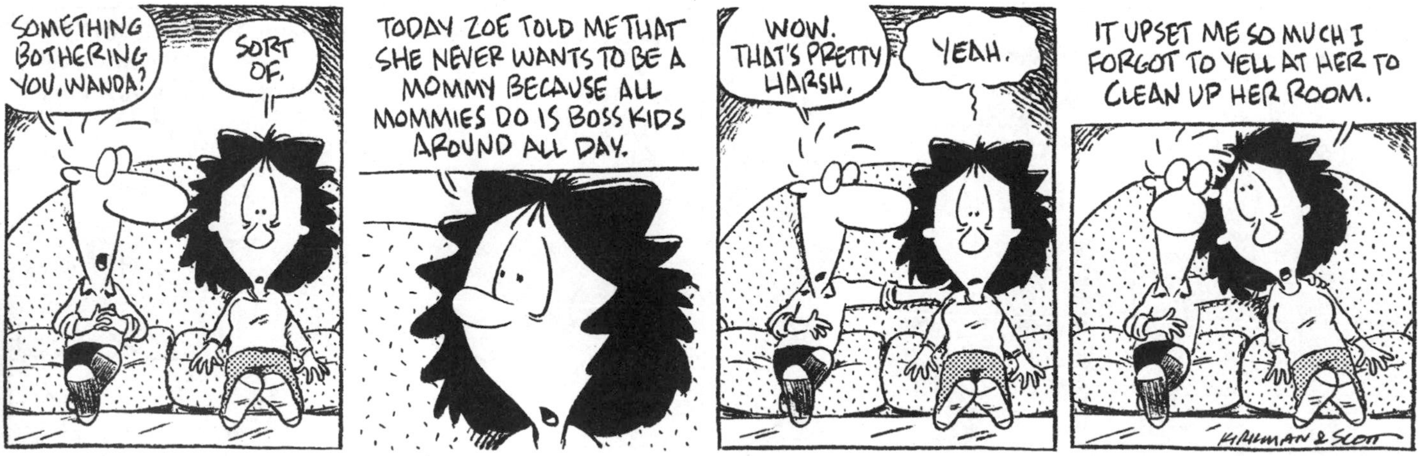
SOMETHING BOTHERING YOU, WANDA?
SORT OF.
TODAY ZOE TOLD ME THAT SHE NEVER WANTS TO BE A MOMMY BECAUSE ALL MOMMIES DO IS BOSS KIDS AROUND ALL DAY.
WOW. THAT'S PRETTY HARSH.
YEAH.
IT UPSET ME SO MUCH I FORGOT TO YELL AT HER TO CLEAN UP HER ROOM.
KIRKMAN & SCOTT

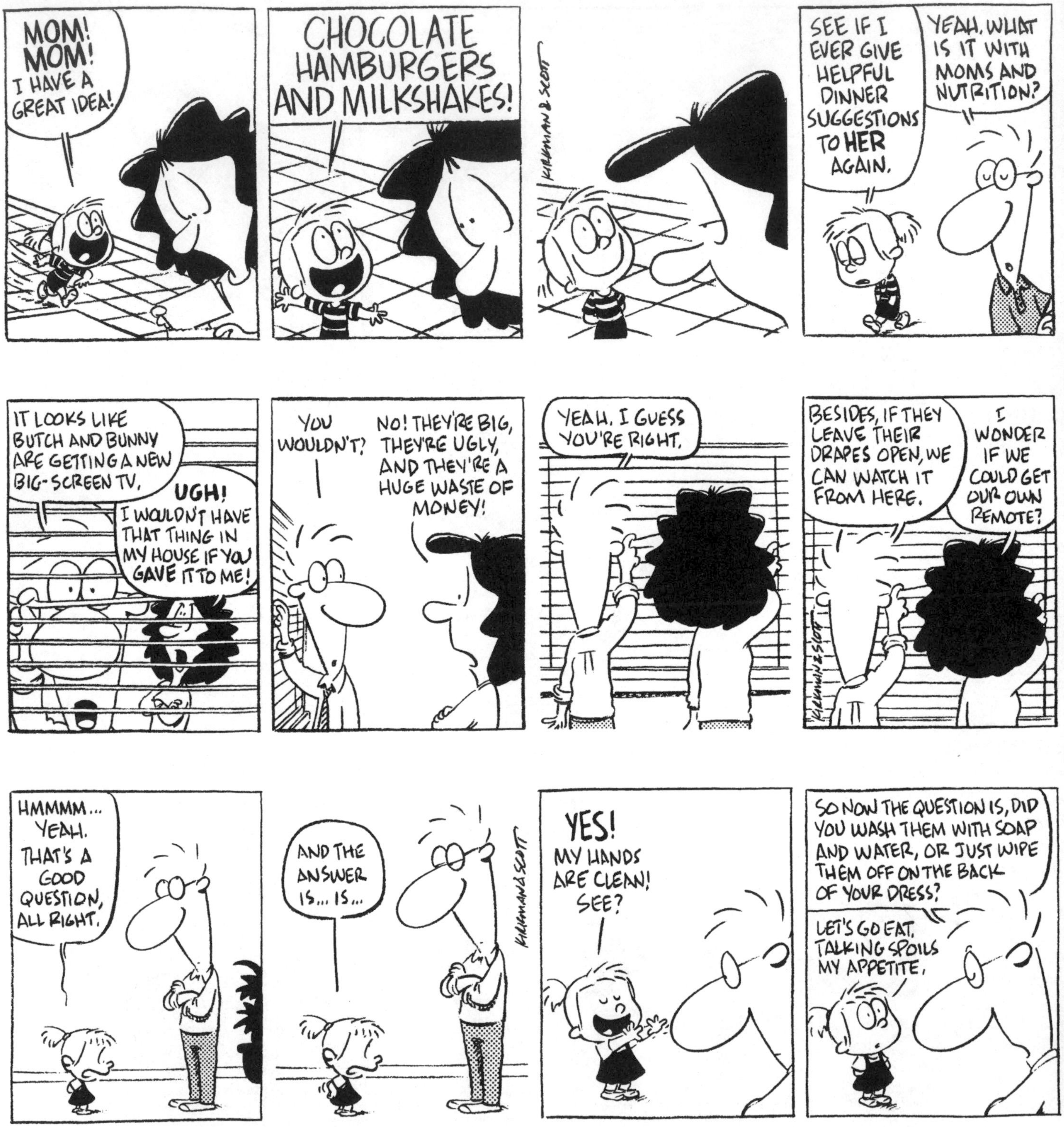
MOM! MOM! I HAVE A GREAT IDEA!
CHOCOLATE HAMBURGERS AND MILKSHAKES!
SEE IF I EVER GIVE HELPFUL DINNER SUGGESTIONS TO HER AGAIN.
YEAH. WHAT IS IT WITH MOMS AND NUTRITION?
IT LOOKS LIKE BUTCH AND BUNNY ARE GETTING A NEW BIG-SCREEN TV.
UGH! I WOULDN'T HAVE THAT THING IN MY HOUSE IF YOU GAVE IT TO ME!
YOU WOULDN'T?
NO! THEY'RE BIG, THEY'RE UGLY, AND THEY'RE A HUGE WASTE OF MONEY!
YEAH. I GUESS YOU'RE RIGHT.
BESIDES, IF THEY LEAVE THEIR DRAPES OPEN, WE CAN WATCH IT FROM HERE.
I WONDER IF WE COULD GET OUR OWN REMOTE?
HMMMM... YEAH. THAT'S A GOOD QUESTION, ALL RIGHT.
AND THE ANSWER IS... IS...
YES! MY HANDS ARE CLEAN! SEE?
SO NOW THE QUESTION IS, DID YOU WASH THEM WITH SOAP AND WATER, OR JUST WIPE THEM OFF ON THE BACK OF YOUR DRESS?
LET'S GO EAT. TALKING SPOILS MY APPETITE.

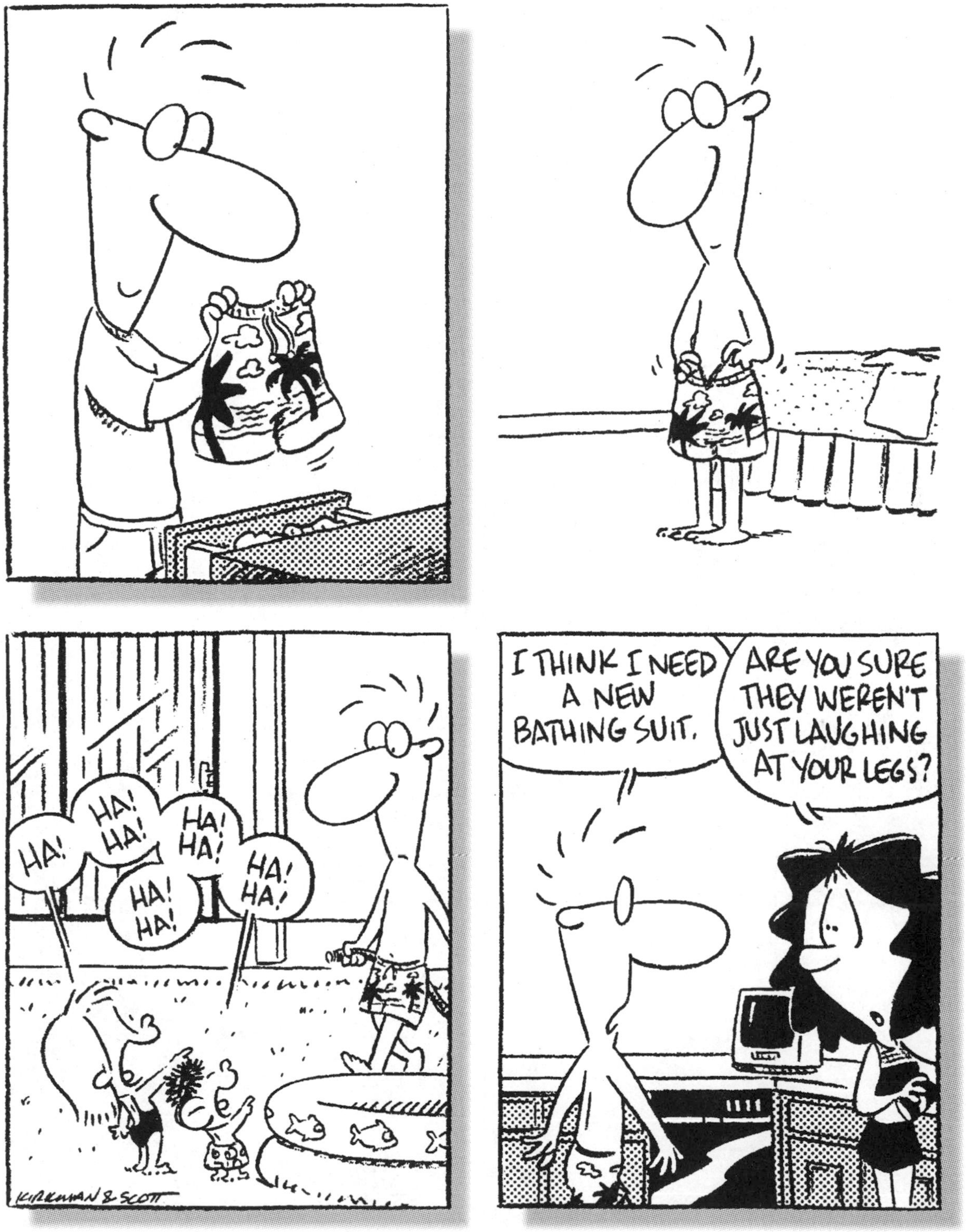
HA!
HA! HA!
HA! HA!
HA! HA!
HA! HA!
KIRKMAN & SCOTT
I THINK I NEED A NEW BATHING SUIT.
ARE YOU SURE THEY WEREN'T JUST LAUGHING AT YOUR LEGS?

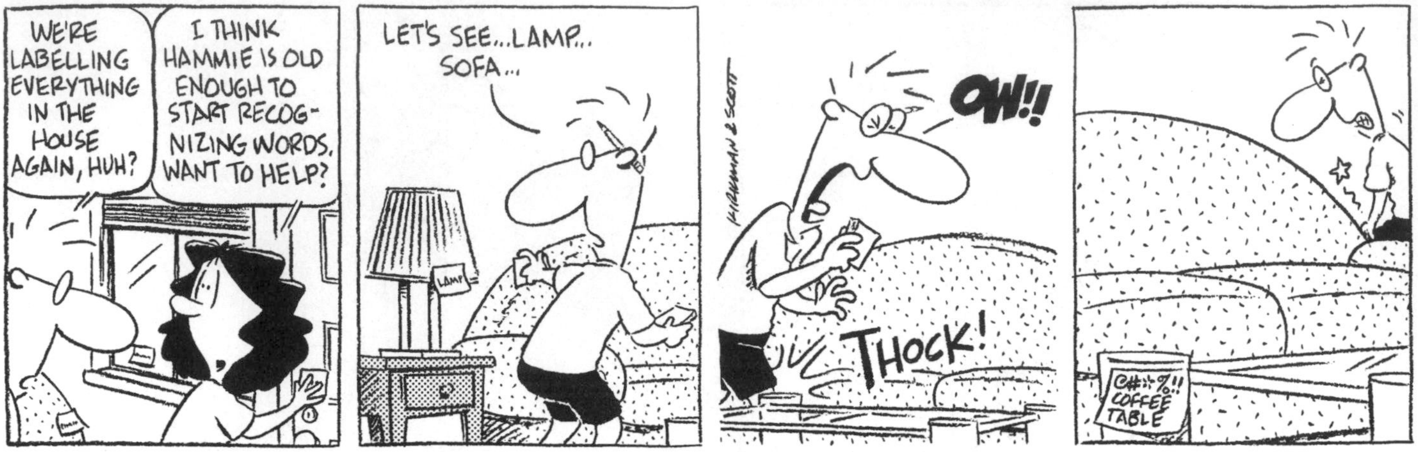
WE'RE LABELLING EVERYTHING IN THE HOUSE AGAIN, HUH?
I THINK HAMMIE IS OLD ENOUGH TO START RECOGNIZING WORDS. WANT TO HELP?
LET'S SEE...LAMP... SOFA...
LAMP
KIRKMAN & SCOTT
OW!!
THOCK!
@#!%!! COFFEE TABLE

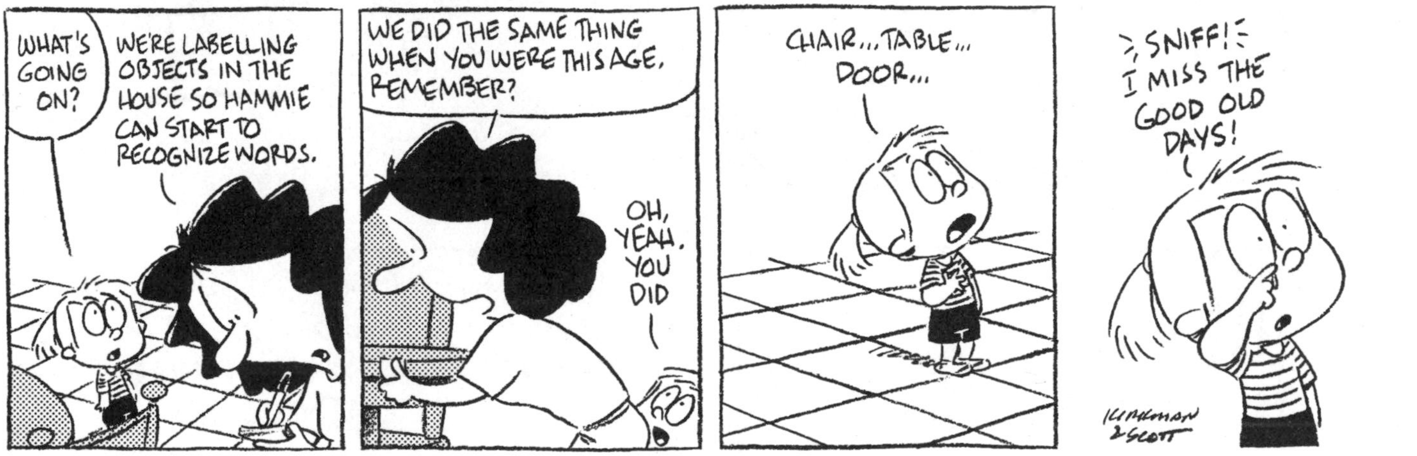
WHAT'S GOING ON?
WE'RE LABELLING OBJECTS IN THE HOUSE SO HAMMIE CAN START TO RECOGNIZE WORDS.
WE DID THE SAME THING WHEN YOU WERE THIS AGE, REMEMBER?
OH, YEAH. YOU DID
CHAIR...TABLE... DOOR...
SNIFF! I MISS THE GOOD OLD DAYS!
KIRKMAN & SCOTT

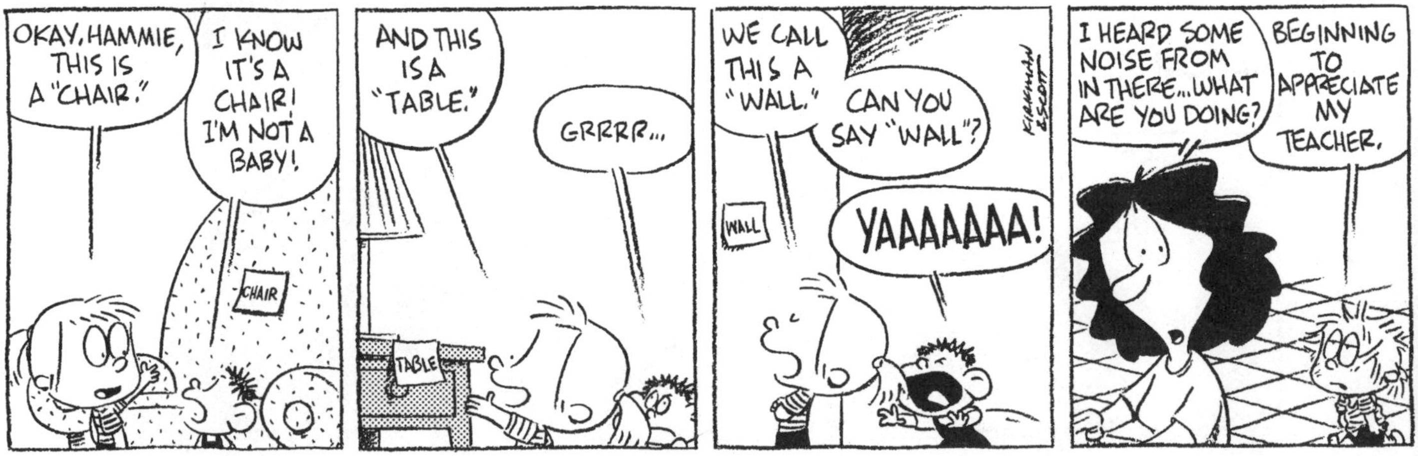
OKAY, HAMMIE, THIS IS A "CHAIR."
I KNOW IT'S A CHAIR! I'M NOT A BABY!
CHAIR
AND THIS IS A "TABLE."
GRRRR...
TABLE
WE CALL THIS A "WALL."
CAN YOU SAY "WALL"?
KIRKMAN & SCOTT
WALL
YAAAAAAA!
I HEARD SOME NOISE FROM IN THERE...WHAT ARE YOU DOING?
BEGINNING TO APPRECIATE MY TEACHER.

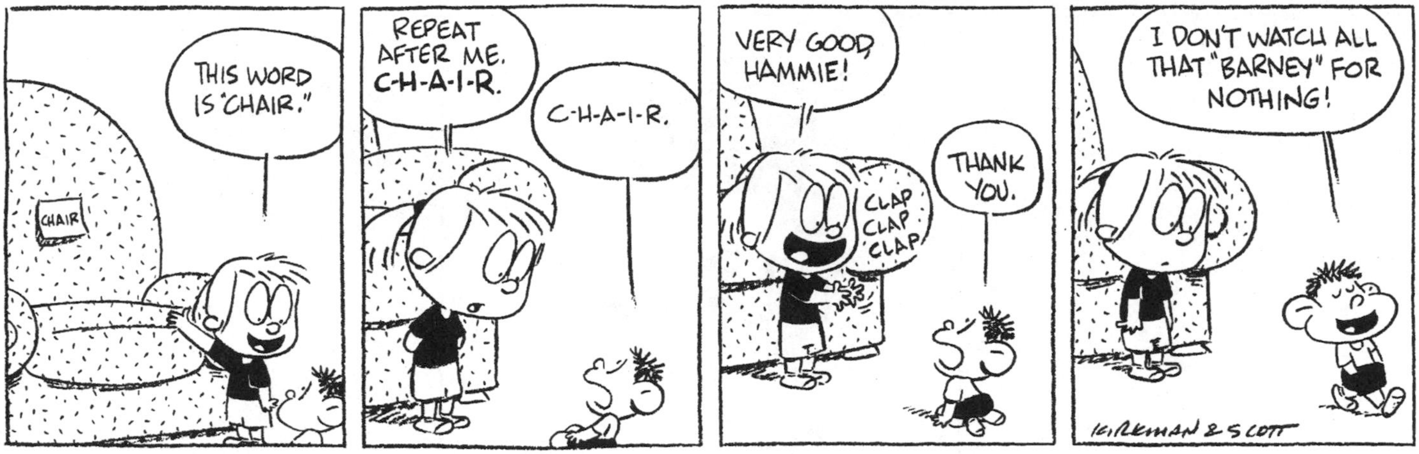
THIS WORD IS "CHAIR."
CHAIR
REPEAT AFTER ME. C-H-A-I-R.
C-H-A-I-R.
VERY GOOD, HAMMIE!
CLAP CLAP CLAP
THANK YOU.
I DON'T WATCH ALL THAT "BARNEY" FOR NOTHING!
KIRKMAN & SCOTT

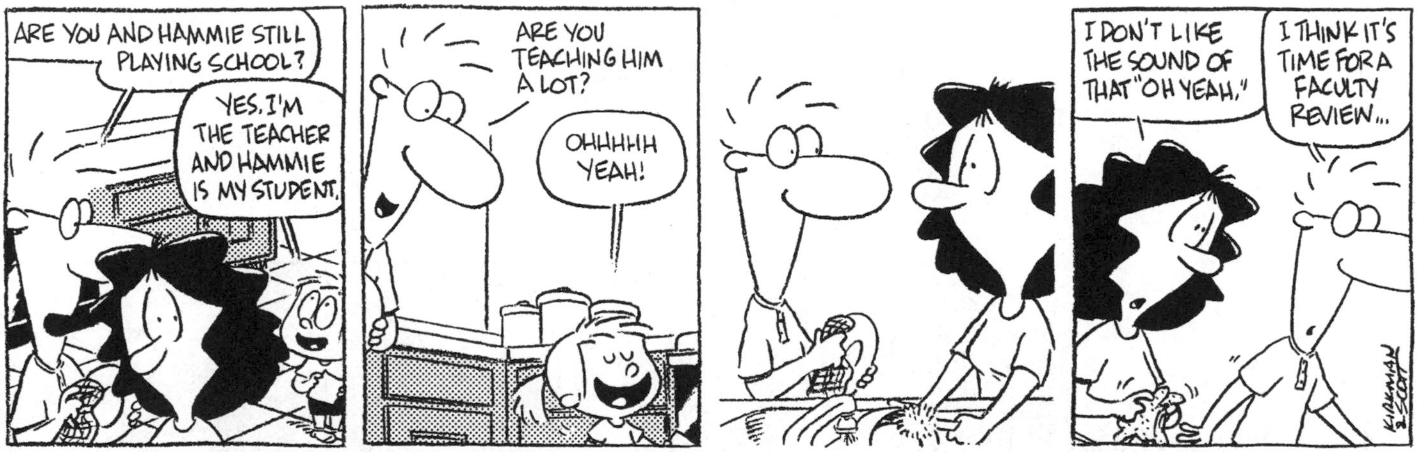
ARE YOU AND HAMMIE STILL PLAYING SCHOOL?
YES. I'M THE TEACHER AND HAMMIE IS MY STUDENT.
ARE YOU TEACHING HIM A LOT?
OHHHHH YEAH!
I DON'T LIKE THE SOUND OF THAT "OH YEAH."
I THINK IT'S TIME FOR A FACULTY REVIEW...
KIRKMAN & SCOTT

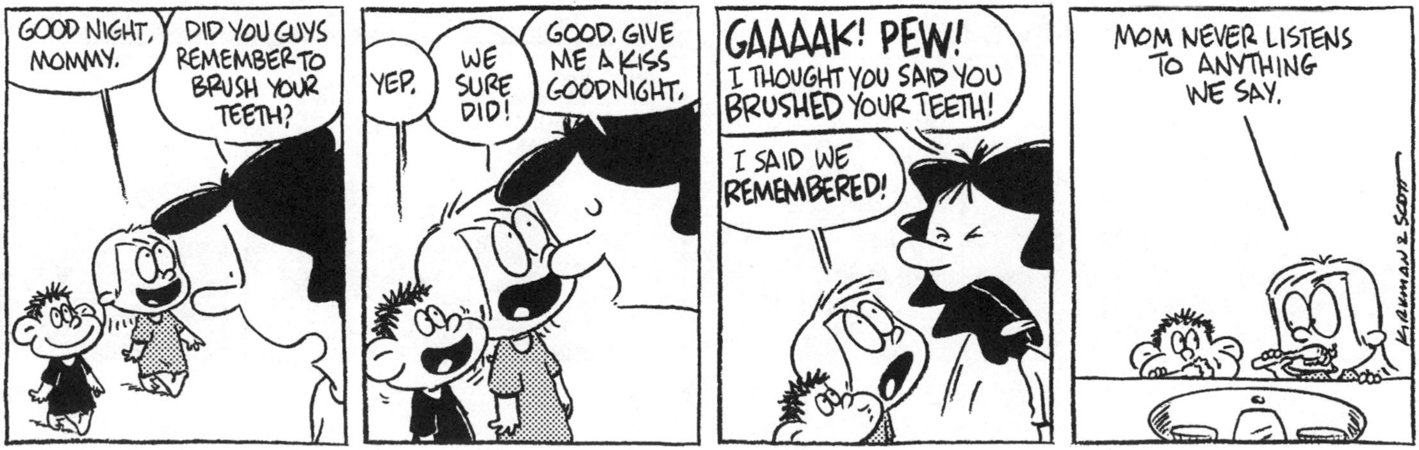
GOOD NIGHT, MOMMY.
DID YOU GUYS REMEMBER TO BRUSH YOUR TEETH?
YEP.
WE SURE DID!
GOOD. GIVE ME A KISS GOODNIGHT.
GAAAAK! PEW! I THOUGHT YOU SAID YOU BRUSHED YOUR TEETH!
I SAID WE REMEMBERED!
MOM NEVER LISTENS TO ANYTHING WE SAY.
KIRKMAN & SCOTT

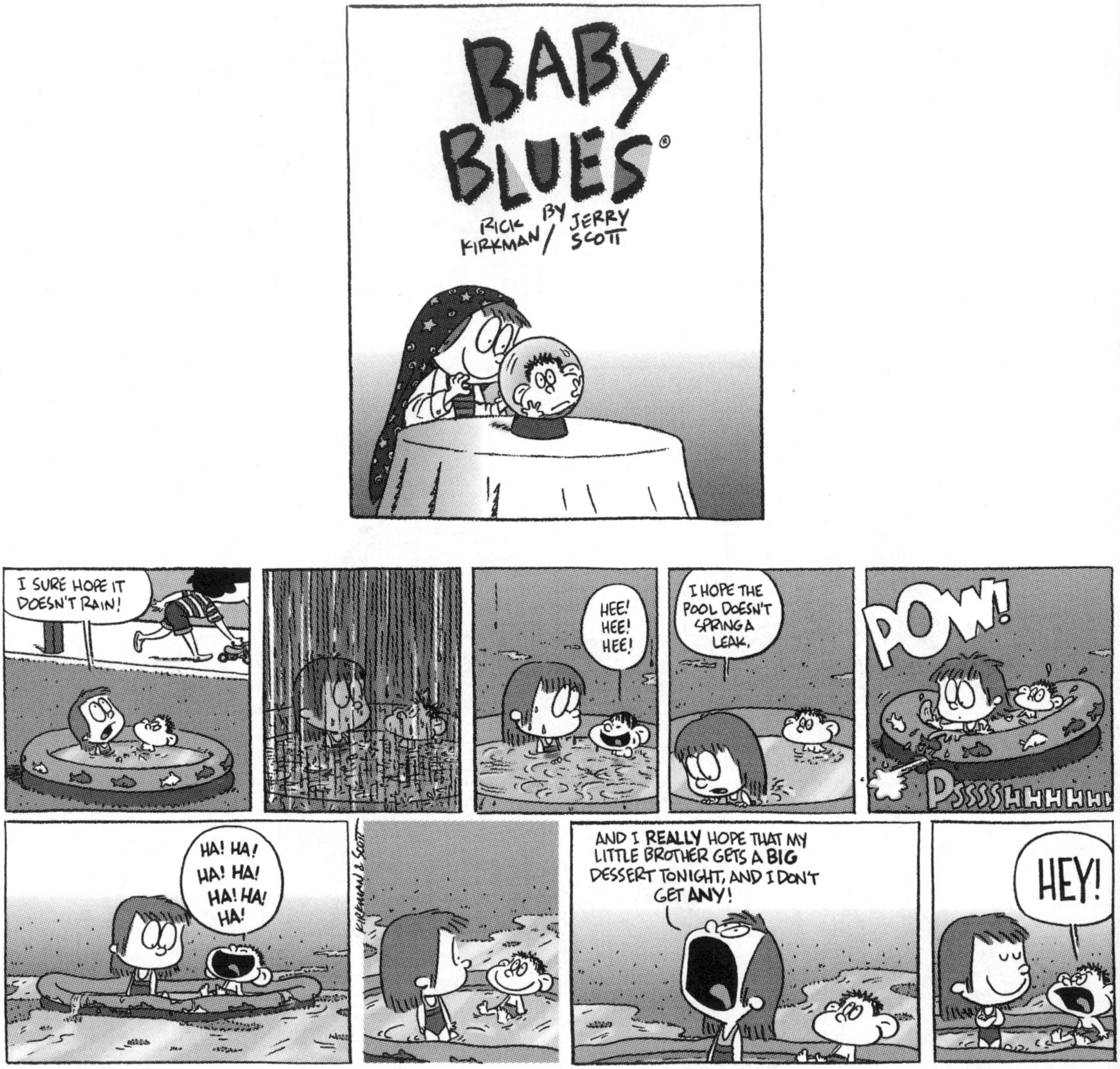
BABY BLUES®
BY RICK KIRKMAN / JERRY SCOTT
I SURE HOPE IT DOESN'T RAIN!
HEE! HEE! HEE!
I HOPE THE POOL DOESN'T SPRING A LEAK.
POW!
PSSSSHHHHHH
HA! HA! HA! HA! HA! HA! HA!
KIRKMAN & SCOTT
AND I REALLY HOPE THAT MY LITTLE BROTHER GETS A BIG DESSERT TONIGHT, AND I DON'T GET ANY!
HEY!

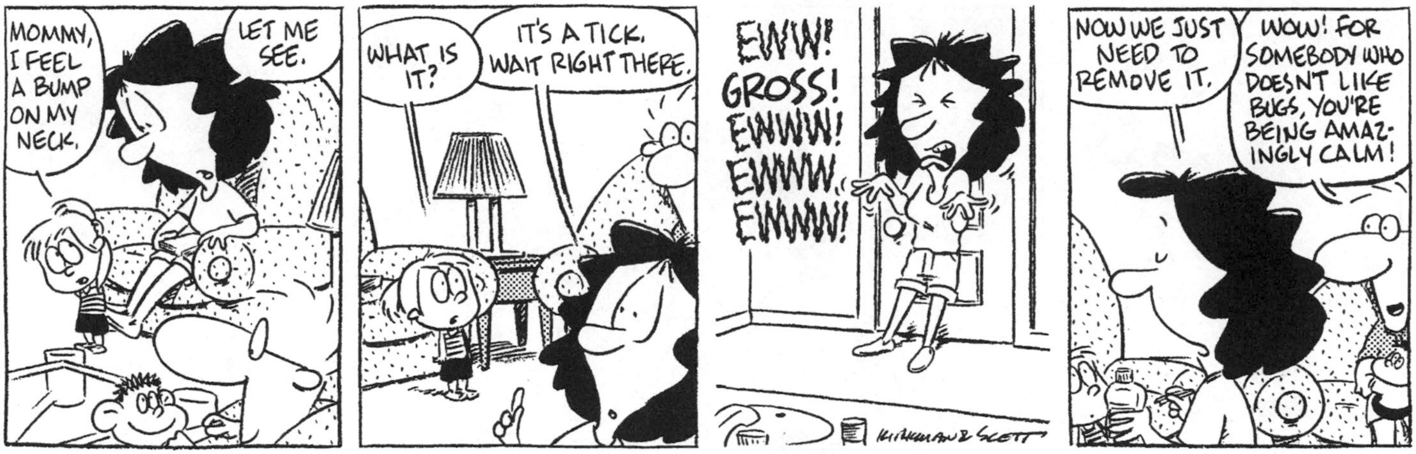
MOMMY, I FEEL A BUMP ON MY NECK.
LET ME SEE.
WHAT IS IT?
IT'S A TICK. WAIT RIGHT THERE.
EWW! GROSS! EWWW! EWWW. EWWW!
KIRKMAN & SCOTT
NOW WE JUST NEED TO REMOVE IT.
WOW! FOR SOMEBODY WHO DOESN'T LIKE BUGS, YOU'RE BEING AMAZINGLY CALM!

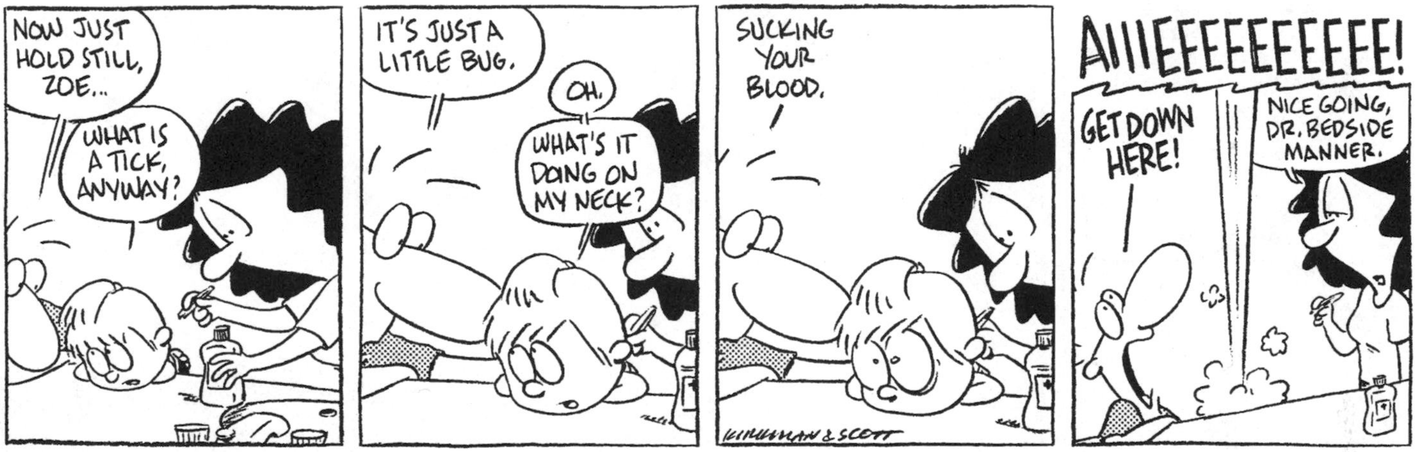
NOW JUST HOLD STILL, ZOE...
WHAT IS A TICK, ANYWAY?
IT'S JUST A LITTLE BUG.
OH.
WHAT'S IT DOING ON MY NECK?
SUCKING YOUR BLOOD.
KIRKMAN & SCOTT
AIIIEEEEEEEEEE!
GET DOWN HERE!
NICE GOING, DR. BEDSIDE MANNER.

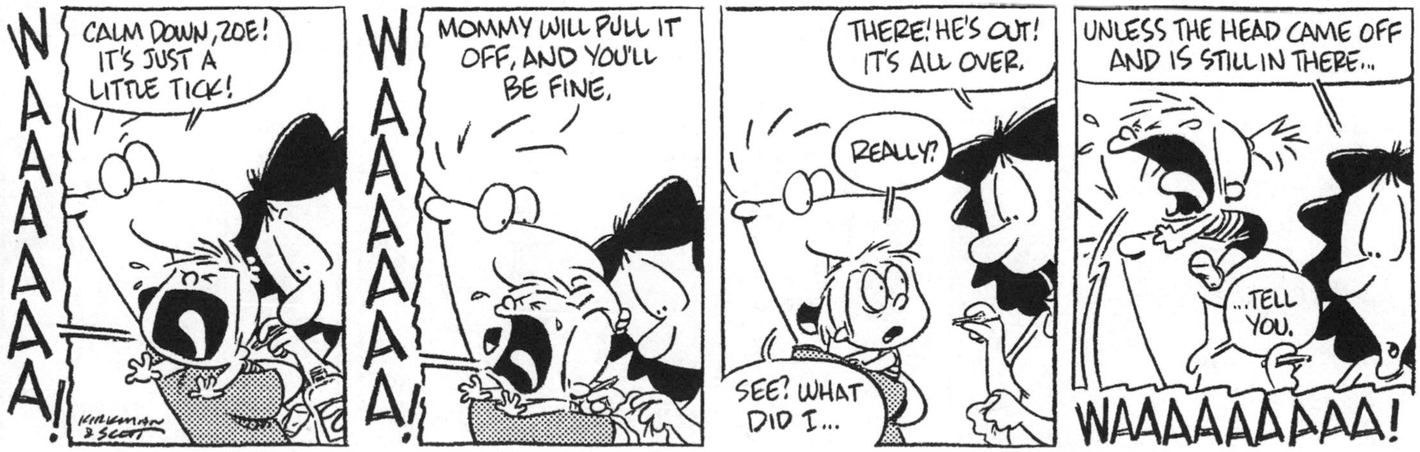
WAAAAAA!
CALM DOWN, ZOE! IT'S JUST A LITTLE TICK!
KIRKMAN & SCOTT
WAAAAAA!
MOMMY WILL PULL IT OFF, AND YOU'LL BE FINE.
THERE! HE'S OUT! IT'S ALL OVER.
REALLY?
SEE? WHAT DID I...
UNLESS THE HEAD CAME OFF AND IS STILL IN THERE...
...TELL YOU.
WAAAAAAAAA!

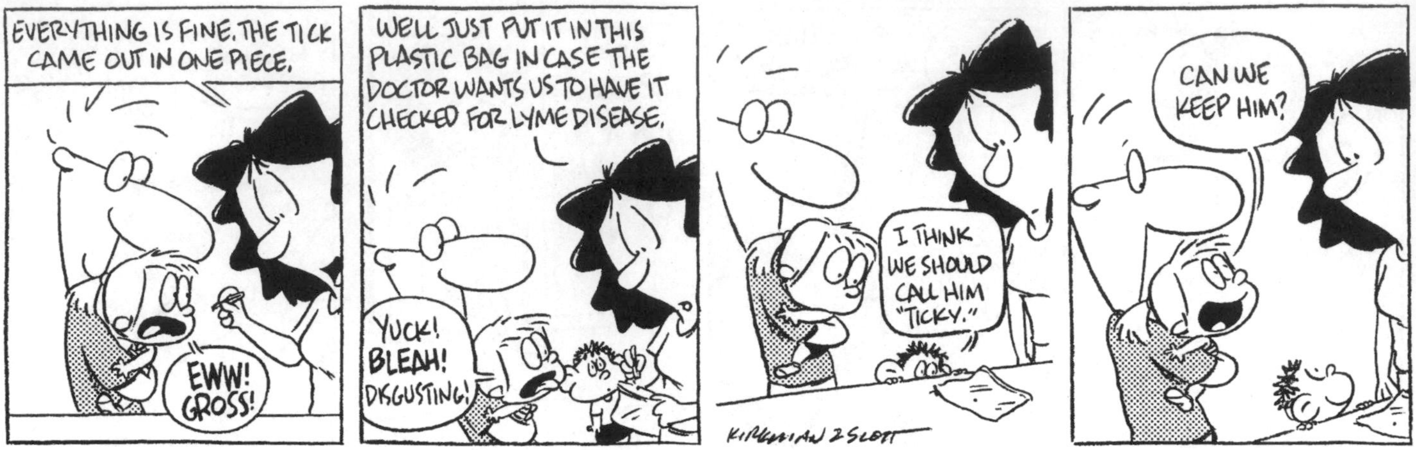
EVERYTHING IS FINE. THE TICK CAME OUT IN ONE PIECE.
EWW! GROSS!
WE'LL JUST PUT IT IN THIS PLASTIC BAG IN CASE THE DOCTOR WANTS US TO HAVE IT CHECKED FOR LYME DISEASE.
YUCK! BLEAH! DISGUSTING!
I THINK WE SHOULD CALL HIM "TICKY."
KIRKMAN & SCOTT
CAN WE KEEP HIM?

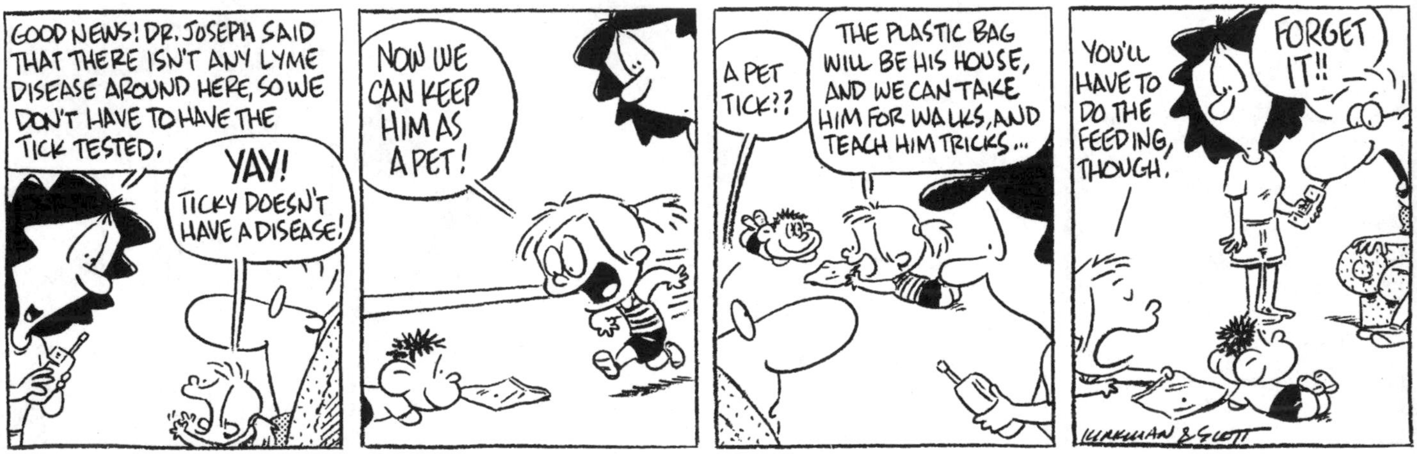
GOOD NEWS! DR. JOSEPH SAID THAT THERE ISN'T ANY LYME DISEASE AROUND HERE, SO WE DON'T HAVE TO HAVE THE TICK TESTED.
YAY! TICKY DOESN'T HAVE A DISEASE!
NOW WE CAN KEEP HIM AS A PET!
A PET TICK??
THE PLASTIC BAG WILL BE HIS HOUSE, AND WE CAN TAKE HIM FOR WALKS, AND TEACH HIM TRICKS...
YOU'LL HAVE TO DO THE FEEDING, THOUGH.
FORGET IT!!
KIRKMAN & SCOTT

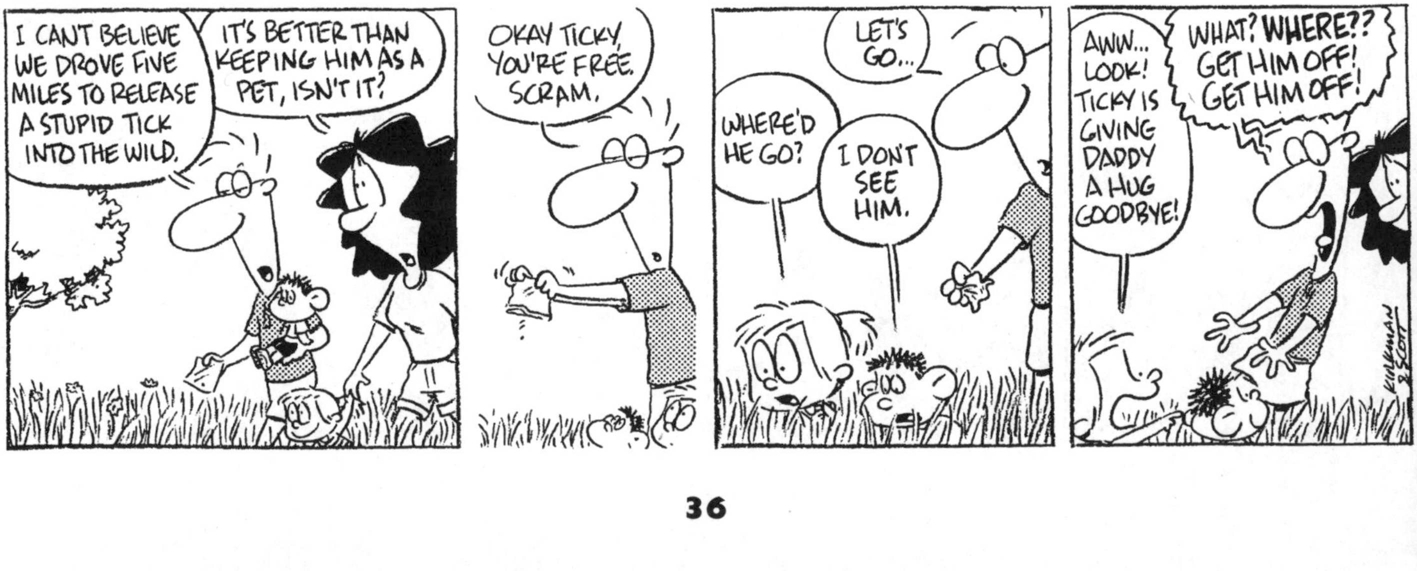
I CAN'T BELIEVE WE DROVE FIVE MILES TO RELEASE A STUPID TICK INTO THE WILD.
IT'S BETTER THAN KEEPING HIM AS A PET, ISN'T IT?
OKAY TICKY, YOU'RE FREE. SCRAM.
LET'S GO...
WHERE'D HE GO?
I DON'T SEE HIM.
AWW... LOOK! TICKY IS GIVING DADDY A HUG GOODBYE!
WHAT? WHERE?? GET HIM OFF! GET HIM OFF!
KIRKMAN & SCOTT

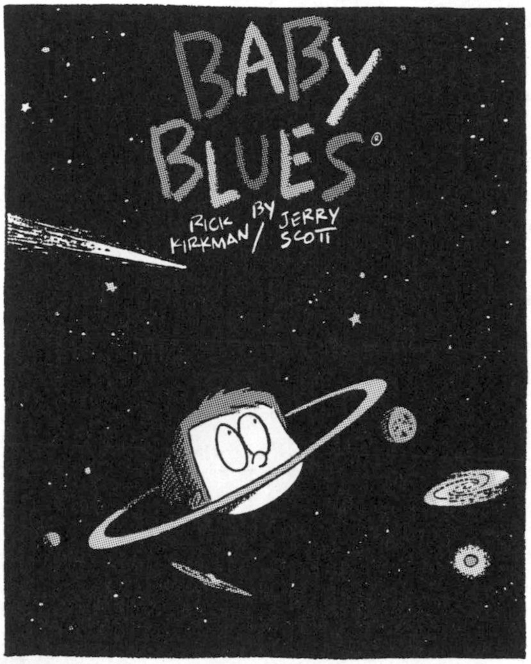

BABY BLUES®
BY RICK KIRKMAN / JERRY SCOTT

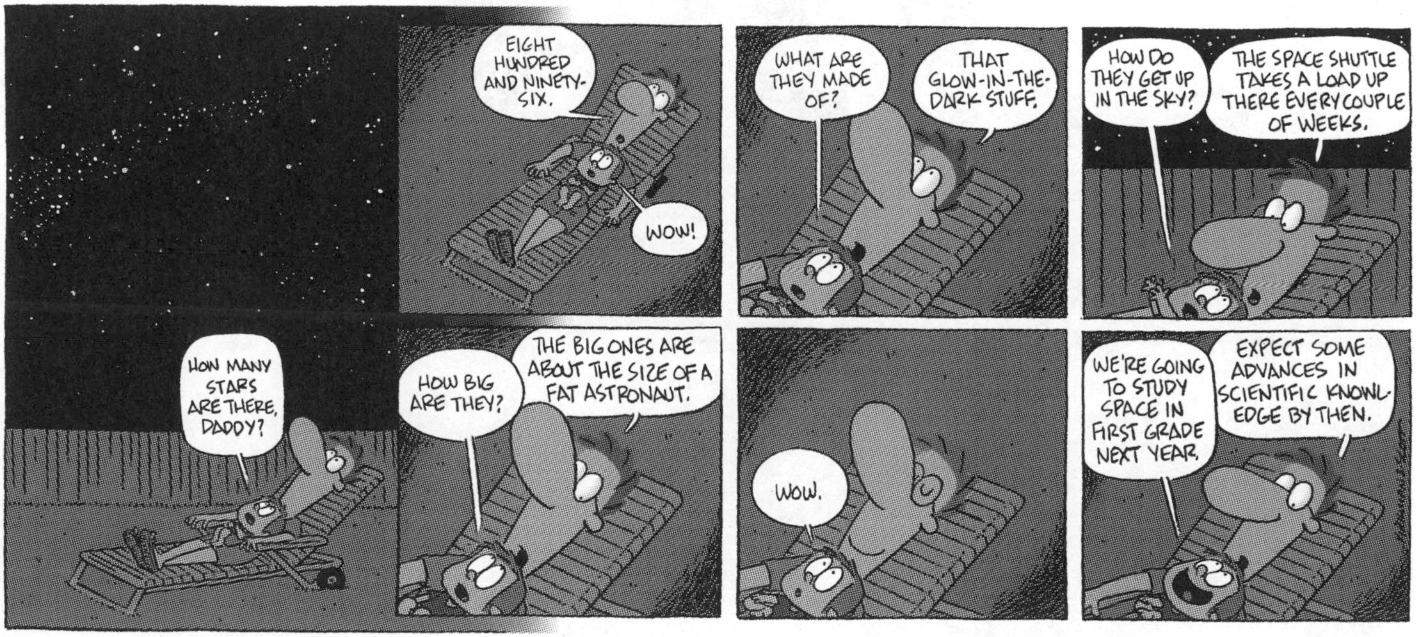

HOW MANY STARS ARE THERE, DADDY?
EIGHT HUNDRED AND NINETY-SIX.
WOW!
WHAT ARE THEY MADE OF?
THAT GLOW-IN-THE-DARK STUFF.
HOW DO THEY GET UP IN THE SKY?
THE SPACE SHUTTLE TAKES A LOAD UP THERE EVERY COUPLE OF WEEKS.
HOW BIG ARE THEY?
THE BIG ONES ARE ABOUT THE SIZE OF A FAT ASTRONAUT.
WOW.
WE'RE GOING TO STUDY SPACE IN FIRST GRADE NEXT YEAR.
EXPECT SOME ADVANCES IN SCIENTIFIC KNOWLEDGE BY THEN.

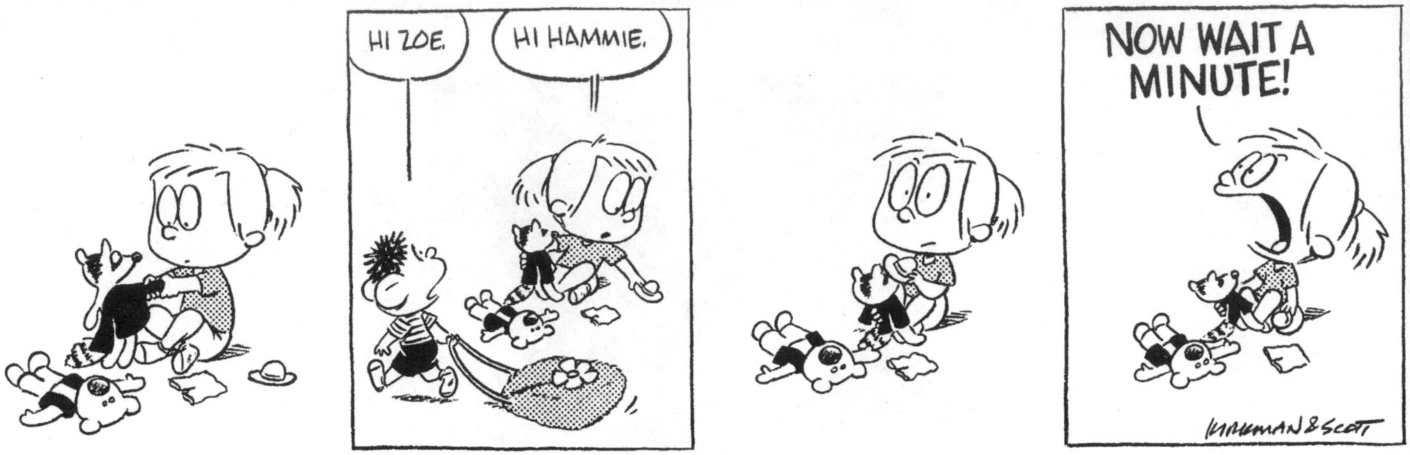
HI ZOE.
HI HAMMIE.
NOW WAIT A MINUTE!
KIRKMAN & SCOTT

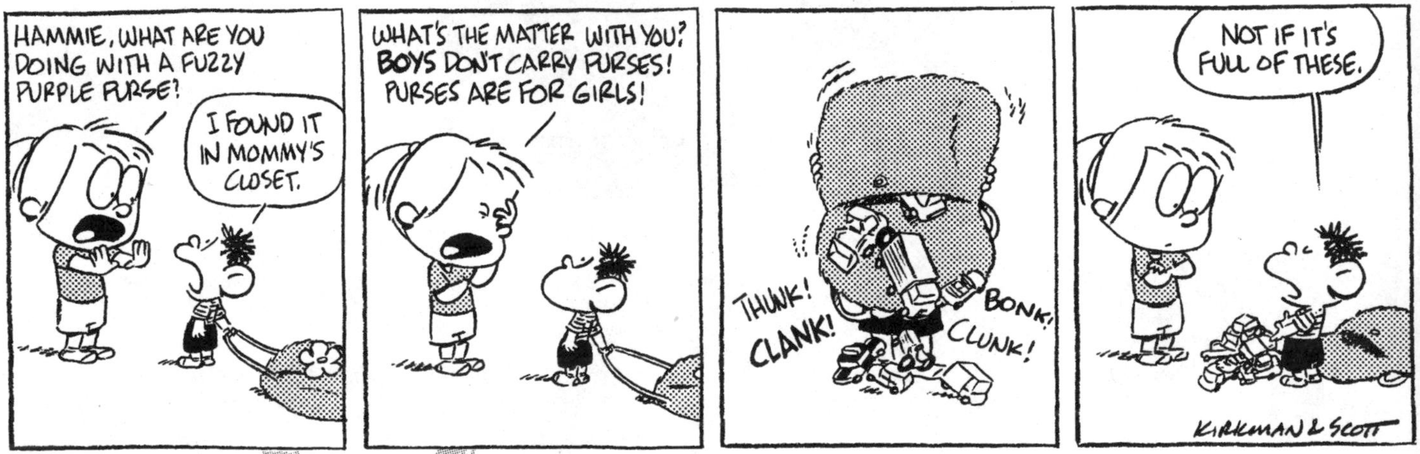
HAMMIE, WHAT ARE YOU DOING WITH A FUZZY PURPLE PURSE?
I FOUND IT IN MOMMY'S CLOSET.
WHAT'S THE MATTER WITH YOU? BOYS DON'T CARRY PURSES! PURSES ARE FOR GIRLS!
THUNK!
CLANK!
BONK!
CLUNK!
NOT IF IT'S FULL OF THESE.
KIRKMAN & SCOTT

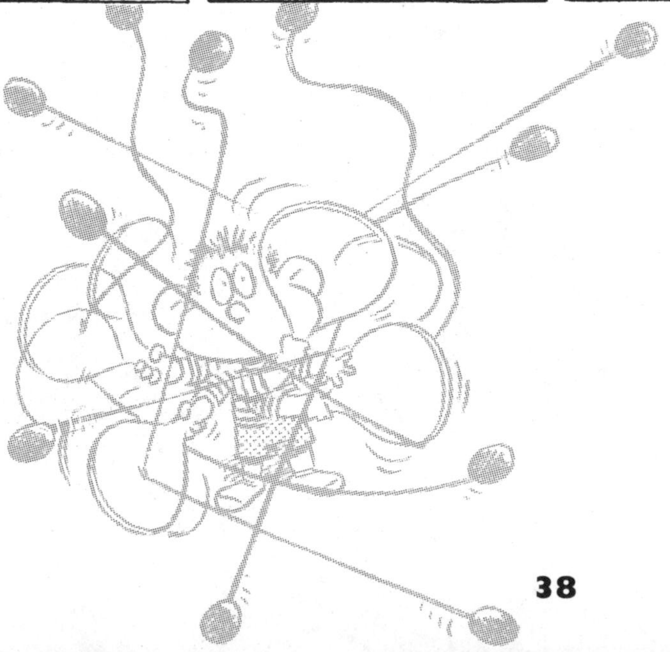

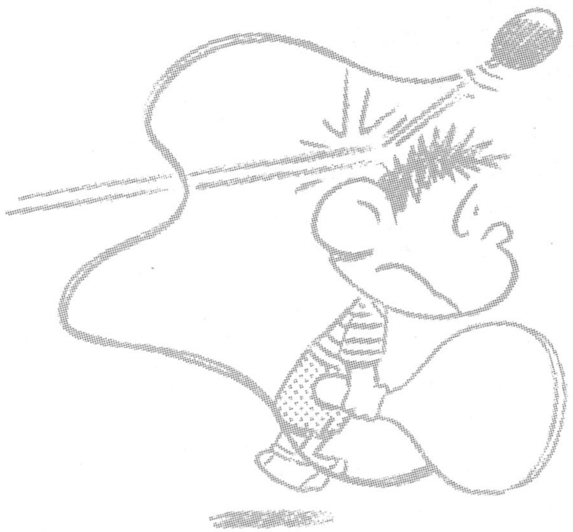

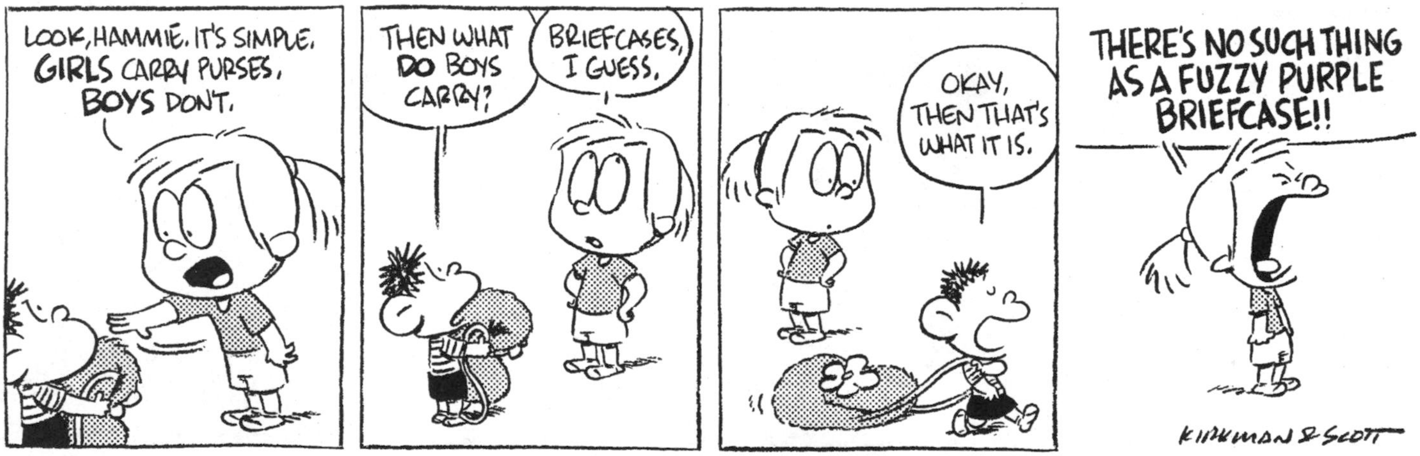

LOOK, HAMMIE. IT'S SIMPLE. GIRLS CARRY PURSES. BOYS DON'T.
THEN WHAT DO BOYS CARRY?
BRIEFCASES, I GUESS.
OKAY, THEN THAT'S WHAT IT IS.
THERE'S NO SUCH THING AS A FUZZY PURPLE BRIEFCASE!!
KIRKMAN & SCOTT

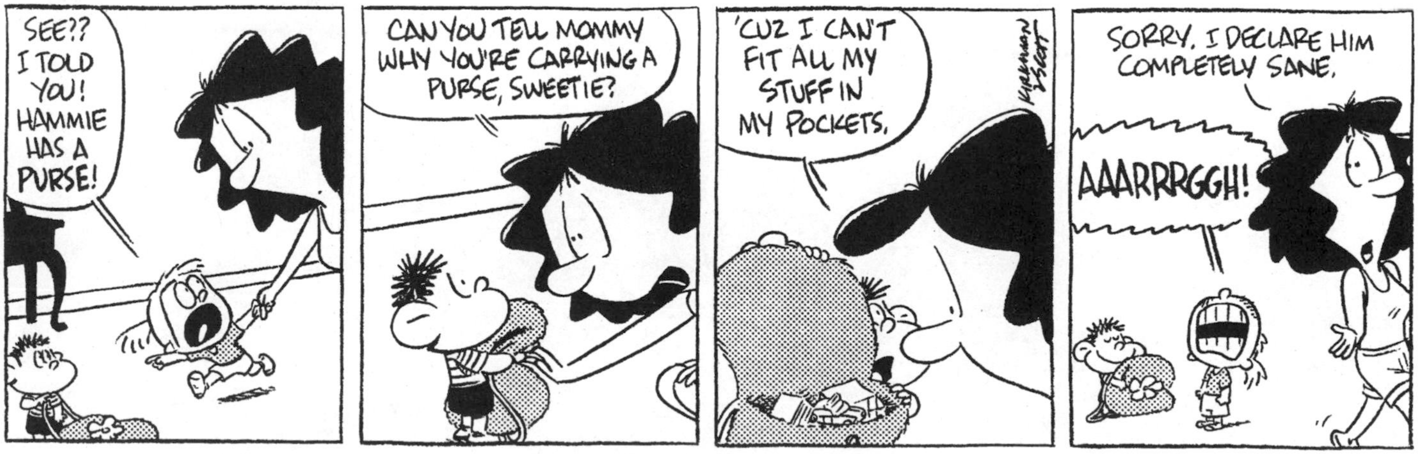

SEE?? I TOLD YOU! HAMMIE HAS A PURSE!
CAN YOU TELL MOMMY WHY YOU'RE CARRYING A PURSE, SWEETIE?
'CUZ I CAN'T FIT ALL MY STUFF IN MY POCKETS.
KIRKMAN & SCOTT
SORRY. I DECLARE HIM COMPLETELY SANE.
AAARRRGGH!

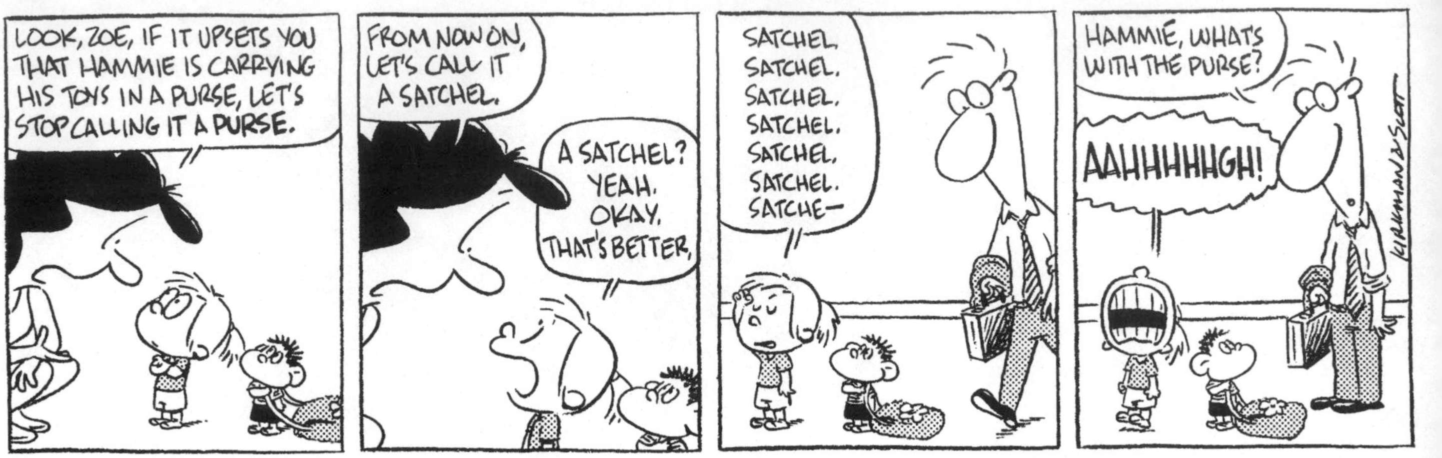
LOOK, ZOE, IF IT UPSETS YOU THAT HAMMIE IS CARRYING HIS TOYS IN A PURSE, LET'S STOP CALLING IT A **PURSE**.
FROM NOW ON, LET'S CALL IT A SATCHEL.
A SATCHEL? YEAH. OKAY. THAT'S BETTER.
SATCHEL. SATCHEL. SATCHEL. SATCHEL. SATCHEL. SATCHEL. SATCHE—
HAMMIE, WHAT'S WITH THE PURSE?
AAHHHHHGH!

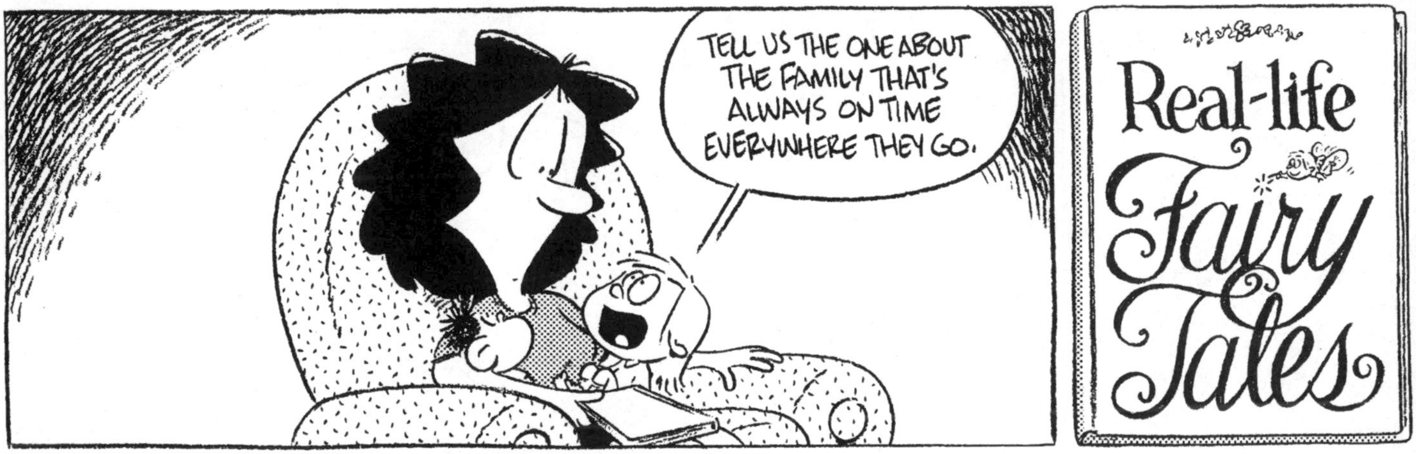
TELL US THE ONE ABOUT THE FAMILY THAT'S ALWAYS ON TIME EVERYWHERE THEY GO.
Real-life Fairy Tales

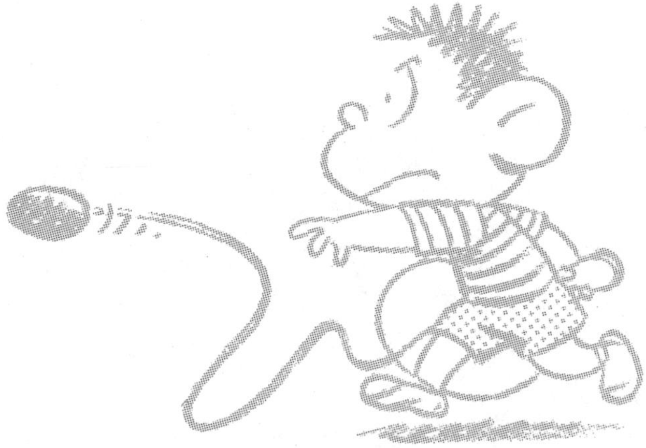

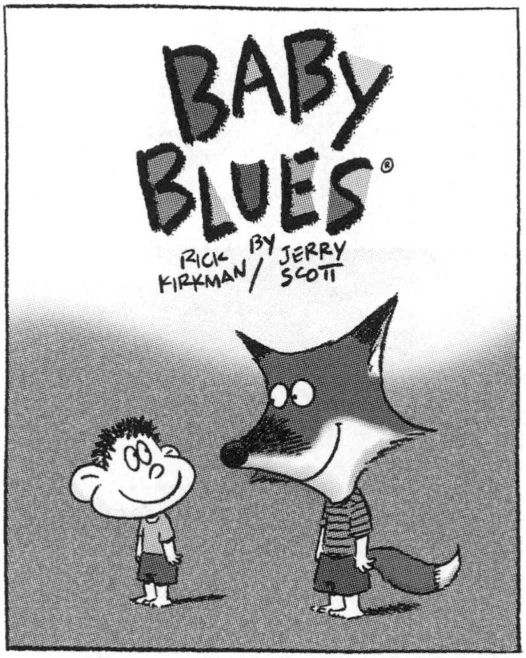
BABY BLUES®
BY RICK KIRKMAN / JERRY SCOTT

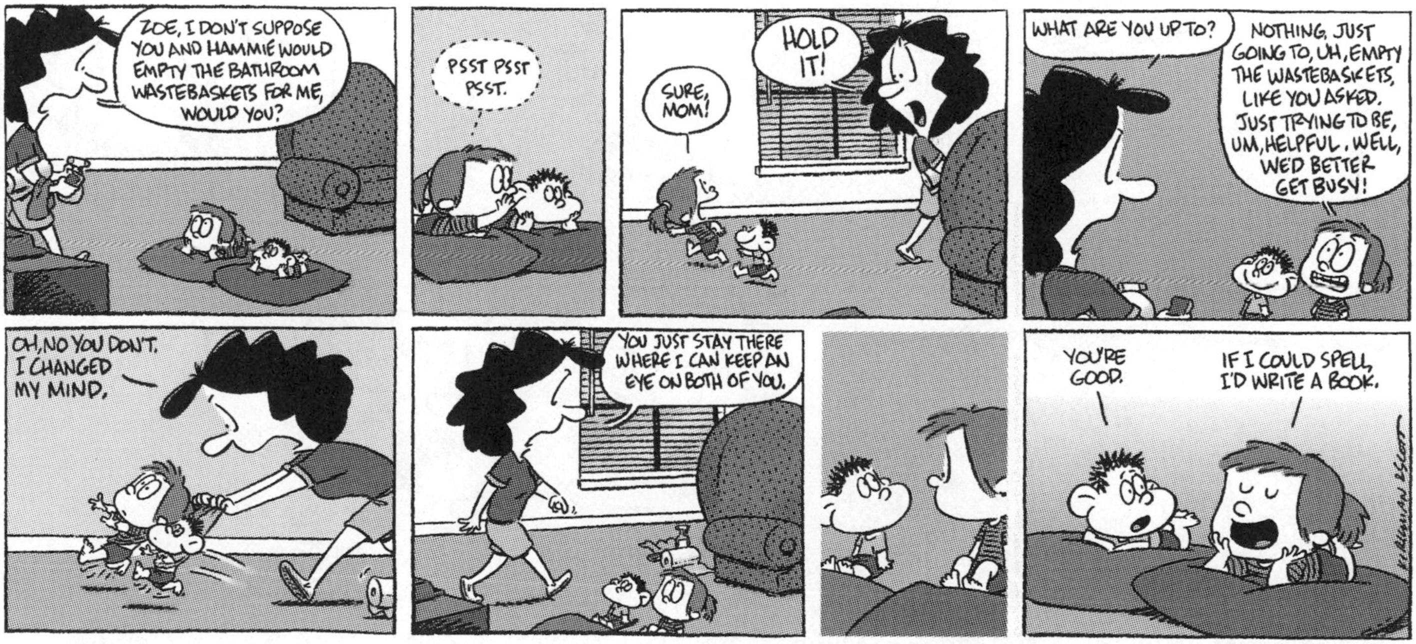
ZOE, I DON'T SUPPOSE YOU AND HAMMIE WOULD EMPTY THE BATHROOM WASTEBASKETS FOR ME, WOULD YOU?
PSST PSST PSST.
SURE, MOM!
HOLD IT!
WHAT ARE YOU UP TO?
NOTHING. JUST GOING TO, UH, EMPTY THE WASTEBASKETS, LIKE YOU ASKED. JUST TRYING TO BE, UM, HELPFUL. WELL, WE'D BETTER GET BUSY!
OH, NO YOU DON'T. I CHANGED MY MIND.
YOU JUST STAY THERE WHERE I CAN KEEP AN EYE ON BOTH OF YOU.
YOU'RE GOOD.
IF I COULD SPELL, I'D WRITE A BOOK.

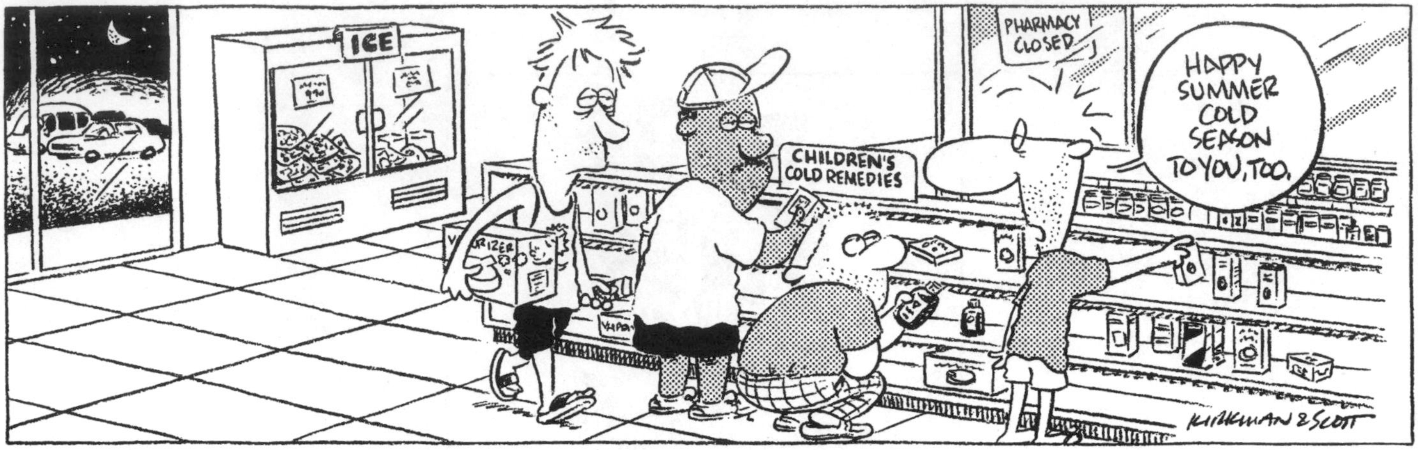
ICE
PHARMACY CLOSED
CHILDREN'S COLD REMEDIES
HAPPY SUMMER COLD SEASON TO YOU, TOO.
KIRKMAN & SCOTT

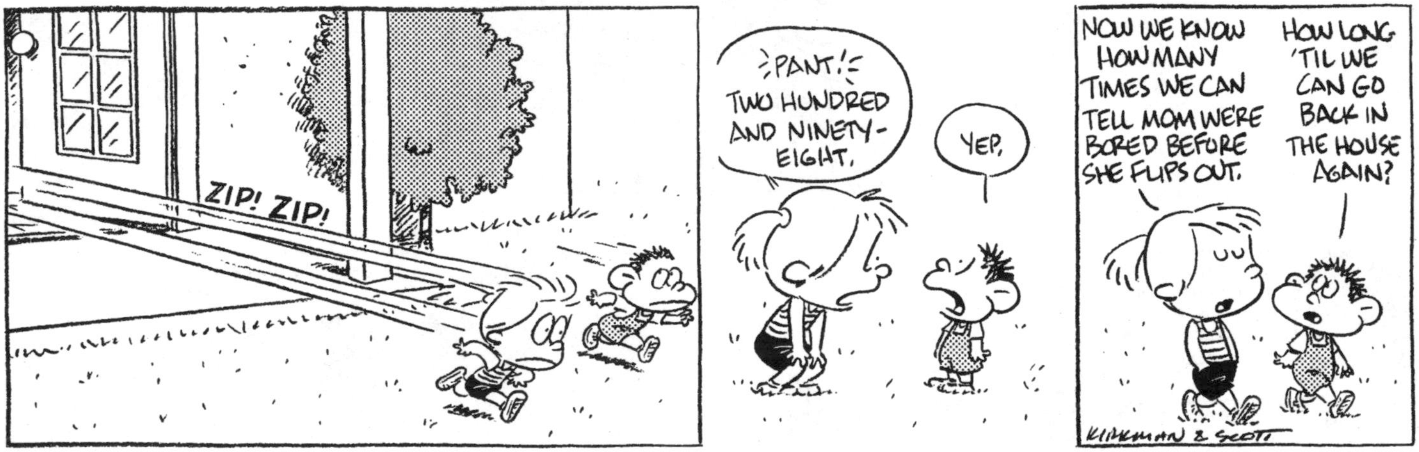
ZIP! ZIP!
PANT! TWO HUNDRED AND NINETY-EIGHT.
YEP.
NOW WE KNOW HOW MANY TIMES WE CAN TELL MOM WE'RE BORED BEFORE SHE FLIPS OUT.
HOW LONG 'TIL WE CAN GO BACK IN THE HOUSE AGAIN?
KIRKMAN & SCOTT

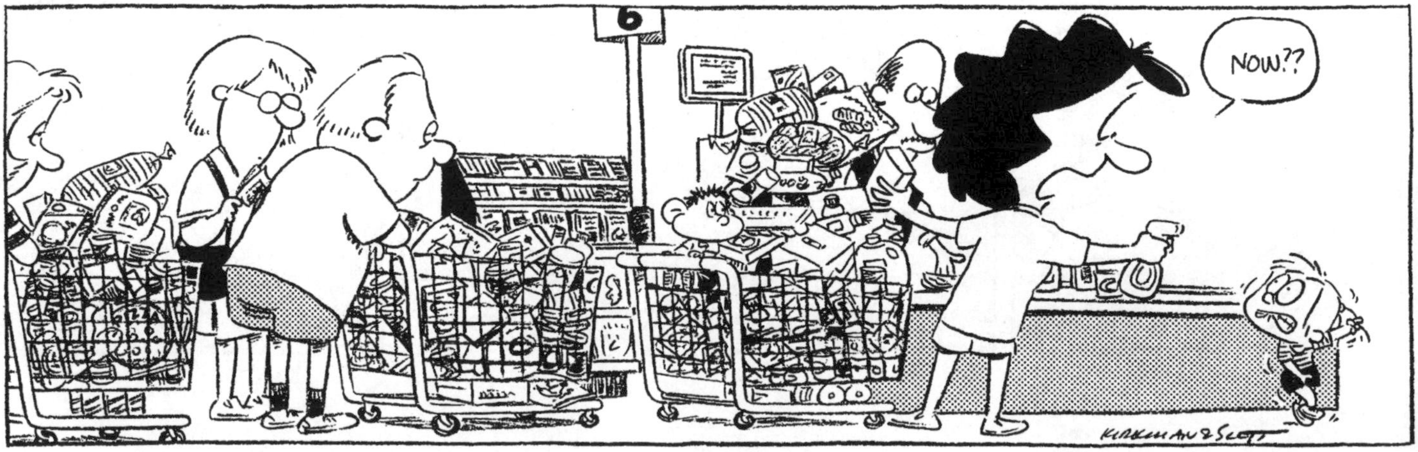
6
NOW??
KIRKMAN & SCOTT

BABY BLUES®
BY JERRY
ZOE, WILL YOU GO GET DADDY A PAPER CLIP?
OKAY.
PAPER CLIP, PAPER CLIP, PAPER CLIP,
OH DEAR! WE'RE OUT OF PEPPER!
PEPPER CLIP, PEPPER CLIP, PEPPER CLIP,
HOW AM I GOING TO MAKE THE SEAFOOD DIP?
PEPPER DIP, PEPPER DIP, PEPPER DIP, PEPPER DIP,
I WONDER HOW PEPPERONI WOULD TASTE WITH CLAMS?
MOMMY, WHERE'S MY ACTION MAN?
PEPPERONI ACTION CLAM, PEPPERONI ACTION CLAM, PEPPERONI ACTION CLAM,
I FORGOT WHAT I WAS SUPPOSED TO GET, SO I JUST BROUGHT YOU A BANANA.
KIRKMAN & SCOTT

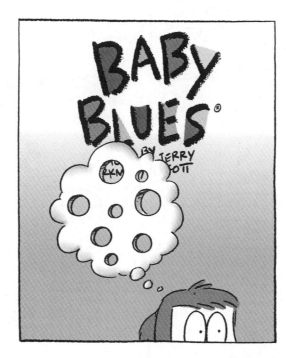

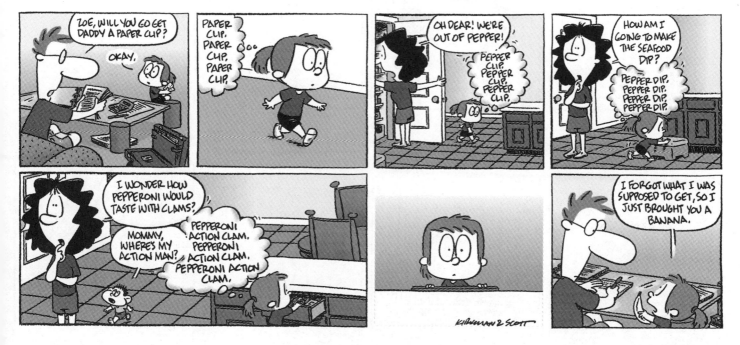

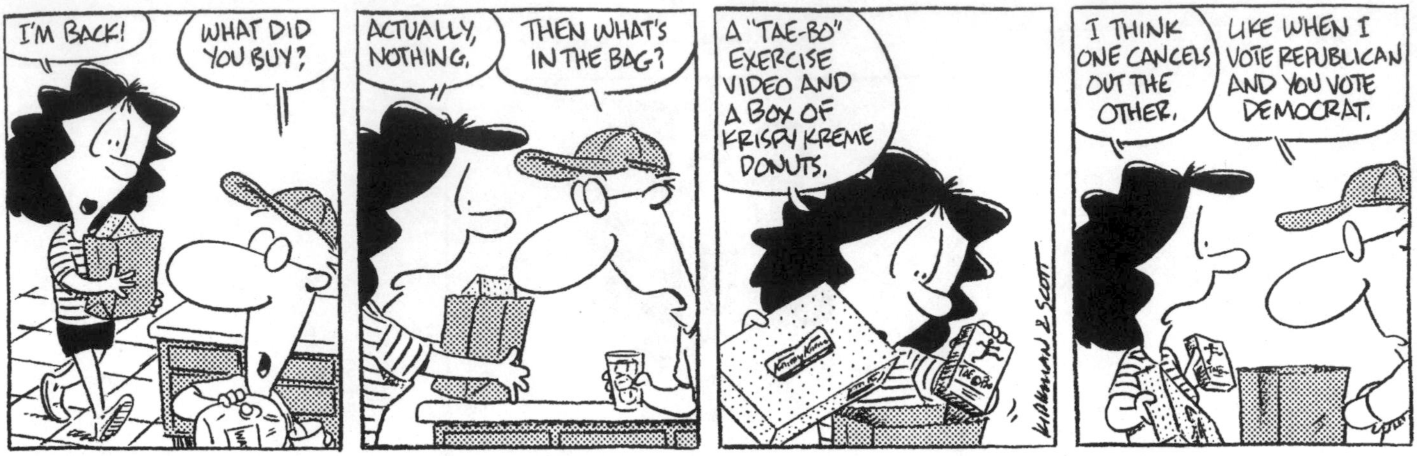
I'M BACK!
WHAT DID YOU BUY?
ACTUALLY, NOTHING.
THEN WHAT'S IN THE BAG?
A "TAE-BO" EXERCISE VIDEO AND A BOX OF KRISPY KREME DONUTS.
I THINK ONE CANCELS OUT THE OTHER.
LIKE WHEN I VOTE REPUBLICAN AND YOU VOTE DEMOCRAT.

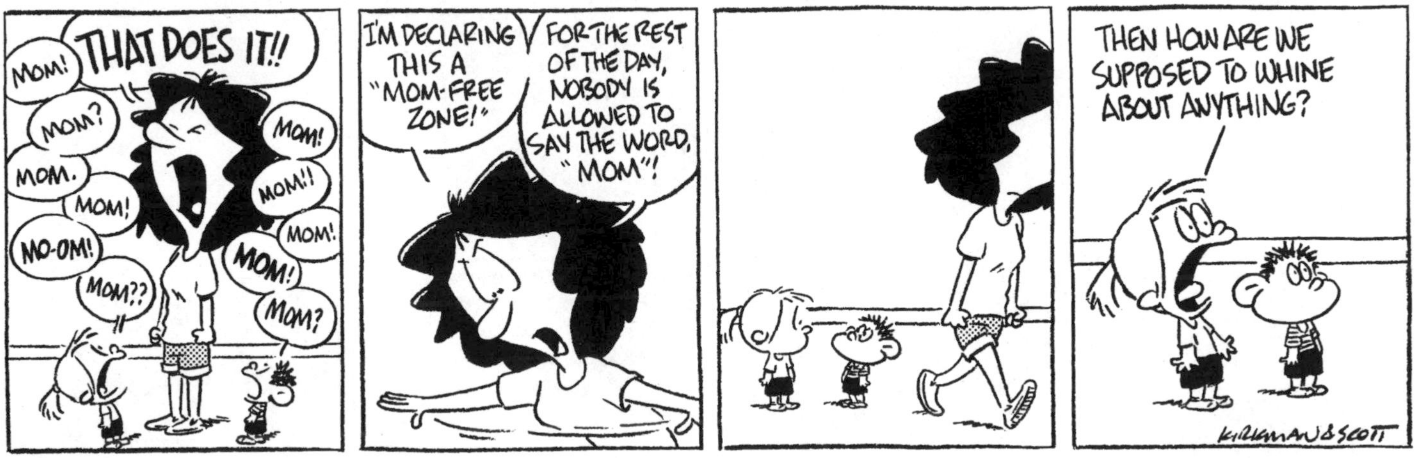
THAT DOES IT!!
MOM!
MOM?
MOM.
MOM!
MO-OM!
MOM??
MOM!
MOM!!
MOM!
MOM!
MOM?
I'M DECLARING THIS A "MOM-FREE ZONE!"
FOR THE REST OF THE DAY, NOBODY IS ALLOWED TO SAY THE WORD, "MOM"!
THEN HOW ARE WE SUPPOSED TO WHINE ABOUT ANYTHING?

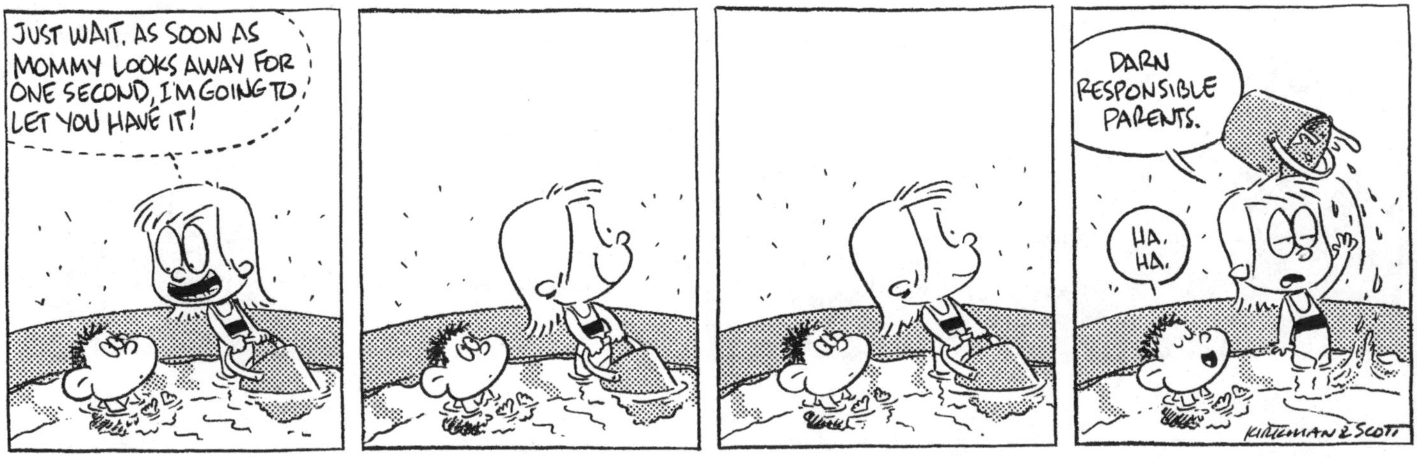
JUST WAIT. AS SOON AS MOMMY LOOKS AWAY FOR ONE SECOND, I'M GOING TO LET YOU HAVE IT!
DARN RESPONSIBLE PARENTS.
HA. HA.

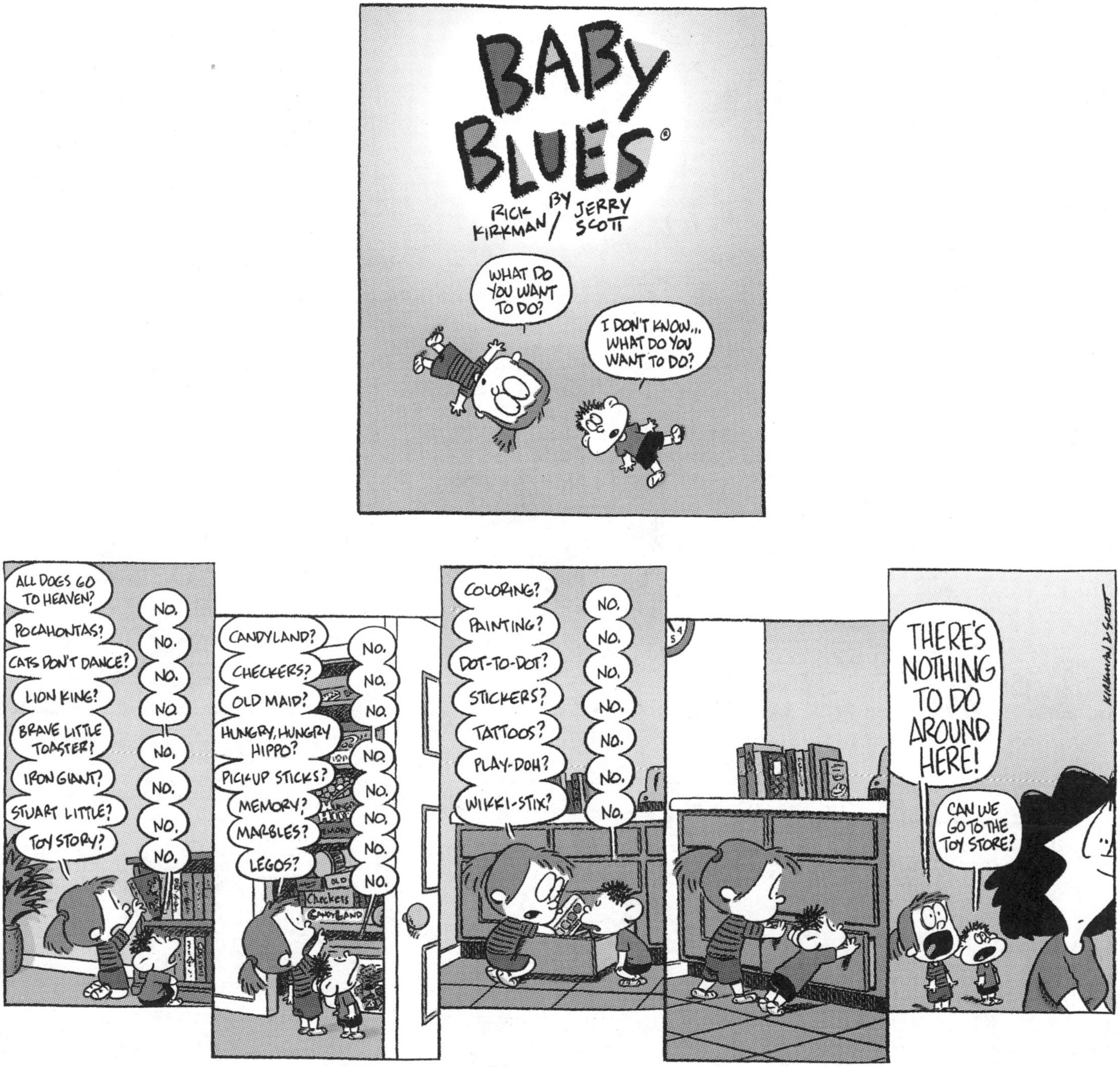
BABY BLUES®
BY RICK KIRKMAN / JERRY SCOTT
WHAT DO YOU WANT TO DO?
I DON'T KNOW... WHAT DO YOU WANT TO DO?
ALL DOGS GO TO HEAVEN?
POCAHONTAS?
CATS DON'T DANCE?
LION KING?
BRAVE LITTLE TOASTER?
IRON GIANT?
STUART LITTLE?
TOY STORY?
NO.
NO.
NO.
NO.
NO.
NO.
NO.
NO.
CANDYLAND?
CHECKERS?
OLD MAID?
HUNGRY, HUNGRY HIPPO?
PICKUP STICKS?
MEMORY?
MARBLES?
LEGOS?
NO.
NO.
NO.
NO.
NO.
NO.
NO.
NO.
COLORING?
PAINTING?
DOT-TO-DOT?
STICKERS?
TATTOOS?
PLAY-DOH?
WIKKI-STIX?
NO.
NO.
NO.
NO.
NO.
NO.
NO.
THERE'S NOTHING TO DO AROUND HERE!
CAN WE GO TO THE TOY STORE?

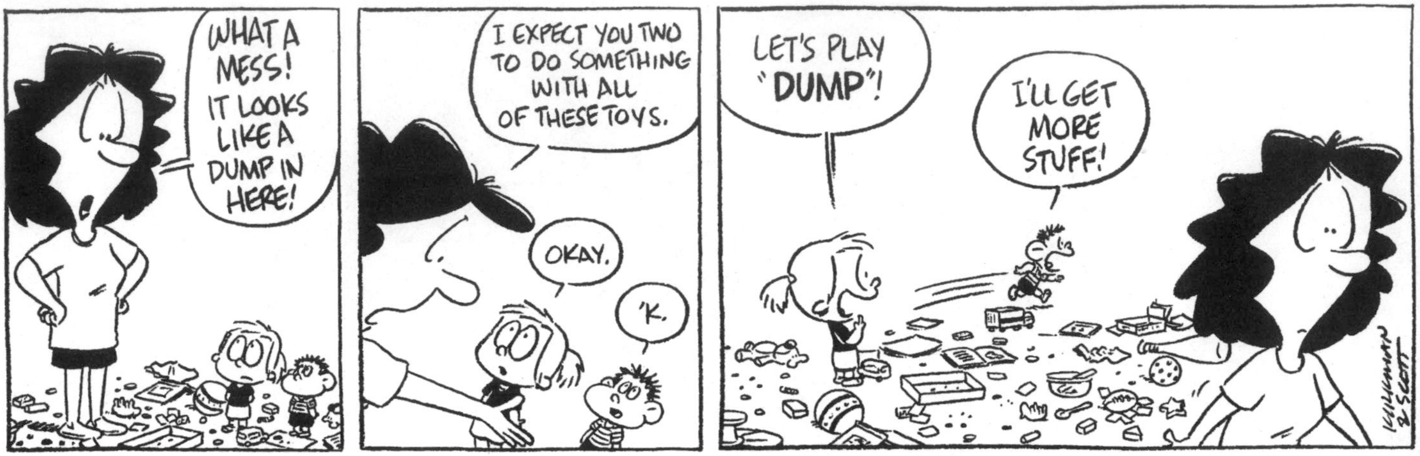
WHAT A MESS! IT LOOKS LIKE A DUMP IN HERE!
I EXPECT YOU TWO TO DO SOMETHING WITH ALL OF THESE TOYS.
OKAY.
'K.
LET'S PLAY "DUMP"!
I'LL GET MORE STUFF!

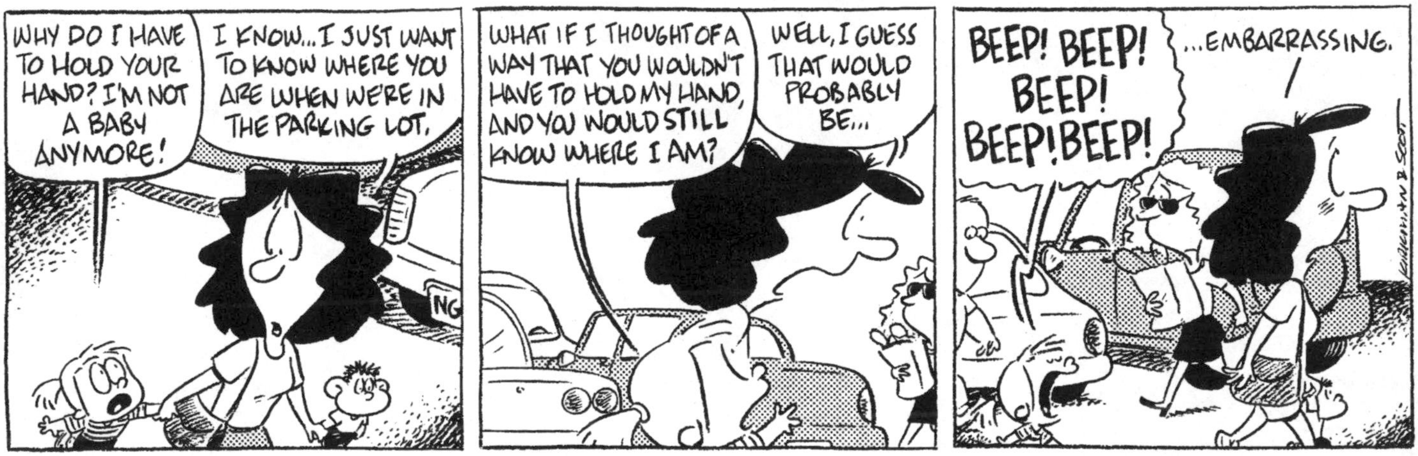
WHY DO I HAVE TO HOLD YOUR HAND? I'M NOT A BABY ANYMORE!
I KNOW... I JUST WANT TO KNOW WHERE YOU ARE WHEN WE'RE IN THE PARKING LOT.
WHAT IF I THOUGHT OF A WAY THAT YOU WOULDN'T HAVE TO HOLD MY HAND, AND YOU WOULD STILL KNOW WHERE I AM?
WELL, I GUESS THAT WOULD PROBABLY BE...
BEEP! BEEP! BEEP! BEEP! BEEP!
...EMBARRASSING.

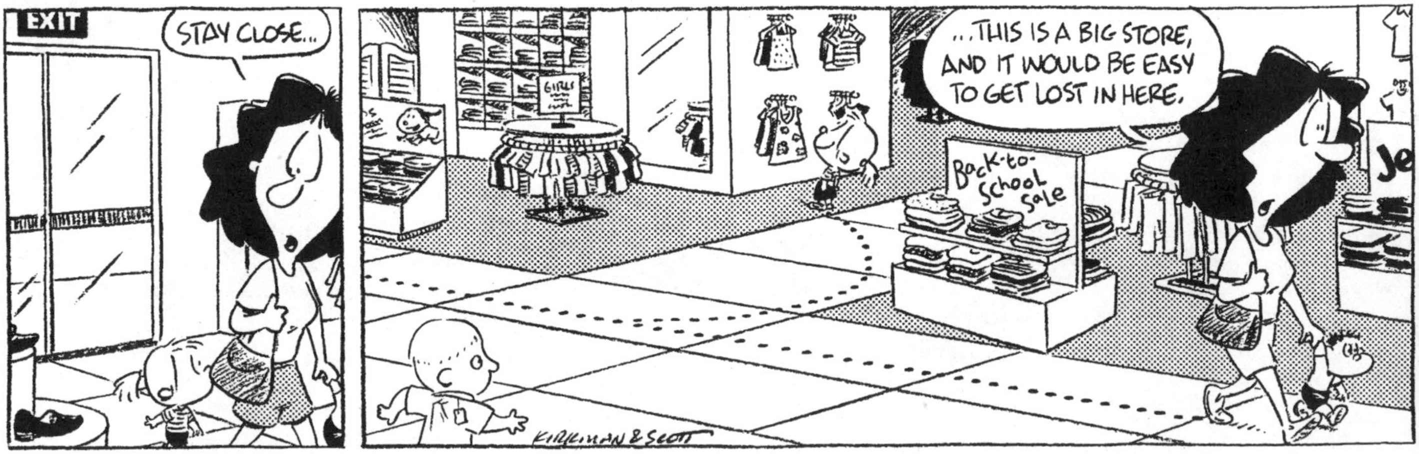
EXIT
STAY CLOSE...
...THIS IS A BIG STORE, AND IT WOULD BE EASY TO GET LOST IN HERE.
Back-to-School Sale
KIRKMAN & SCOTT

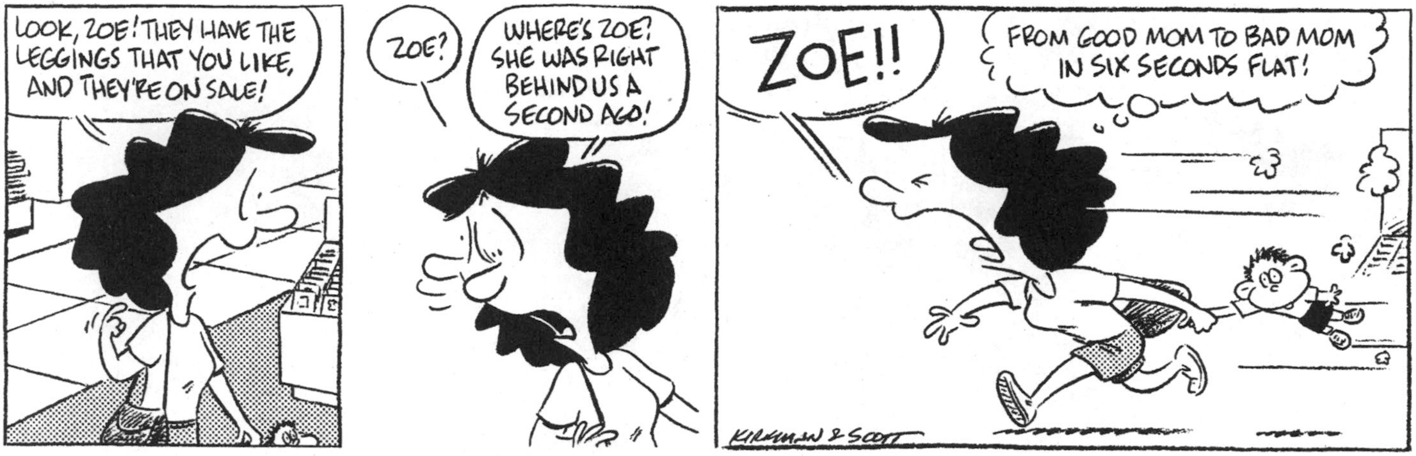
LOOK, ZOE! THEY HAVE THE LEGGINGS THAT YOU LIKE, AND THEY'RE ON SALE!
ZOE?
WHERE'S ZOE? SHE WAS RIGHT BEHIND US A SECOND AGO!
ZOE!!
FROM GOOD MOM TO BAD MOM IN SIX SECONDS FLAT!
KIRKMAN & SCOTT

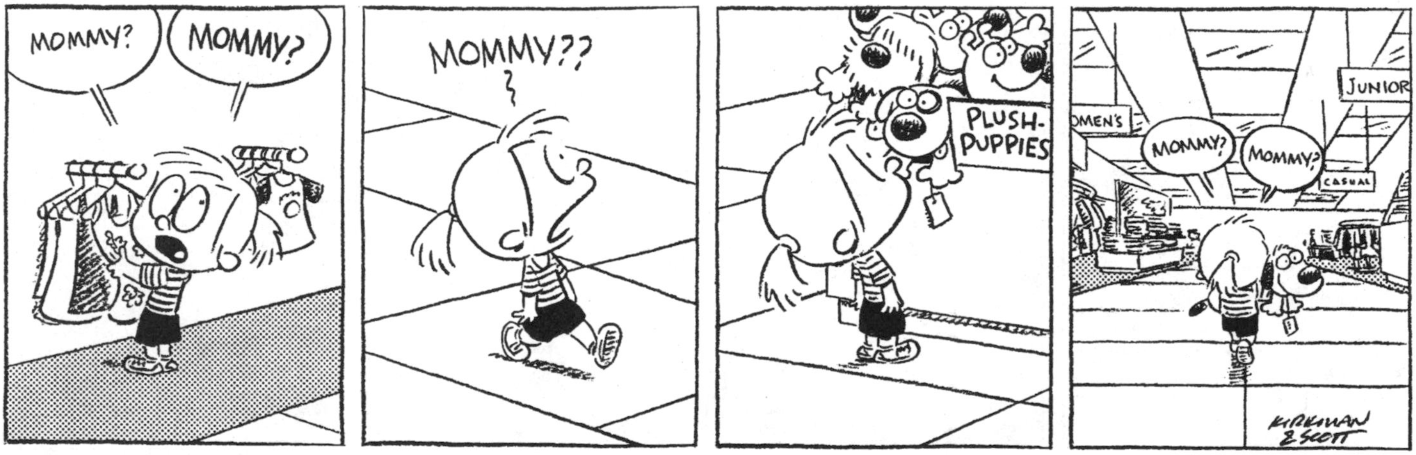
MOMMY?
MOMMY?
MOMMY??
PLUSH-PUPPIES
JUNIOR
OMEN'S
MOMMY?
MOMMY?
CASUAL
KIRKMAN & SCOTT

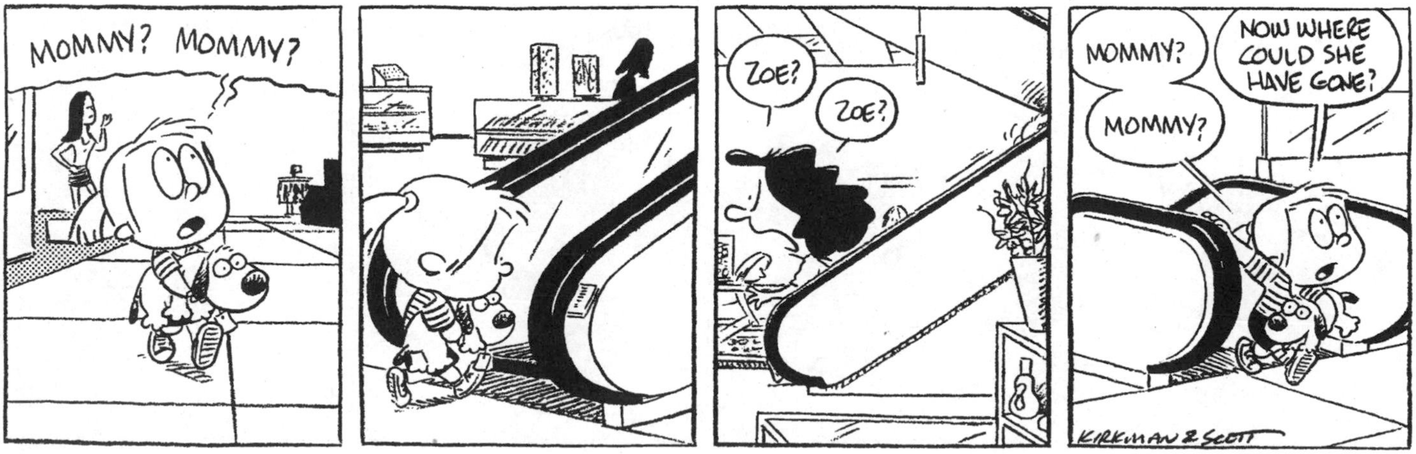
MOMMY? MOMMY?
ZOE?
ZOE?
MOMMY?
MOMMY?
NOW WHERE COULD SHE HAVE GONE?
KIRKMAN & SCOTT

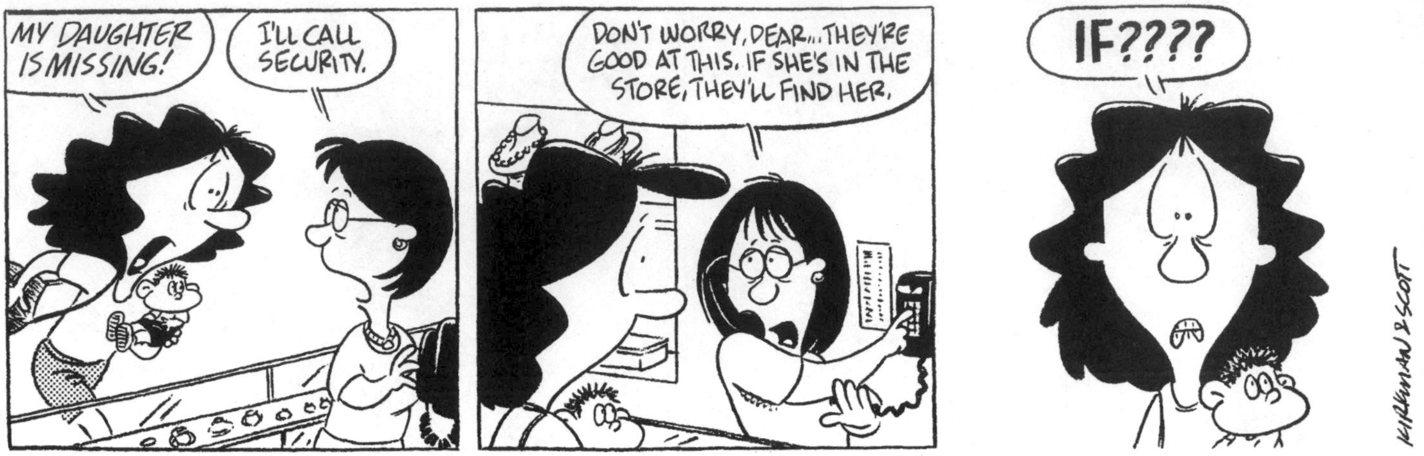
MY DAUGHTER IS MISSING!
I'LL CALL SECURITY.
DON'T WORRY, DEAR... THEY'RE GOOD AT THIS. IF SHE'S IN THE STORE, THEY'LL FIND HER.
IF????
KIRKMAN & SCOTT

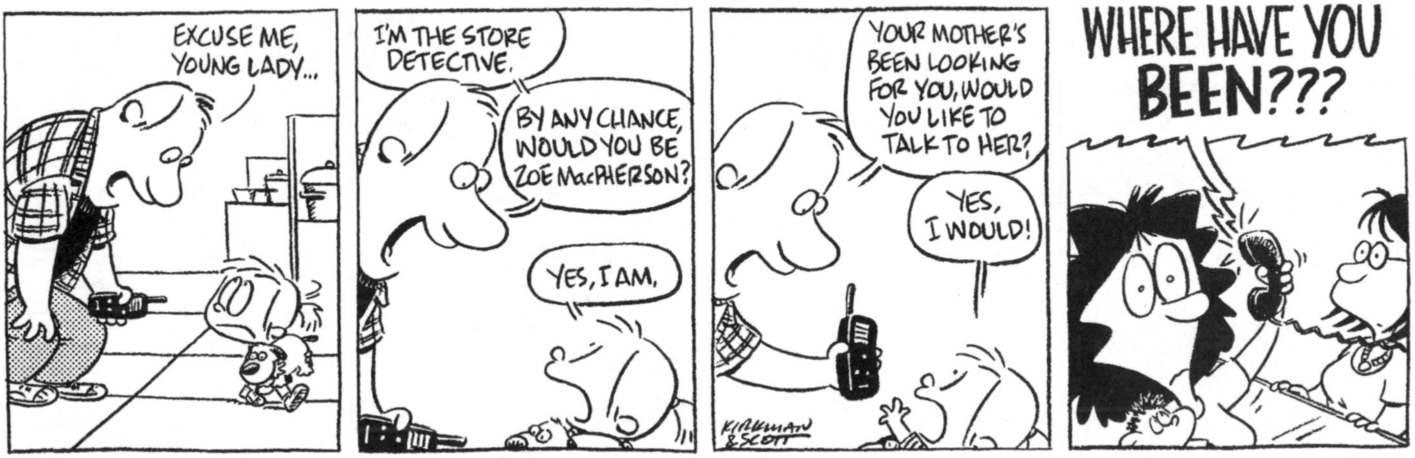
EXCUSE ME, YOUNG LADY...
I'M THE STORE DETECTIVE.
BY ANY CHANCE, WOULD YOU BE ZOE MacPHERSON?
YES, I AM.
YOUR MOTHER'S BEEN LOOKING FOR YOU, WOULD YOU LIKE TO TALK TO HER?
YES, I WOULD!
KIRKMAN & SCOTT
WHERE HAVE YOU BEEN???

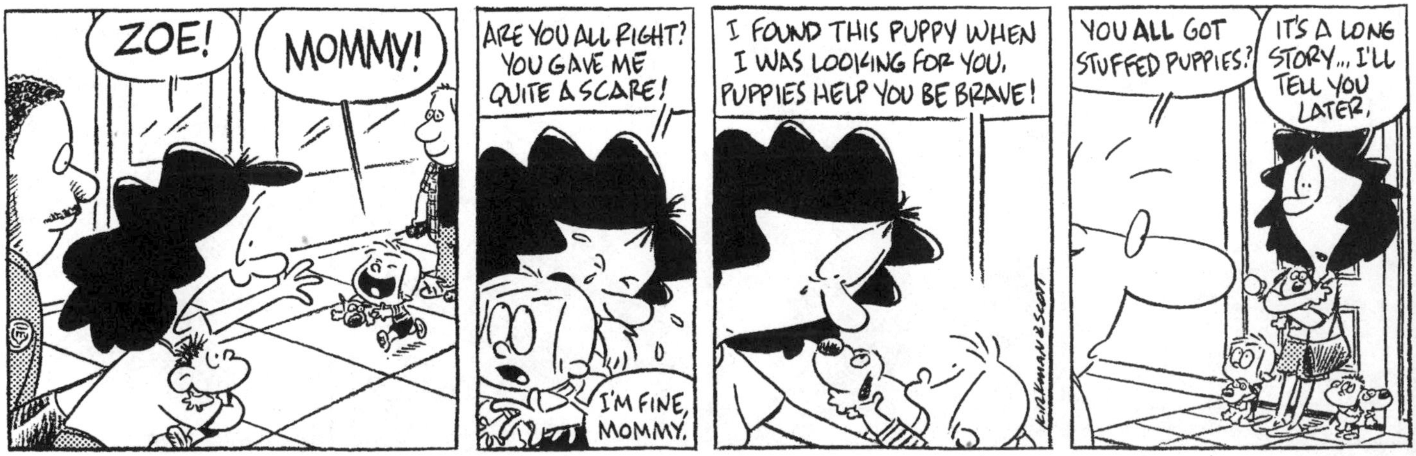
ZOE!
MOMMY!
ARE YOU ALL RIGHT? YOU GAVE ME QUITE A SCARE!
I'M FINE, MOMMY.
I FOUND THIS PUPPY WHEN I WAS LOOKING FOR YOU. PUPPIES HELP YOU BE BRAVE!
KIRKMAN & SCOTT
YOU ALL GOT STUFFED PUPPIES?
IT'S A LONG STORY... I'LL TELL YOU LATER.

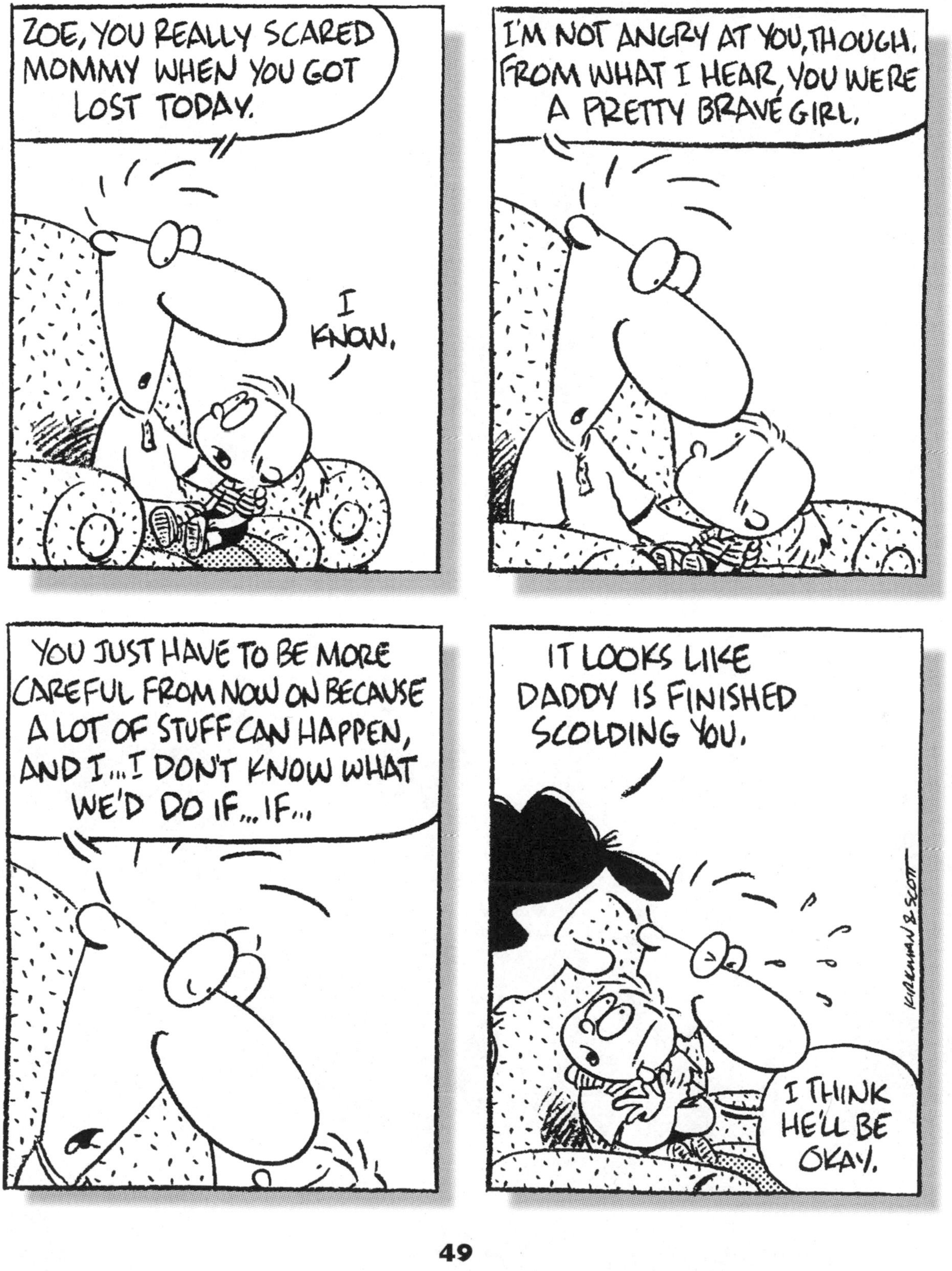
ZOE, YOU REALLY SCARED MOMMY WHEN YOU GOT LOST TODAY.
I KNOW.
I'M NOT ANGRY AT YOU, THOUGH. FROM WHAT I HEAR, YOU WERE A PRETTY BRAVE GIRL.
YOU JUST HAVE TO BE MORE CAREFUL FROM NOW ON BECAUSE A LOT OF STUFF CAN HAPPEN, AND I... I DON'T KNOW WHAT WE'D DO IF... IF...
IT LOOKS LIKE DADDY IS FINISHED SCOLDING YOU.
I THINK HE'LL BE OKAY.
KIRKMAN & SCOTT

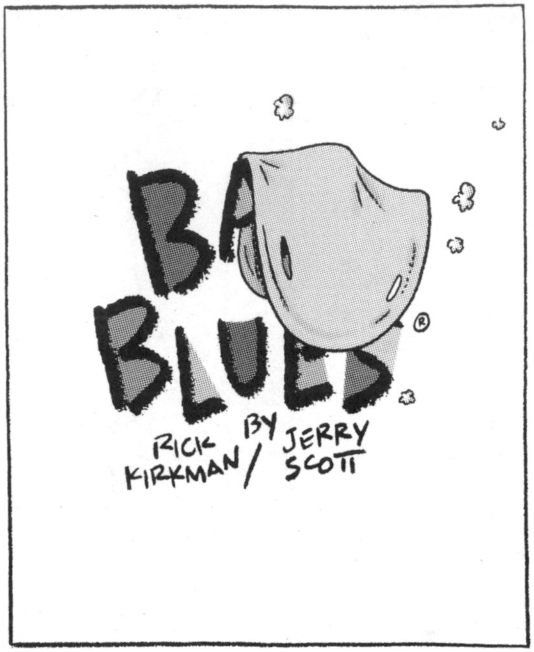
BABY BLUES®
BY
RICK KIRKMAN / JERRY SCOTT

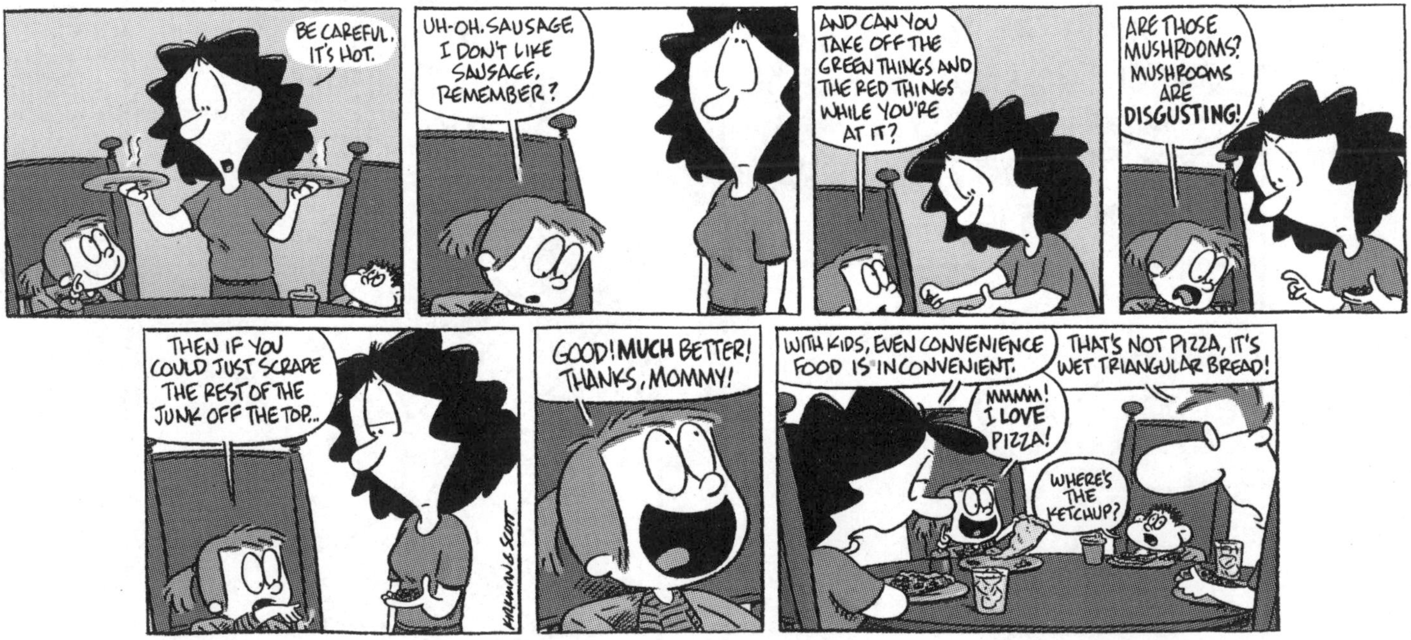
BE CAREFUL. IT'S HOT.
UH-OH. SAUSAGE. I DON'T LIKE SAUSAGE, REMEMBER?
AND CAN YOU TAKE OFF THE GREEN THINGS AND THE RED THINGS WHILE YOU'RE AT IT?
ARE THOSE MUSHROOMS? MUSHROOMS ARE **DISGUSTING**!
THEN IF YOU COULD JUST SCRAPE THE REST OF THE JUNK OFF THE TOP...
KIRKMAN & SCOTT
GOOD! **MUCH** BETTER! THANKS, MOMMY!
WITH KIDS, EVEN CONVENIENCE FOOD IS INCONVENIENT.
MMMM! I **LOVE** PIZZA!
THAT'S NOT PIZZA, IT'S WET TRIANGULAR BREAD!
WHERE'S THE KETCHUP?

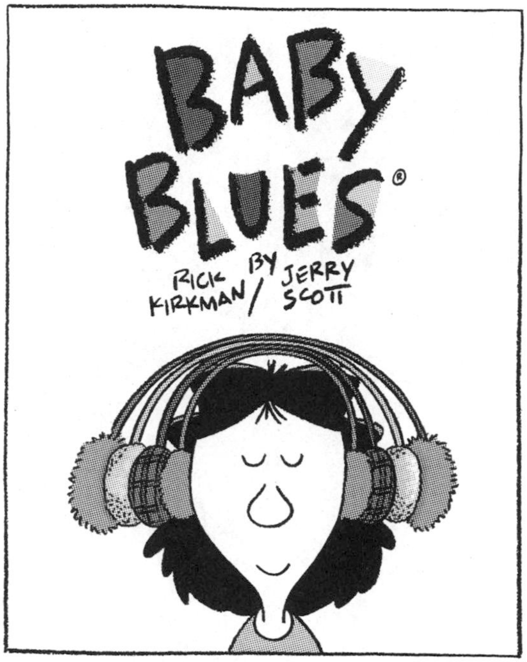
BABY BLUES®
BY RICK KIRKMAN / JERRY SCOTT

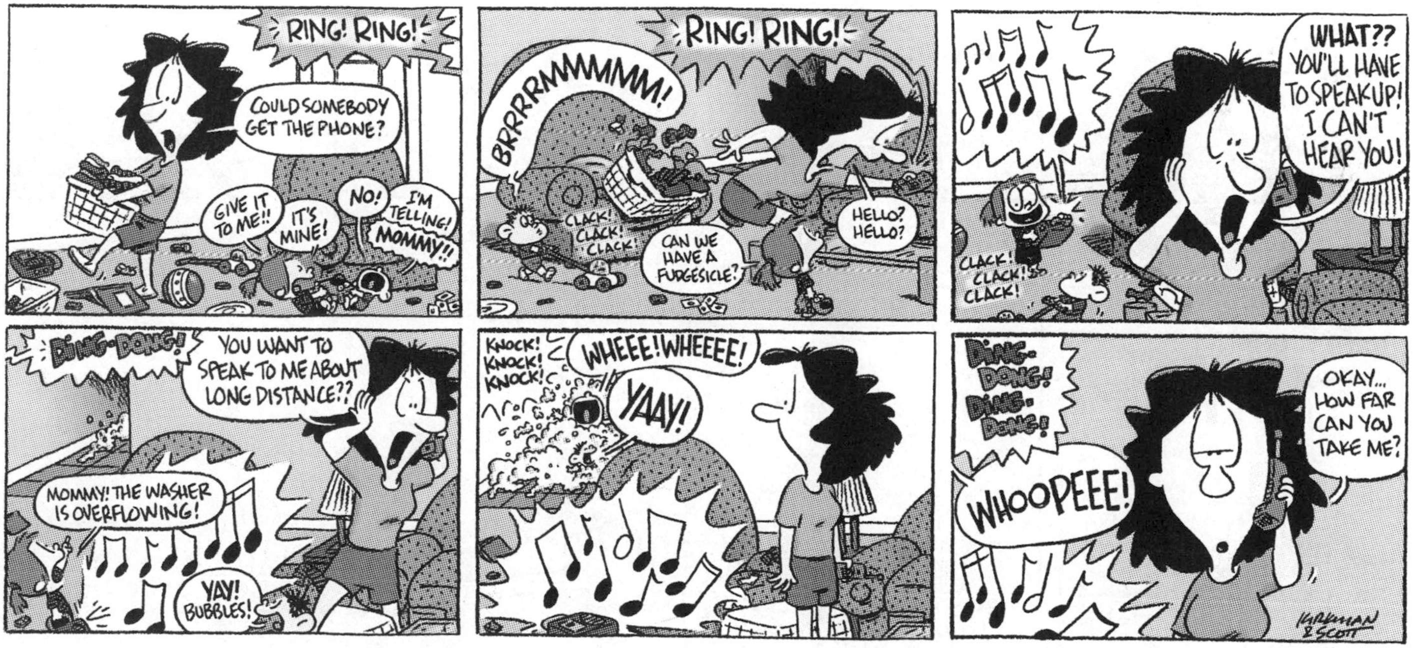
RING! RING!
COULD SOMEBODY GET THE PHONE?
GIVE IT TO ME!!
IT'S MINE!
NO!
I'M TELLING! MOMMY!!
RING! RING!
BRRRRMMMMMM!
CLACK! CLACK! CLACK!
CAN WE HAVE A FUDGESICLE?
HELLO? HELLO?
WHAT?? YOU'LL HAVE TO SPEAK UP! I CAN'T HEAR YOU!
CLACK! CLACK! CLACK!
DING-DONG!
YOU WANT TO SPEAK TO ME ABOUT LONG DISTANCE??
MOMMY! THE WASHER IS OVERFLOWING!
YAY! BUBBLES!
KNOCK! KNOCK! KNOCK!
WHEEE! WHEEEE!
YAAY!
DING-DONG! DING-DONG!
WHOOPEEE!
OKAY... HOW FAR CAN YOU TAKE ME?
KIRKMAN & SCOTT

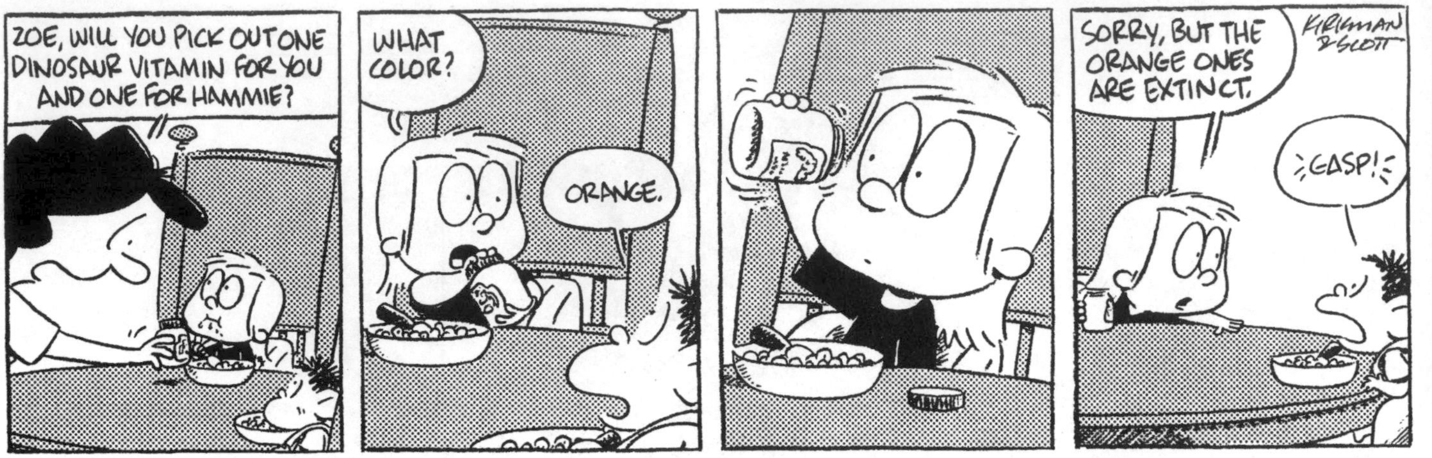
ZOE, WILL YOU PICK OUT ONE DINOSAUR VITAMIN FOR YOU AND ONE FOR HAMMIE?
WHAT COLOR?
ORANGE.
SORRY, BUT THE ORANGE ONES ARE EXTINCT.
KIRKMAN & SCOTT
GASP!

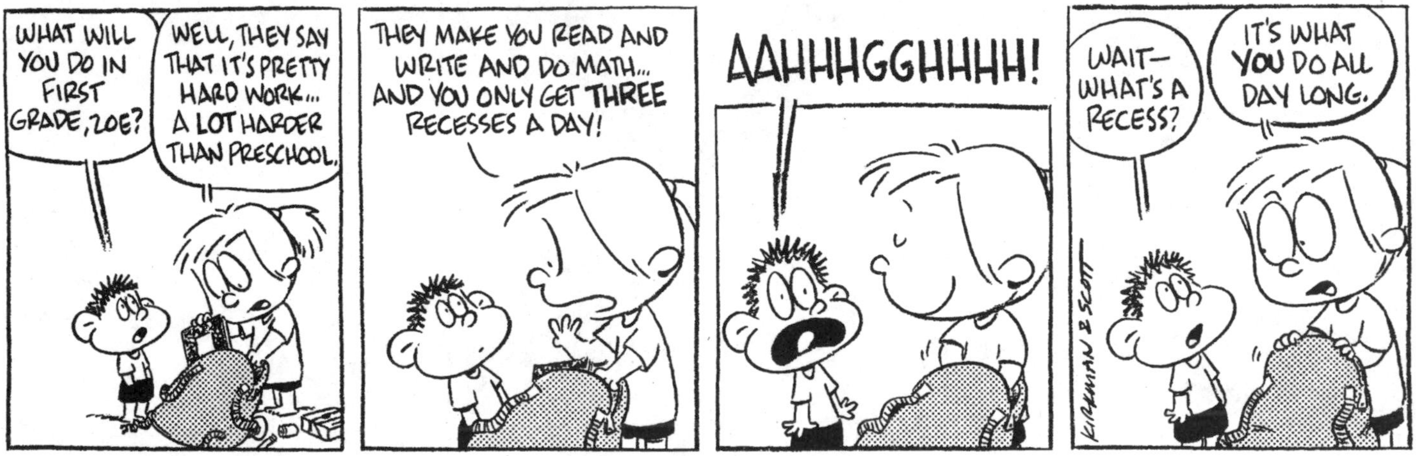
WHAT WILL YOU DO IN FIRST GRADE, ZOE?
WELL, THEY SAY THAT IT'S PRETTY HARD WORK... A **LOT** HARDER THAN PRESCHOOL.
THEY MAKE YOU READ AND WRITE AND DO MATH... AND YOU ONLY GET **THREE** RECESSES A DAY!
AAHHHGGHHHH!
WAIT— WHAT'S A RECESS?
IT'S WHAT **YOU** DO ALL DAY LONG.
KIRKMAN & SCOTT

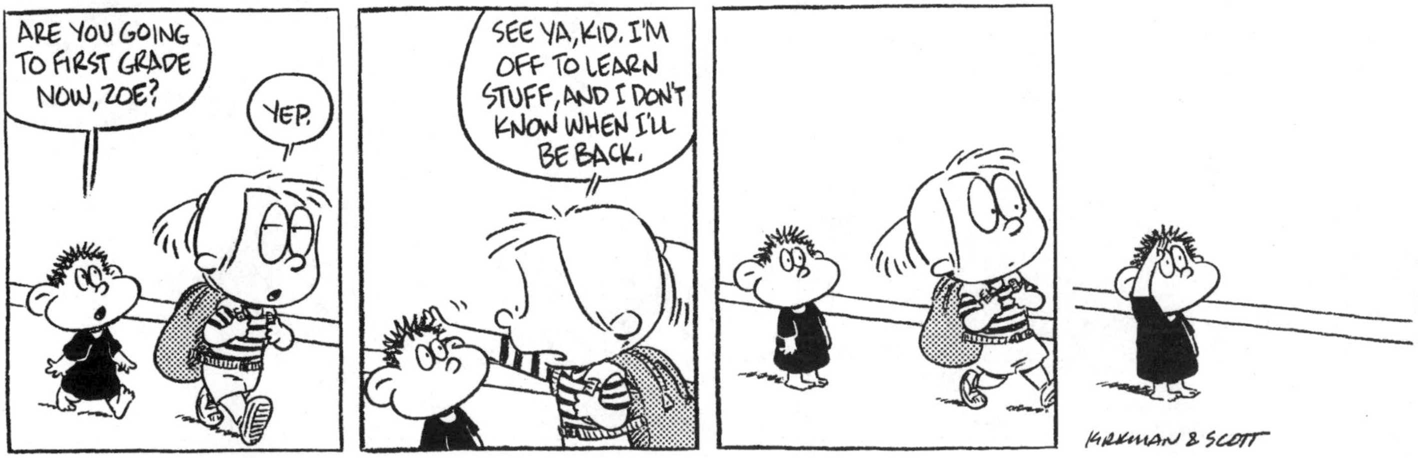
ARE YOU GOING TO FIRST GRADE NOW, ZOE?
YEP.
SEE YA, KID. I'M OFF TO LEARN STUFF, AND I DON'T KNOW WHEN I'LL BE BACK.
KIRKMAN & SCOTT

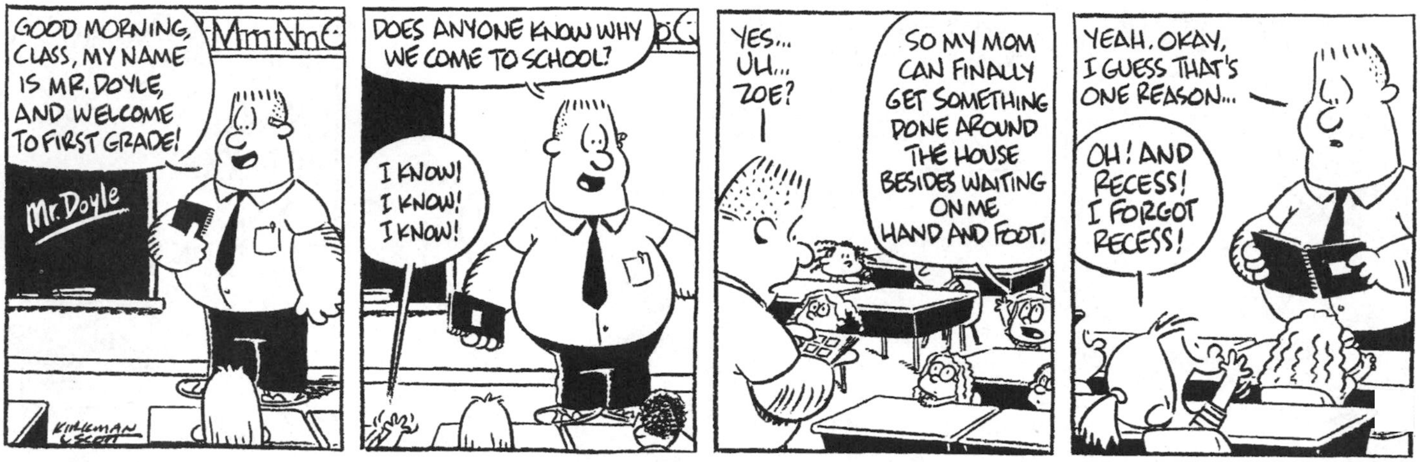
GOOD MORNING, CLASS, MY NAME IS MR. DOYLE, AND WELCOME TO FIRST GRADE!
Mr. Doyle
KIRKMAN & SCOTT
DOES ANYONE KNOW WHY WE COME TO SCHOOL?
I KNOW! I KNOW! I KNOW!
YES... UH... ZOE?
SO MY MOM CAN FINALLY GET SOMETHING DONE AROUND THE HOUSE BESIDES WAITING ON ME HAND AND FOOT.
YEAH, OKAY, I GUESS THAT'S ONE REASON...
OH! AND RECESS! I FORGOT RECESS!

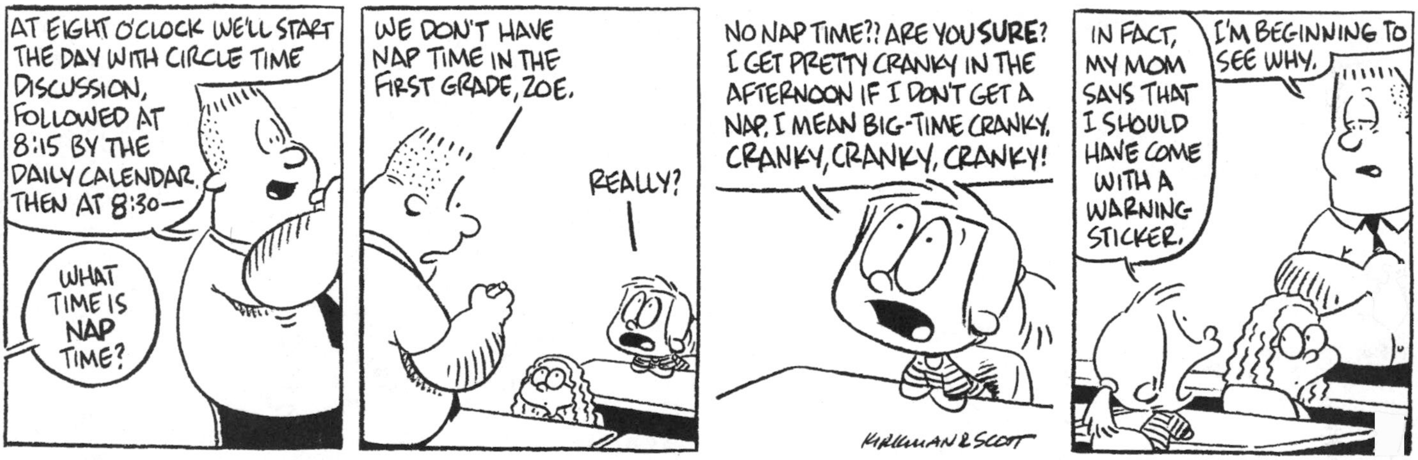
AT EIGHT O'CLOCK WE'LL START THE DAY WITH CIRCLE TIME DISCUSSION, FOLLOWED AT 8:15 BY THE DAILY CALENDAR. THEN AT 8:30—
WHAT TIME IS NAP TIME?
WE DON'T HAVE NAP TIME IN THE FIRST GRADE, ZOE.
REALLY?
NO NAP TIME?? ARE YOU SURE? I GET PRETTY CRANKY IN THE AFTERNOON IF I DON'T GET A NAP. I MEAN BIG-TIME CRANKY. CRANKY, CRANKY, CRANKY!
KIRKMAN & SCOTT
IN FACT, MY MOM SAYS THAT I SHOULD HAVE COME WITH A WARNING STICKER.
I'M BEGINNING TO SEE WHY.

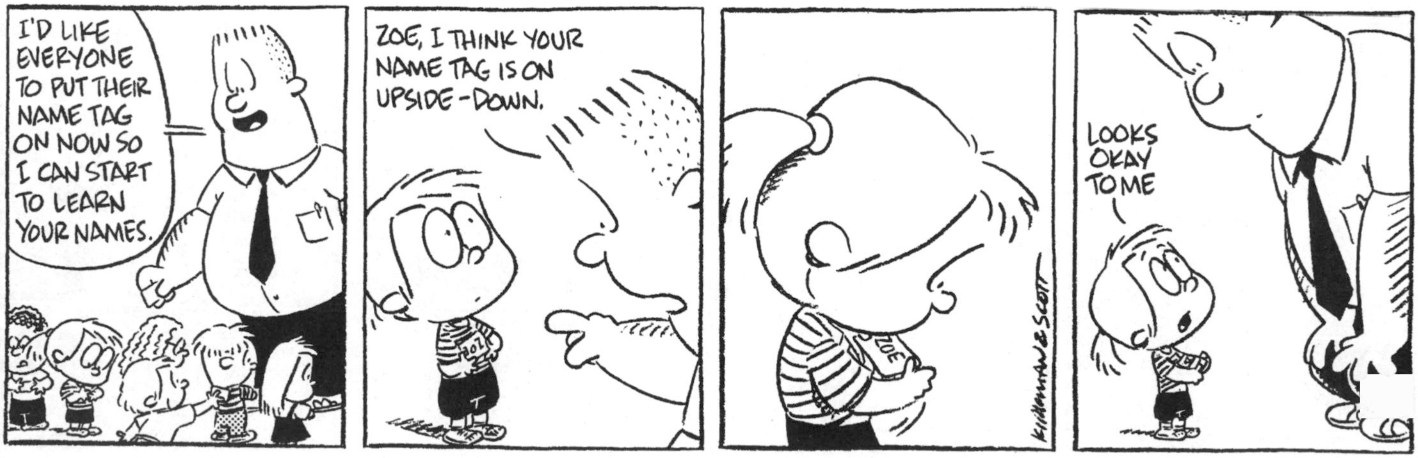
I'D LIKE EVERYONE TO PUT THEIR NAME TAG ON NOW SO I CAN START TO LEARN YOUR NAMES.
ZOE, I THINK YOUR NAME TAG IS ON UPSIDE-DOWN.
ZOE
KIRKMAN & SCOTT
LOOKS OKAY TO ME

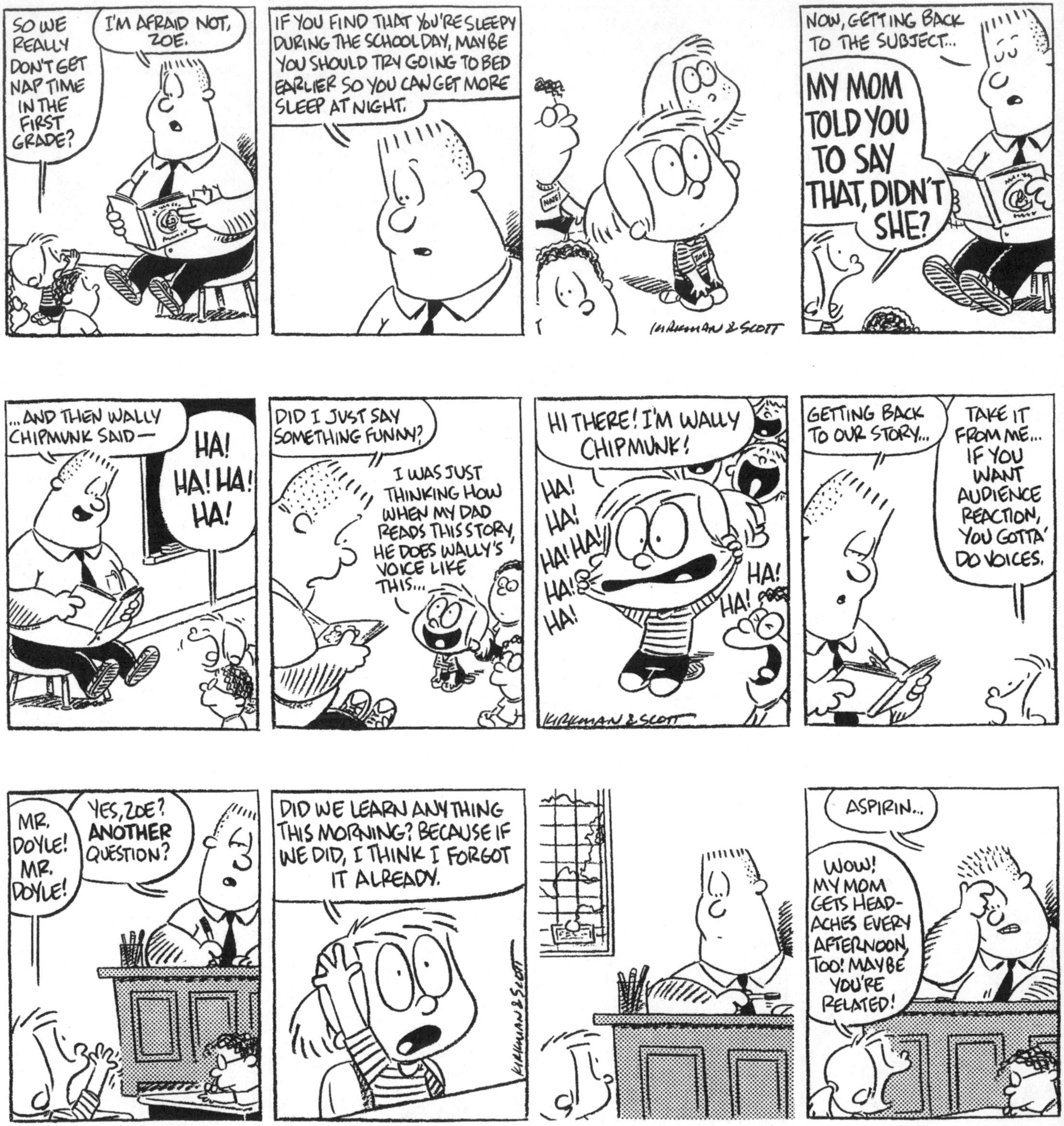
SO WE REALLY DON'T GET NAP TIME IN THE FIRST GRADE?
I'M AFRAID NOT, ZOE.
IF YOU FIND THAT YOU'RE SLEEPY DURING THE SCHOOL DAY, MAYBE YOU SHOULD TRY GOING TO BED EARLIER SO YOU CAN GET MORE SLEEP AT NIGHT.
NATE
ZOE
KIRKMAN & SCOTT
NOW, GETTING BACK TO THE SUBJECT...
MY MOM TOLD YOU TO SAY THAT, DIDN'T SHE?
...AND THEN WALLY CHIPMUNK SAID—
HA! HA! HA! HA!
DID I JUST SAY SOMETHING FUNNY?
I WAS JUST THINKING HOW WHEN MY DAD READS THIS STORY, HE DOES WALLY'S VOICE LIKE THIS...
HI THERE! I'M WALLY CHIPMUNK!
HA! HA! HA! HA! HA! HA!
HA! HA!
KIRKMAN & SCOTT
GETTING BACK TO OUR STORY...
TAKE IT FROM ME... IF YOU WANT AUDIENCE REACTION, YOU GOTTA' DO VOICES.
MR. DOYLE! MR. DOYLE!
YES, ZOE? ANOTHER QUESTION?
DID WE LEARN ANYTHING THIS MORNING? BECAUSE IF WE DID, I THINK I FORGOT IT ALREADY.
KIRKMAN & SCOTT
ASPIRIN...
WOW! MY MOM GETS HEADACHES EVERY AFTERNOON, TOO! MAYBE YOU'RE RELATED!

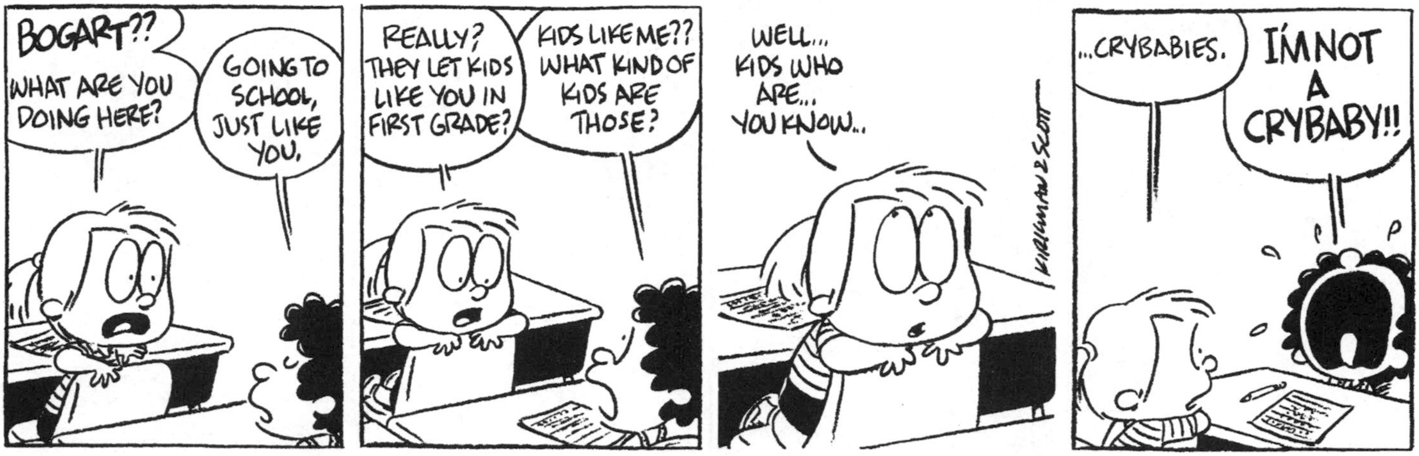
BOGART??
WHAT ARE YOU DOING HERE?
GOING TO SCHOOL, JUST LIKE YOU.
REALLY? THEY LET KIDS LIKE YOU IN FIRST GRADE?
KIDS LIKE ME?? WHAT KIND OF KIDS ARE THOSE?
WELL... KIDS WHO ARE... YOU KNOW...
...CRYBABIES.
I'M NOT A CRYBABY!!
KIRKMAN & SCOTT

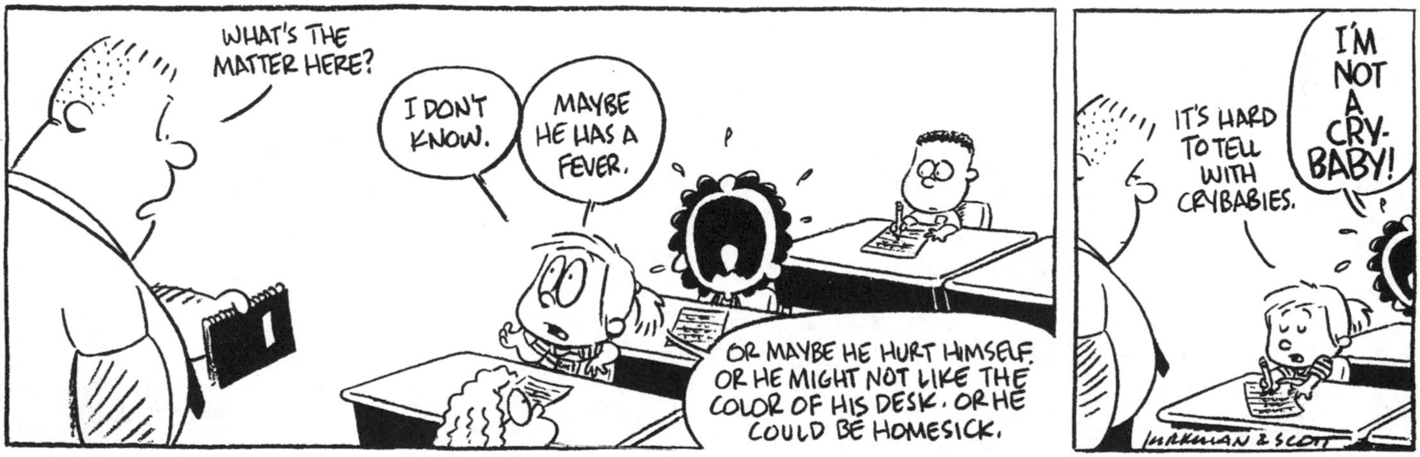
WHAT'S THE MATTER HERE?
I DON'T KNOW.
MAYBE HE HAS A FEVER.
OR MAYBE HE HURT HIMSELF. OR HE MIGHT NOT LIKE THE COLOR OF HIS DESK. OR HE COULD BE HOMESICK.
IT'S HARD TO TELL WITH CRYBABIES.
I'M NOT A CRY-BABY!
KIRKMAN & SCOTT

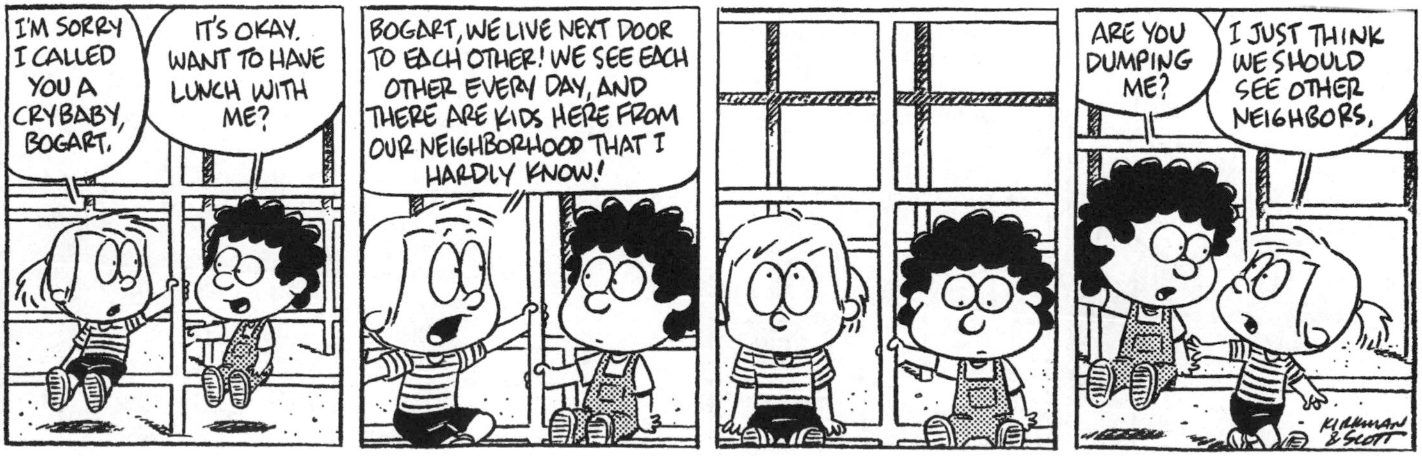
I'M SORRY I CALLED YOU A CRYBABY, BOGART.
IT'S OKAY. WANT TO HAVE LUNCH WITH ME?
BOGART, WE LIVE NEXT DOOR TO EACH OTHER! WE SEE EACH OTHER EVERY DAY, AND THERE ARE KIDS HERE FROM OUR NEIGHBORHOOD THAT I HARDLY KNOW!
ARE YOU DUMPING ME?
I JUST THINK WE SHOULD SEE OTHER NEIGHBORS.
KIRKMAN & SCOTT

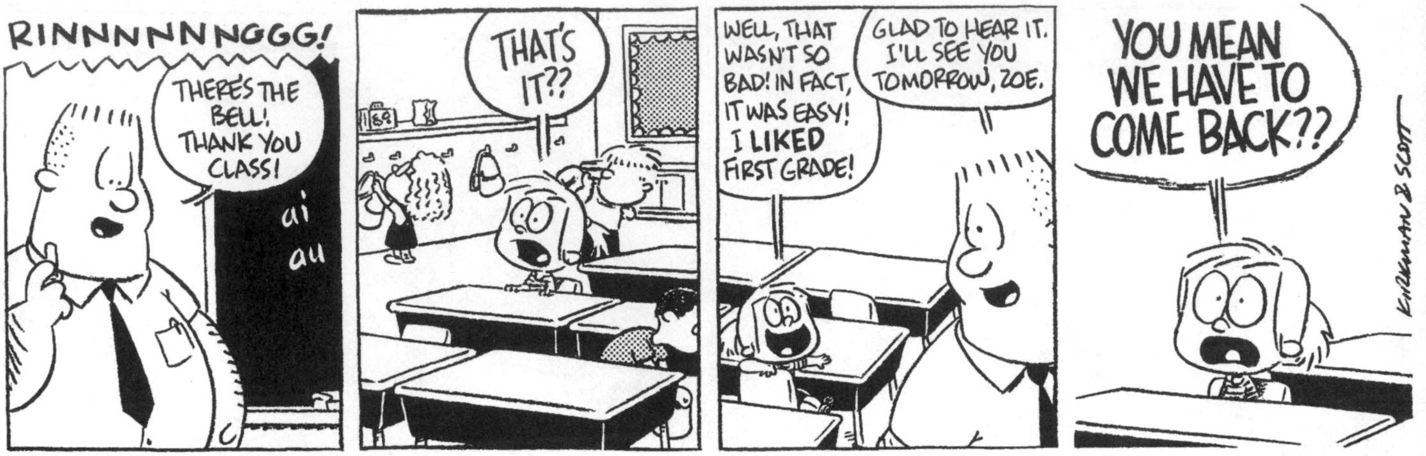
RINNNNNNGGG!
THERE'S THE BELL! THANK YOU CLASS!
ai
au
THAT'S IT??
WELL, THAT WASN'T SO BAD! IN FACT, IT WAS EASY! I **LIKED** FIRST GRADE!
GLAD TO HEAR IT. I'LL SEE YOU TOMORROW, ZOE.
YOU MEAN WE HAVE TO COME BACK??
KIRKMAN & SCOTT

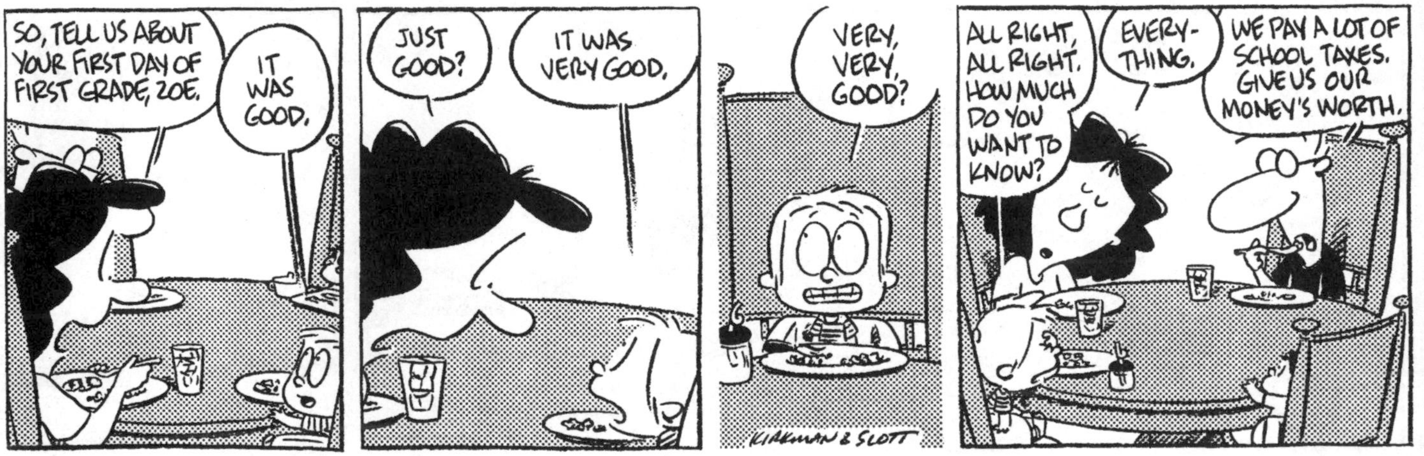
SO, TELL US ABOUT YOUR FIRST DAY OF FIRST GRADE, ZOE.
IT WAS GOOD.
JUST GOOD?
IT WAS VERY GOOD.
VERY, VERY, GOOD?
KIRKMAN & SCOTT
ALL RIGHT, ALL RIGHT. HOW MUCH DO YOU WANT TO KNOW?
EVERY-THING.
WE PAY A LOT OF SCHOOL TAXES. GIVE US OUR MONEY'S WORTH.

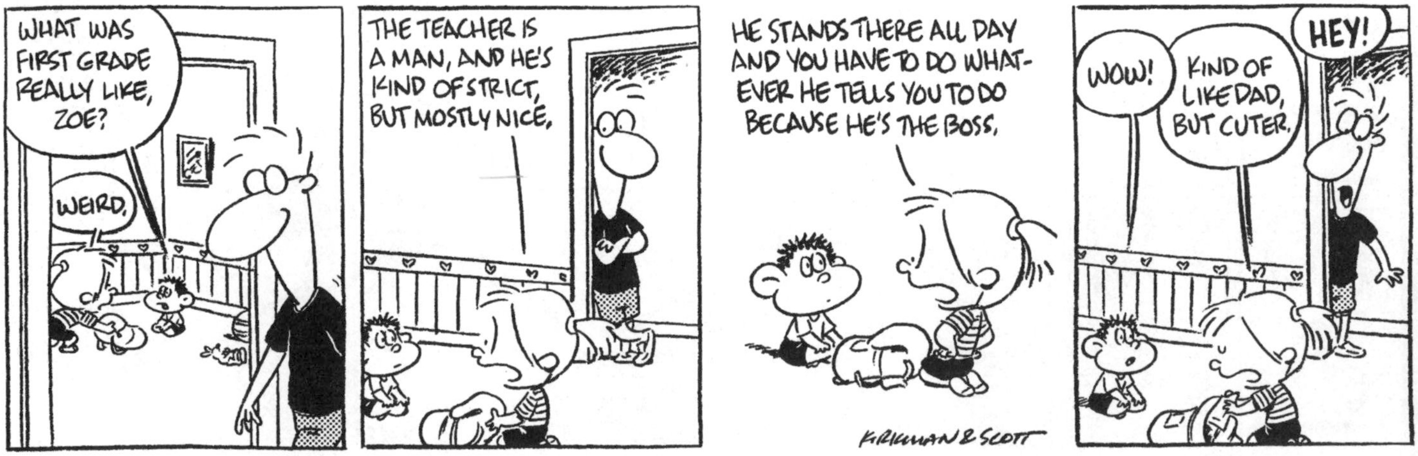
WHAT WAS FIRST GRADE REALLY LIKE, ZOE?
WEIRD.
THE TEACHER IS A MAN, AND HE'S KIND OF STRICT, BUT MOSTLY NICE.
HE STANDS THERE ALL DAY AND YOU HAVE TO DO WHAT-EVER HE TELLS YOU TO DO BECAUSE HE'S THE BOSS.
KIRKMAN & SCOTT
WOW!
KIND OF LIKE DAD, BUT CUTER.
HEY!

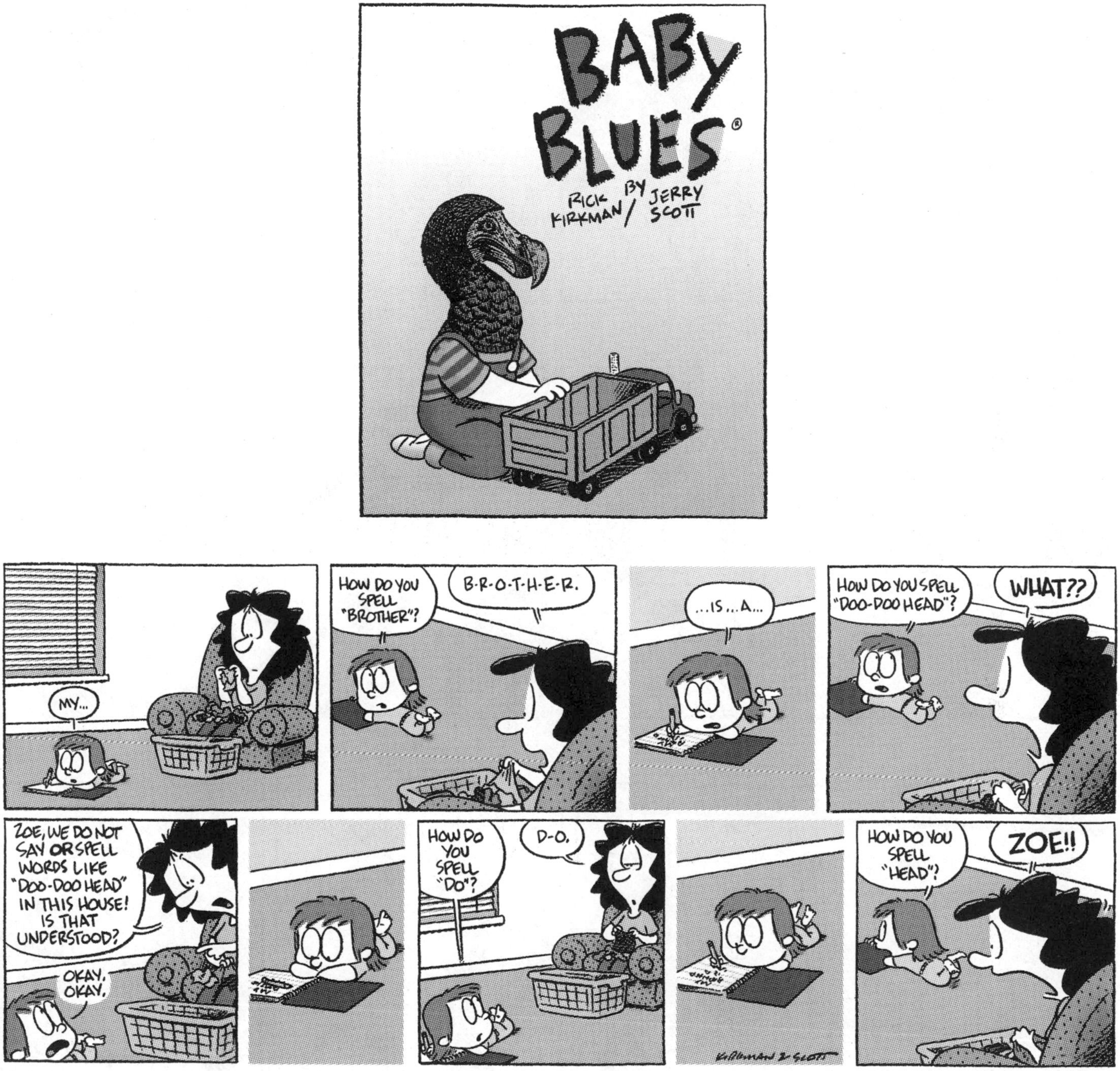
BABY BLUES®
BY RICK KIRKMAN / JERRY SCOTT
MY...
HOW DO YOU SPELL "BROTHER"?
B-R-O-T-H-E-R.
...IS...A...
HOW DO YOU SPELL "DOO-DOO HEAD"?
WHAT??
ZOE, WE DO NOT SAY OR SPELL WORDS LIKE "DOO-DOO HEAD" IN THIS HOUSE! IS THAT UNDERSTOOD?
OKAY, OKAY.
HOW DO YOU SPELL "DO"?
D-O.
KIRKMAN & SCOTT
HOW DO YOU SPELL "HEAD"?
ZOE!!

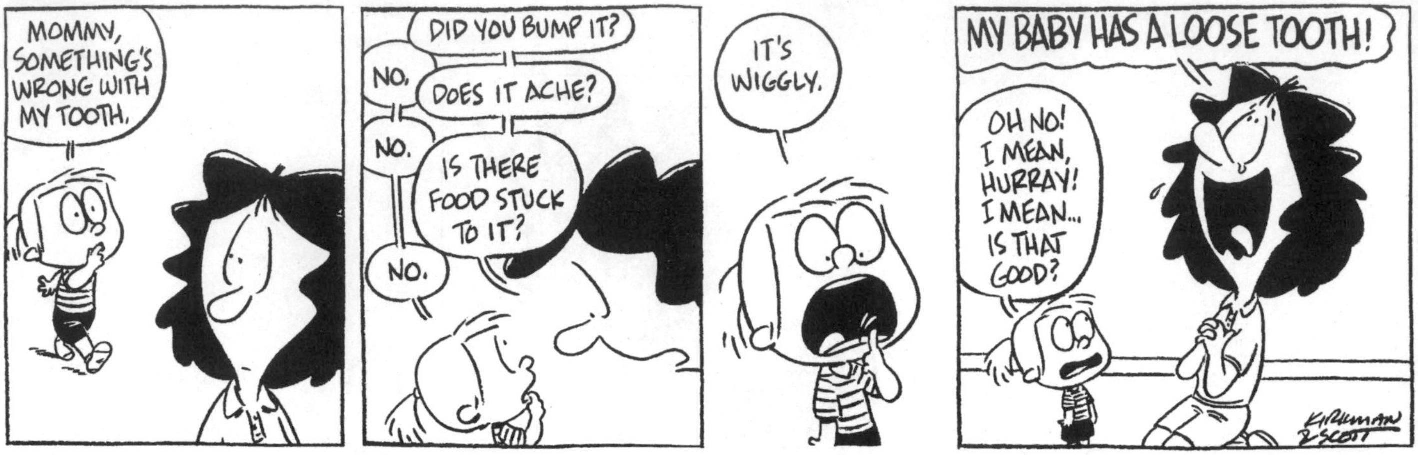
MOMMY, SOMETHING'S WRONG WITH MY TOOTH.
DID YOU BUMP IT?
NO.
DOES IT ACHE?
NO.
IS THERE FOOD STUCK TO IT?
NO.
IT'S WIGGLY.
MY BABY HAS A LOOSE TOOTH!
OH NO! I MEAN, HURRAY! I MEAN... IS THAT GOOD?
KIRKMAN & SCOTT

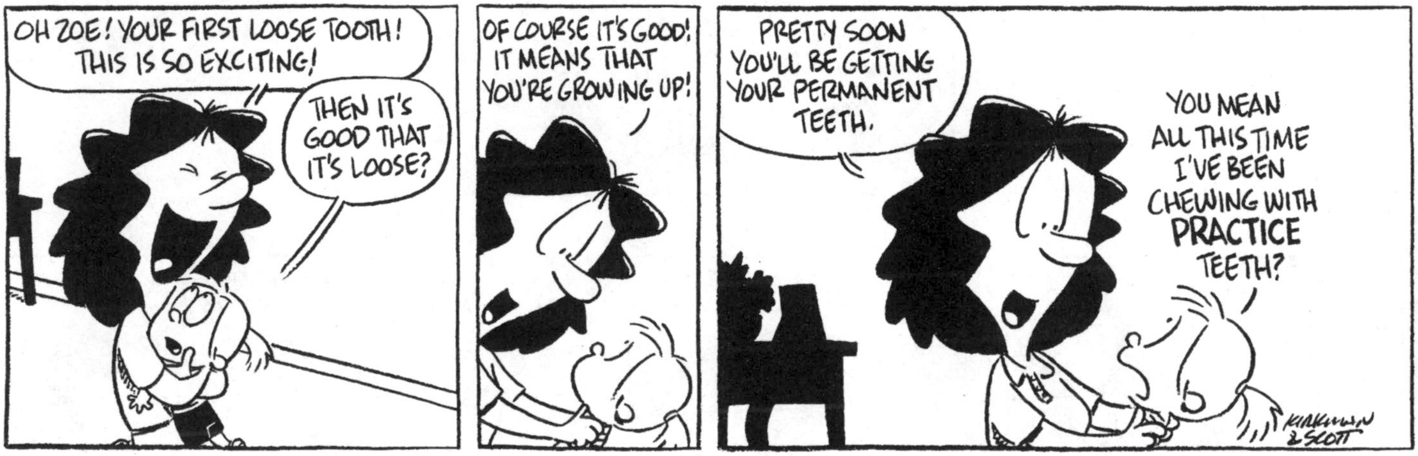
OH ZOE! YOUR FIRST LOOSE TOOTH! THIS IS SO EXCITING!
THEN IT'S GOOD THAT IT'S LOOSE?
OF COURSE IT'S GOOD! IT MEANS THAT YOU'RE GROWING UP!
PRETTY SOON YOU'LL BE GETTING YOUR PERMANENT TEETH.
YOU MEAN ALL THIS TIME I'VE BEEN CHEWING WITH PRACTICE TEETH?
KIRKMAN & SCOTT

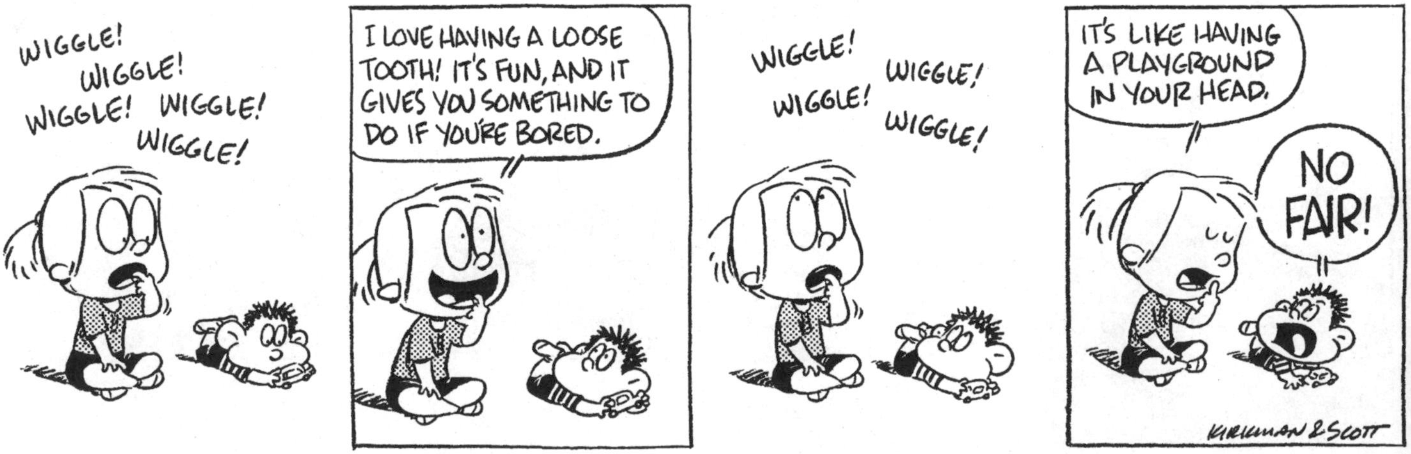
WIGGLE! WIGGLE! WIGGLE! WIGGLE! WIGGLE!
I LOVE HAVING A LOOSE TOOTH! IT'S FUN, AND IT GIVES YOU SOMETHING TO DO IF YOU'RE BORED.
WIGGLE! WIGGLE! WIGGLE! WIGGLE!
IT'S LIKE HAVING A PLAYGROUND IN YOUR HEAD.
NO FAIR!
KIRKMAN & SCOTT

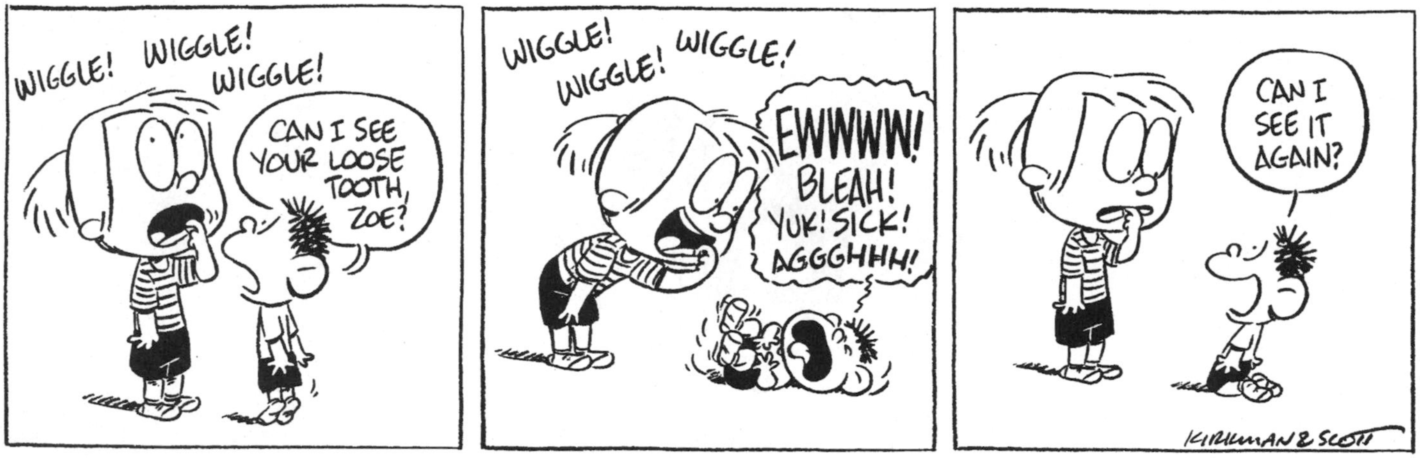

WIGGLE! WIGGLE! WIGGLE!
CAN I SEE YOUR LOOSE TOOTH, ZOE?
WIGGLE! WIGGLE! WIGGLE!
EWWWW! BLEAH! YUK! SICK! AGGGHHH!
CAN I SEE IT AGAIN?
KIRKMAN & SCOTT

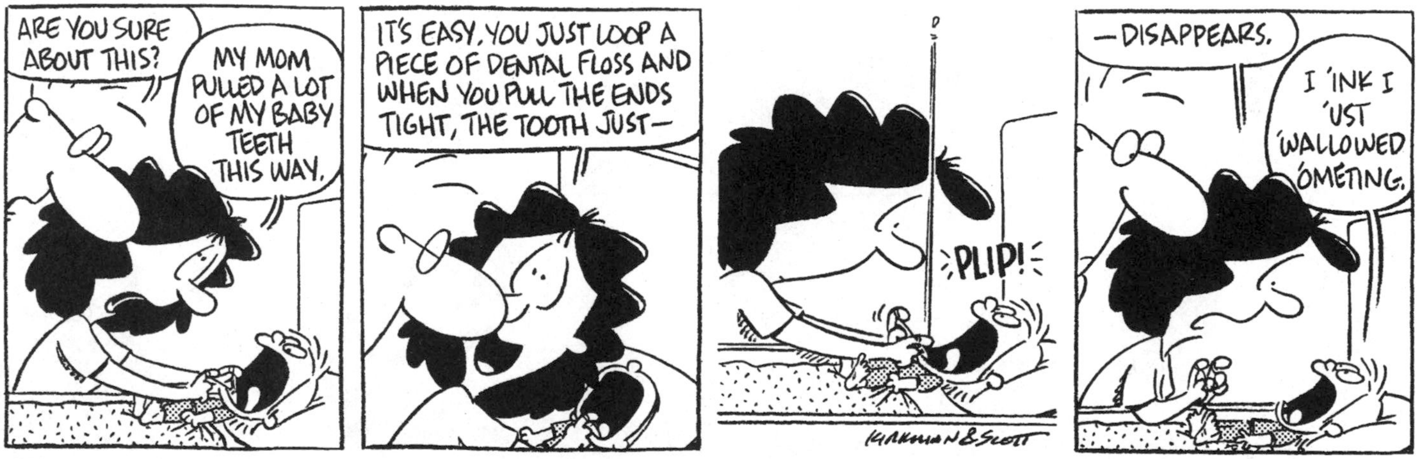

ARE YOU SURE ABOUT THIS?
MY MOM PULLED A LOT OF MY BABY TEETH THIS WAY.
IT'S EASY. YOU JUST LOOP A PIECE OF DENTAL FLOSS AND WHEN YOU PULL THE ENDS TIGHT, THE TOOTH JUST—
PLIP!
KIRKMAN & SCOTT
—DISAPPEARS.
I 'INK I 'UST 'WALLOWED 'OMETING.

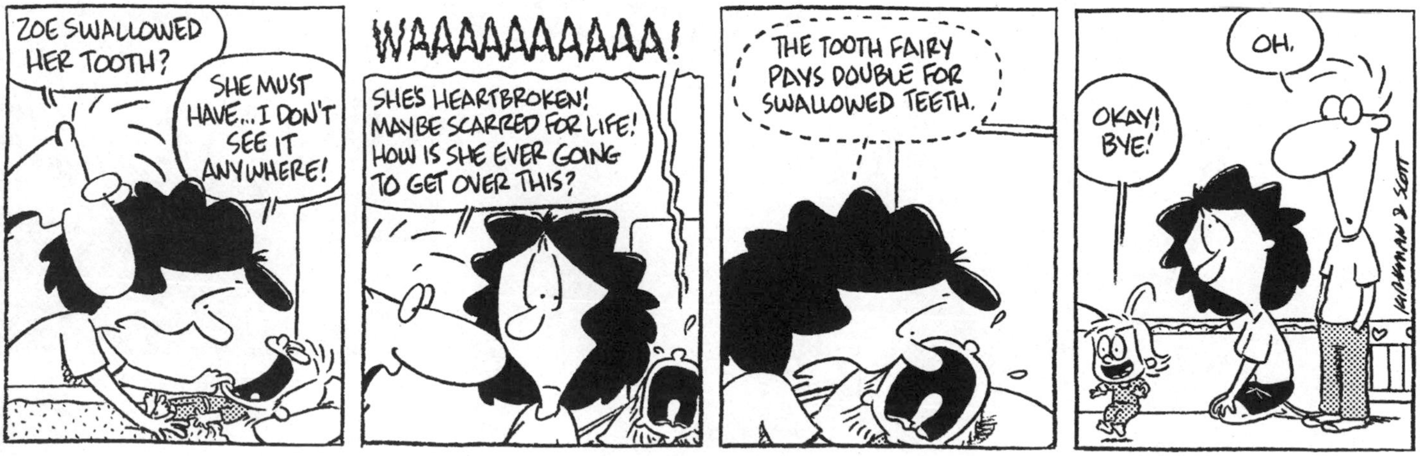

ZOE SWALLOWED HER TOOTH?
SHE MUST HAVE... I DON'T SEE IT ANYWHERE!
WAAAAAAAAAA!
SHE'S HEARTBROKEN! MAYBE SCARRED FOR LIFE! HOW IS SHE EVER GOING TO GET OVER THIS?
THE TOOTH FAIRY PAYS DOUBLE FOR SWALLOWED TEETH.
OH.
OKAY! BYE!
KIRKMAN & SCOTT

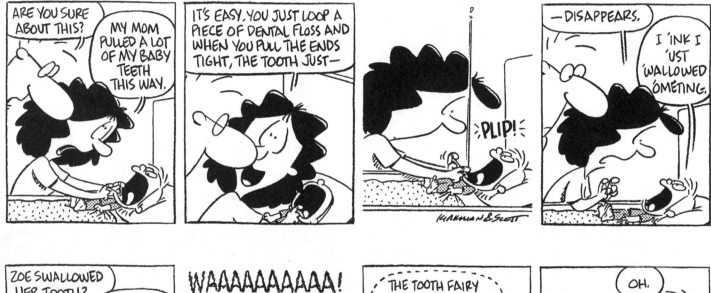

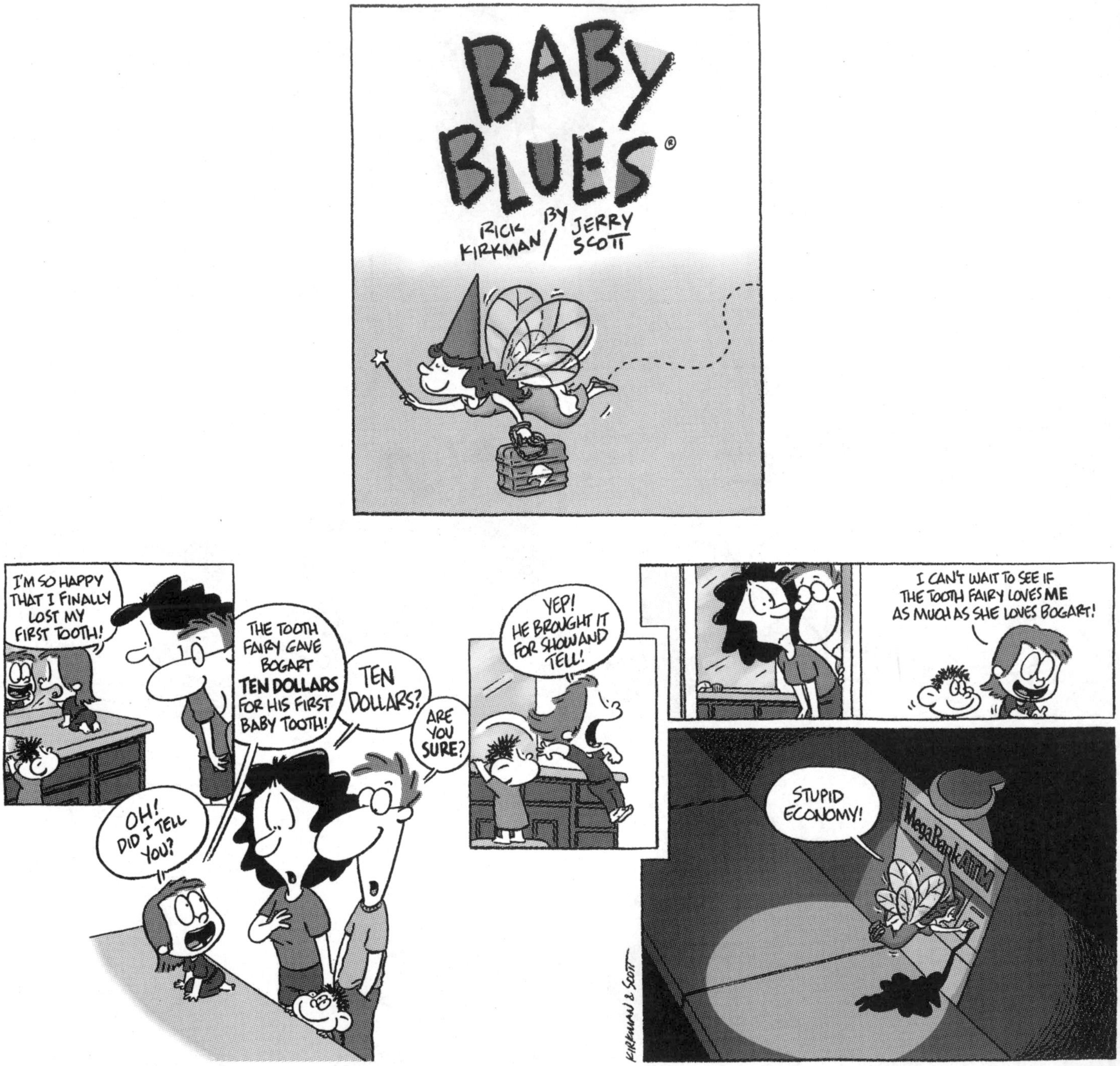
BABY BLUES®
BY RICK KIRKMAN / JERRY SCOTT
I'M SO HAPPY THAT I FINALLY LOST MY FIRST TOOTH!
THE TOOTH FAIRY GAVE BOGART **TEN DOLLARS** FOR HIS FIRST BABY TOOTH!
TEN DOLLARS?
ARE YOU **SURE**?
OH! DID I TELL YOU?
YEP! HE BROUGHT IT FOR SHOW AND TELL!
I CAN'T WAIT TO SEE IF THE TOOTH FAIRY LOVES **ME** AS MUCH AS SHE LOVES BOGART!
STUPID ECONOMY!
MegaBank ATM
KIRKMAN & SCOTT

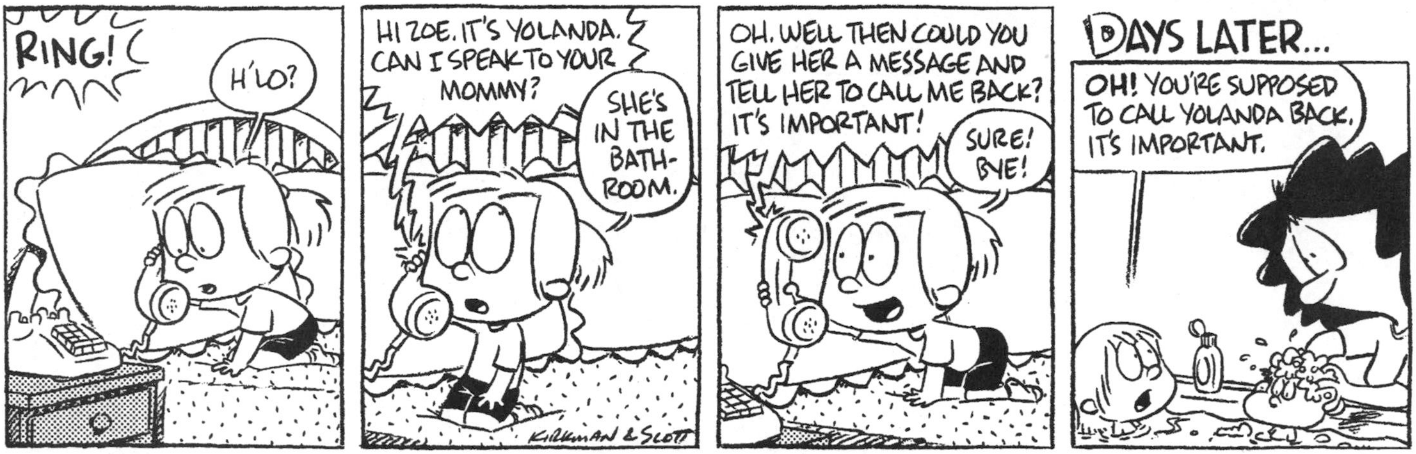
RING!
H'LO?
HI ZOE. IT'S YOLANDA. CAN I SPEAK TO YOUR MOMMY?
SHE'S IN THE BATH-ROOM.
OH. WELL THEN COULD YOU GIVE HER A MESSAGE AND TELL HER TO CALL ME BACK? IT'S IMPORTANT!
SURE! BYE!
DAYS LATER...
OH! YOU'RE SUPPOSED TO CALL YOLANDA BACK. IT'S IMPORTANT.
KIRKMAN & SCOTT

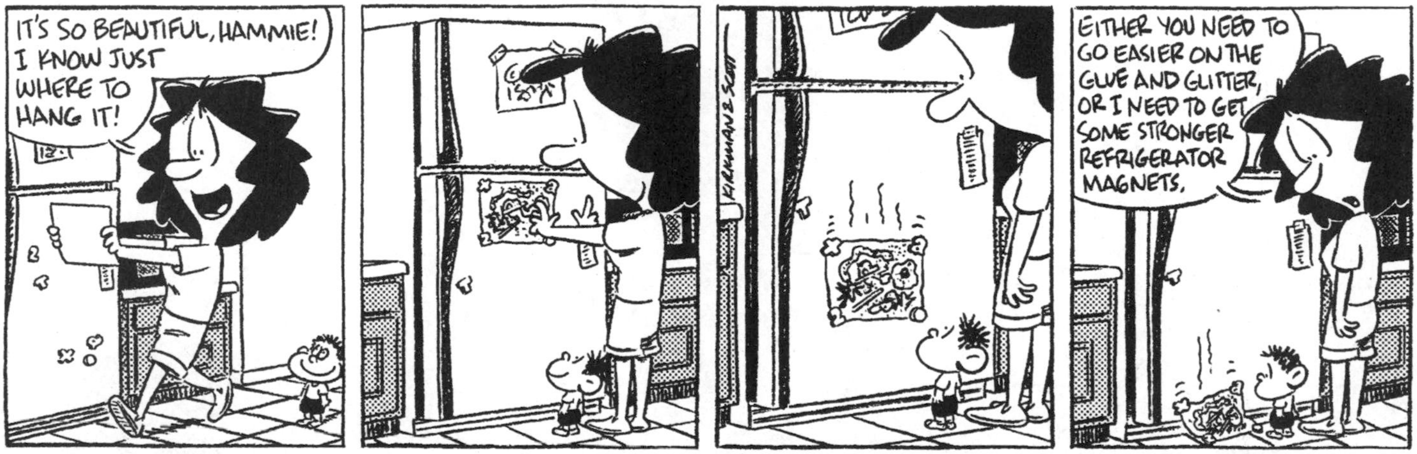
IT'S SO BEAUTIFUL, HAMMIE! I KNOW JUST WHERE TO HANG IT!
KIRKMAN & SCOTT
EITHER YOU NEED TO GO EASIER ON THE GLUE AND GLITTER, OR I NEED TO GET SOME STRONGER REFRIGERATOR MAGNETS.

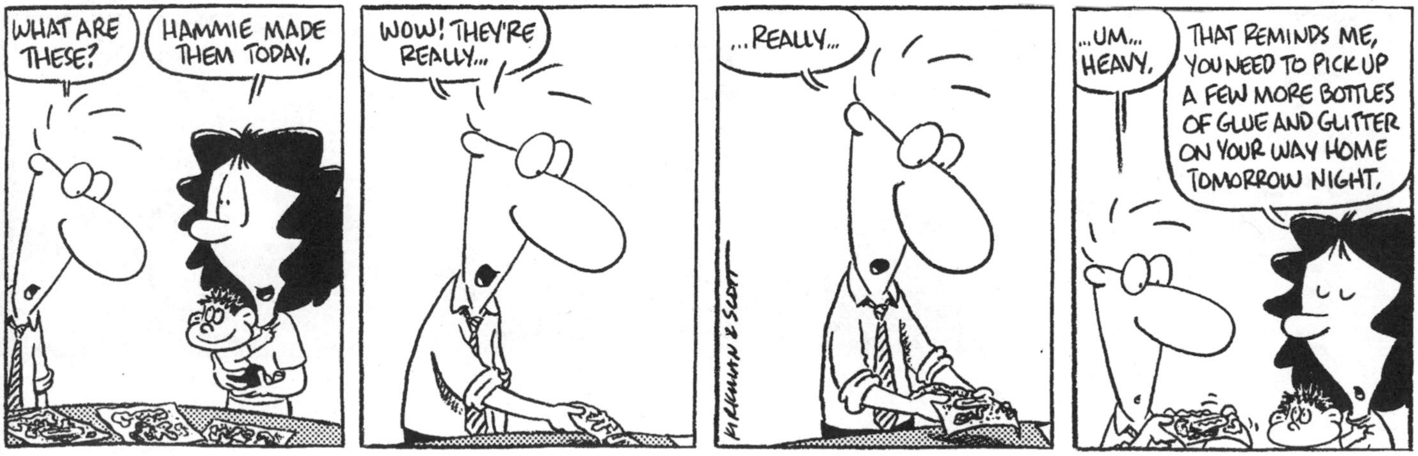
WHAT ARE THESE?
HAMMIE MADE THEM TODAY.
WOW! THEY'RE REALLY...
...REALLY...
KIRKMAN & SCOTT
...UM... HEAVY.
THAT REMINDS ME, YOU NEED TO PICK UP A FEW MORE BOTTLES OF GLUE AND GLITTER ON YOUR WAY HOME TOMORROW NIGHT.

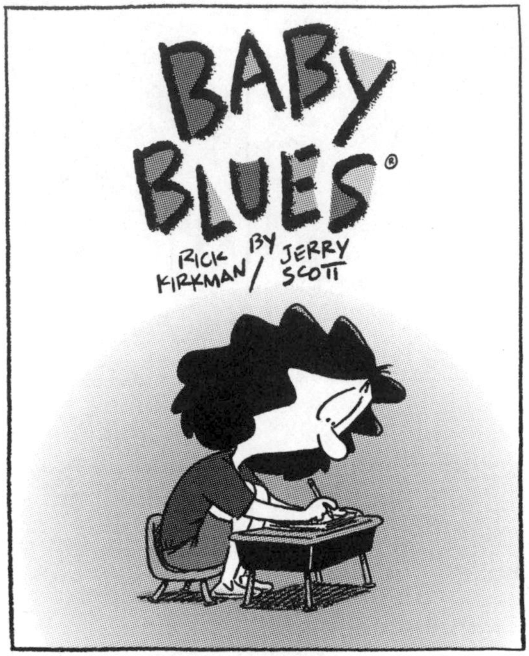
BABY BLUES®
BY RICK KIRKMAN / JERRY SCOTT

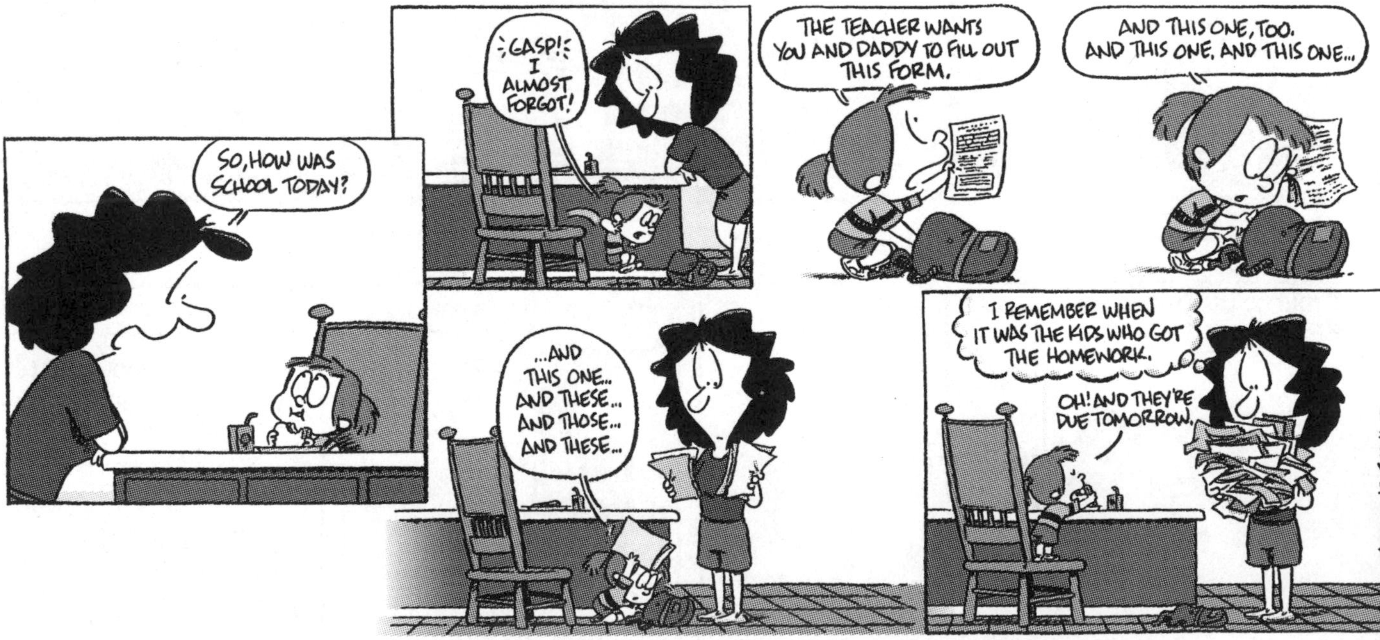
SO, HOW WAS SCHOOL TODAY?
GASP! I ALMOST FORGOT!
THE TEACHER WANTS YOU AND DADDY TO FILL OUT THIS FORM.
AND THIS ONE, TOO. AND THIS ONE. AND THIS ONE...
...AND THIS ONE... AND THESE... AND THOSE... AND THESE...
I REMEMBER WHEN IT WAS THE KIDS WHO GOT THE HOMEWORK.
OH! AND THEY'RE DUE TOMORROW.
KIRKMAN & SCOTT

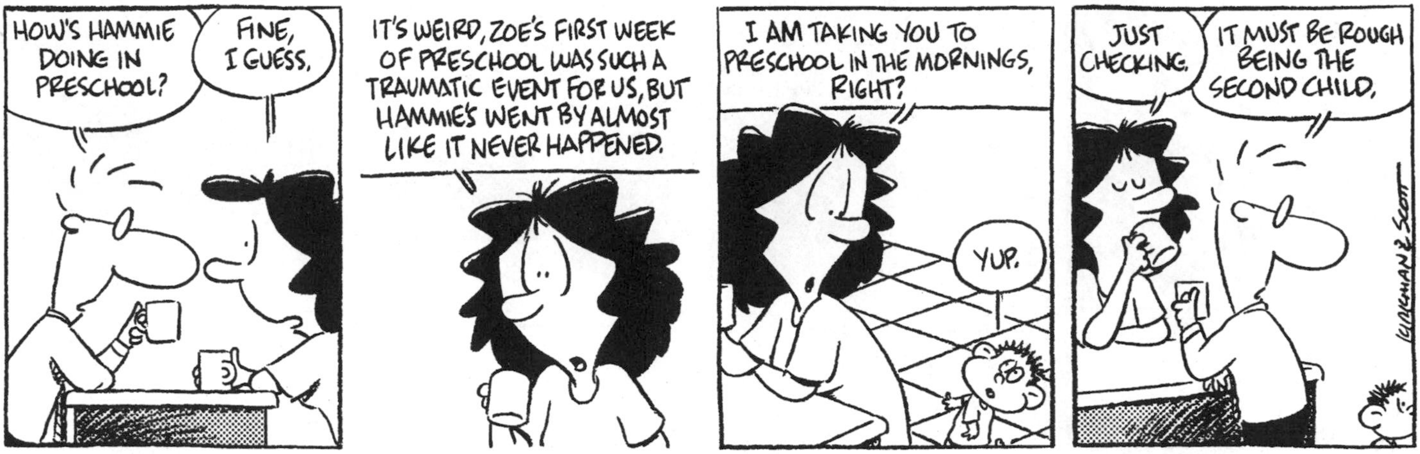
HOW'S HAMMIE DOING IN PRESCHOOL?
FINE, I GUESS.
IT'S WEIRD, ZOE'S FIRST WEEK OF PRESCHOOL WAS SUCH A TRAUMATIC EVENT FOR US, BUT HAMMIE'S WENT BY ALMOST LIKE IT NEVER HAPPENED.
I AM TAKING YOU TO PRESCHOOL IN THE MORNINGS, RIGHT?
YUP.
JUST CHECKING.
IT MUST BE ROUGH BEING THE SECOND CHILD.
KIRKMAN & SCOTT

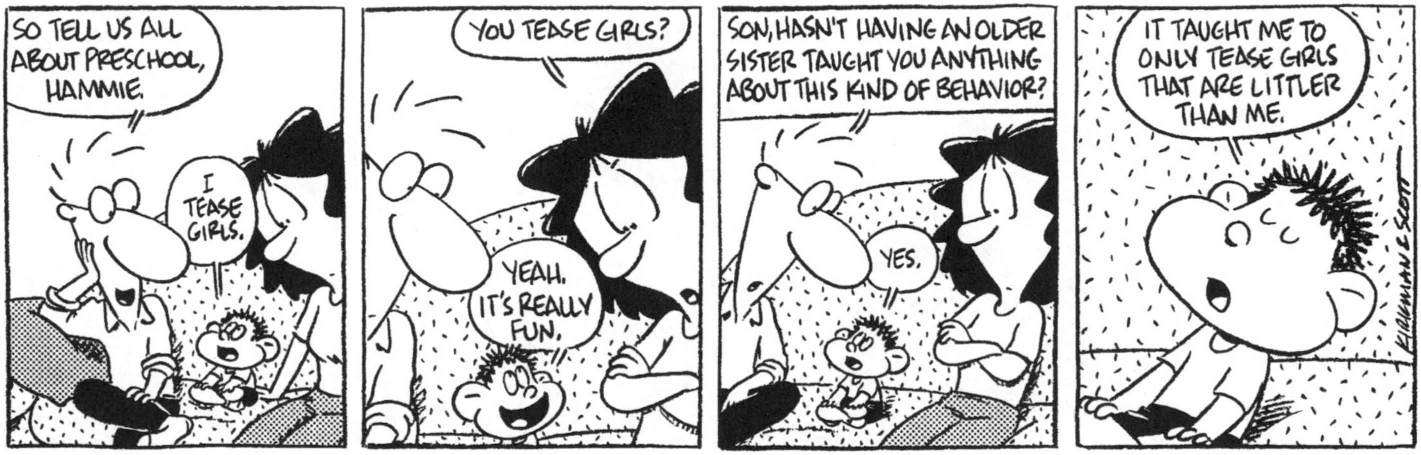
SO TELL US ALL ABOUT PRESCHOOL, HAMMIE.
I TEASE GIRLS.
YOU TEASE GIRLS?
YEAH. IT'S REALLY FUN.
SON, HASN'T HAVING AN OLDER SISTER TAUGHT YOU ANYTHING ABOUT THIS KIND OF BEHAVIOR?
YES.
IT TAUGHT ME TO ONLY TEASE GIRLS THAT ARE LITTLER THAN ME.
KIRKMAN & SCOTT

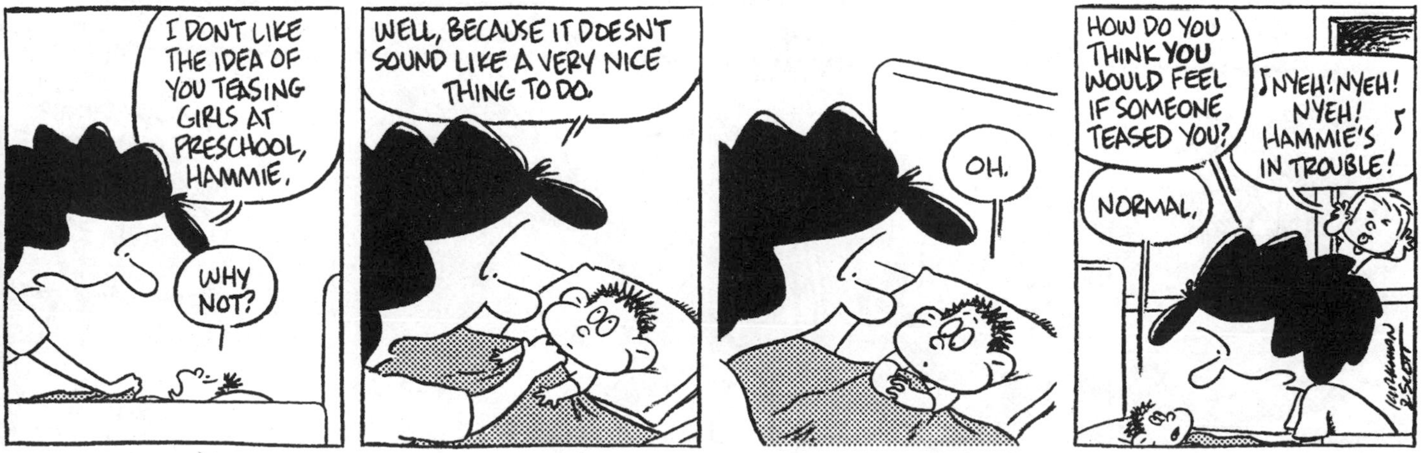
I DON'T LIKE THE IDEA OF YOU TEASING GIRLS AT PRESCHOOL, HAMMIE.
WHY NOT?
WELL, BECAUSE IT DOESN'T SOUND LIKE A VERY NICE THING TO DO.
OH.
HOW DO YOU THINK YOU WOULD FEEL IF SOMEONE TEASED YOU?
NORMAL.
NYEH! NYEH! NYEH! HAMMIE'S IN TROUBLE!

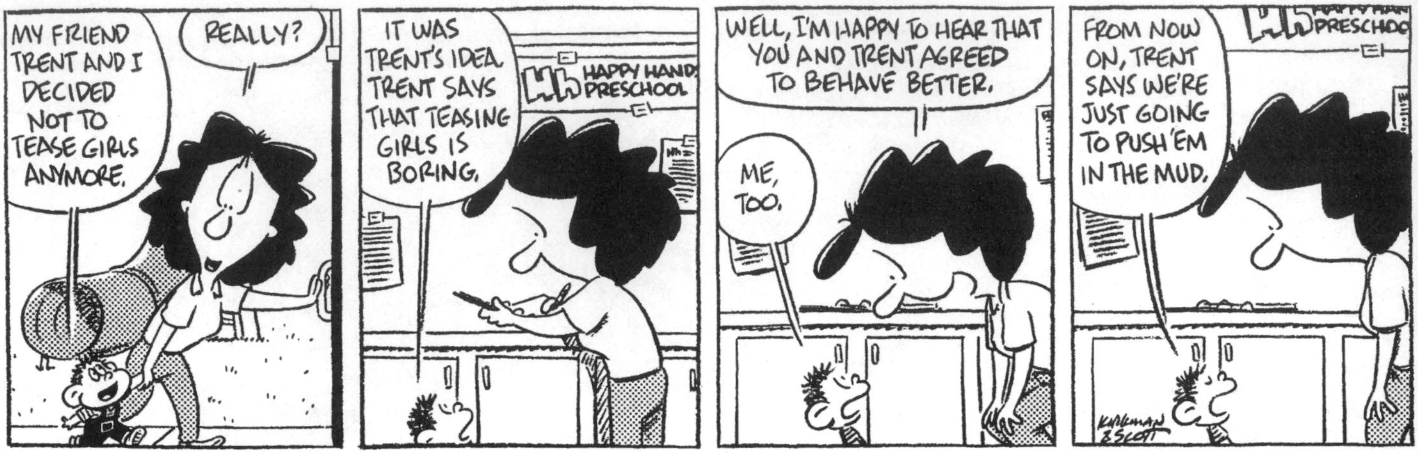
MY FRIEND TRENT AND I DECIDED NOT TO TEASE GIRLS ANYMORE.
REALLY?
IT WAS TRENT'S IDEA. TRENT SAYS THAT TEASING GIRLS IS BORING.
HAPPY HANDS PRESCHOOL
WELL, I'M HAPPY TO HEAR THAT YOU AND TRENT AGREED TO BEHAVE BETTER.
ME, TOO.
FROM NOW ON, TRENT SAYS WE'RE JUST GOING TO PUSH 'EM IN THE MUD.
KIRKMAN & SCOTT

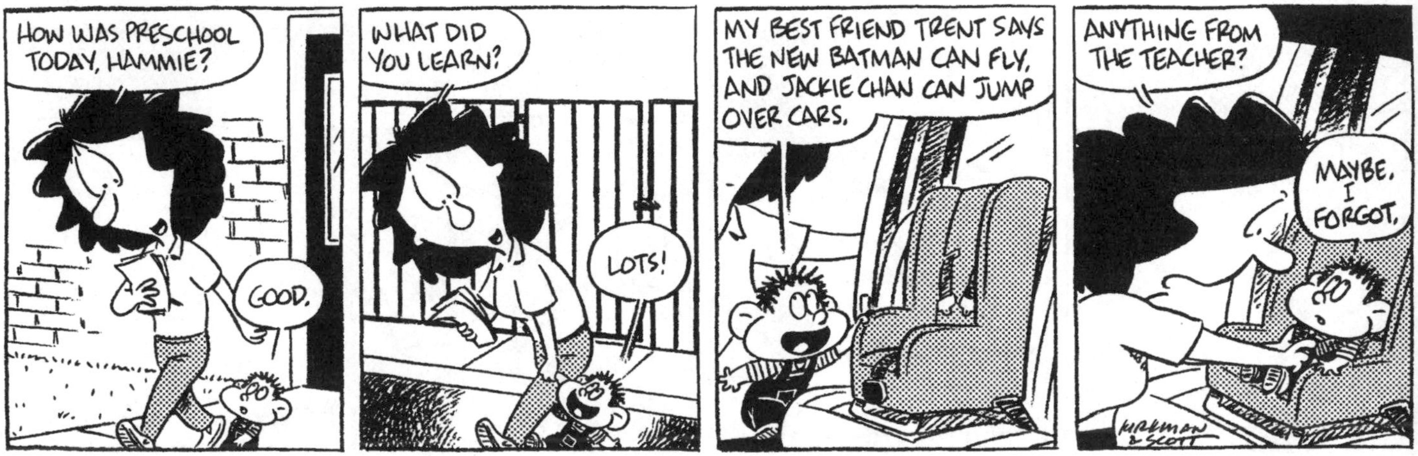
HOW WAS PRESCHOOL TODAY, HAMMIE?
GOOD.
WHAT DID YOU LEARN?
LOTS!
MY BEST FRIEND TRENT SAYS THE NEW BATMAN CAN FLY, AND JACKIE CHAN CAN JUMP OVER CARS.
ANYTHING FROM THE TEACHER?
MAYBE. I FORGOT.
KIRKMAN & SCOTT

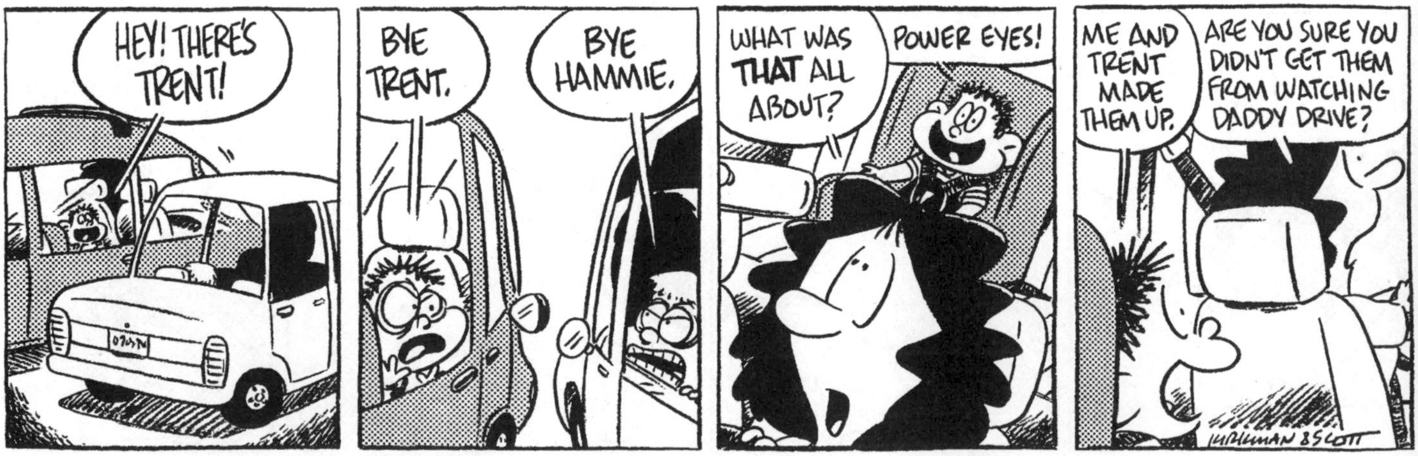
HEY! THERE'S TRENT!
BYE TRENT.
BYE HAMMIE.
WHAT WAS THAT ALL ABOUT?
POWER EYES!
ME AND TRENT MADE THEM UP.
ARE YOU SURE YOU DIDN'T GET THEM FROM WATCHING DADDY DRIVE?
KIRKMAN & SCOTT

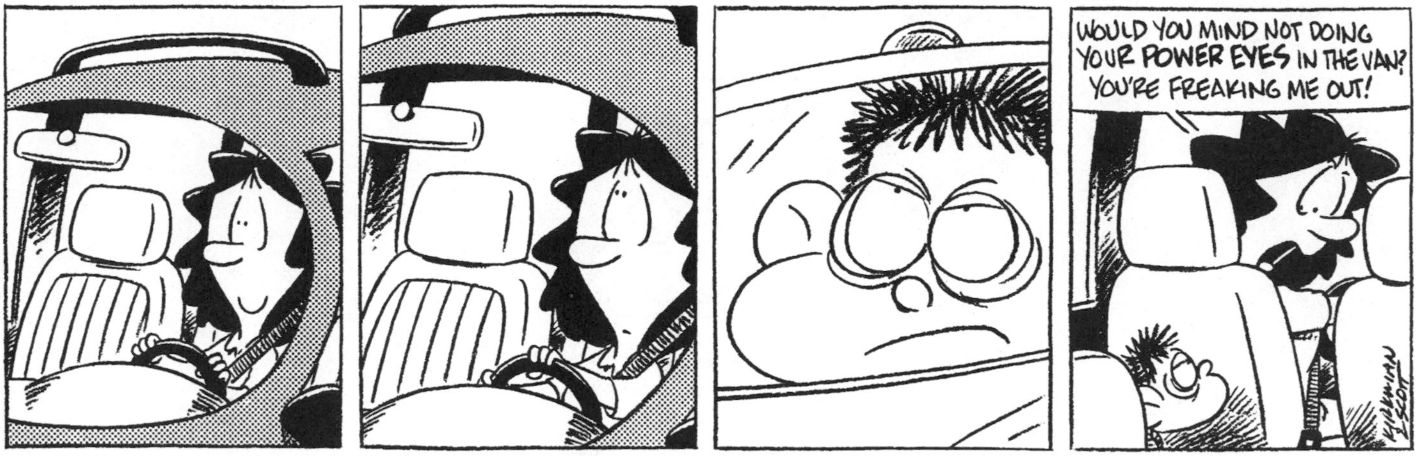
WOULD YOU MIND NOT DOING YOUR POWER EYES IN THE VAN? YOU'RE FREAKING ME OUT!
KIRKMAN & SCOTT

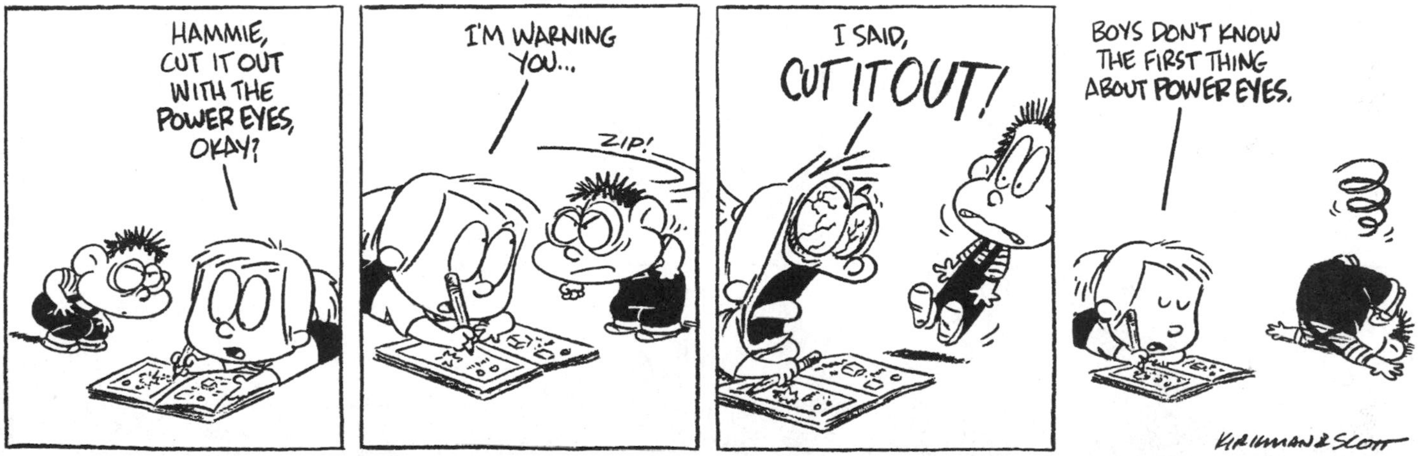
HAMMIE, CUT IT OUT WITH THE POWER EYES, OKAY?
I'M WARNING YOU...
ZIP!
I SAID, CUT IT OUT!
BOYS DON'T KNOW THE FIRST THING ABOUT POWER EYES.
KIRKMAN & SCOTT

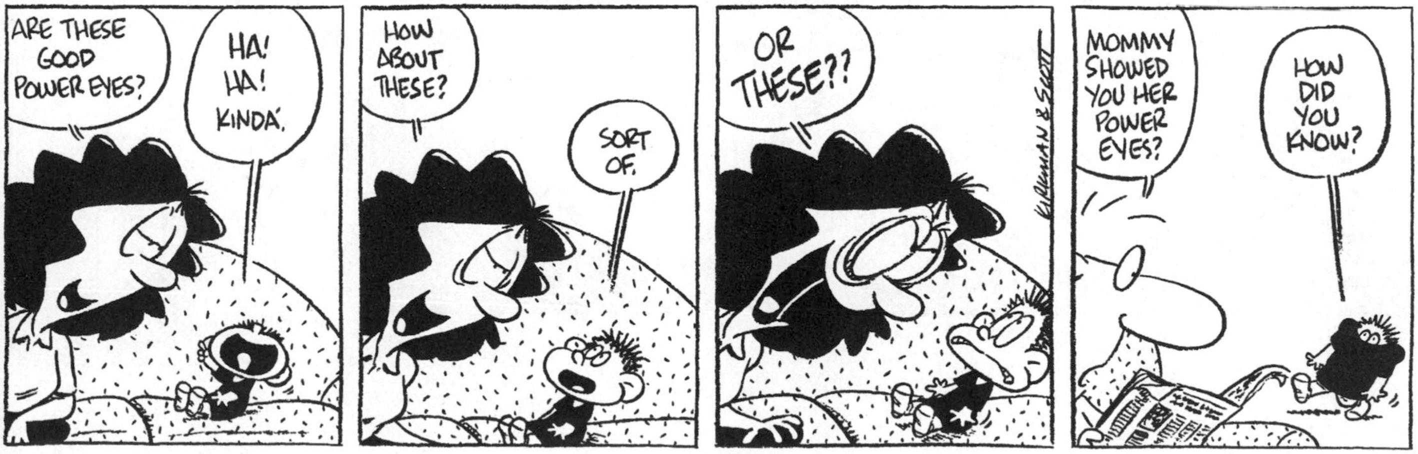
ARE THESE GOOD POWER EYES?
HA! HA! KINDA'.
HOW ABOUT THESE?
SORT OF.
OR THESE??
KIRKMAN & SCOTT
MOMMY SHOWED YOU HER POWER EYES?
HOW DID YOU KNOW?

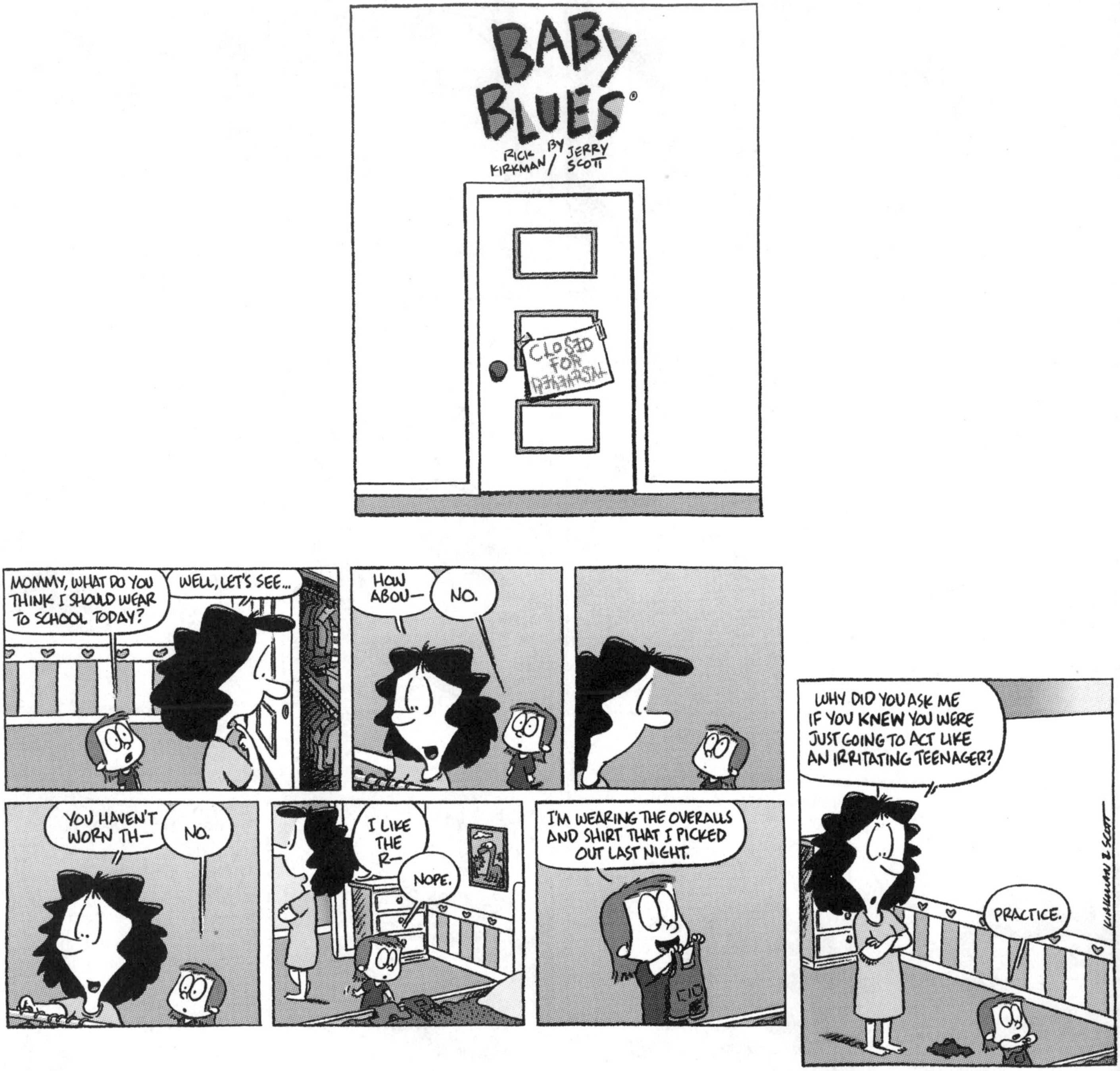
BABY BLUES®
BY RICK KIRKMAN / JERRY SCOTT
MOMMY, WHAT DO YOU THINK I SHOULD WEAR TO SCHOOL TODAY?
WELL, LET'S SEE...
HOW ABOU—
NO.
YOU HAVEN'T WORN TH—
NO.
I LIKE THE R—
NOPE.
I'M WEARING THE OVERALLS AND SHIRT THAT I PICKED OUT LAST NIGHT.
WHY DID YOU ASK ME IF YOU KNEW YOU WERE JUST GOING TO ACT LIKE AN IRRITATING TEENAGER?
PRACTICE.
KIRKMAN & SCOTT

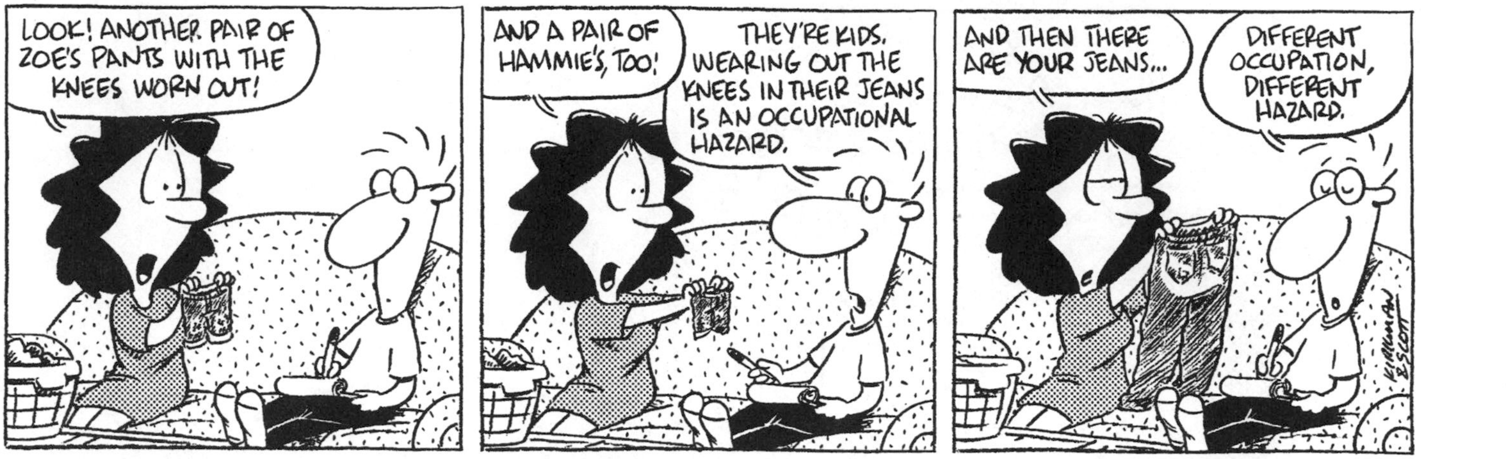
LOOK! ANOTHER PAIR OF ZOE'S PANTS WITH THE KNEES WORN OUT!
AND A PAIR OF HAMMIE'S, TOO!
THEY'RE KIDS. WEARING OUT THE KNEES IN THEIR JEANS IS AN OCCUPATIONAL HAZARD.
AND THEN THERE ARE **YOUR** JEANS...
DIFFERENT OCCUPATION, DIFFERENT HAZARD.
KIRKMAN & SCOTT

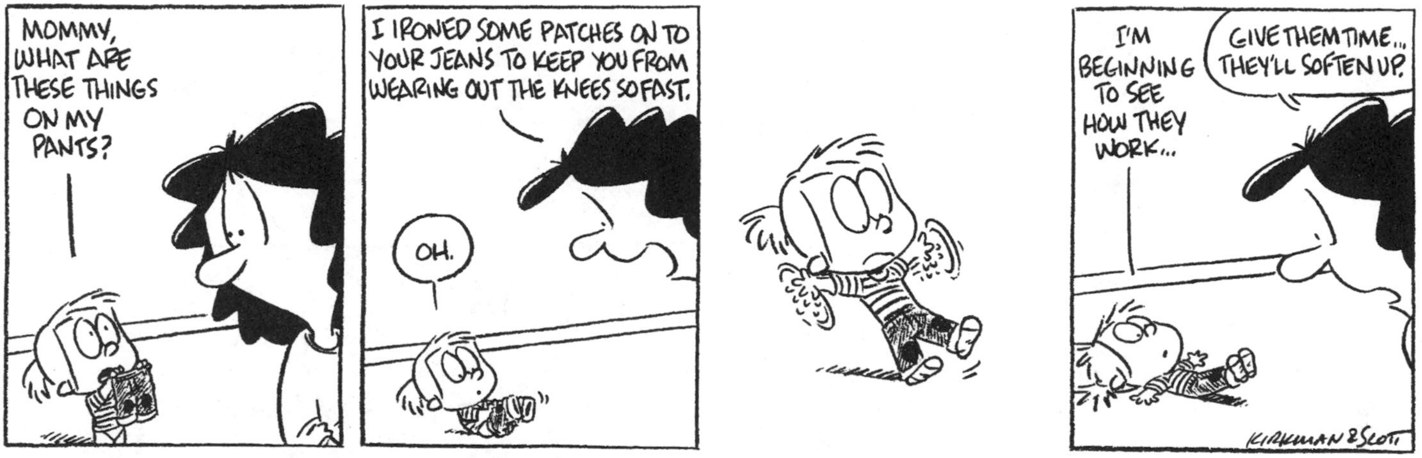
MOMMY, WHAT ARE THESE THINGS ON MY PANTS?
I IRONED SOME PATCHES ON TO YOUR JEANS TO KEEP YOU FROM WEARING OUT THE KNEES SO FAST.
OH.
I'M BEGINNING TO SEE HOW THEY WORK...
GIVE THEM TIME... THEY'LL SOFTEN UP.
KIRKMAN & SCOTT

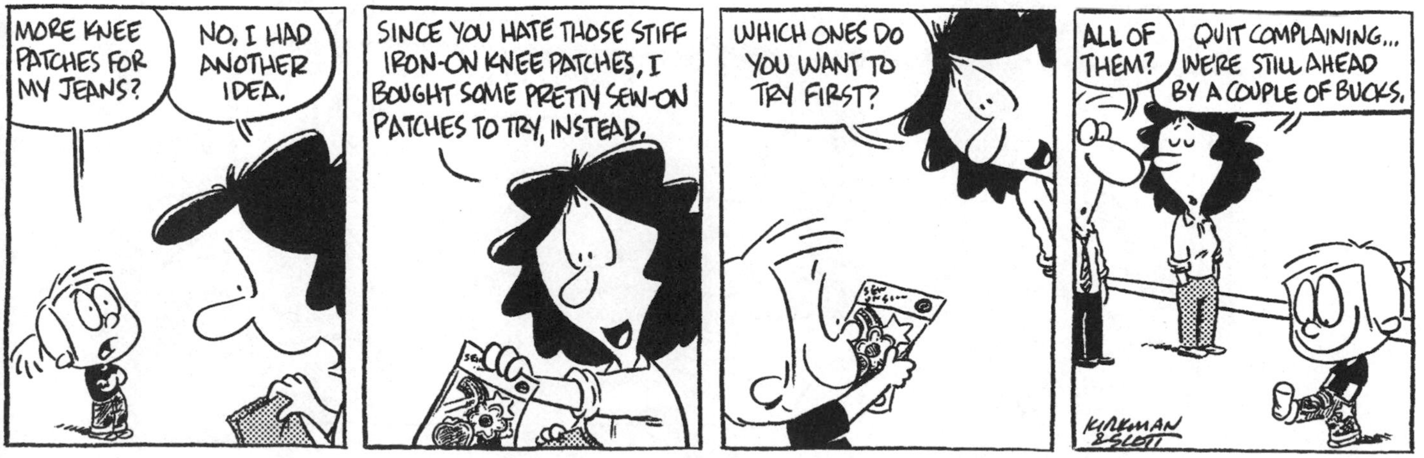
MORE KNEE PATCHES FOR MY JEANS?
NO, I HAD ANOTHER IDEA.
SINCE YOU HATE THOSE STIFF IRON-ON KNEE PATCHES, I BOUGHT SOME PRETTY SEW-ON PATCHES TO TRY, INSTEAD.
WHICH ONES DO YOU WANT TO TRY FIRST?
ALL OF THEM?
QUIT COMPLAINING... WE'RE STILL AHEAD BY A COUPLE OF BUCKS.
KIRKMAN & SCOTT

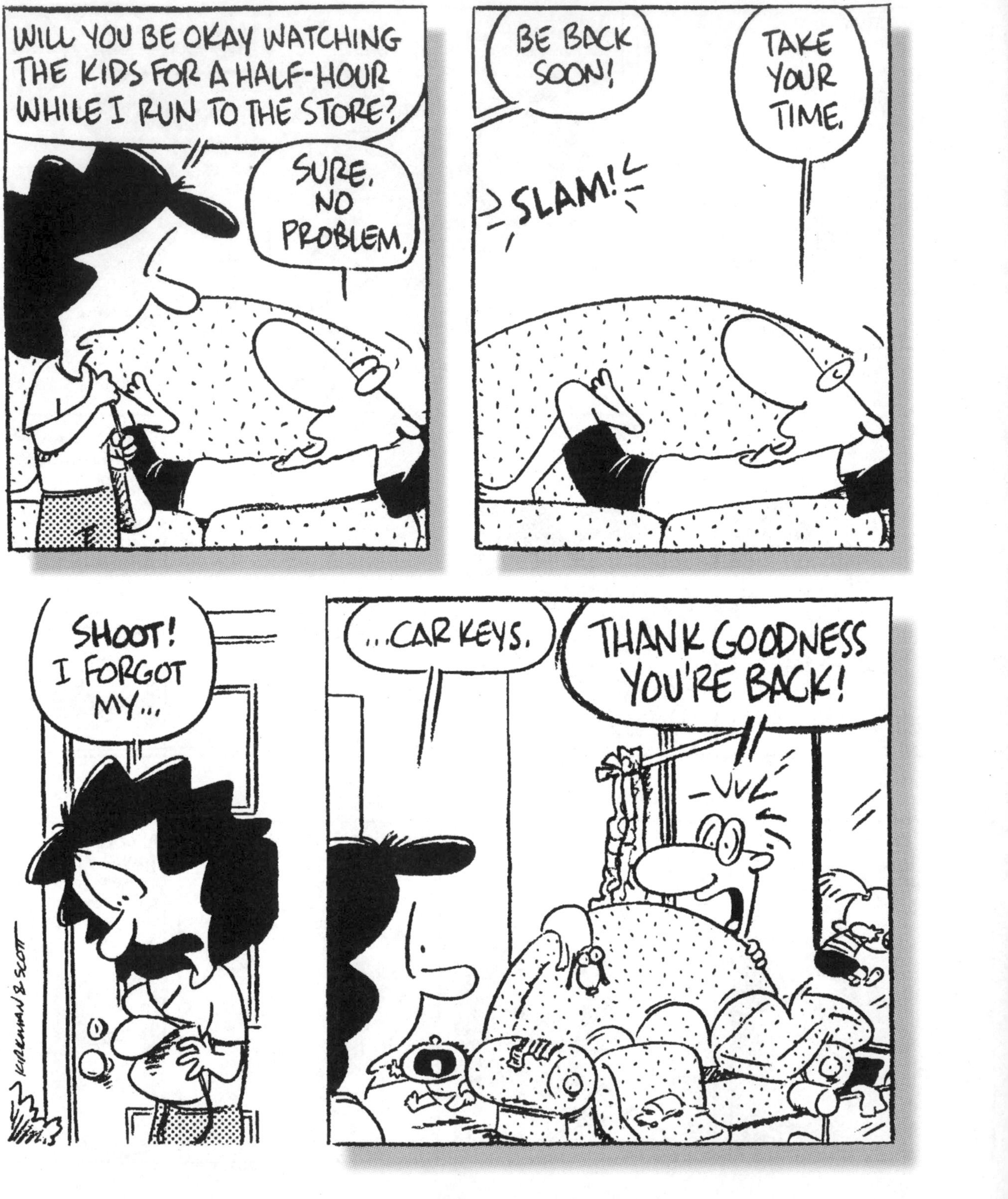
WILL YOU BE OKAY WATCHING THE KIDS FOR A HALF-HOUR WHILE I RUN TO THE STORE?
SURE. NO PROBLEM.
BE BACK SOON!
SLAM!
TAKE YOUR TIME.
SHOOT! I FORGOT MY...
...CAR KEYS.
THANK GOODNESS YOU'RE BACK!
KIRKMAN & SCOTT

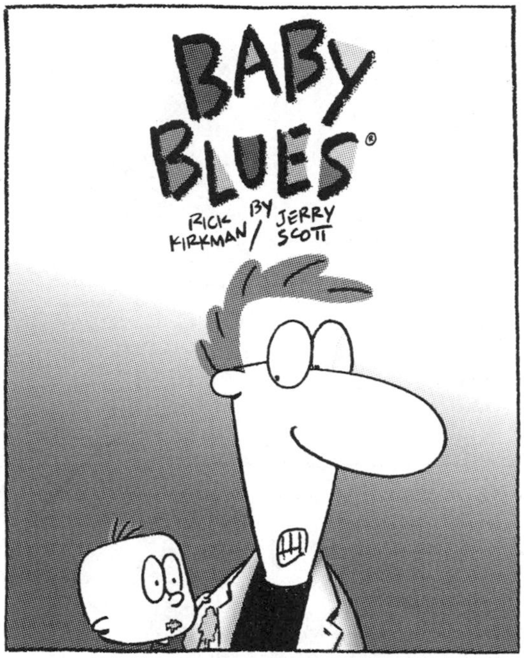
BABY BLUES®
BY RICK KIRKMAN / JERRY SCOTT

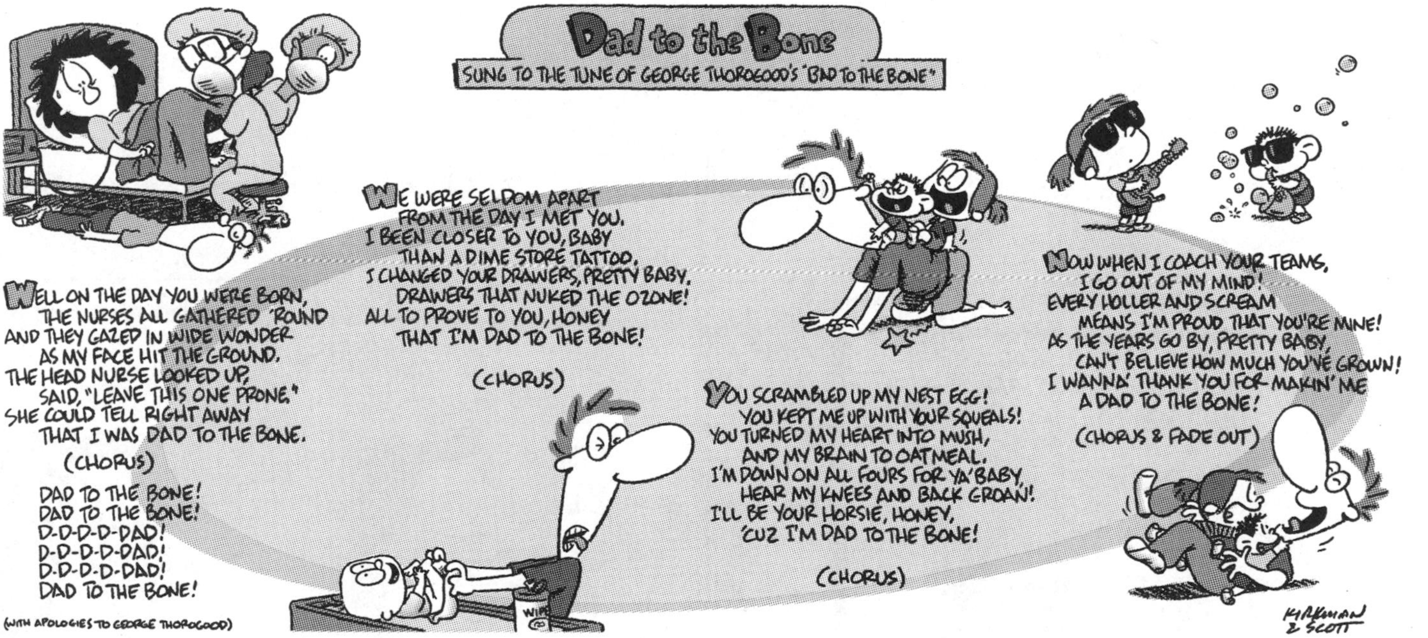
Dad to the Bone
SUNG TO THE TUNE OF GEORGE THOROGOOD'S "BAD TO THE BONE"
WELL ON THE DAY YOU WERE BORN,
THE NURSES ALL GATHERED 'ROUND
AND THEY GAZED IN WIDE WONDER
AS MY FACE HIT THE GROUND.
THE HEAD NURSE LOOKED UP,
SAID, "LEAVE THIS ONE PRONE."
SHE COULD TELL RIGHT AWAY
THAT I WAS DAD TO THE BONE.
(CHORUS)
DAD TO THE BONE!
DAD TO THE BONE!
D-D-D-D-DAD!
D-D-D-D-DAD!
D-D-D-D-DAD!
DAD TO THE BONE!
(WITH APOLOGIES TO GEORGE THOROGOOD)
WE WERE SELDOM APART
FROM THE DAY I MET YOU.
I BEEN CLOSER TO YOU, BABY
THAN A DIME STORE TATTOO.
I CHANGED YOUR DRAWERS, PRETTY BABY.
DRAWERS THAT NUKED THE OZONE!
ALL TO PROVE TO YOU, HONEY
THAT I'M DAD TO THE BONE!
(CHORUS)
YOU SCRAMBLED UP MY NEST EGG!
YOU KEPT ME UP WITH YOUR SQUEALS!
YOU TURNED MY HEART INTO MUSH,
AND MY BRAIN TO OATMEAL.
I'M DOWN ON ALL FOURS FOR YA' BABY,
HEAR MY KNEES AND BACK GROAN!
I'LL BE YOUR HORSIE, HONEY,
'CUZ I'M DAD TO THE BONE!
(CHORUS)
NOW WHEN I COACH YOUR TEAMS,
I GO OUT OF MY MIND!
EVERY HOLLER AND SCREAM
MEANS I'M PROUD THAT YOU'RE MINE!
AS THE YEARS GO BY, PRETTY BABY,
CAN'T BELIEVE HOW MUCH YOU'VE GROWN!
I WANNA' THANK YOU FOR MAKIN' ME
A DAD TO THE BONE!
(CHORUS & FADE OUT)
KIRKMAN & SCOTT

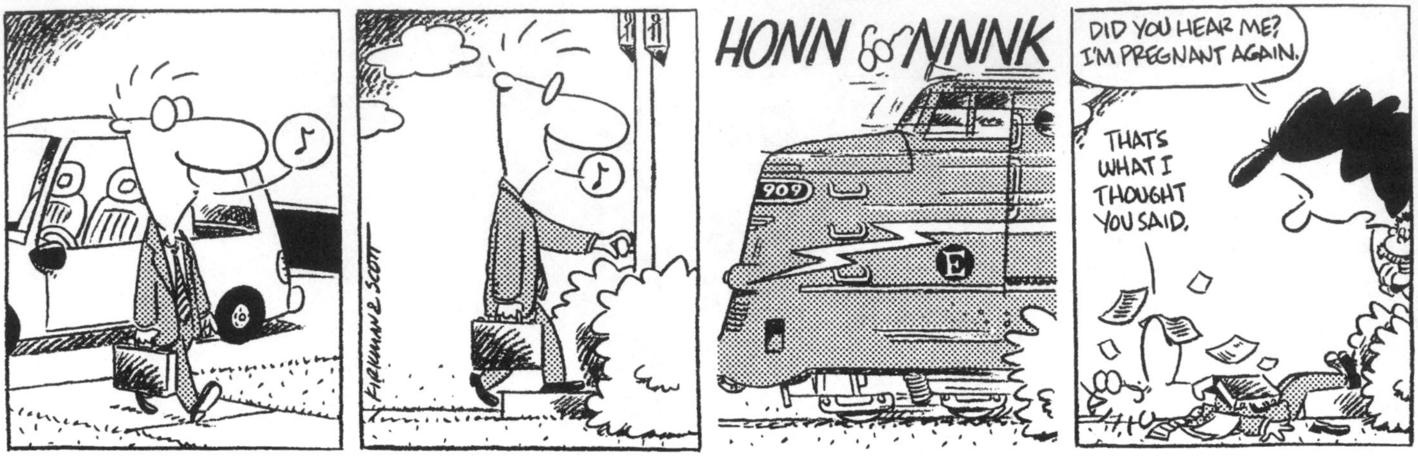
KIRKMAN & SCOTT
HONN NNNK
DID YOU HEAR ME? I'M PREGNANT AGAIN.
THAT'S WHAT I THOUGHT YOU SAID.

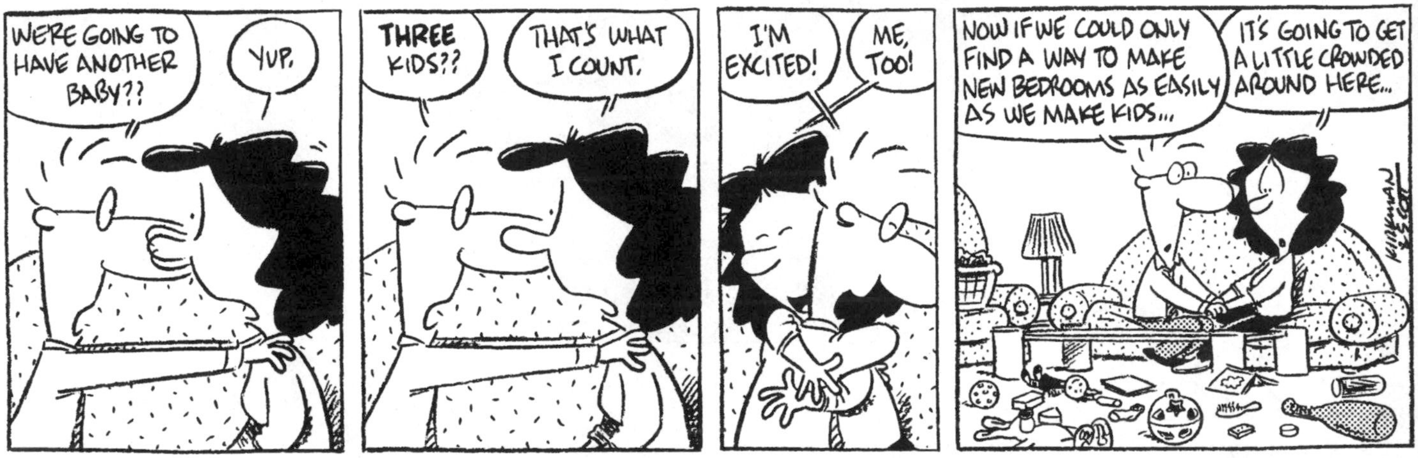
WE'RE GOING TO HAVE ANOTHER BABY??
YUP.
THREE KIDS??
THAT'S WHAT I COUNT.
I'M EXCITED!
ME, TOO!
NOW IF WE COULD ONLY FIND A WAY TO MAKE NEW BEDROOMS AS EASILY AS WE MAKE KIDS...
IT'S GOING TO GET A LITTLE CROWDED AROUND HERE...
KIRKMAN & SCOTT

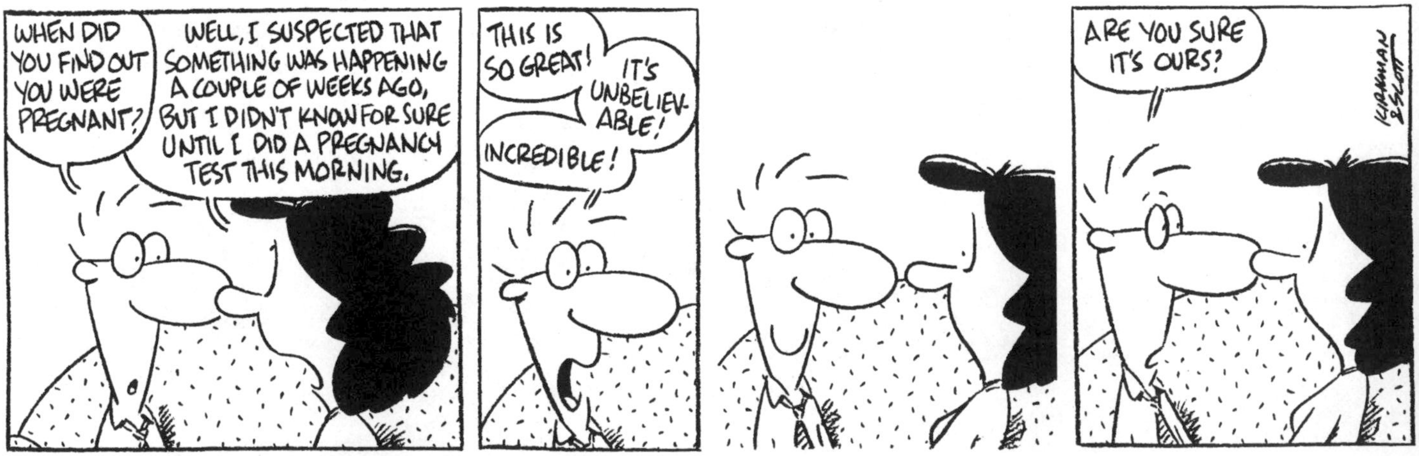
WHEN DID YOU FIND OUT YOU WERE PREGNANT?
WELL, I SUSPECTED THAT SOMETHING WAS HAPPENING A COUPLE OF WEEKS AGO, BUT I DIDN'T KNOW FOR SURE UNTIL I DID A PREGNANCY TEST THIS MORNING.
THIS IS SO GREAT!
IT'S UNBELIEVABLE!
INCREDIBLE!
ARE YOU SURE IT'S OURS?
KIRKMAN & SCOTT

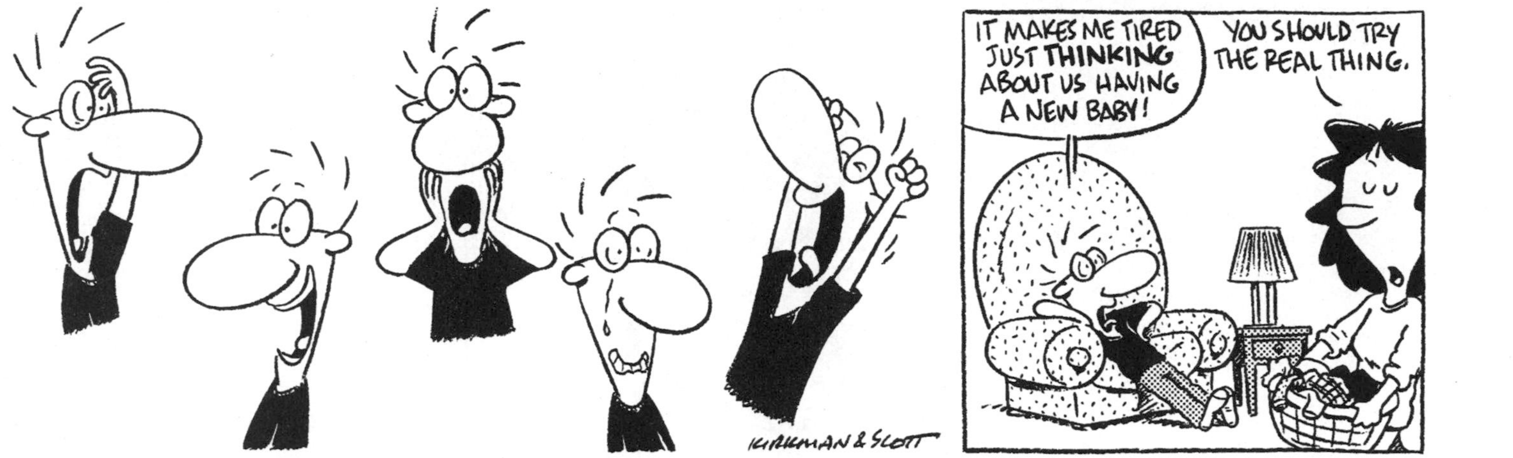
KIRKMAN & SCOTT
IT MAKES ME TIRED JUST **THINKING** ABOUT US HAVING A NEW BABY!
YOU SHOULD TRY THE REAL THING.

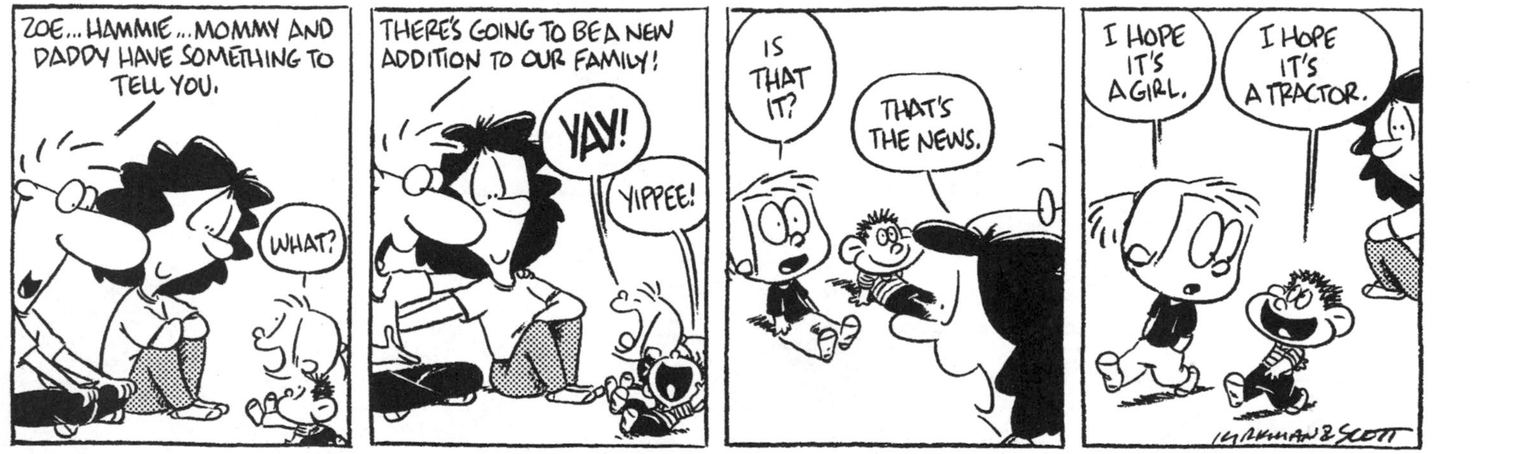
ZOE... HAMMIE... MOMMY AND DADDY HAVE SOMETHING TO TELL YOU.
WHAT?
THERE'S GOING TO BE A NEW ADDITION TO OUR FAMILY!
YAY!
YIPPEE!
IS THAT IT?
THAT'S THE NEWS.
I HOPE IT'S A GIRL.
I HOPE IT'S A TRACTOR.
KIRKMAN & SCOTT

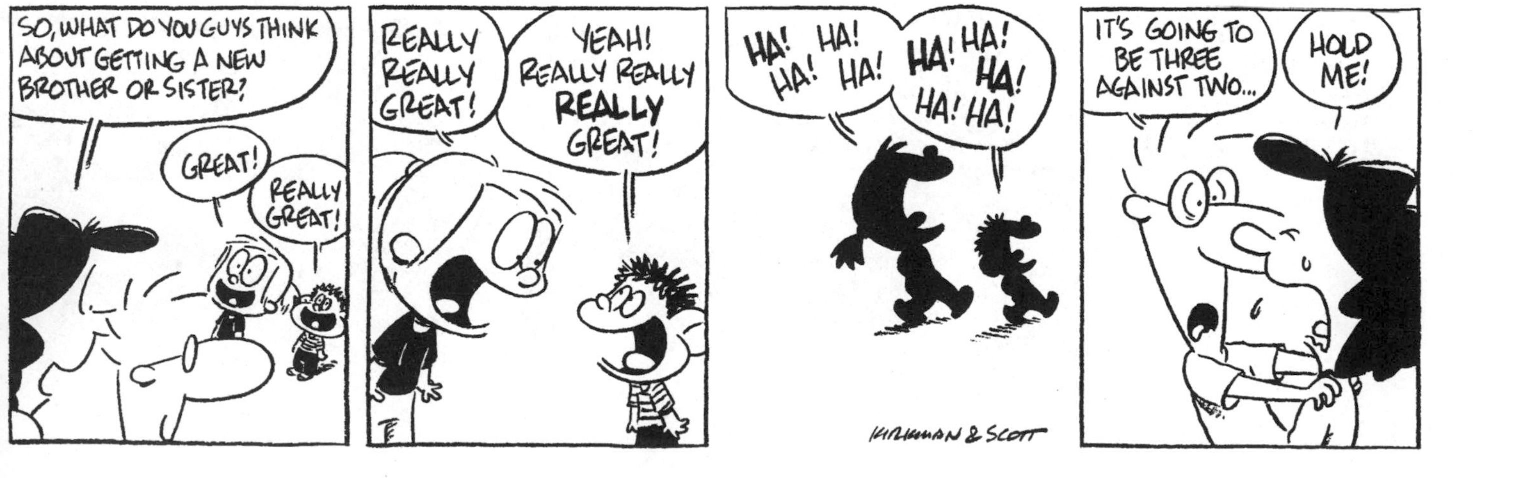
SO, WHAT DO YOU GUYS THINK ABOUT GETTING A NEW BROTHER OR SISTER?
GREAT!
REALLY GREAT!
REALLY REALLY GREAT!
YEAH! REALLY REALLY **REALLY** GREAT!
HA! HA! HA! HA!
HA! HA! **HA!** HA! HA!
KIRKMAN & SCOTT
IT'S GOING TO BE THREE AGAINST TWO...
HOLD ME!

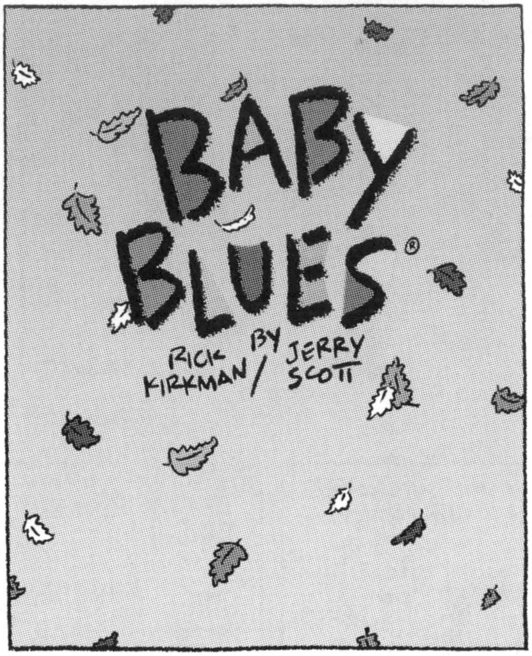
BABY BLUES®
BY
RICK KIRKMAN / JERRY SCOTT

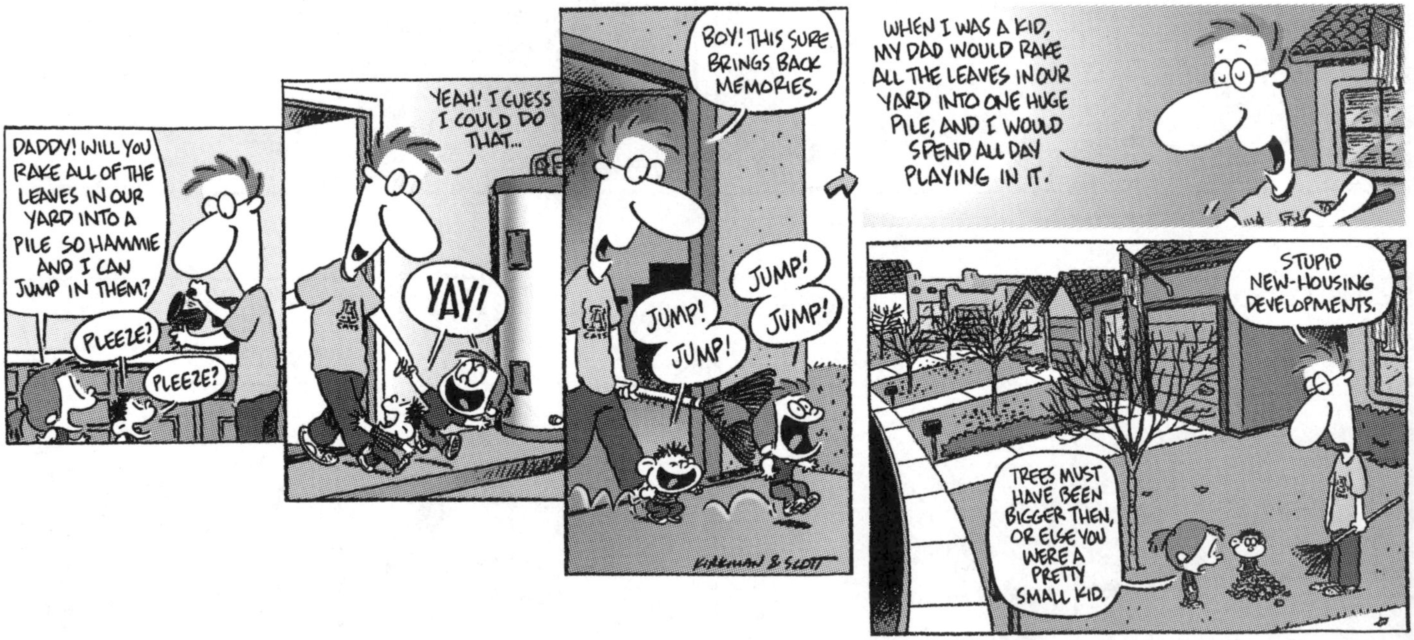
DADDY! WILL YOU RAKE ALL OF THE LEAVES IN OUR YARD INTO A PILE SO HAMMIE AND I CAN JUMP IN THEM?
PLEEZE?
PLEEZE?
YEAH! I GUESS I COULD DO THAT...
YAY!
BOY! THIS SURE BRINGS BACK MEMORIES.
JUMP! JUMP!
JUMP! JUMP!
KIRKMAN & SCOTT
WHEN I WAS A KID, MY DAD WOULD RAKE ALL THE LEAVES IN OUR YARD INTO ONE HUGE PILE, AND I WOULD SPEND ALL DAY PLAYING IN IT.
TREES MUST HAVE BEEN BIGGER THEN, OR ELSE YOU WERE A PRETTY SMALL KID.
STUPID NEW-HOUSING DEVELOPMENTS.

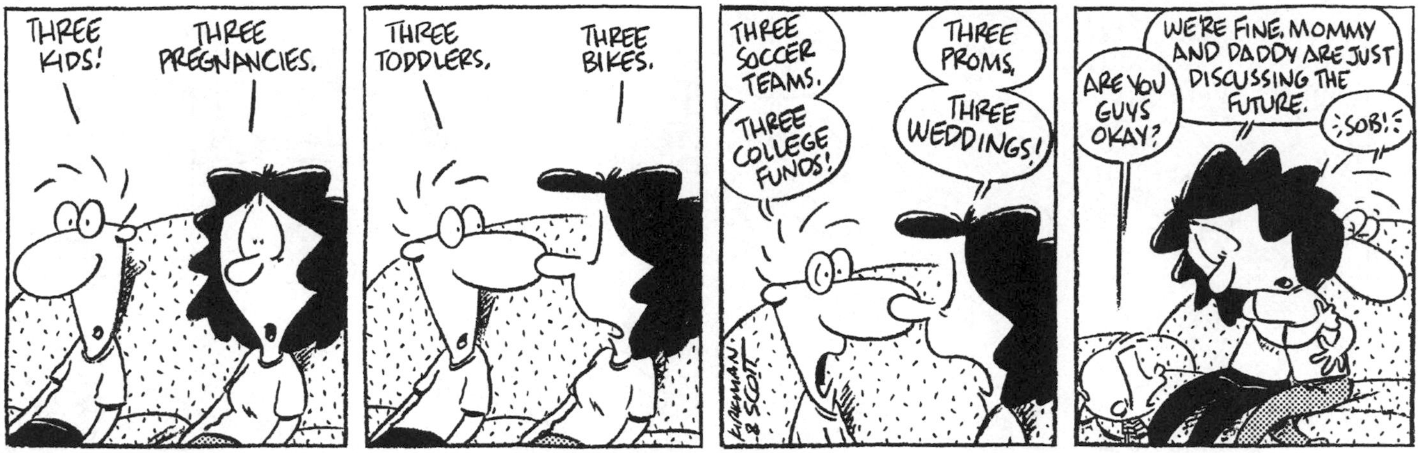

THREE KIDS!
THREE PREGNANCIES.
THREE TODDLERS.
THREE BIKES.
THREE SOCCER TEAMS.
THREE COLLEGE FUNDS!
THREE PROMS,
THREE WEDDINGS!
KIRKMAN & SCOTT
ARE YOU GUYS OKAY?
WE'RE FINE, MOMMY AND DADDY ARE JUST DISCUSSING THE FUTURE.
SOB!

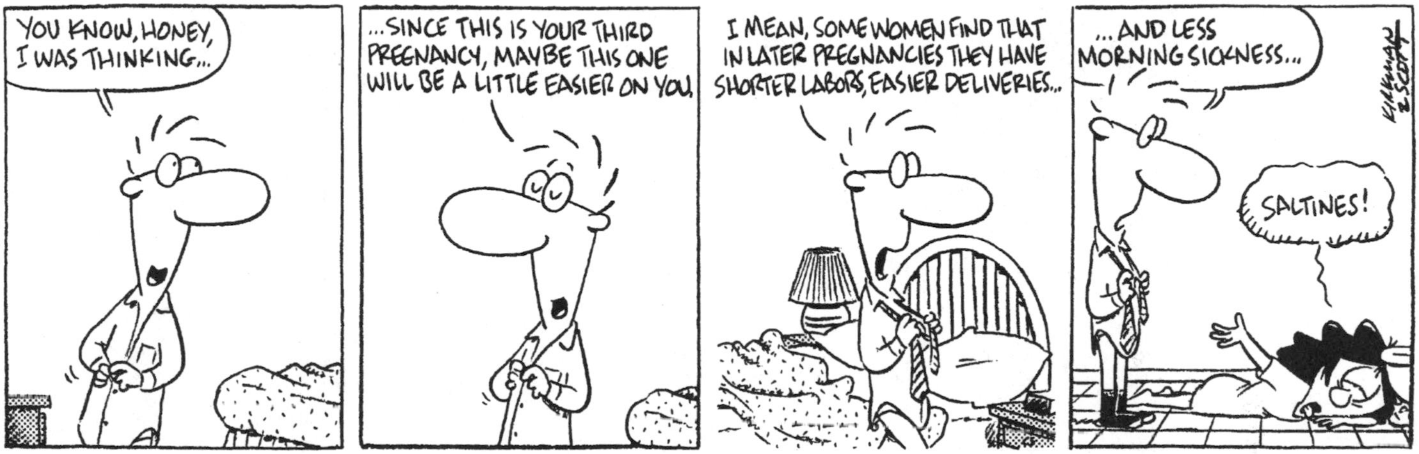

YOU KNOW, HONEY, I WAS THINKING...
...SINCE THIS IS YOUR THIRD PREGNANCY, MAYBE THIS ONE WILL BE A LITTLE EASIER ON YOU.
I MEAN, SOME WOMEN FIND THAT IN LATER PREGNANCIES THEY HAVE SHORTER LABORS, EASIER DELIVERIES...
...AND LESS MORNING SICKNESS...
KIRKMAN & SCOTT
SALTINES!

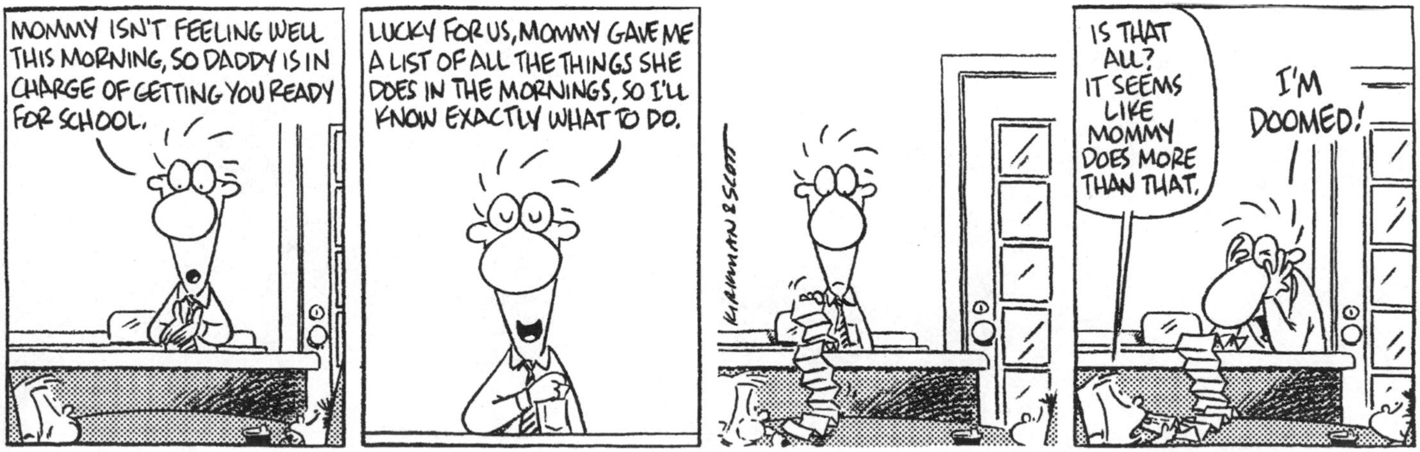

MOMMY ISN'T FEELING WELL THIS MORNING, SO DADDY IS IN CHARGE OF GETTING YOU READY FOR SCHOOL.
LUCKY FOR US, MOMMY GAVE ME A LIST OF ALL THE THINGS SHE DOES IN THE MORNINGS, SO I'LL KNOW EXACTLY WHAT TO DO.
KIRKMAN & SCOTT
IS THAT ALL? IT SEEMS LIKE MOMMY DOES MORE THAN THAT.
I'M DOOMED!

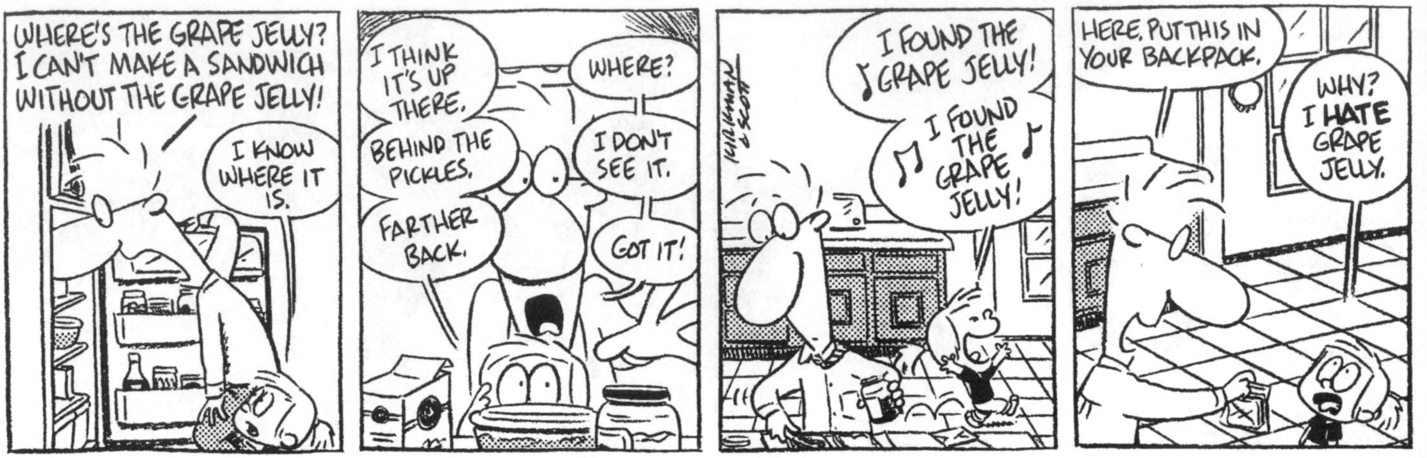
WHERE'S THE GRAPE JELLY? I CAN'T MAKE A SANDWICH WITHOUT THE GRAPE JELLY!
I KNOW WHERE IT IS.
I THINK IT'S UP THERE.
WHERE?
BEHIND THE PICKLES.
I DON'T SEE IT.
FARTHER BACK.
GOT IT!
I FOUND THE GRAPE JELLY!
I FOUND THE GRAPE JELLY!
HERE, PUT THIS IN YOUR BACKPACK.
WHY? I HATE GRAPE JELLY.

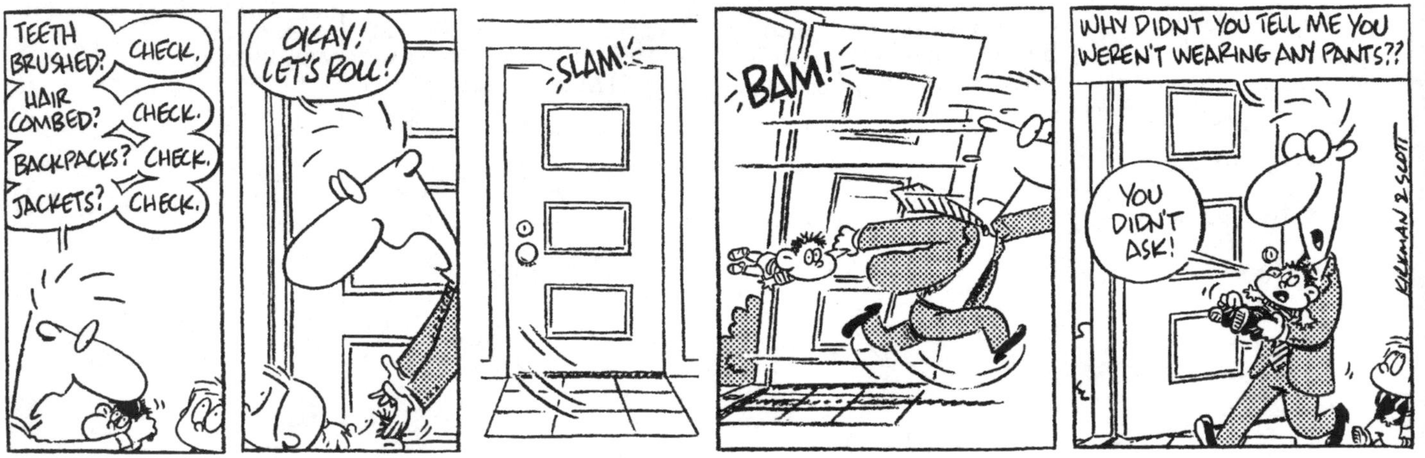
TEETH BRUSHED?
CHECK.
HAIR COMBED?
CHECK.
BACKPACKS?
CHECK.
JACKETS?
CHECK.
OKAY! LET'S ROLL!
SLAM!
BAM!
WHY DIDN'T YOU TELL ME YOU WEREN'T WEARING ANY PANTS??
YOU DIDN'T ASK!
KIRKMAN & SCOTT

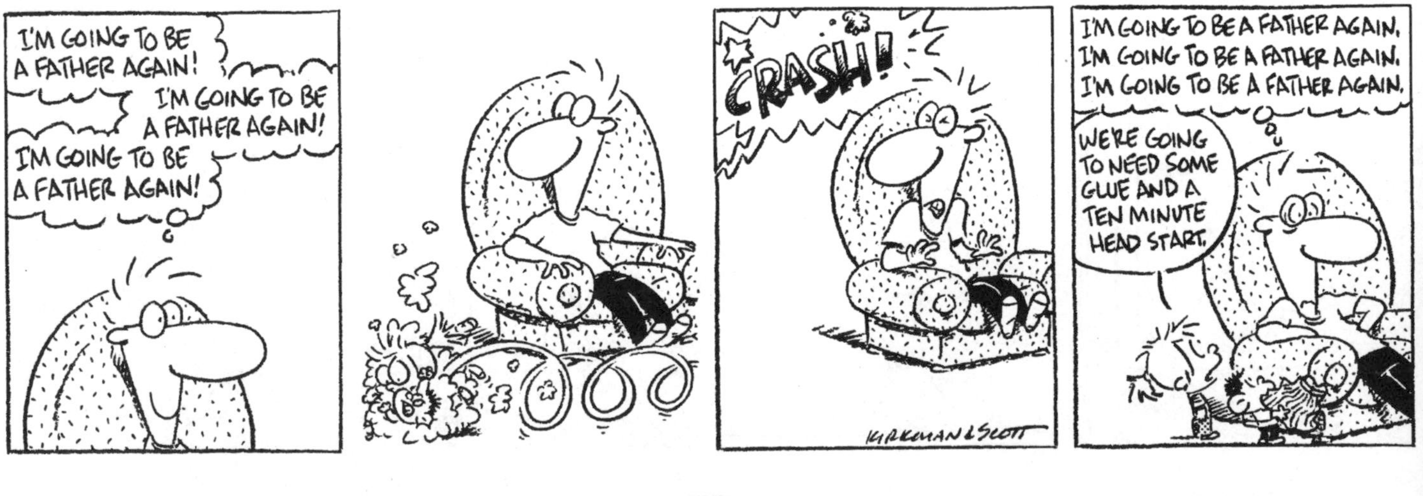
I'M GOING TO BE A FATHER AGAIN!
I'M GOING TO BE A FATHER AGAIN!
I'M GOING TO BE A FATHER AGAIN!
CRASH!
KIRKMAN & SCOTT
I'M GOING TO BE A FATHER AGAIN. I'M GOING TO BE A FATHER AGAIN. I'M GOING TO BE A FATHER AGAIN.
WE'RE GOING TO NEED SOME GLUE AND A TEN MINUTE HEAD START.

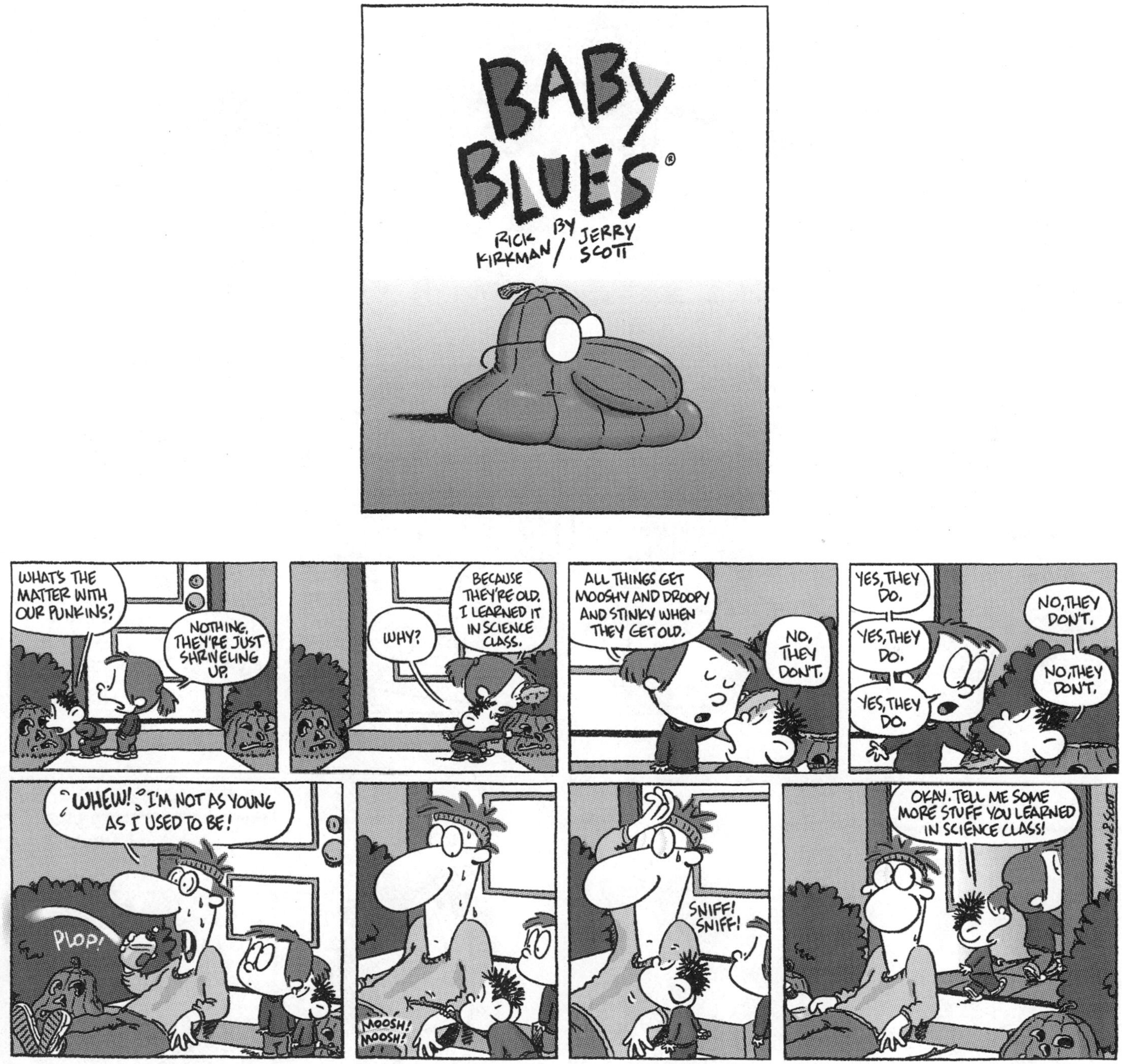
BABY BLUES®
BY RICK KIRKMAN / JERRY SCOTT
WHAT'S THE MATTER WITH OUR PUNKINS?
NOTHING. THEY'RE JUST SHRIVELING UP.
WHY?
BECAUSE THEY'RE OLD. I LEARNED IT IN SCIENCE CLASS.
ALL THINGS GET MOOSHY AND DROOPY AND STINKY WHEN THEY GET OLD.
NO, THEY DON'T.
YES, THEY DO.
NO, THEY DON'T.
YES, THEY DO.
NO, THEY DON'T.
YES, THEY DO.
WHEW! I'M NOT AS YOUNG AS I USED TO BE!
PLOP!
MOOSH! MOOSH!
SNIFF! SNIFF!
OKAY. TELL ME SOME MORE STUFF YOU LEARNED IN SCIENCE CLASS!

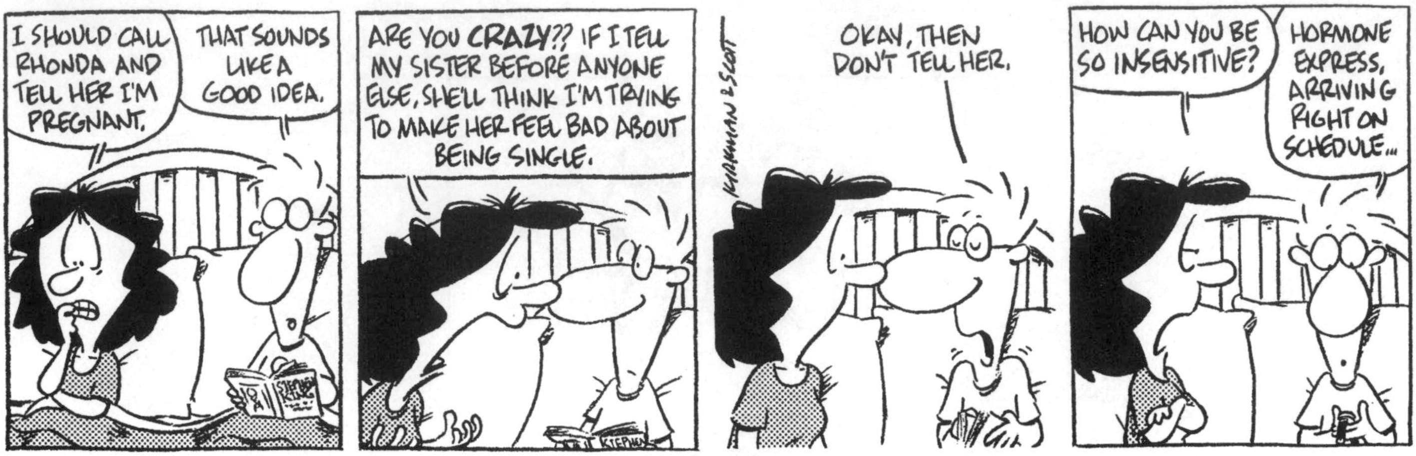
I SHOULD CALL RHONDA AND TELL HER I'M PREGNANT.
THAT SOUNDS LIKE A GOOD IDEA.
ARE YOU **CRAZY**?? IF I TELL MY SISTER BEFORE ANYONE ELSE, SHE'LL THINK I'M TRYING TO MAKE HER FEEL BAD ABOUT BEING SINGLE.
KIRKMAN & SCOTT
OKAY, THEN DON'T TELL HER.
HOW CAN YOU BE SO INSENSITIVE?
HORMONE EXPRESS, ARRIVING RIGHT ON SCHEDULE...

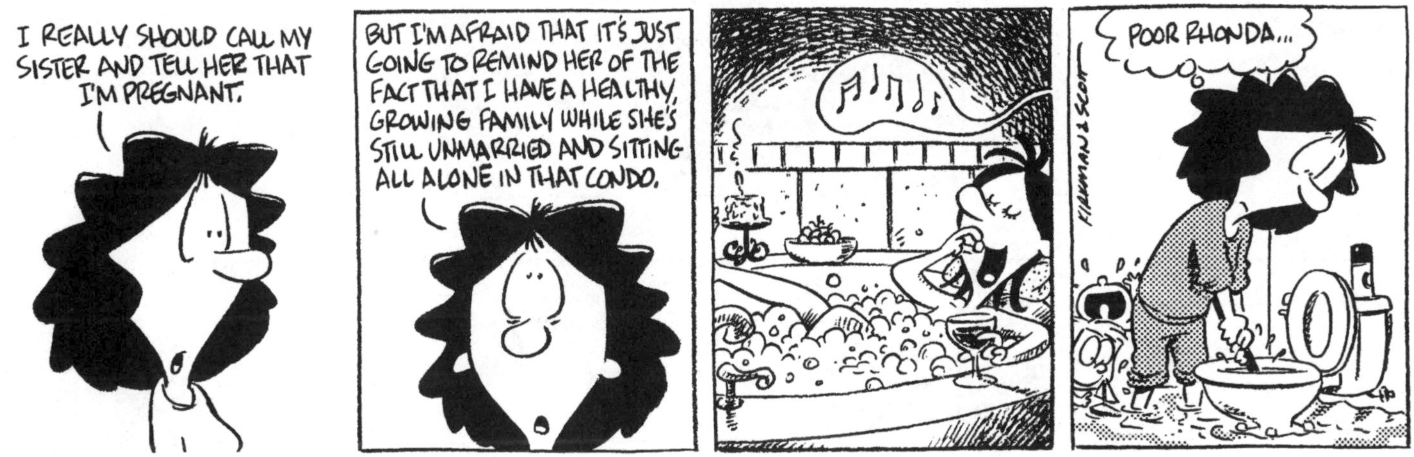
I REALLY SHOULD CALL MY SISTER AND TELL HER THAT I'M PREGNANT.
BUT I'M AFRAID THAT IT'S JUST GOING TO REMIND HER OF THE FACT THAT I HAVE A HEALTHY, GROWING FAMILY WHILE SHE'S STILL UNMARRIED AND SITTING ALL ALONE IN THAT CONDO.
KIRKMAN & SCOTT
POOR RHONDA...

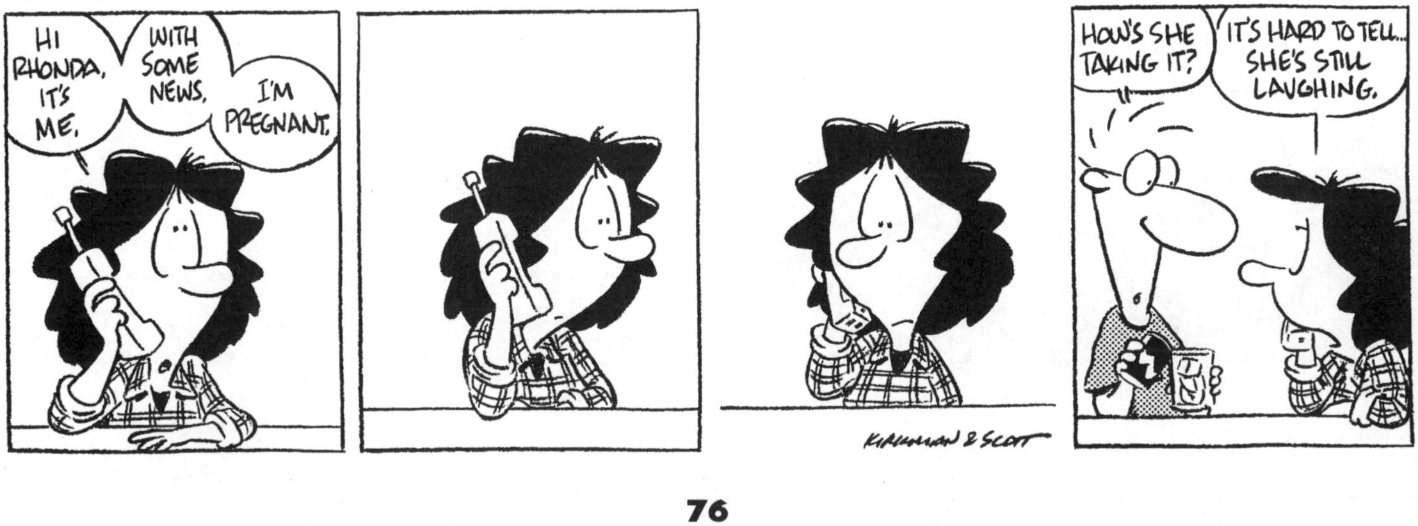
HI RHONDA, IT'S ME.
WITH SOME NEWS.
I'M PREGNANT.
HOW'S SHE TAKING IT?
IT'S HARD TO TELL... SHE'S STILL LAUGHING.
KIRKMAN & SCOTT

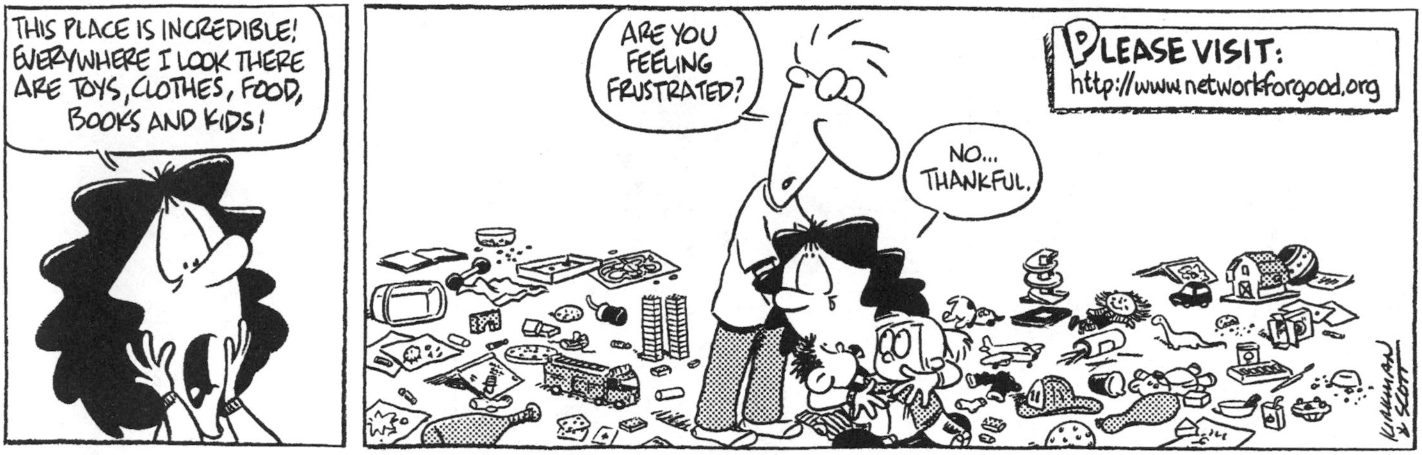
THIS PLACE IS INCREDIBLE! EVERYWHERE I LOOK THERE ARE TOYS, CLOTHES, FOOD, BOOKS AND KIDS!
ARE YOU FEELING FRUSTRATED?
NO... THANKFUL.
PLEASE VISIT:
http://www.networkforgood.org
KIRKMAN & SCOTT

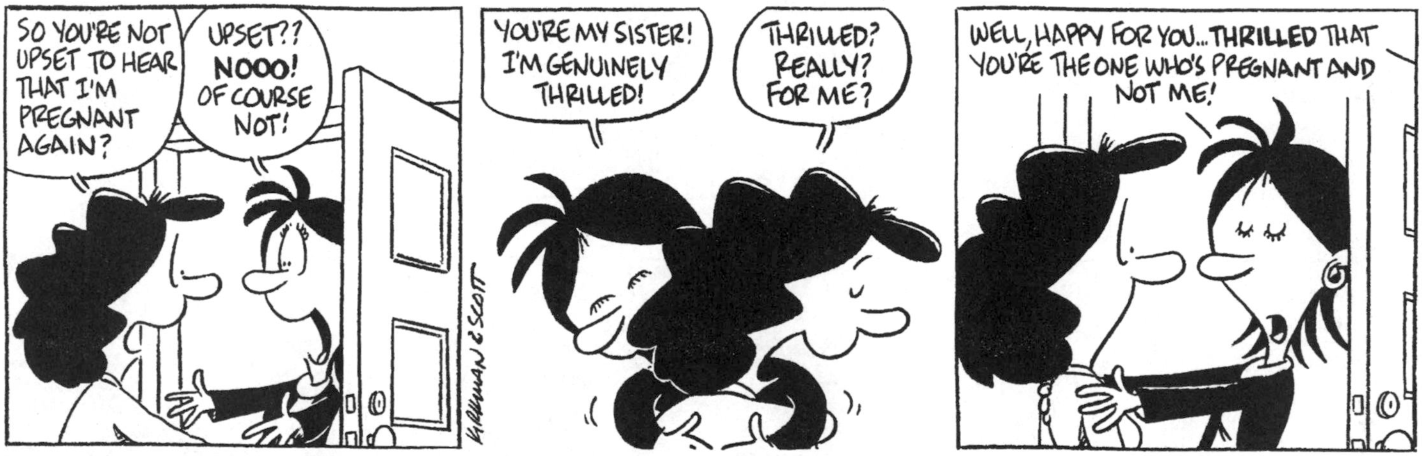
SO YOU'RE NOT UPSET TO HEAR THAT I'M PREGNANT AGAIN?
UPSET?? NOOO! OF COURSE NOT!
KIRKMAN & SCOTT
YOU'RE MY SISTER! I'M GENUINELY THRILLED!
THRILLED? REALLY? FOR ME?
WELL, HAPPY FOR YOU... THRILLED THAT YOU'RE THE ONE WHO'S PREGNANT AND NOT ME!

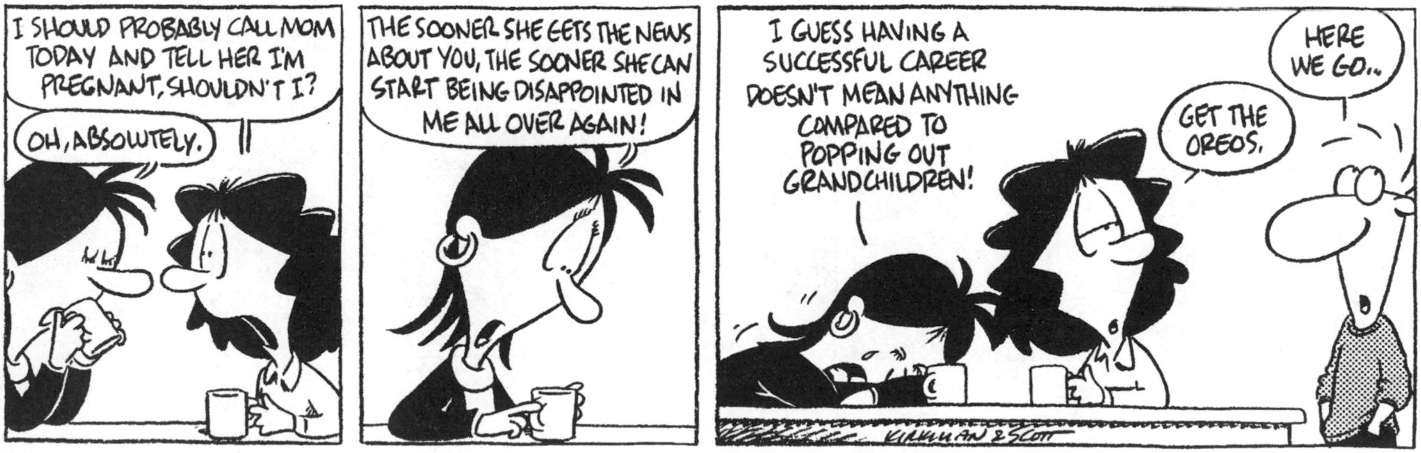
I SHOULD PROBABLY CALL MOM TODAY AND TELL HER I'M PREGNANT, SHOULDN'T I?
OH, ABSOLUTELY.
THE SOONER SHE GETS THE NEWS ABOUT YOU, THE SOONER SHE CAN START BEING DISAPPOINTED IN ME ALL OVER AGAIN!
I GUESS HAVING A SUCCESSFUL CAREER DOESN'T MEAN ANYTHING COMPARED TO POPPING OUT GRANDCHILDREN!
GET THE OREOS.
HERE WE GO...
KIRKMAN & SCOTT

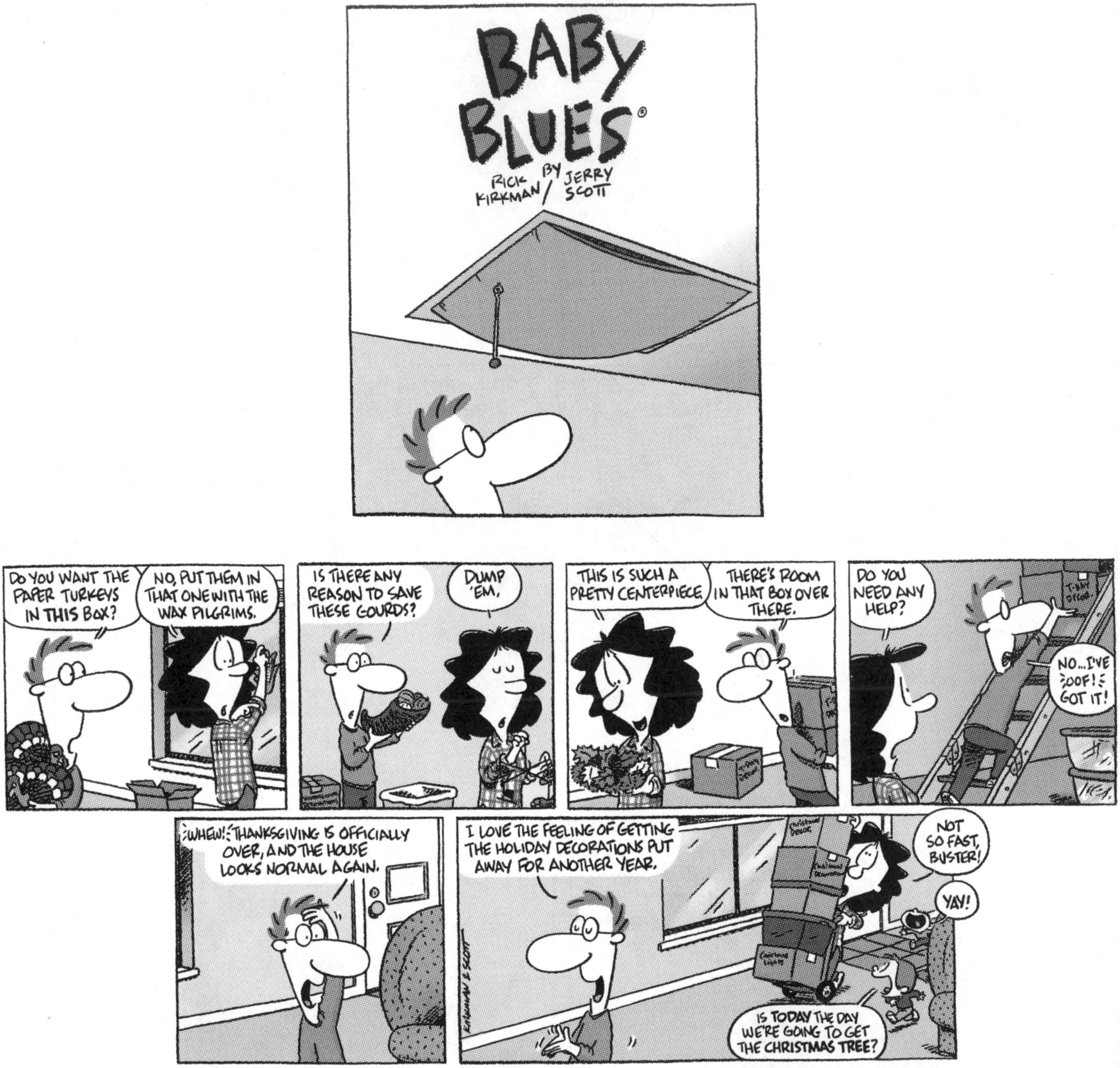

BABY BLUES®
BY RICK KIRKMAN / JERRY SCOTT
DO YOU WANT THE PAPER TURKEYS IN THIS BOX?
NO, PUT THEM IN THAT ONE WITH THE WAX PILGRIMS.
IS THERE ANY REASON TO SAVE THESE GOURDS?
DUMP 'EM.
THIS IS SUCH A PRETTY CENTERPIECE.
THERE'S ROOM IN THAT BOX OVER THERE.
DO YOU NEED ANY HELP?
NO... I'VE OOF! GOT IT!
WHEW! THANKSGIVING IS OFFICIALLY OVER, AND THE HOUSE LOOKS NORMAL AGAIN.
I LOVE THE FEELING OF GETTING THE HOLIDAY DECORATIONS PUT AWAY FOR ANOTHER YEAR.
NOT SO FAST, BUSTER!
YAY!
IS TODAY THE DAY WE'RE GOING TO GET THE CHRISTMAS TREE?

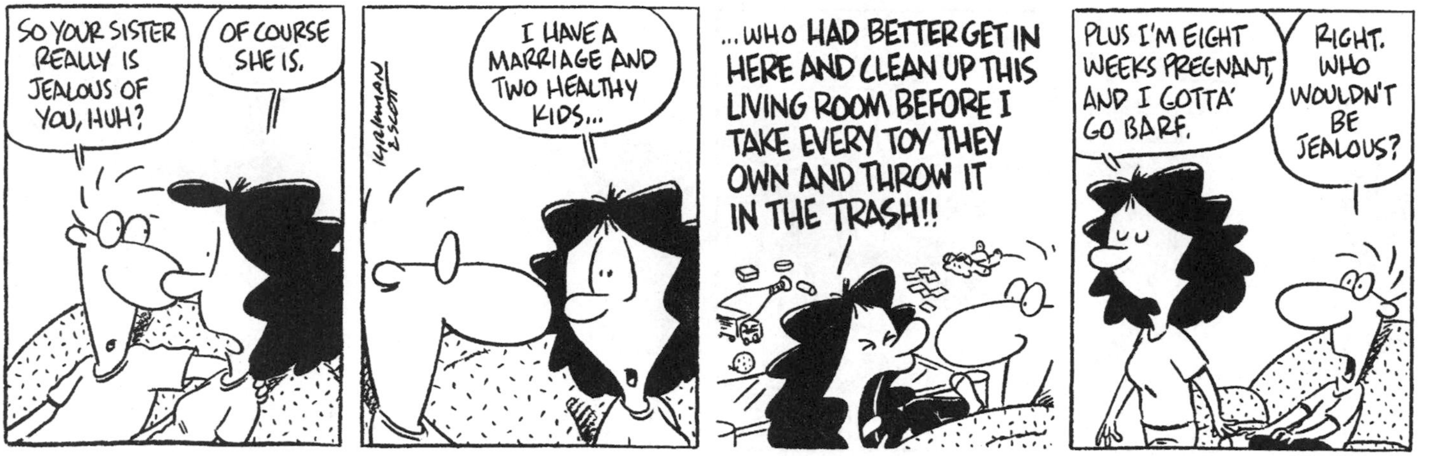
SO YOUR SISTER REALLY IS JEALOUS OF YOU, HUH?
OF COURSE SHE IS.
I HAVE A MARRIAGE AND TWO HEALTHY KIDS...
...WHO HAD BETTER GET IN HERE AND CLEAN UP THIS LIVING ROOM BEFORE I TAKE EVERY TOY THEY OWN AND THROW IT IN THE TRASH!!
PLUS I'M EIGHT WEEKS PREGNANT, AND I GOTTA' GO BARF.
RIGHT. WHO WOULDN'T BE JEALOUS?

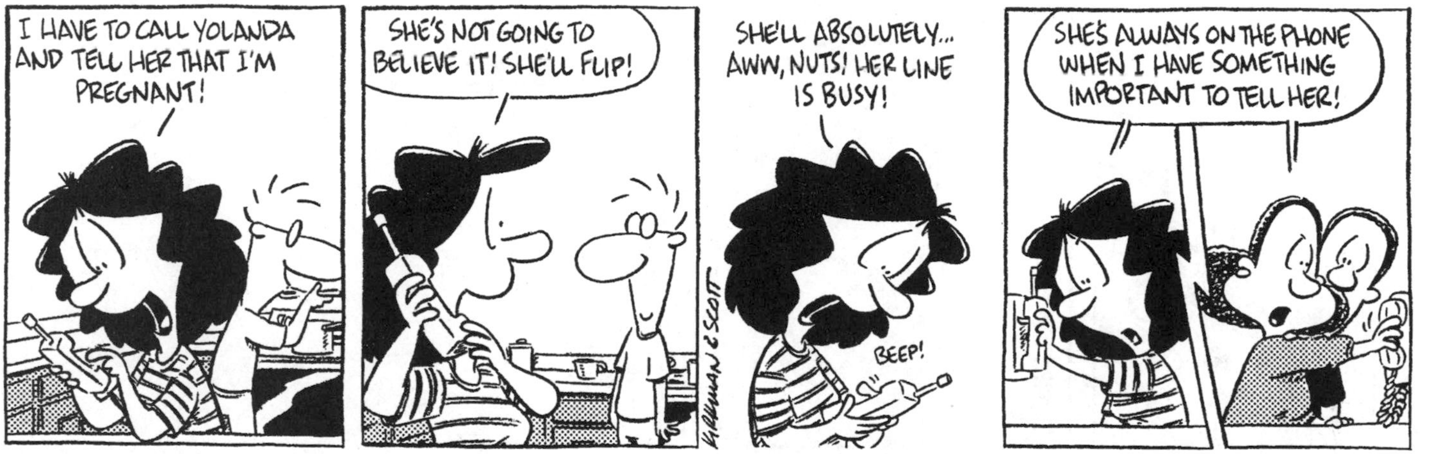
I HAVE TO CALL YOLANDA AND TELL HER THAT I'M PREGNANT!
SHE'S NOT GOING TO BELIEVE IT! SHE'LL FLIP!
SHE'LL ABSOLUTELY... AWW, NUTS! HER LINE IS BUSY!
BEEP!
SHE'S ALWAYS ON THE PHONE WHEN I HAVE SOMETHING IMPORTANT TO TELL HER!

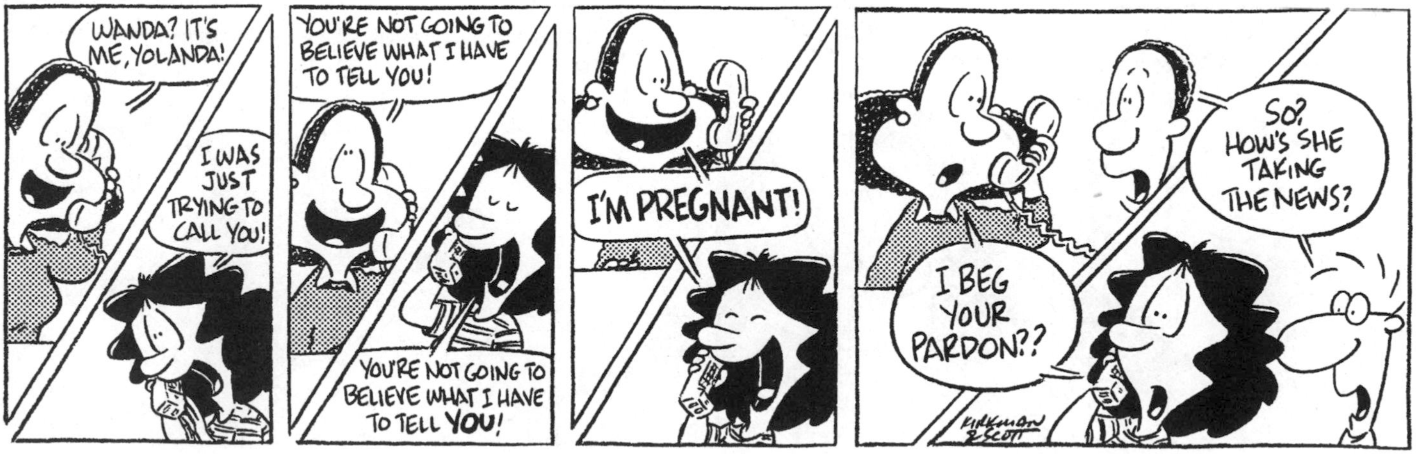
WANDA? IT'S ME, YOLANDA!
I WAS JUST TRYING TO CALL YOU!
YOU'RE NOT GOING TO BELIEVE WHAT I HAVE TO TELL YOU!
YOU'RE NOT GOING TO BELIEVE WHAT I HAVE TO TELL YOU!
I'M PREGNANT!
SO? HOW'S SHE TAKING THE NEWS?
I BEG YOUR PARDON??

WHAT DO YOU MEAN YOU'RE PREGNANT? I'M PREGNANT!
I'M PREGNANT, TOO!
WHEN DID YOU FIND OUT?
LAST WEEK!
SAME HERE! HOW FAR ALONG ARE YOU?
EIGHT WEEKS!
SAME HERE!
WE GET TO GET FAT TOGETHER!
BEN AND JERRY'S, HERE WE COME!
KIRKMAN & SCOTT
YOU GUYS ARE PREGNANT, TOO?
YES!
CAN YOU BELIEVE IT?
THIS IS SO GREAT! WE'LL BE LIKE A CLUB!
WE'LL GO THROUGH OUR PREGNANCIES LIKE A TEAM!
KIRKMAN & SCOTT
NATURALLY, I'LL BE HERE TO GIVE YOU TWO GUIDANCE AND ADVICE ALL ALONG THE WAY...
I FEEL NAUSEATED. AND THIS TIME IT'S NOT MORNING SICKNESS.
HAND-ME-DOWNS ARE COOL.
VEGETABLES ARE YUMMY.
YOUR PARENTS ARE WISE AND KNOWLEDGEABLE.
HELPING WITH THE DISHES WILL MAKE YOU POPULAR.
IN-STATE COLLEGES ARE THE BEST!
I'M ONLY EIGHT WEEKS PREGNANT. I DON'T THINK THE BABY CAN HEAR YOU YET.
KIRKMAN & SCOTT

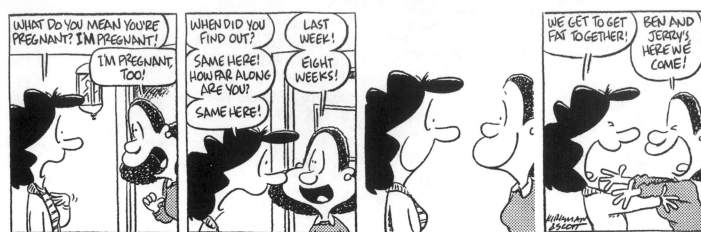

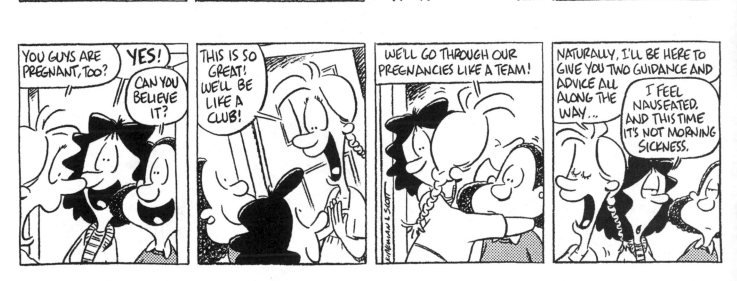

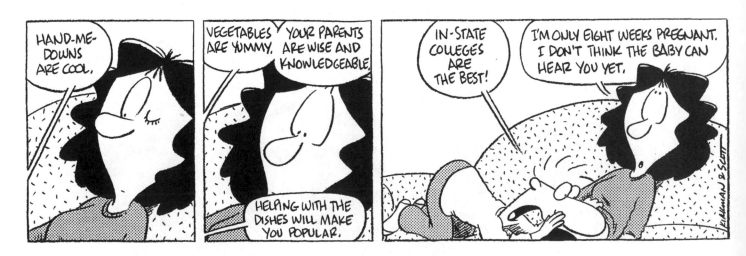

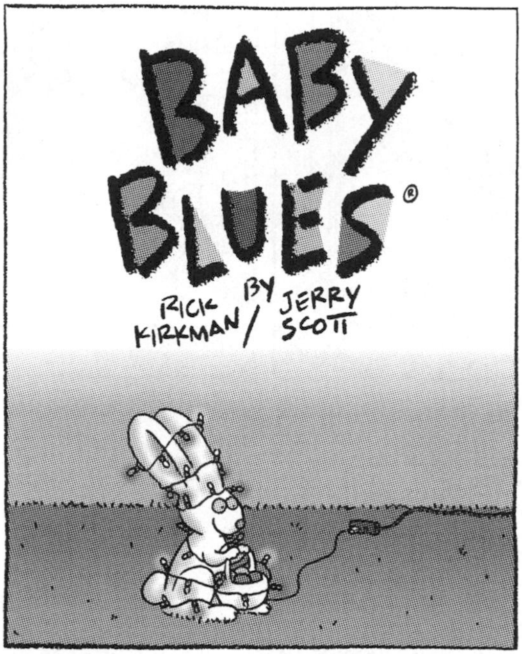
BABY BLUES®
BY RICK KIRKMAN / JERRY SCOTT

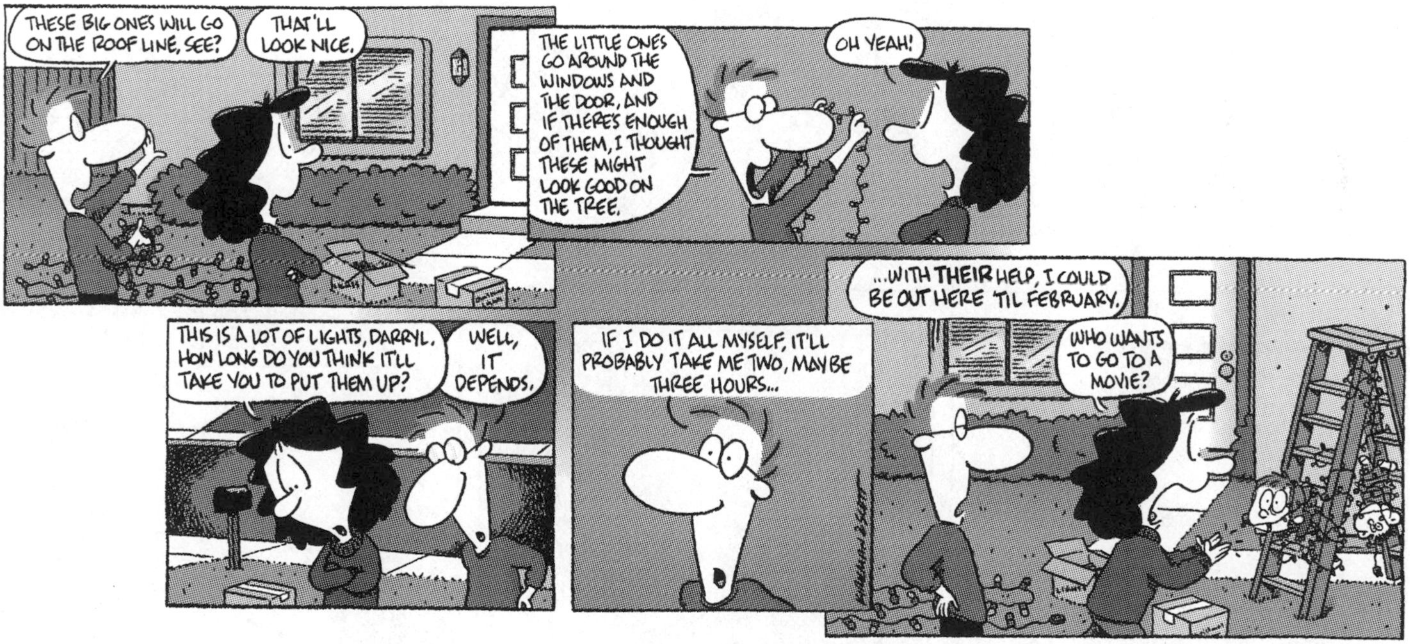
THESE BIG ONES WILL GO ON THE ROOF LINE, SEE?
THAT'LL LOOK NICE.
THE LITTLE ONES GO AROUND THE WINDOWS AND THE DOOR, AND IF THERE'S ENOUGH OF THEM, I THOUGHT THESE MIGHT LOOK GOOD ON THE TREE.
OH YEAH!
THIS IS A LOT OF LIGHTS, DARRYL. HOW LONG DO YOU THINK IT'LL TAKE YOU TO PUT THEM UP?
WELL, IT DEPENDS.
IF I DO IT ALL MYSELF, IT'LL PROBABLY TAKE ME TWO, MAYBE THREE HOURS...
...WITH THEIR HELP, I COULD BE OUT HERE 'TIL FEBRUARY.
WHO WANTS TO GO TO A MOVIE?

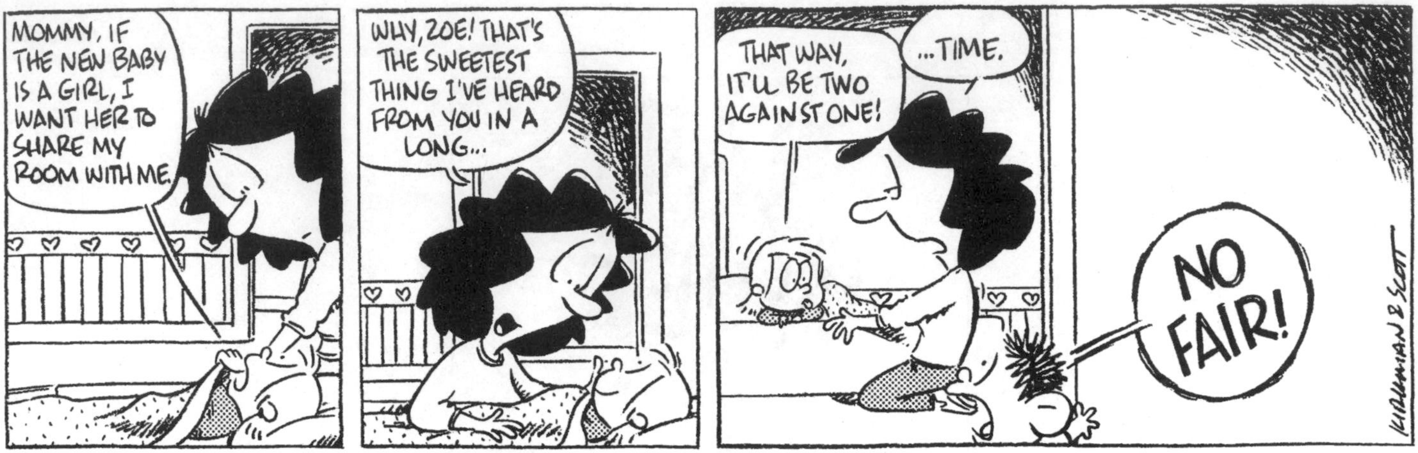
MOMMY, IF THE NEW BABY IS A GIRL, I WANT HER TO SHARE MY ROOM WITH ME.
WHY, ZOE! THAT'S THE SWEETEST THING I'VE HEARD FROM YOU IN A LONG...
THAT WAY, IT'LL BE TWO AGAINST ONE!
...TIME.
NO FAIR!
KIRKMAN & SCOTT

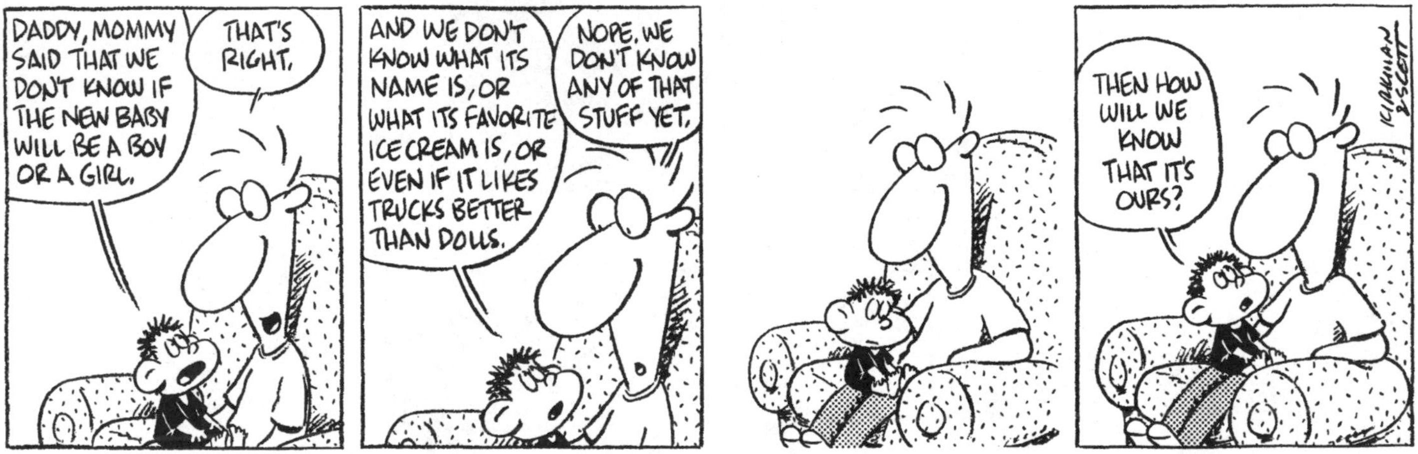
DADDY, MOMMY SAID THAT WE DON'T KNOW IF THE NEW BABY WILL BE A BOY OR A GIRL.
THAT'S RIGHT.
AND WE DON'T KNOW WHAT ITS NAME IS, OR WHAT ITS FAVORITE ICE CREAM IS, OR EVEN IF IT LIKES TRUCKS BETTER THAN DOLLS.
NOPE. WE DON'T KNOW ANY OF THAT STUFF YET.
KIRKMAN & SCOTT
THEN HOW WILL WE KNOW THAT IT'S OURS?

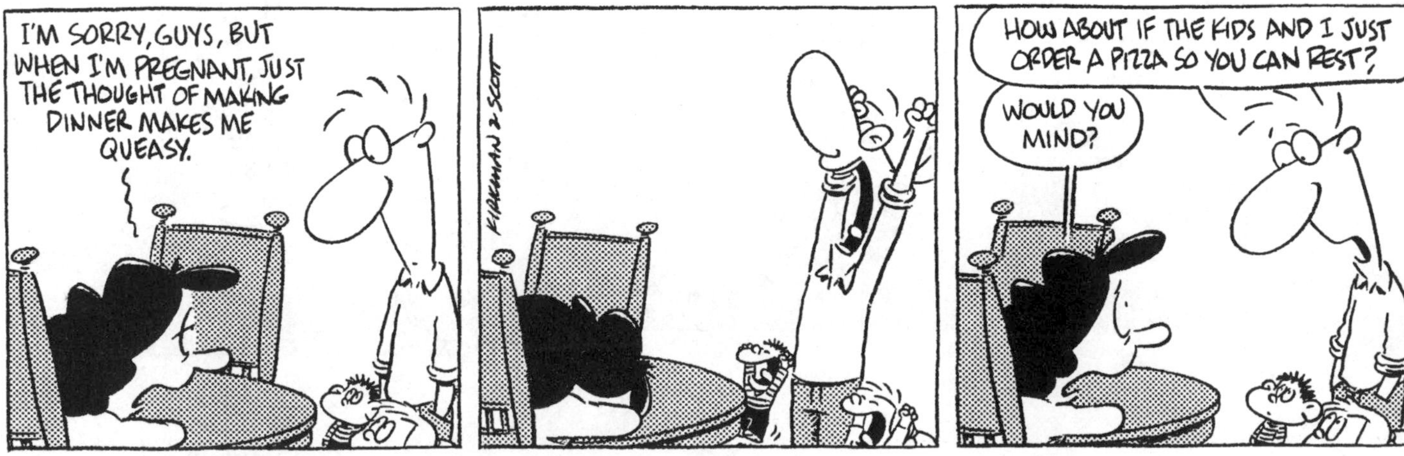
I'M SORRY, GUYS, BUT WHEN I'M PREGNANT, JUST THE THOUGHT OF MAKING DINNER MAKES ME QUEASY.
KIRKMAN & SCOTT
HOW ABOUT IF THE KIDS AND I JUST ORDER A PIZZA SO YOU CAN REST?
WOULD YOU MIND?

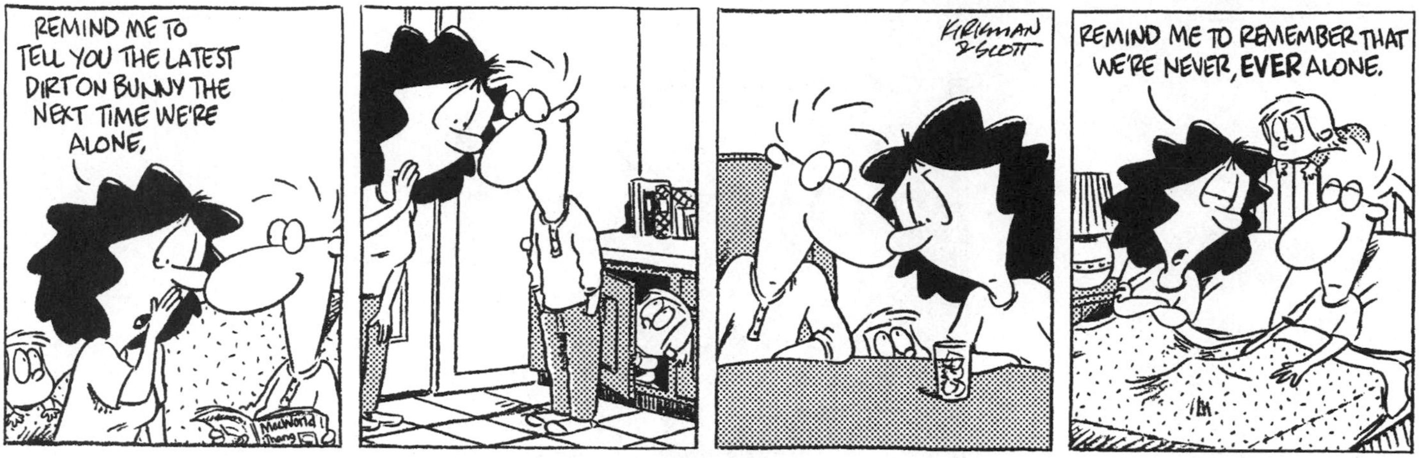
REMIND ME TO TELL YOU THE LATEST DIRT ON BUNNY THE NEXT TIME WE'RE ALONE.
KIRKMAN & SCOTT
REMIND ME TO REMEMBER THAT WE'RE NEVER, **EVER** ALONE.

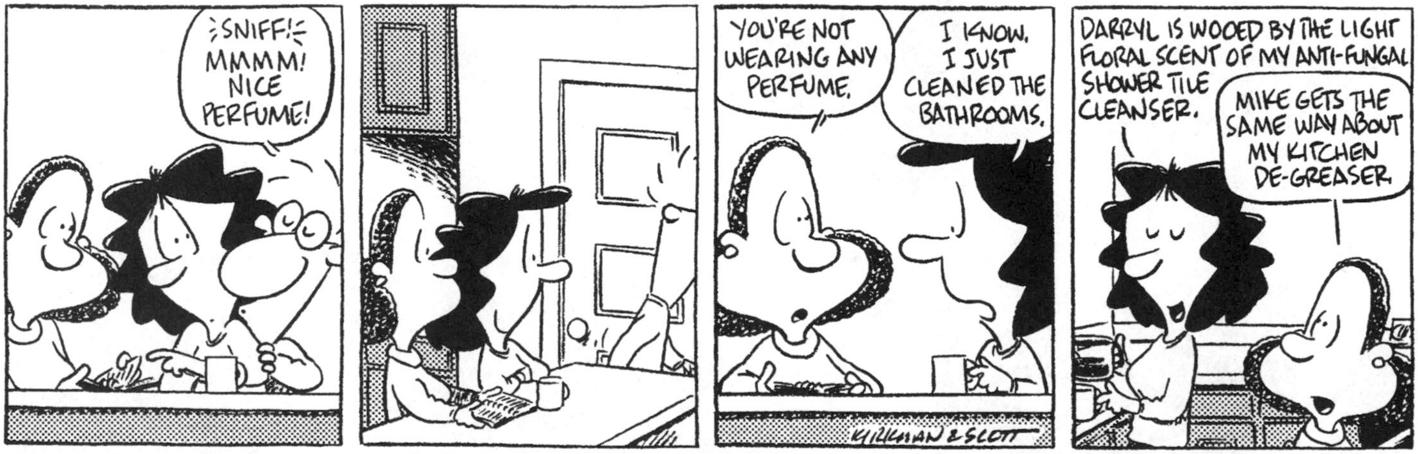
SNIFF!
MMMMM! NICE PERFUME!
YOU'RE NOT WEARING ANY PERFUME.
I KNOW. I JUST CLEANED THE BATHROOMS.
KIRKMAN & SCOTT
DARRYL IS WOOED BY THE LIGHT FLORAL SCENT OF MY ANTI-FUNGAL SHOWER TILE CLEANSER.
MIKE GETS THE SAME WAY ABOUT MY KITCHEN DE-GREASER.

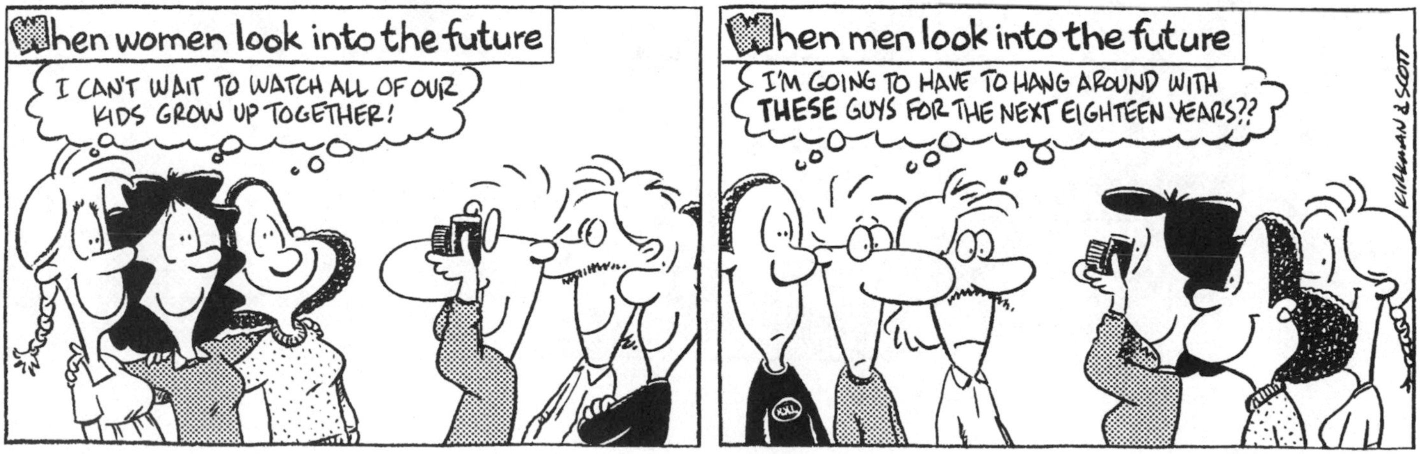
When women look into the future
I CAN'T WAIT TO WATCH ALL OF OUR KIDS GROW UP TOGETHER!
When men look into the future
I'M GOING TO HAVE TO HANG AROUND WITH **THESE** GUYS FOR THE NEXT EIGHTEEN YEARS??
KIRKMAN & SCOTT

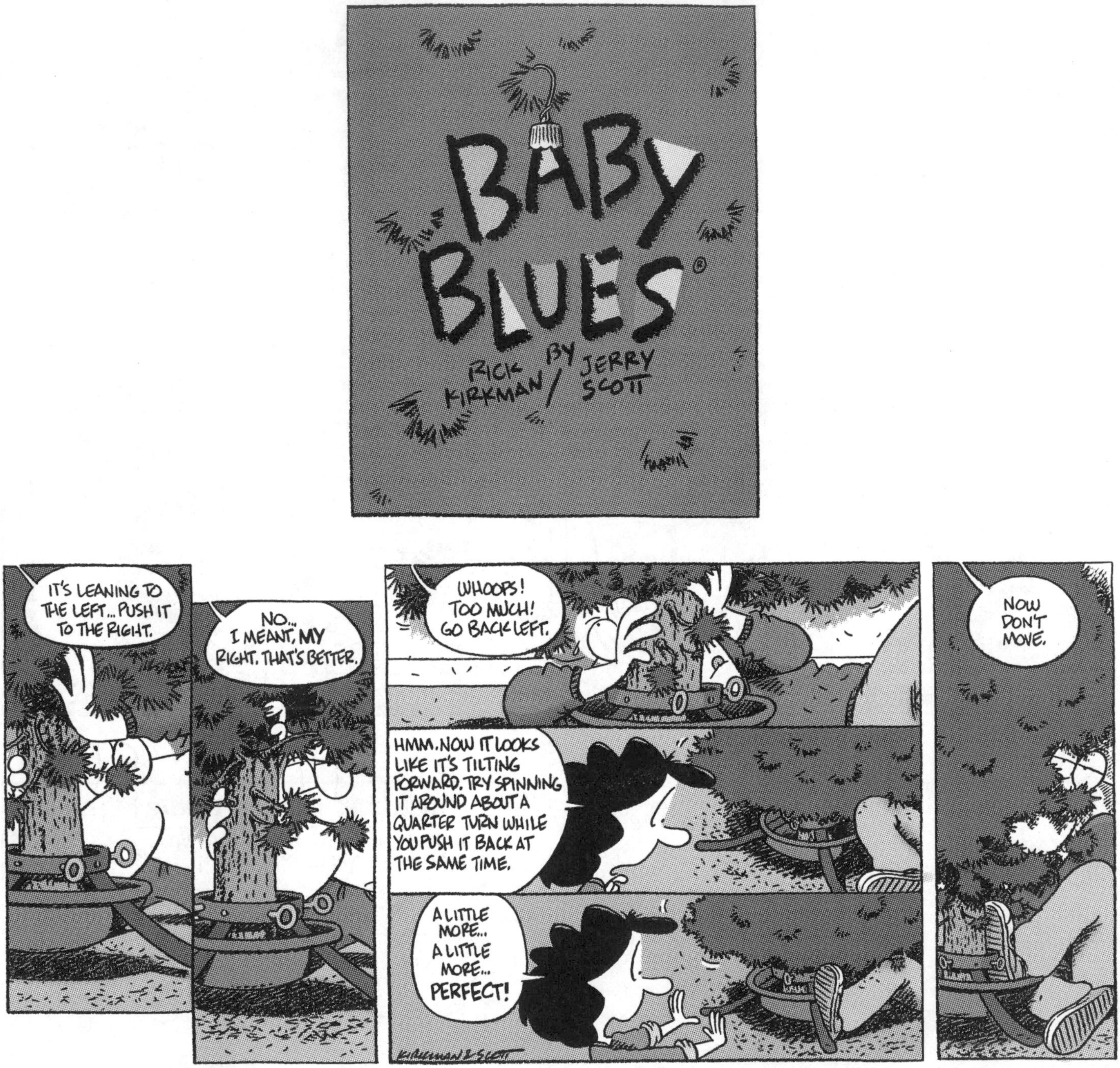
BABY BLUES®
BY RICK KIRKMAN / JERRY SCOTT
IT'S LEANING TO THE LEFT... PUSH IT TO THE RIGHT.
NO... I MEANT, MY RIGHT. THAT'S BETTER.
WHOOPS! TOO MUCH! GO BACK LEFT.
HMM. NOW IT LOOKS LIKE IT'S TILTING FORWARD. TRY SPINNING IT AROUND ABOUT A QUARTER TURN WHILE YOU PUSH IT BACK AT THE SAME TIME.
A LITTLE MORE... A LITTLE MORE... PERFECT!
NOW DON'T MOVE.
KIRKMAN & SCOTT

Panel 1: MOMMY IS GOING TO HAVE ANOTHER BABY.

I KNOW.

Panel 2: I'M WISHING FOR A GIRL!

I'M WISHING FOR A BOY OR A GIRL.

Panel 4: SOMETIMES YOU DON'T MAKE ANY SENSE AT ALL.

I BET I GET MY WISH, THOUGH.

KIRKMAN & SCOTT

Panel 1: CRUNCH! CRUNCH! CRUNCH! SLURP!

Panel 2: ZOE, WHAT IS OUR RULE ABOUT EATING IN THE LIVING ROOM?

NO EATING ALLOWED IN THE LIVING ROOM.

Panel 3: THEN CAN YOU TELL ME WHY I JUST CAUGHT YOU EATING IN THE LIVING ROOM?

KIRKMAN & SCOTT

Panel 4: BECAUSE I CHEW WITH MY MOUTH OPEN?

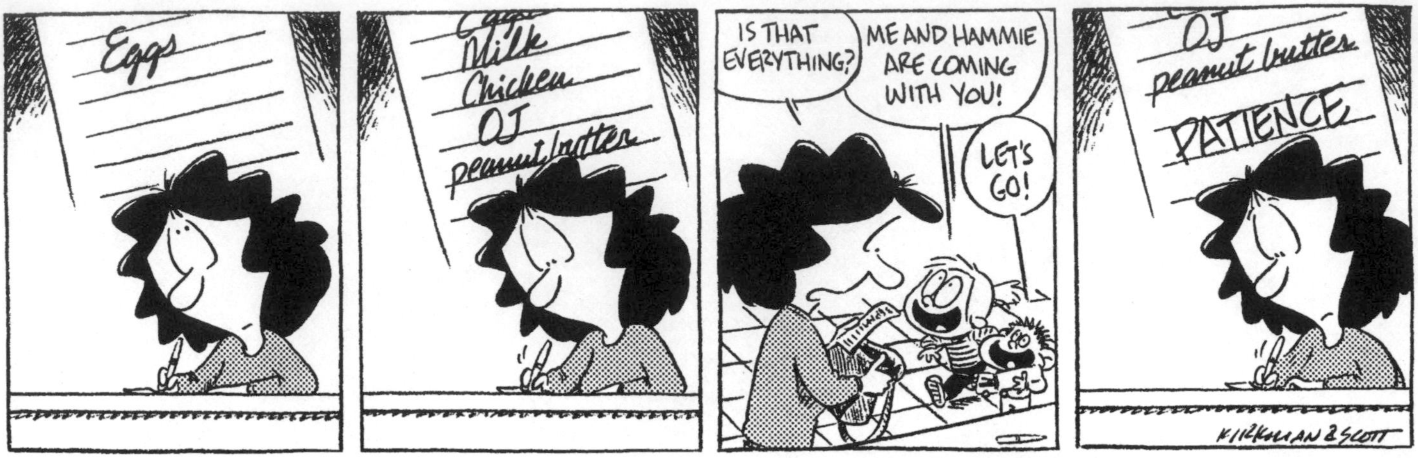
Eggs
Milk
Chicken
OJ
peanut butter
IS THAT EVERYTHING?
ME AND HAMMIE ARE COMING WITH YOU!
LET'S GO!
OJ
peanut butter
PATIENCE
KIRKMAN & SCOTT

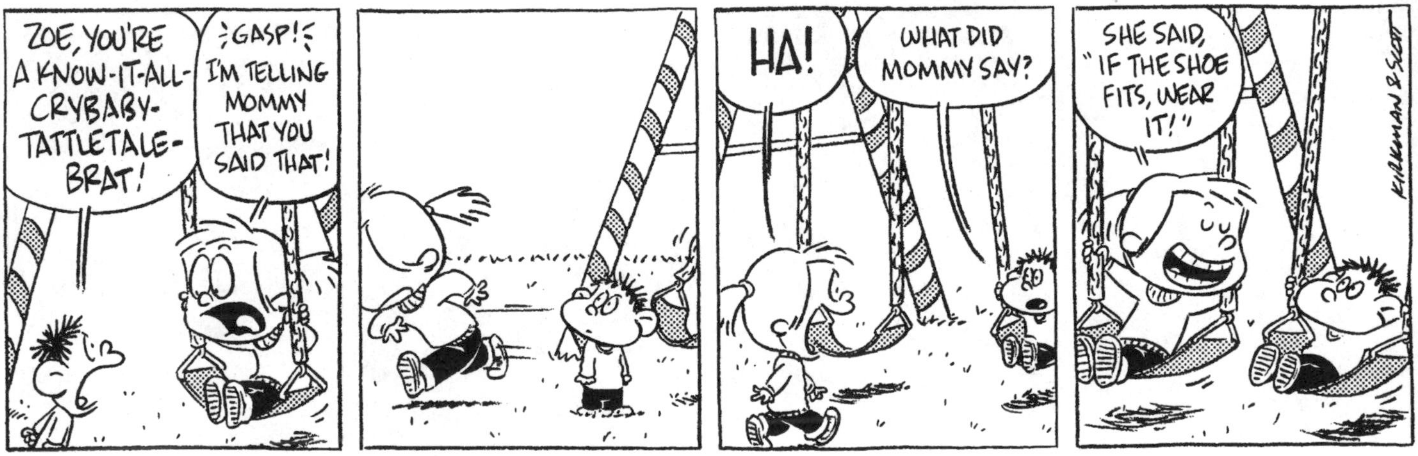
ZOE, YOU'RE A KNOW-IT-ALL-CRYBABY-TATTLETALE-BRAT!
GASP! I'M TELLING MOMMY THAT YOU SAID THAT!
HA!
WHAT DID MOMMY SAY?
SHE SAID, "IF THE SHOE FITS, WEAR IT!"
KIRKMAN & SCOTT

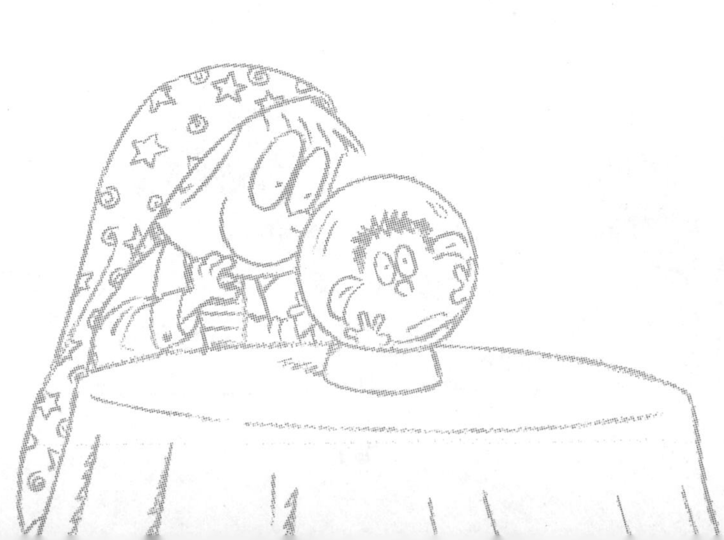

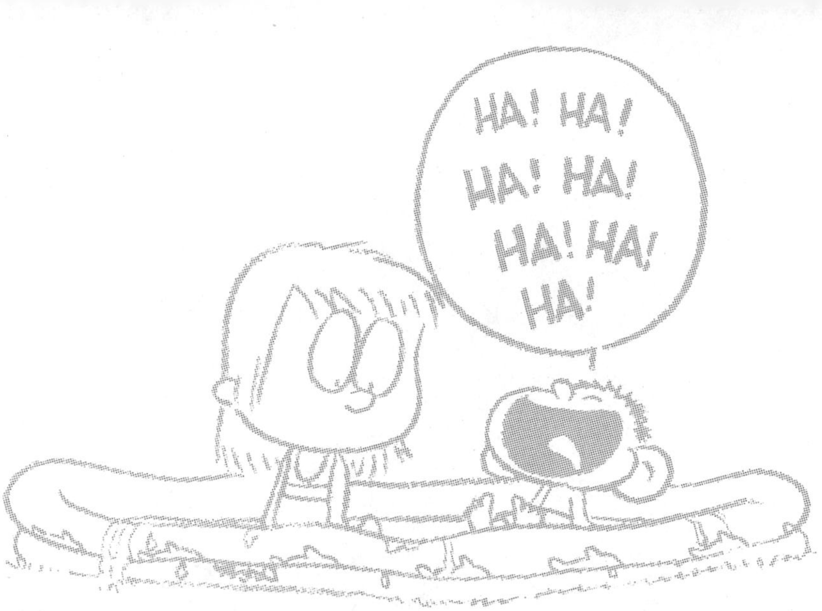
HA! HA!
HA! HA!
HA! HA!
HA!

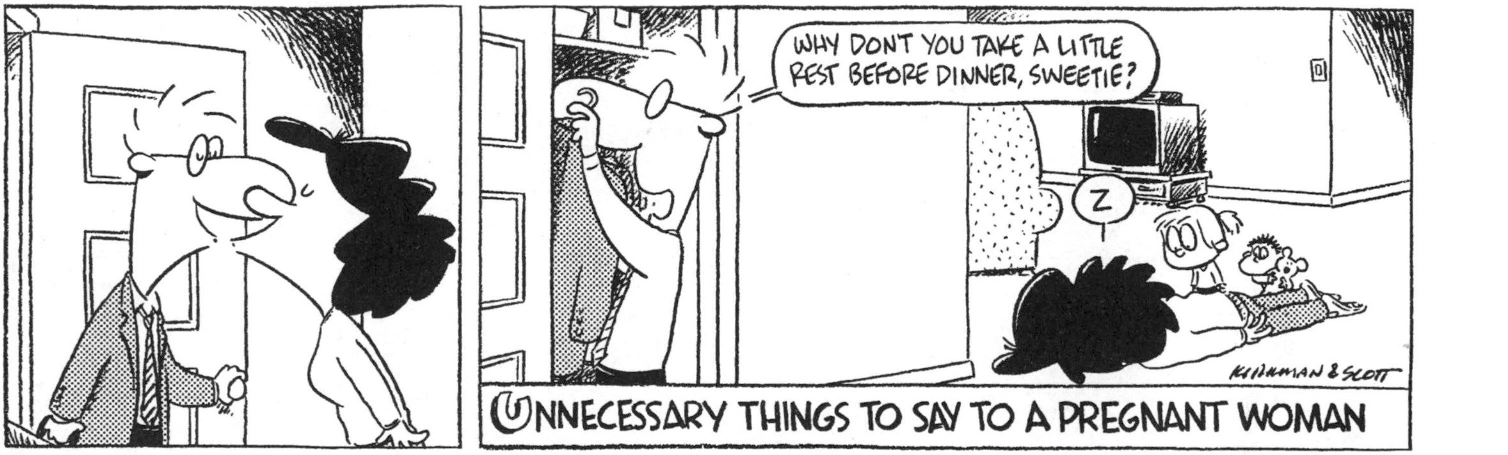
WHY DON'T YOU TAKE A LITTLE REST BEFORE DINNER, SWEETIE?
Z
KIRKMAN & SCOTT
UNNECESSARY THINGS TO SAY TO A PREGNANT WOMAN

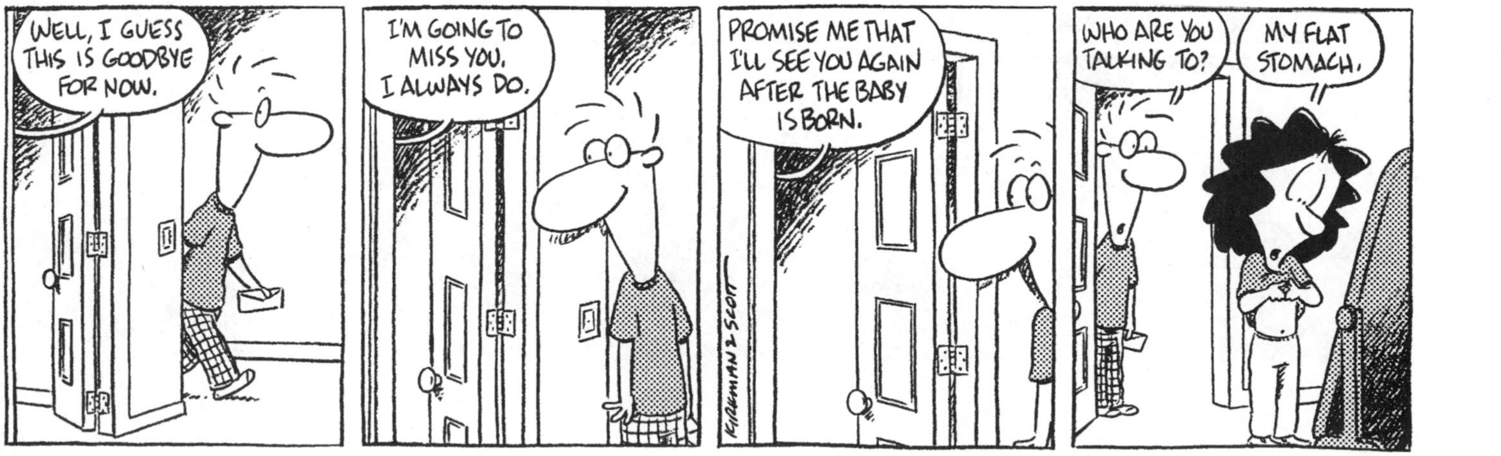
WELL, I GUESS THIS IS GOODBYE FOR NOW.
I'M GOING TO MISS YOU. I ALWAYS DO.
KIRKMAN & SCOTT
PROMISE ME THAT I'LL SEE YOU AGAIN AFTER THE BABY IS BORN.
WHO ARE YOU TALKING TO?
MY FLAT STOMACH.

BABY BLUES®
BY RICK KIRKMAN / JERRY SCOTT
OUTWIT OUTPLAY
SURVIVOR
PARENTHOOD
OUTLAST

HURRY, GUYS! WE'RE GOING TO BE LATE!
FASTER! FASTER!
EAT! EAT! EAT!
AAAAAGHHH!
TIME TO GO! GETINTHECAR! GETINTHECAR!
HI GUYS. I THINK MY MORNING SICKNESS IS A LITTLE BETTER TODAY.
THE REAL MIRACLE OF HUMAN REPRODUCTION IS THAT HUSBANDS ACTUALLY SURVIVE IT.
WHEN MOMMY DRESSES ME, MY SHOES ALWAYS MATCH.
KIRKMAN & SCOTT

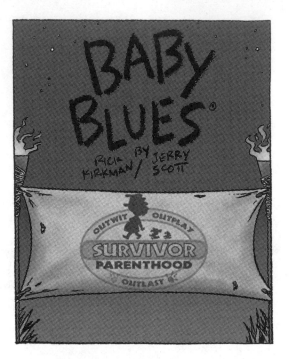

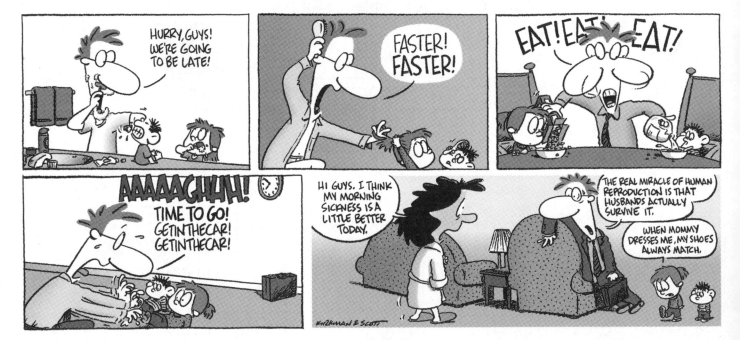

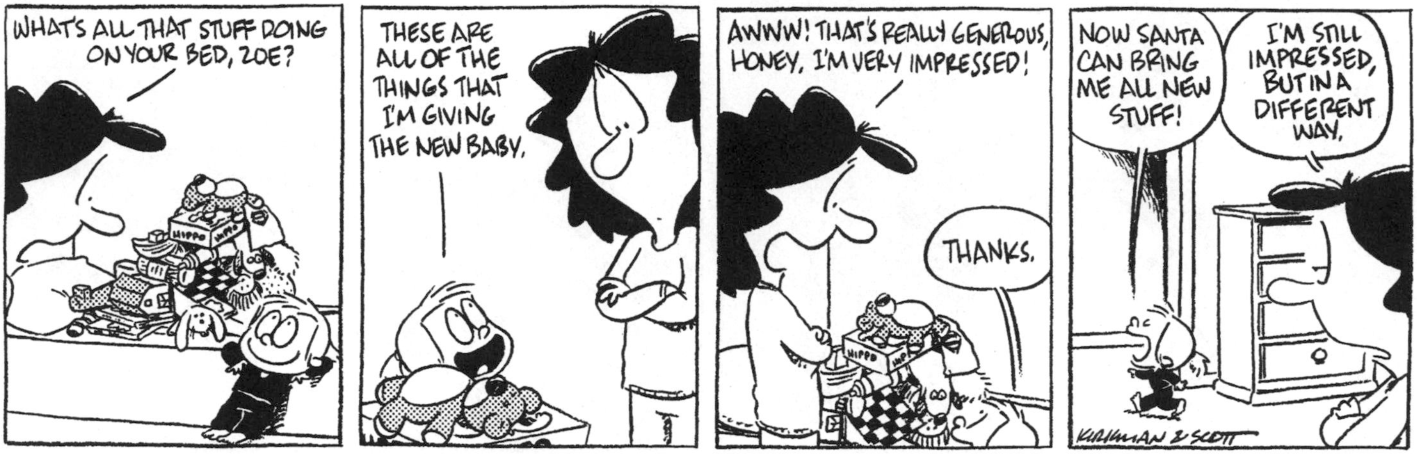
WHAT'S ALL THAT STUFF DOING ON YOUR BED, ZOE?
THESE ARE ALL OF THE THINGS THAT I'M GIVING THE NEW BABY.
AWWW! THAT'S REALLY GENEROUS, HONEY. I'M VERY IMPRESSED!
THANKS.
NOW SANTA CAN BRING ME ALL NEW STUFF!
I'M STILL IMPRESSED, BUT IN A DIFFERENT WAY.
KIRKMAN & SCOTT

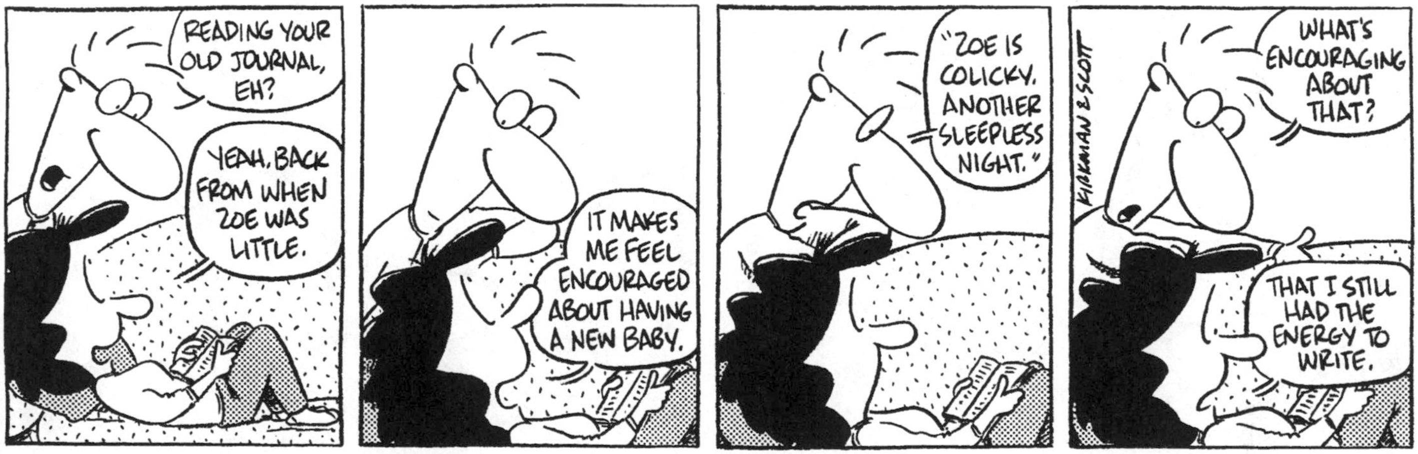
READING YOUR OLD JOURNAL, EH?
YEAH. BACK FROM WHEN ZOE WAS LITTLE.
IT MAKES ME FEEL ENCOURAGED ABOUT HAVING A NEW BABY.
"ZOE IS COLICKY. ANOTHER SLEEPLESS NIGHT."
KIRKMAN & SCOTT
WHAT'S ENCOURAGING ABOUT THAT?
THAT I STILL HAD THE ENERGY TO WRITE.

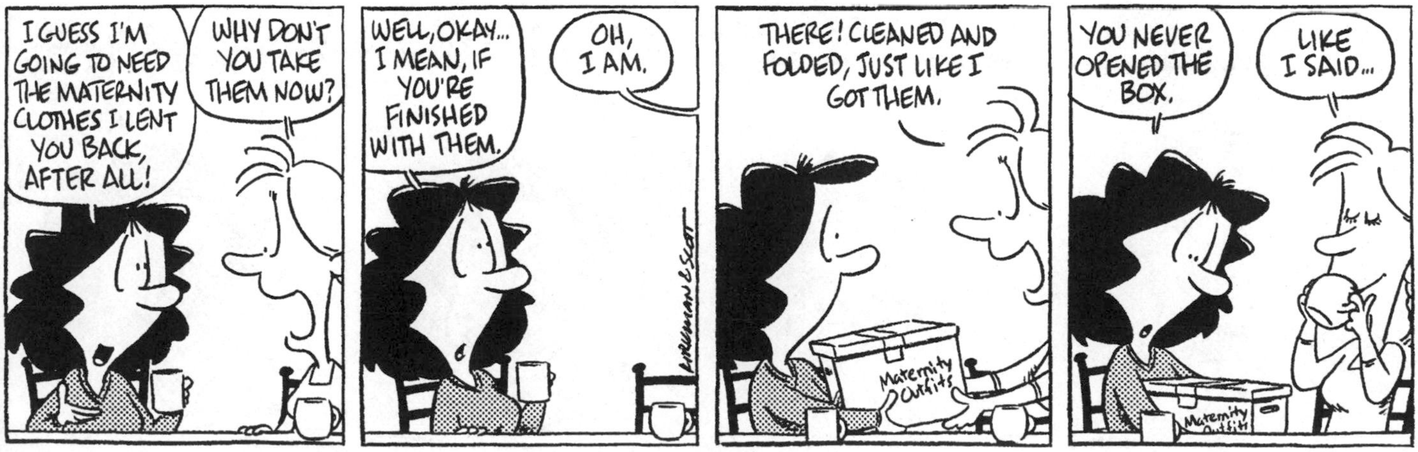
I GUESS I'M GOING TO NEED THE MATERNITY CLOTHES I LENT YOU BACK, AFTER ALL!
WHY DON'T YOU TAKE THEM NOW?
WELL, OKAY... I MEAN, IF YOU'RE FINISHED WITH THEM.
OH, I AM.
KIRKMAN & SCOTT
THERE! CLEANED AND FOLDED, JUST LIKE I GOT THEM.
Maternity Outfits
YOU NEVER OPENED THE BOX.
LIKE I SAID...
Maternity Outfits

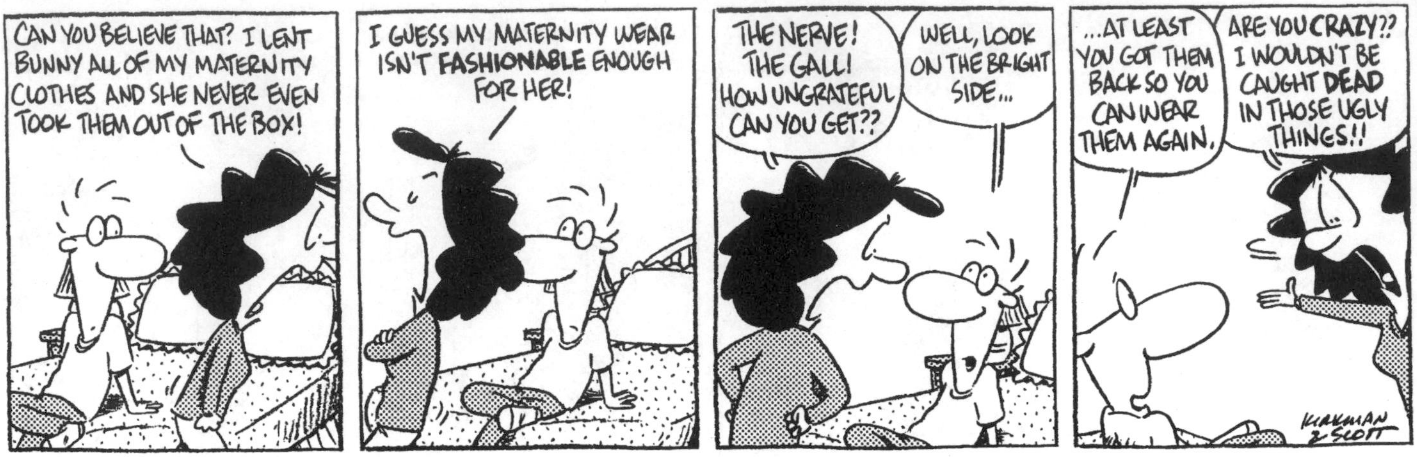
CAN YOU BELIEVE THAT? I LENT BUNNY ALL OF MY MATERNITY CLOTHES AND SHE NEVER EVEN TOOK THEM OUT OF THE BOX!
I GUESS MY MATERNITY WEAR ISN'T **FASHIONABLE** ENOUGH FOR HER!
THE NERVE! THE GALL! HOW UNGRATEFUL CAN YOU GET??
WELL, LOOK ON THE BRIGHT SIDE...
...AT LEAST YOU GOT THEM BACK SO YOU CAN WEAR THEM AGAIN.
ARE YOU **CRAZY**?? I WOULDN'T BE CAUGHT **DEAD** IN THOSE UGLY THINGS!!
KIRKMAN & SCOTT

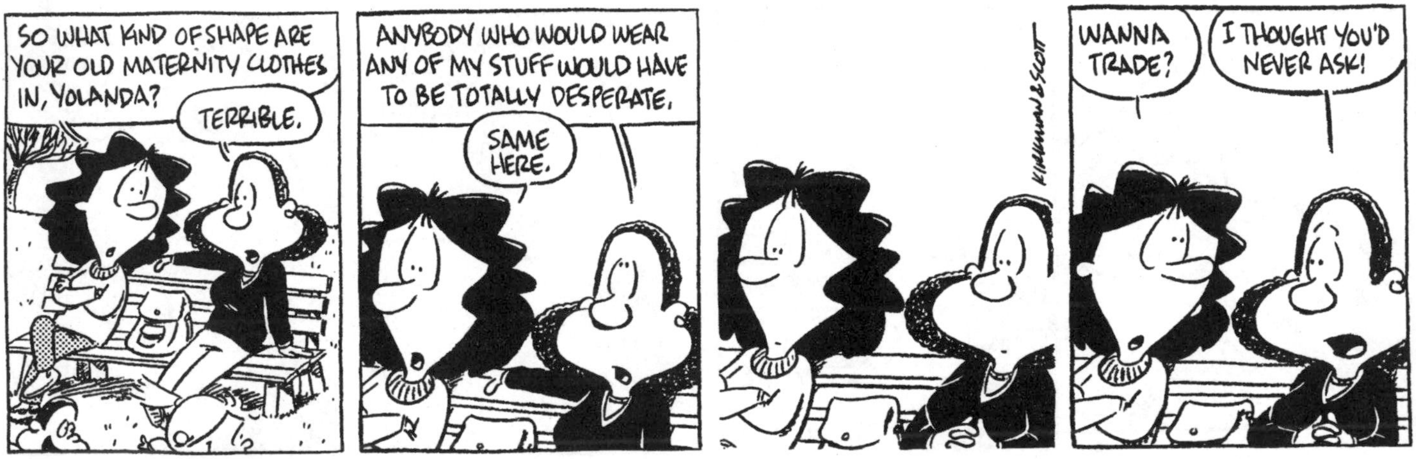
SO WHAT KIND OF SHAPE ARE YOUR OLD MATERNITY CLOTHES IN, YOLANDA?
TERRIBLE.
ANYBODY WHO WOULD WEAR ANY OF MY STUFF WOULD HAVE TO BE TOTALLY DESPERATE.
SAME HERE.
KIRKMAN & SCOTT
WANNA TRADE?
I THOUGHT YOU'D NEVER ASK!

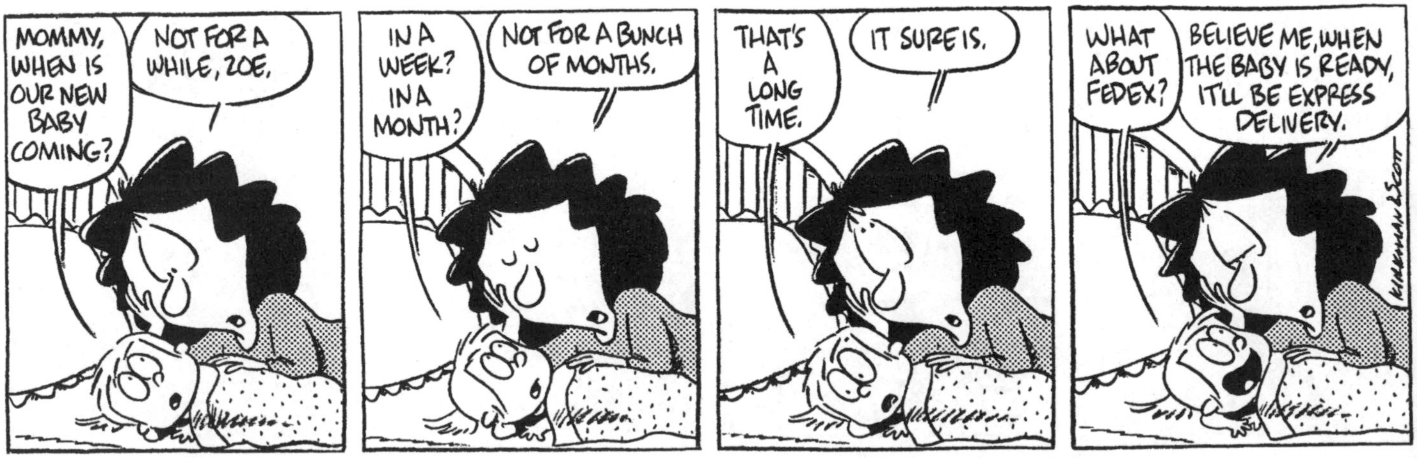
MOMMY, WHEN IS OUR NEW BABY COMING?
NOT FOR A WHILE, ZOE.
IN A WEEK? IN A MONTH?
NOT FOR A BUNCH OF MONTHS.
THAT'S A LONG TIME.
IT SURE IS.
WHAT ABOUT FEDEX?
BELIEVE ME, WHEN THE BABY IS READY, IT'LL BE EXPRESS DELIVERY.
KIRKMAN & SCOTT

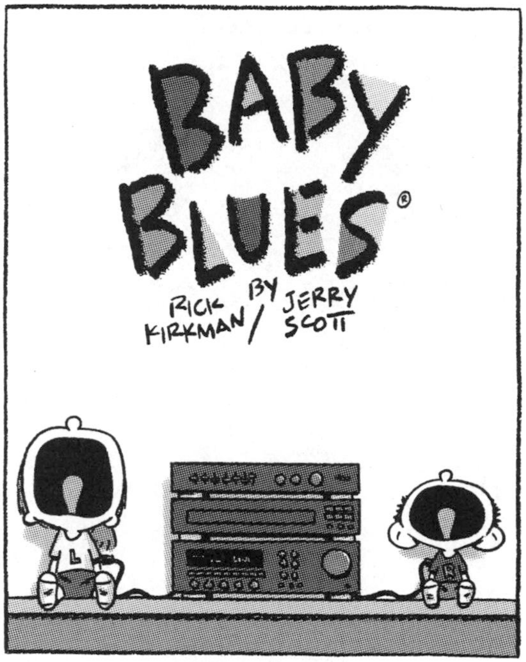
BABY BLUES®
BY
RICK KIRKMAN / JERRY SCOTT

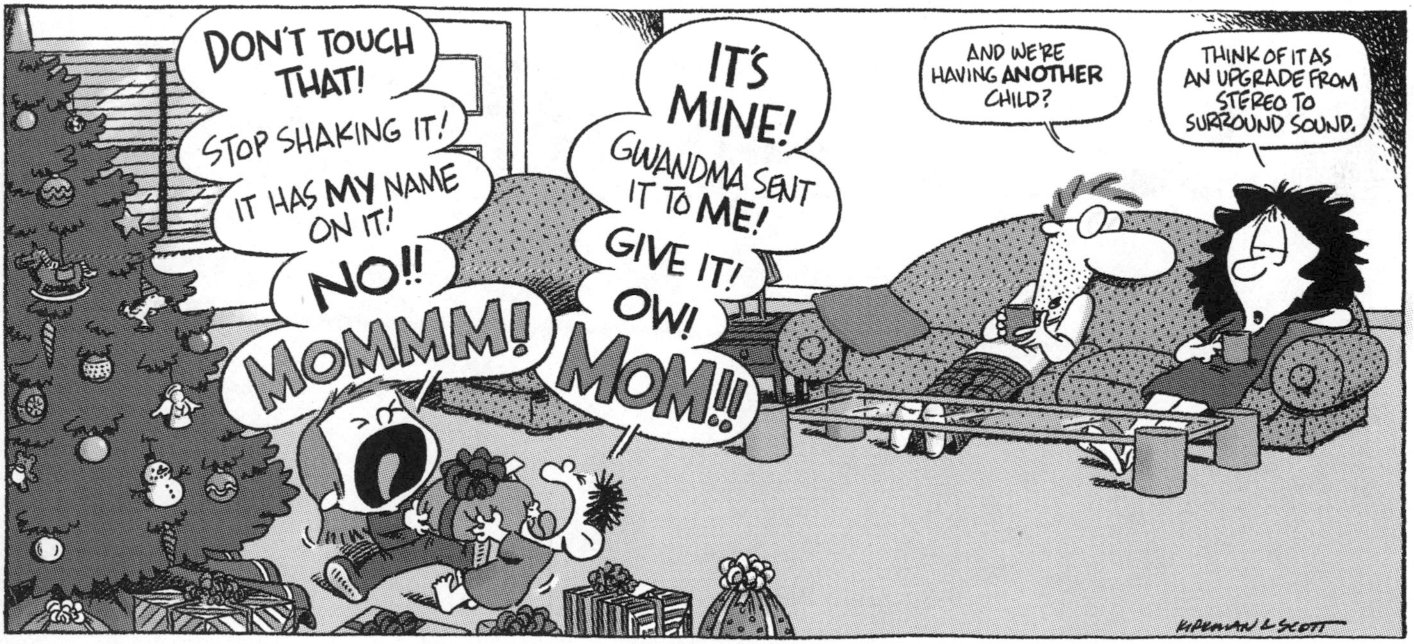
DON'T TOUCH THAT!
STOP SHAKING IT!
IT HAS MY NAME ON IT!
NO!!
MOMMM!
IT'S MINE!
GWANDMA SENT IT TO ME!
GIVE IT!
OW!
MOM!!
AND WE'RE HAVING ANOTHER CHILD?
THINK OF IT AS AN UPGRADE FROM STEREO TO SURROUND SOUND.
KIRKMAN & SCOTT

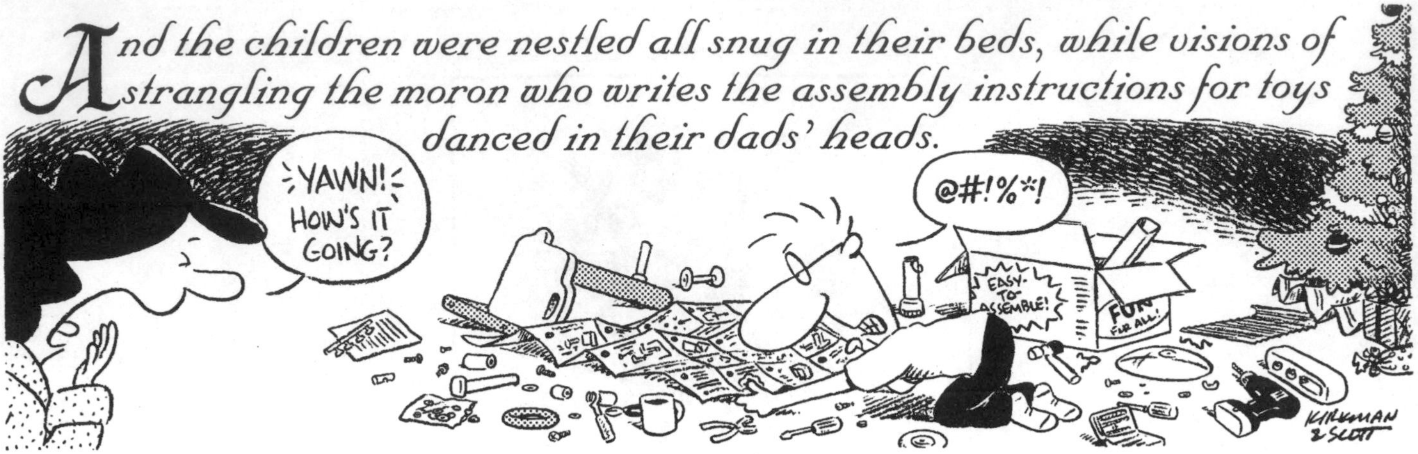
And the children were nestled all snug in their beds, while visions of strangling the moron who writes the assembly instructions for toys danced in their dads' heads.
YAWN! HOW'S IT GOING?
@#!%*!
EASY-TO-ASSEMBLE!
FUN FOR ALL!
KIRKMAN & SCOTT

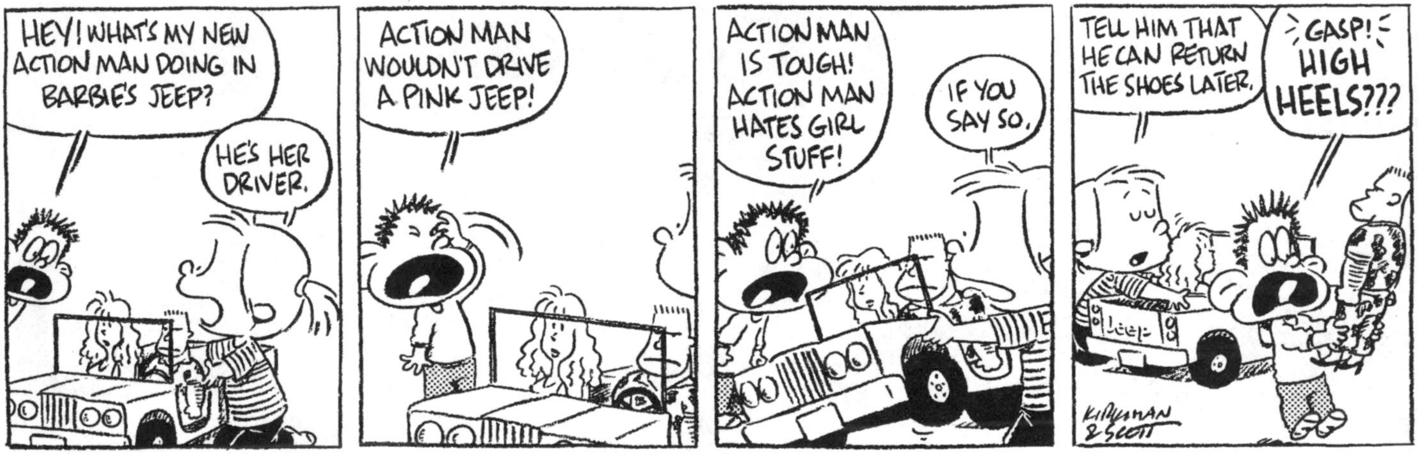
HEY! WHAT'S MY NEW ACTION MAN DOING IN BARBIE'S JEEP?
HE'S HER DRIVER.
ACTION MAN WOULDN'T DRIVE A PINK JEEP!
ACTION MAN IS TOUGH! ACTION MAN HATES GIRL STUFF!
IF YOU SAY SO.
TELL HIM THAT HE CAN RETURN THE SHOES LATER.
GASP! HIGH HEELS???
Jeep
KIRKMAN & SCOTT

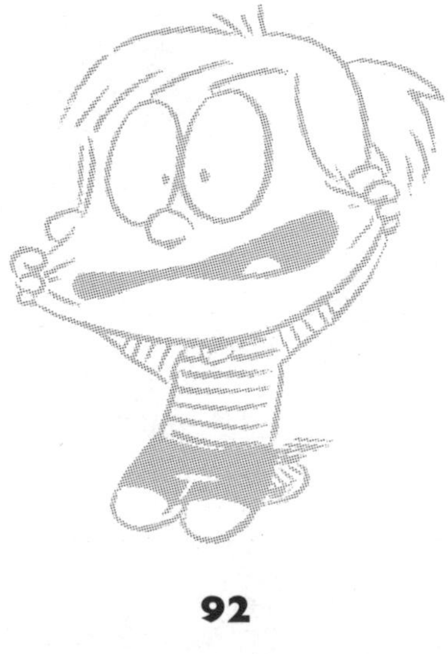

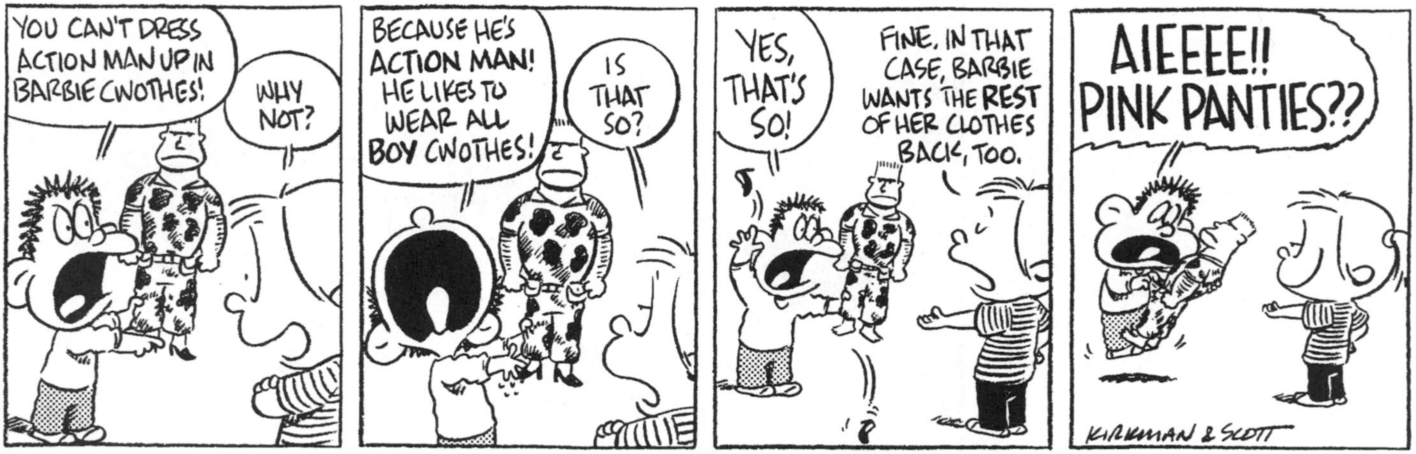
YOU CAN'T DRESS ACTION MAN UP IN BARBIE CWOTHES!
WHY NOT?
BECAUSE HE'S ACTION MAN! HE LIKES TO WEAR ALL BOY CWOTHES!
IS THAT SO?
YES, THAT'S SO!
FINE. IN THAT CASE, BARBIE WANTS THE REST OF HER CLOTHES BACK, TOO.
AIEEEE!! PINK PANTIES??
KIRKMAN & SCOTT

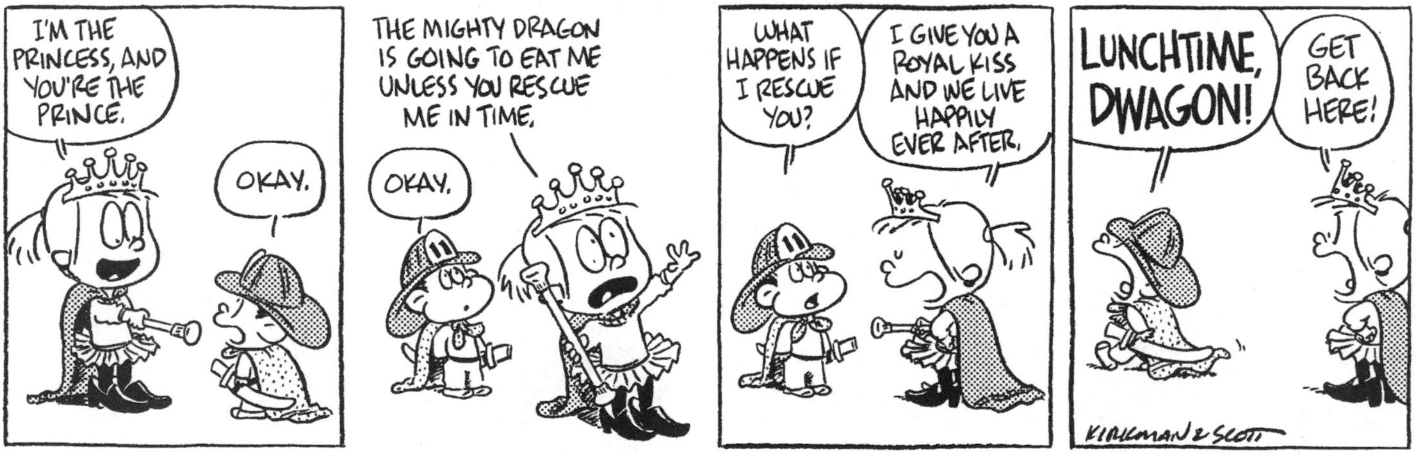
I'M THE PRINCESS, AND YOU'RE THE PRINCE.
OKAY.
THE MIGHTY DRAGON IS GOING TO EAT ME UNLESS YOU RESCUE ME IN TIME.
OKAY.
WHAT HAPPENS IF I RESCUE YOU?
I GIVE YOU A ROYAL KISS AND WE LIVE HAPPILY EVER AFTER.
LUNCHTIME, DWAGON!
GET BACK HERE!
KIRKMAN & SCOTT

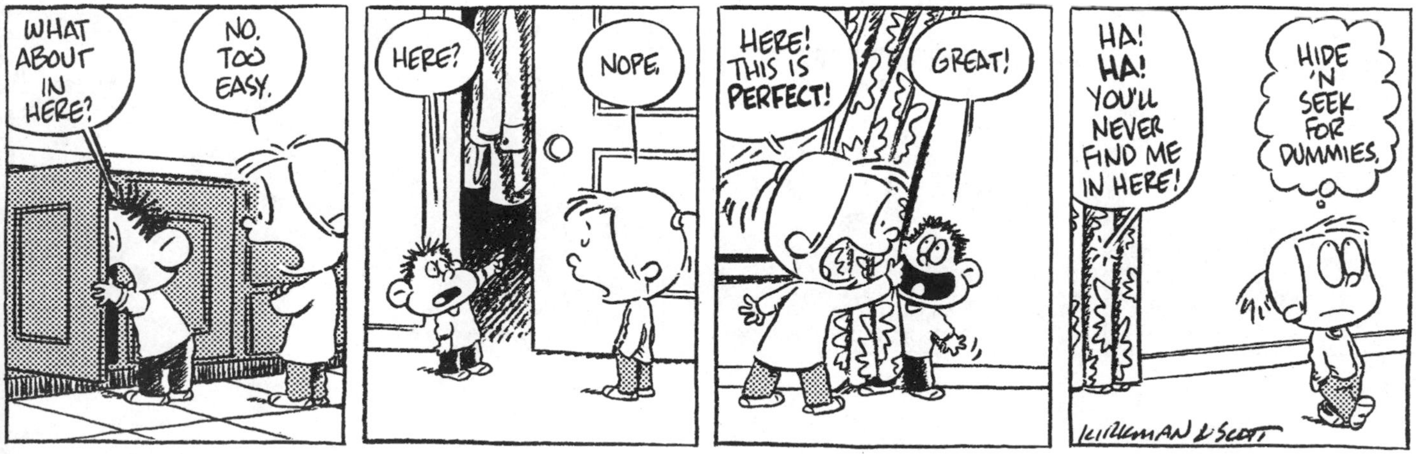
WHAT ABOUT IN HERE?
NO. TOO EASY.
HERE?
NOPE.
HERE! THIS IS PERFECT!
GREAT!
HA! HA! YOU'LL NEVER FIND ME IN HERE!
HIDE 'N SEEK FOR DUMMIES.
KIRKMAN & SCOTT

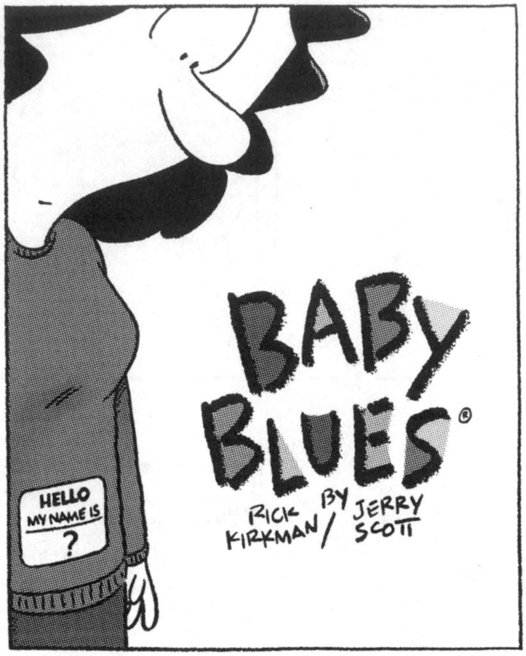
HELLO
MY NAME IS
?
BABY BLUES®
BY RICK KIRKMAN / JERRY SCOTT

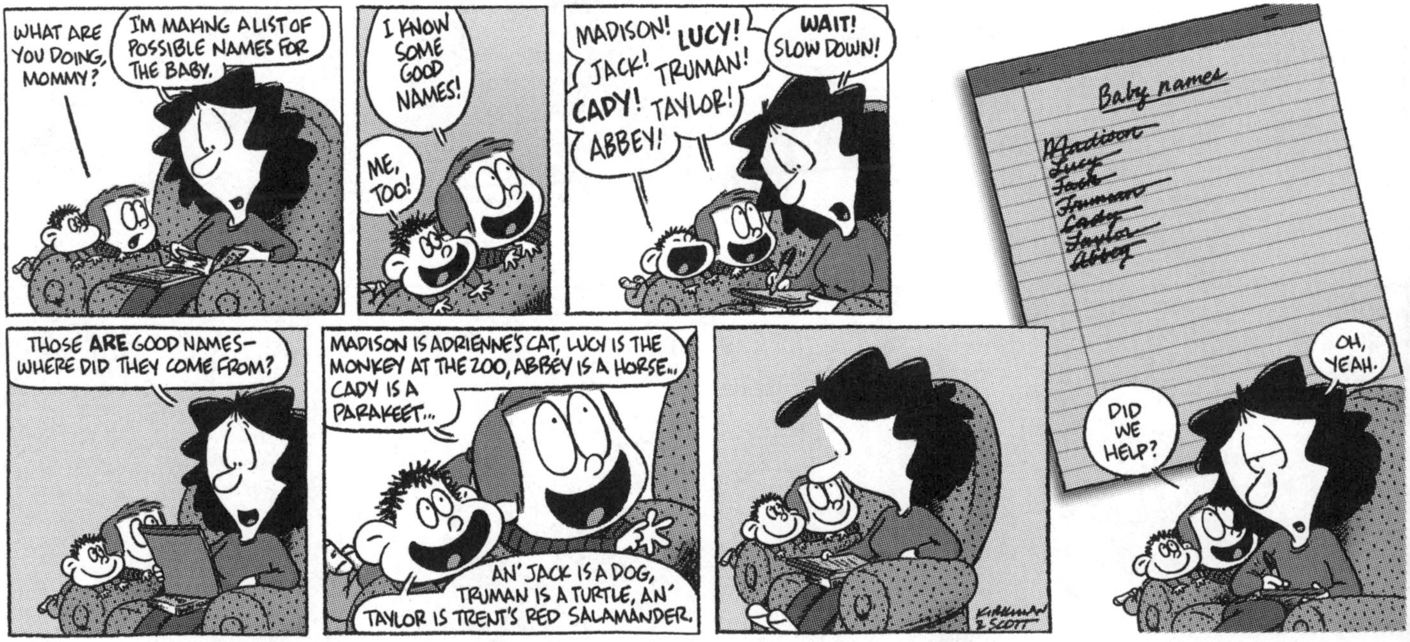
WHAT ARE YOU DOING, MOMMY?
I'M MAKING A LIST OF POSSIBLE NAMES FOR THE BABY.
I KNOW SOME GOOD NAMES!
ME, TOO!
MADISON! JACK! CADY! ABBEY!
LUCY! TRUMAN! TAYLOR!
WAIT! SLOW DOWN!
THOSE ARE GOOD NAMES— WHERE DID THEY COME FROM?
MADISON IS ADRIENNE'S CAT, LUCY IS THE MONKEY AT THE ZOO, ABBEY IS A HORSE... CADY IS A PARAKEET...
AN' JACK IS A DOG, TRUMAN IS A TURTLE, AN' TAYLOR IS TRENT'S RED SALAMANDER.
KIRKMAN & SCOTT
Baby names
Madison
Lucy
Jack
Truman
Cady
Taylor
Abbey
DID WE HELP?
OH, YEAH.

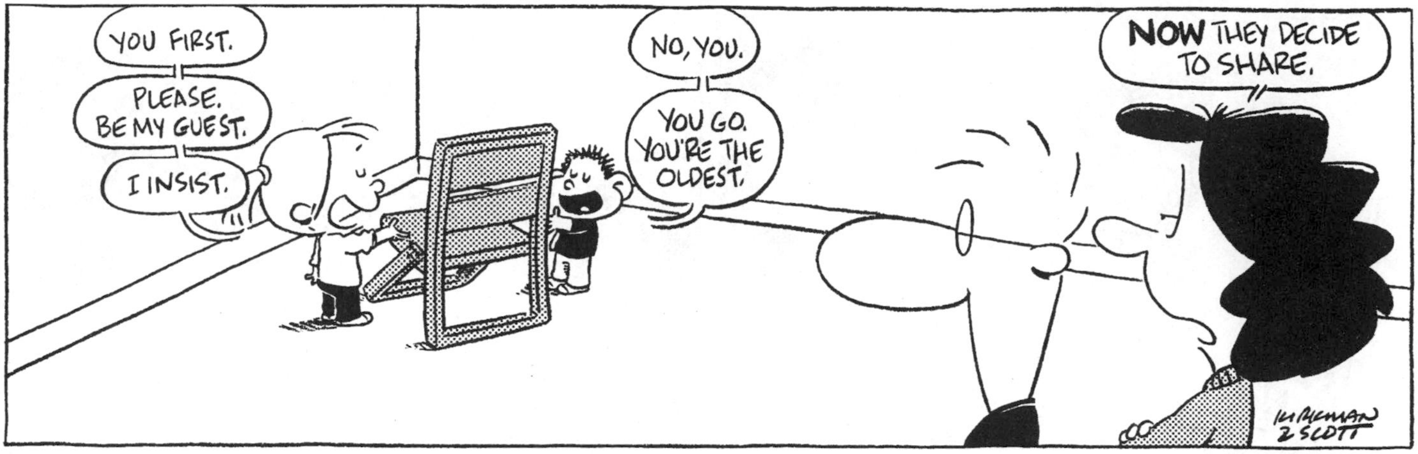
YOU FIRST.
PLEASE. BE MY GUEST.
I INSIST.
NO, YOU.
YOU GO. YOU'RE THE OLDEST.
NOW THEY DECIDE TO SHARE.
KIRKMAN & SCOTT

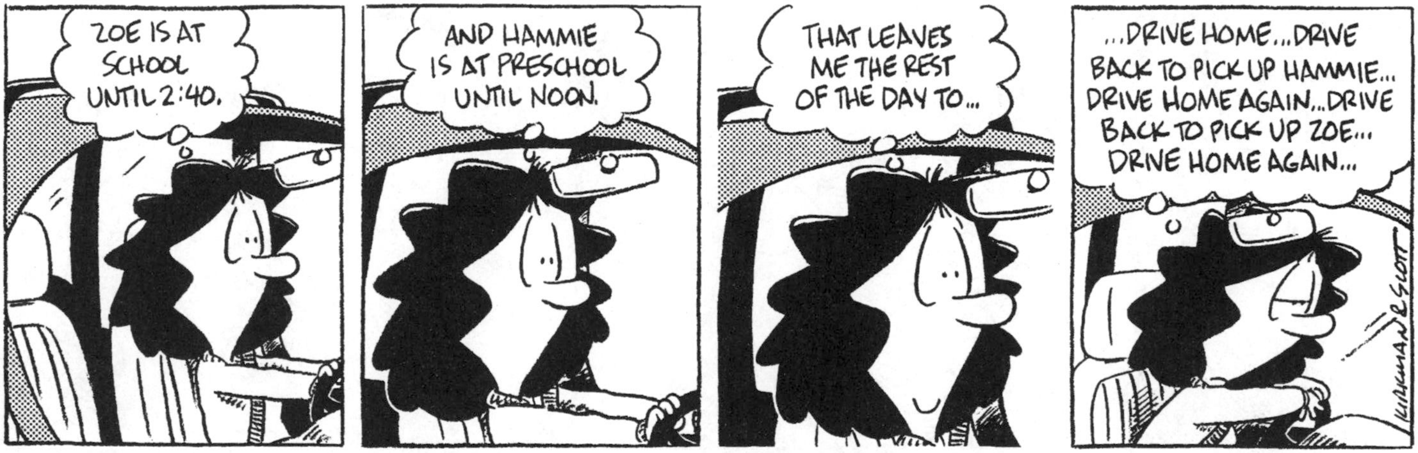
ZOE IS AT SCHOOL UNTIL 2:40.
AND HAMMIE IS AT PRESCHOOL UNTIL NOON.
THAT LEAVES ME THE REST OF THE DAY TO...
...DRIVE HOME...DRIVE BACK TO PICK UP HAMMIE... DRIVE HOME AGAIN...DRIVE BACK TO PICK UP ZOE... DRIVE HOME AGAIN...
KIRKMAN & SCOTT

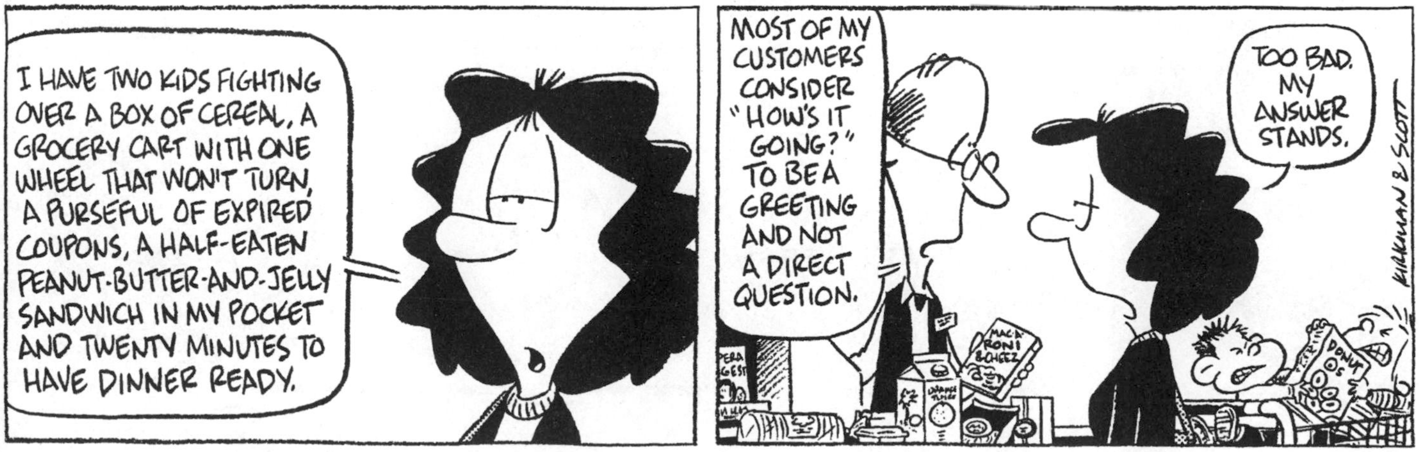
I HAVE TWO KIDS FIGHTING OVER A BOX OF CEREAL, A GROCERY CART WITH ONE WHEEL THAT WON'T TURN, A PURSEFUL OF EXPIRED COUPONS, A HALF-EATEN PEANUT-BUTTER-AND-JELLY SANDWICH IN MY POCKET AND TWENTY MINUTES TO HAVE DINNER READY.
MOST OF MY CUSTOMERS CONSIDER "HOW'S IT GOING?" TO BE A GREETING AND NOT A DIRECT QUESTION.
TOO BAD. MY ANSWER STANDS.
KIRKMAN & SCOTT

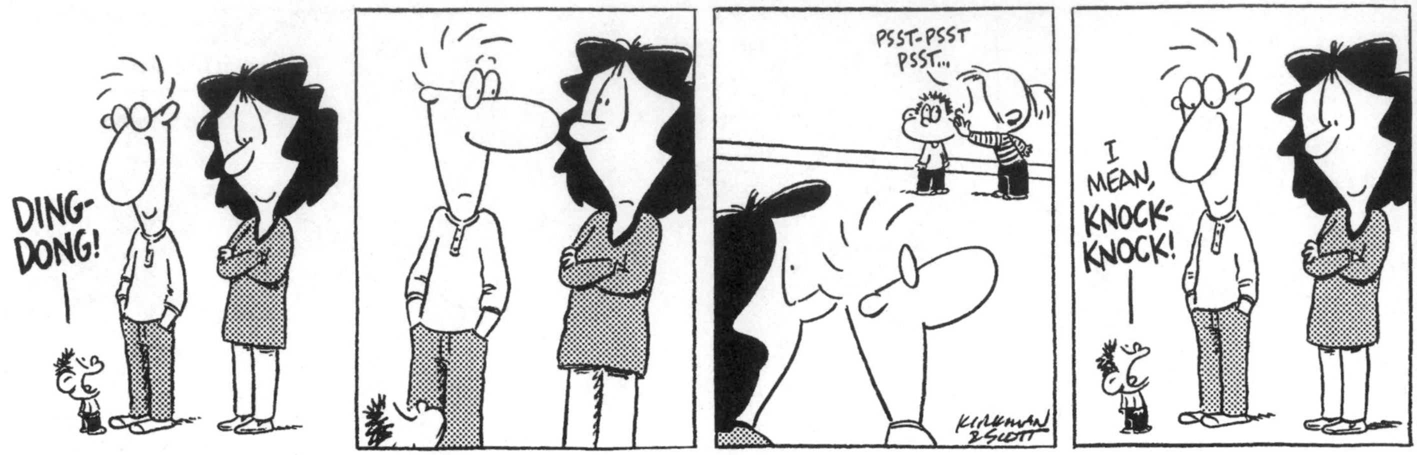
DING-DONG!
PSST-PSST PSST...
I MEAN, KNOCK-KNOCK!

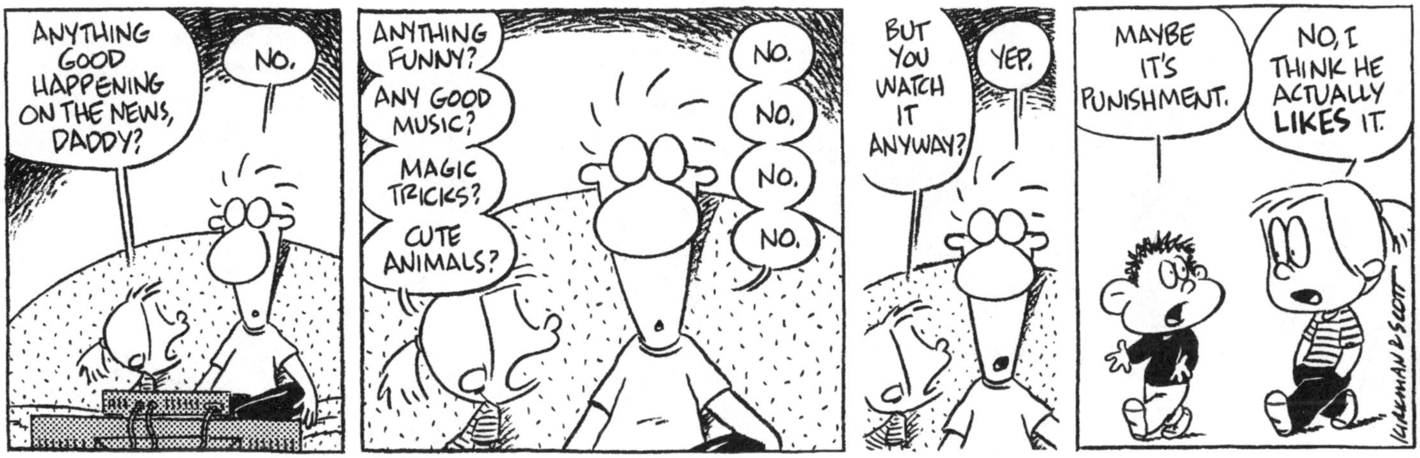
ANYTHING GOOD HAPPENING ON THE NEWS, DADDY?
NO.
ANYTHING FUNNY?
ANY GOOD MUSIC?
MAGIC TRICKS?
CUTE ANIMALS?
NO.
NO.
NO.
NO.
BUT YOU WATCH IT ANYWAY?
YEP.
MAYBE IT'S PUNISHMENT.
NO, I THINK HE ACTUALLY LIKES IT.

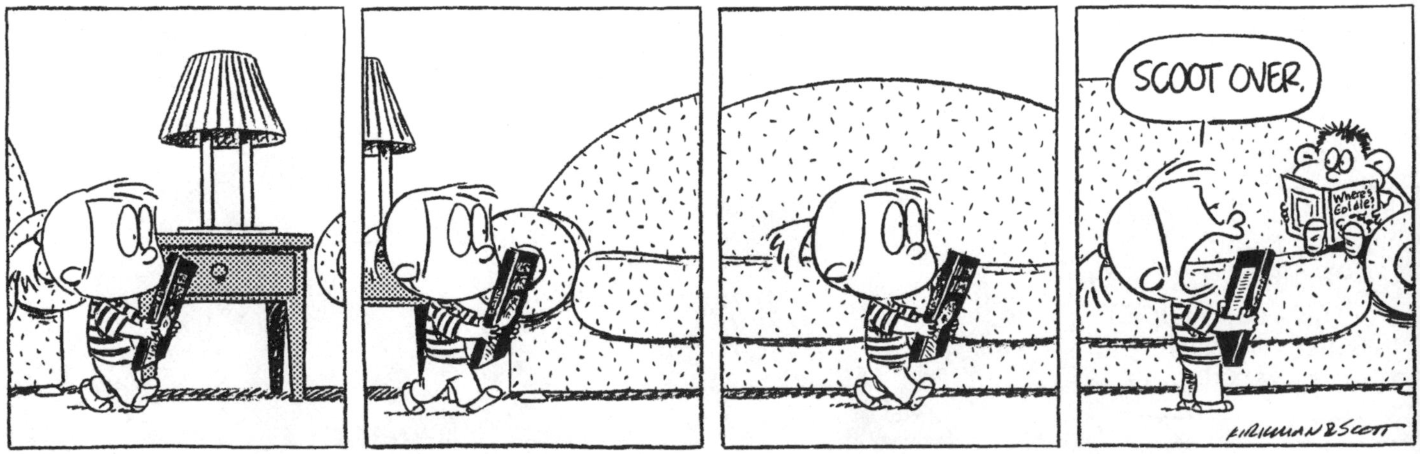
SCOOT OVER.
Where's Goldie?

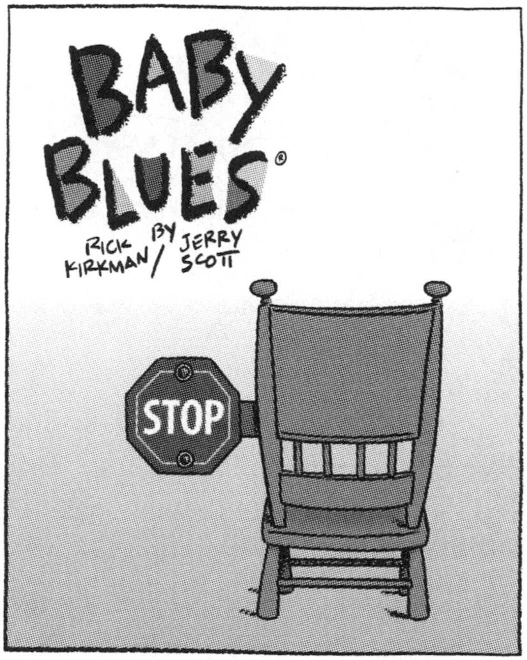
BABY BLUES®
BY RICK KIRKMAN / JERRY SCOTT
STOP

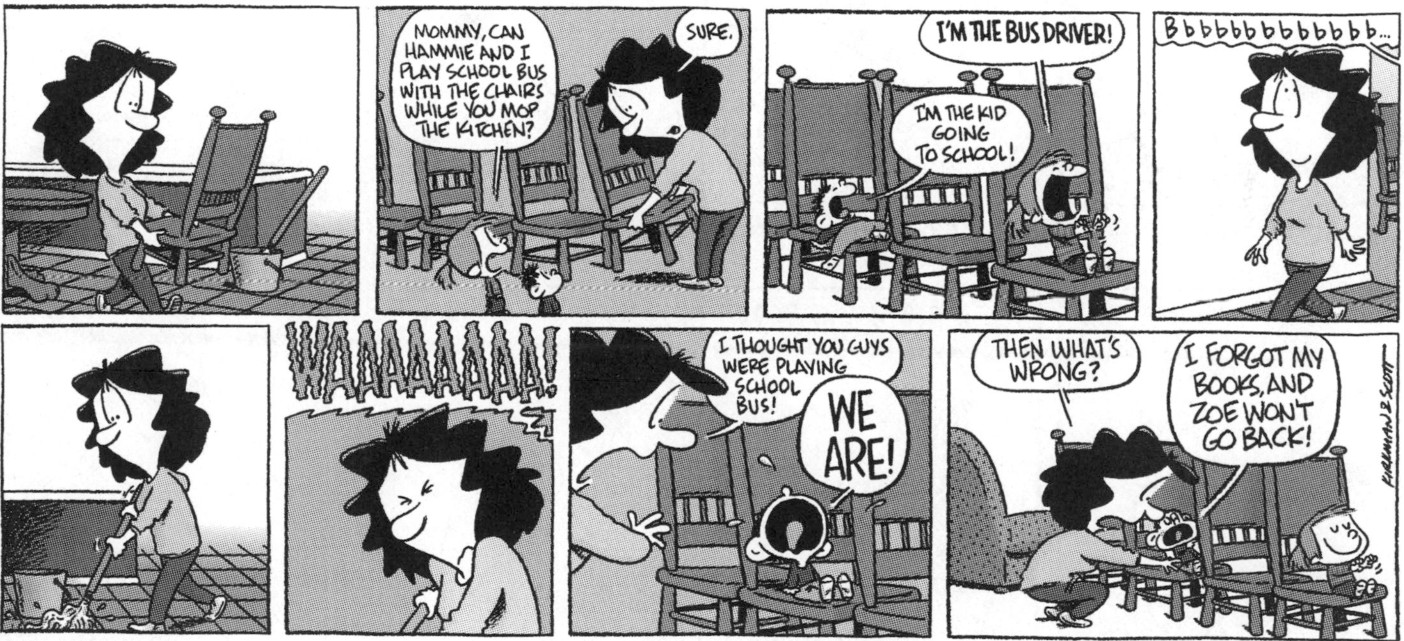
MOMMY, CAN HAMMIE AND I PLAY SCHOOL BUS WITH THE CHAIRS WHILE YOU MOP THE KITCHEN?
SURE.
I'M THE BUS DRIVER!
I'M THE KID GOING TO SCHOOL!
Bbbbbbbbbbbbb...
WAAAAAAAA!
I THOUGHT YOU GUYS WERE PLAYING SCHOOL BUS!
WE ARE!
THEN WHAT'S WRONG?
I FORGOT MY BOOKS, AND ZOE WON'T GO BACK!
KIRKMAN & SCOTT

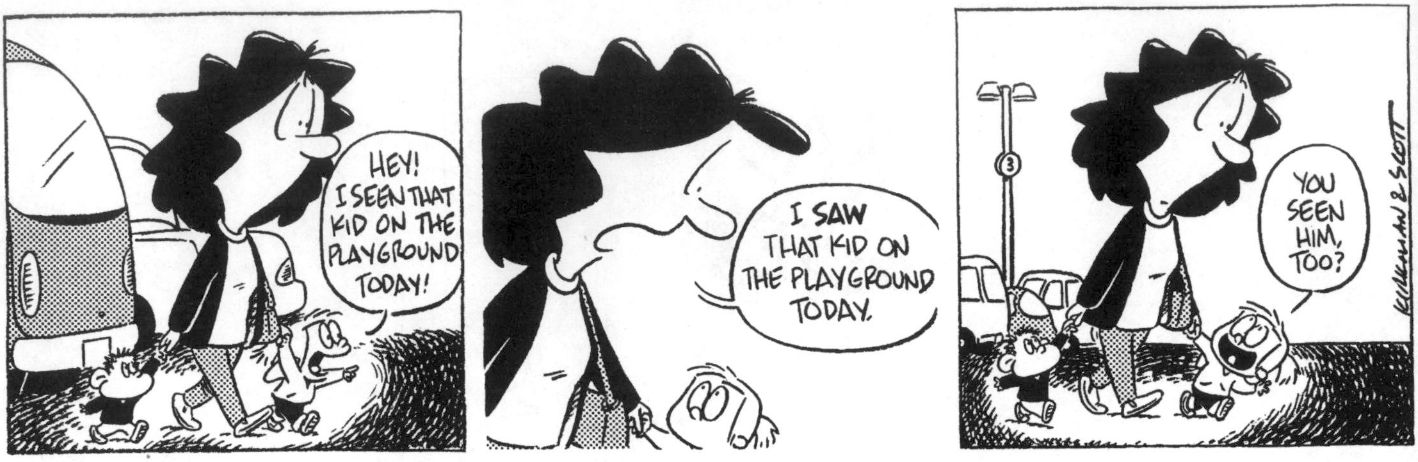
HEY! I SEEN THAT KID ON THE PLAYGROUND TODAY!
I SAW THAT KID ON THE PLAYGROUND TODAY.
YOU SEEN HIM, TOO?
KIRKMAN & SCOTT

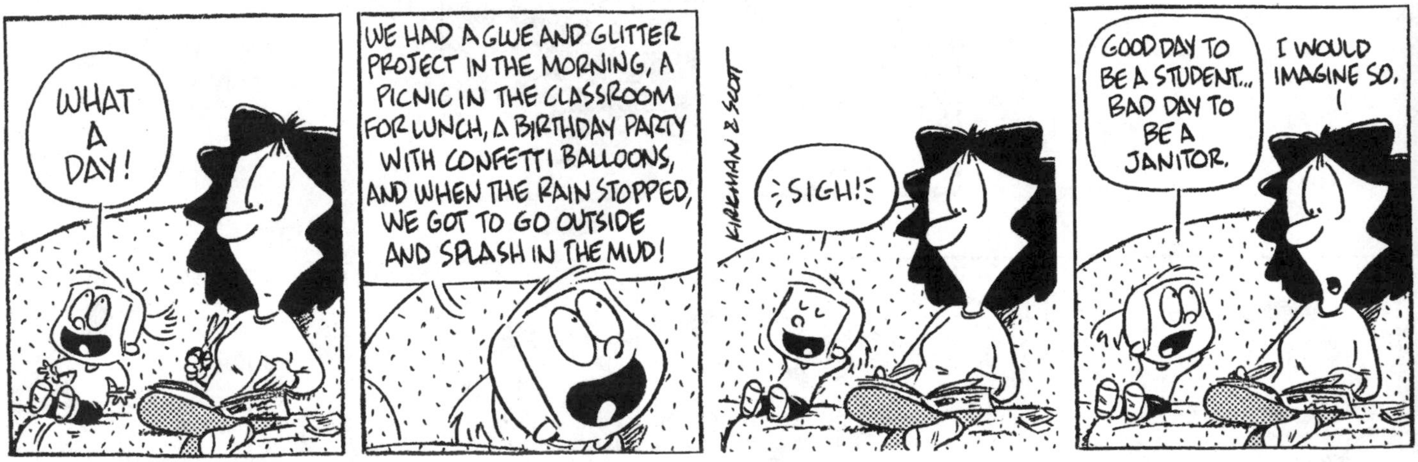
WHAT A DAY!
WE HAD A GLUE AND GLITTER PROJECT IN THE MORNING, A PICNIC IN THE CLASSROOM FOR LUNCH, A BIRTHDAY PARTY WITH CONFETTI BALLOONS, AND WHEN THE RAIN STOPPED, WE GOT TO GO OUTSIDE AND SPLASH IN THE MUD!
KIRKMAN & SCOTT
SIGH!
GOOD DAY TO BE A STUDENT... BAD DAY TO BE A JANITOR.
I WOULD IMAGINE SO.

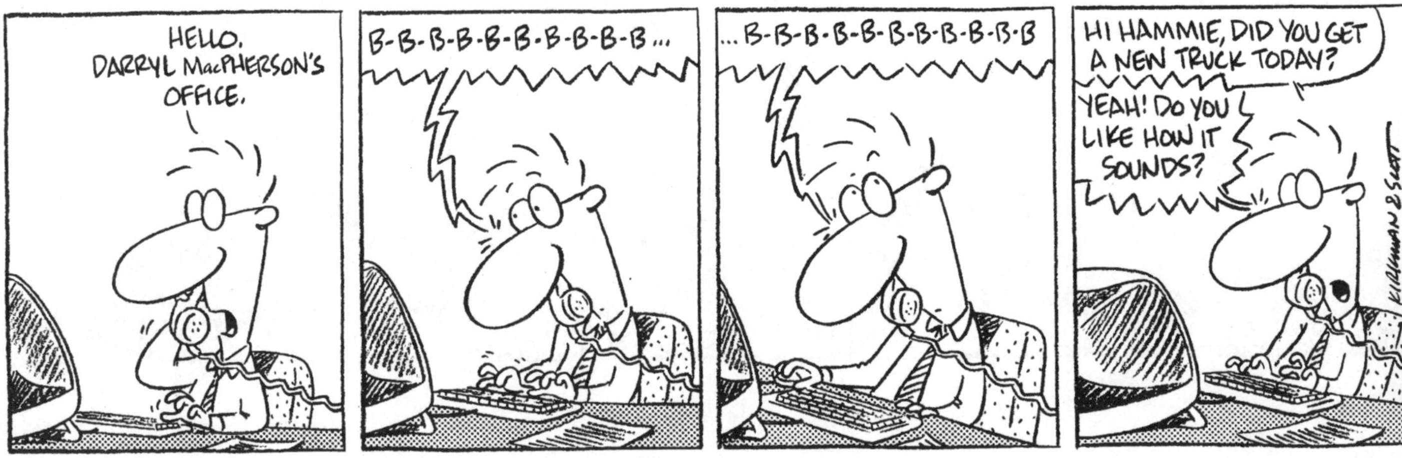
HELLO. DARRYL MacPHERSON'S OFFICE.
B-B-B-B-B-B-B-B-B-B-B...
...B-B-B-B-B-B-B-B-B-B-B-B
HI HAMMIE, DID YOU GET A NEW TRUCK TODAY?
YEAH! DO YOU LIKE HOW IT SOUNDS?
KIRKMAN & SCOTT

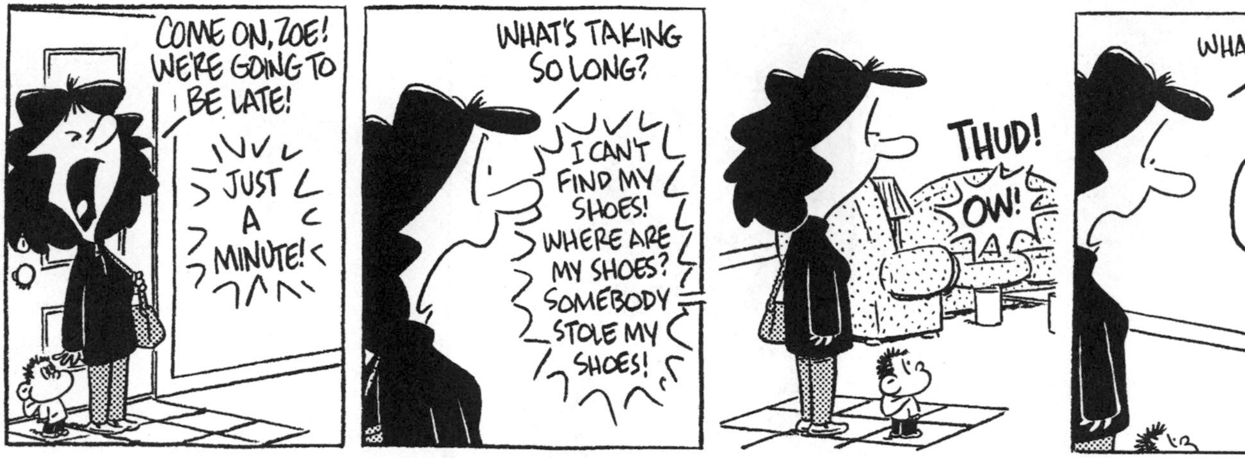
COME ON, ZOE! WE'RE GOING TO BE LATE!
JUST A MINUTE!
WHAT'S TAKING SO LONG?
I CAN'T FIND MY SHOES! WHERE ARE MY SHOES? SOMEBODY STOLE MY SHOES!
THUD!
OW!
WHAT HAPPENED?
I TRIPPED OVER MY SHOES.
KIRKMAN & SCOTT

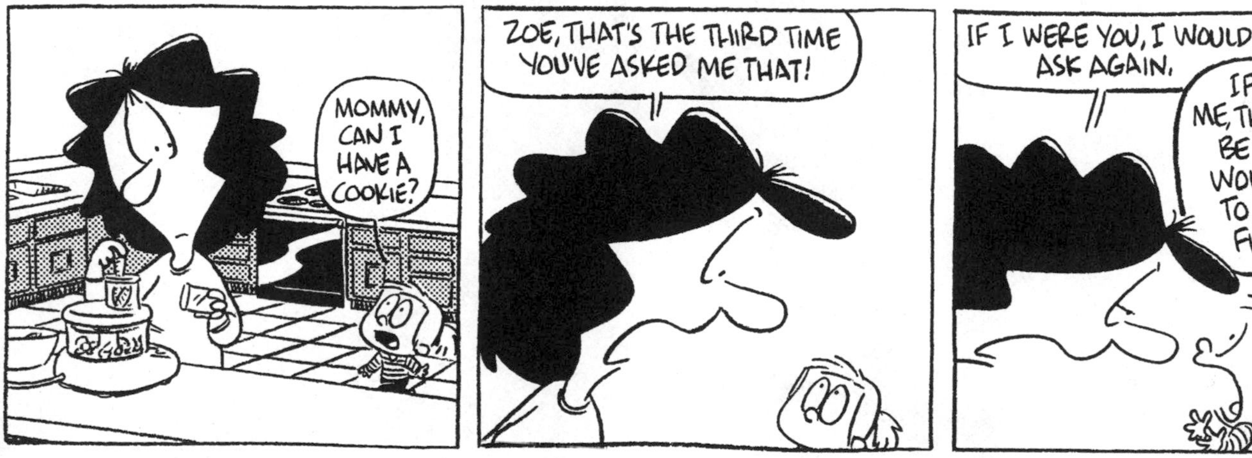
MOMMY, CAN I HAVE A COOKIE?
ZOE, THAT'S THE THIRD TIME YOU'VE ASKED ME THAT!
IF I WERE YOU, I WOULDN'T ASK AGAIN.
IF YOU WERE ME, THEN I WOULD BE YOU, AND I WOULDN'T HAVE TO ASK IN THE FIRST PLACE!
KIRKMAN & SCOTT

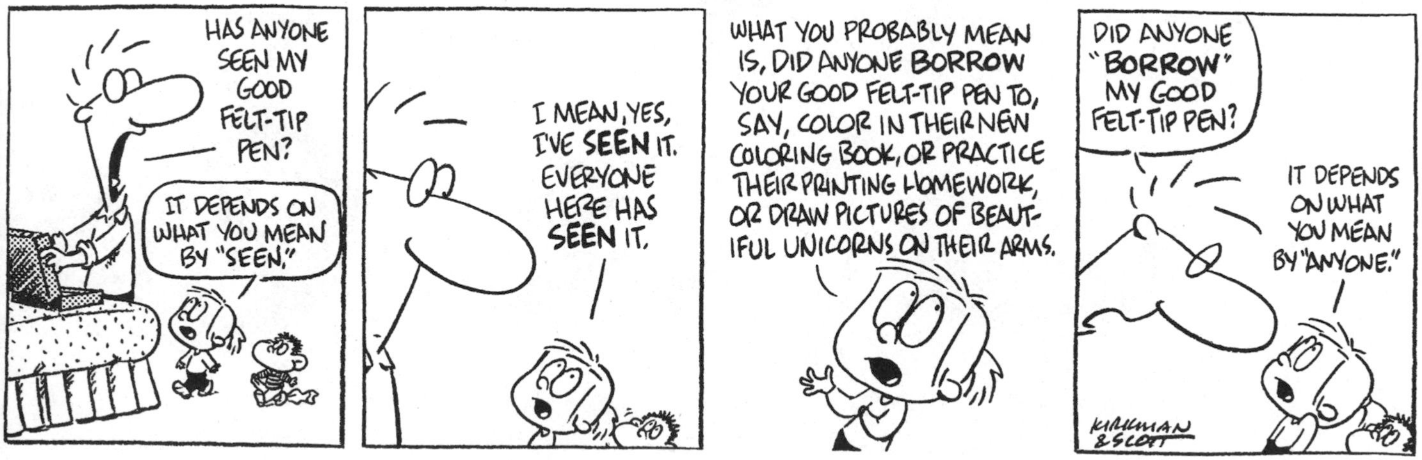
HAS ANYONE SEEN MY GOOD FELT-TIP PEN?
IT DEPENDS ON WHAT YOU MEAN BY "SEEN."
I MEAN, YES, I'VE SEEN IT. EVERYONE HERE HAS SEEN IT.
WHAT YOU PROBABLY MEAN IS, DID ANYONE BORROW YOUR GOOD FELT-TIP PEN TO, SAY, COLOR IN THEIR NEW COLORING BOOK, OR PRACTICE THEIR PRINTING HOMEWORK, OR DRAW PICTURES OF BEAUTIFUL UNICORNS ON THEIR ARMS.
DID ANYONE "BORROW" MY GOOD FELT-TIP PEN?
IT DEPENDS ON WHAT YOU MEAN BY "ANYONE."
KIRKMAN & SCOTT

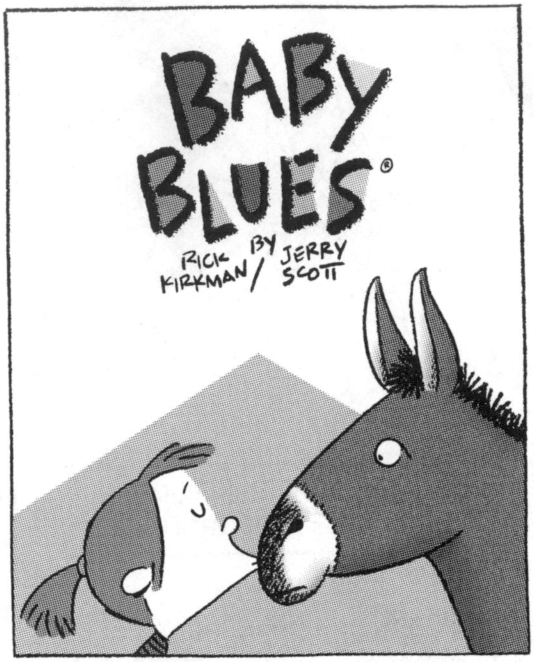
BABY BLUES®
BY RICK KIRKMAN / JERRY SCOTT

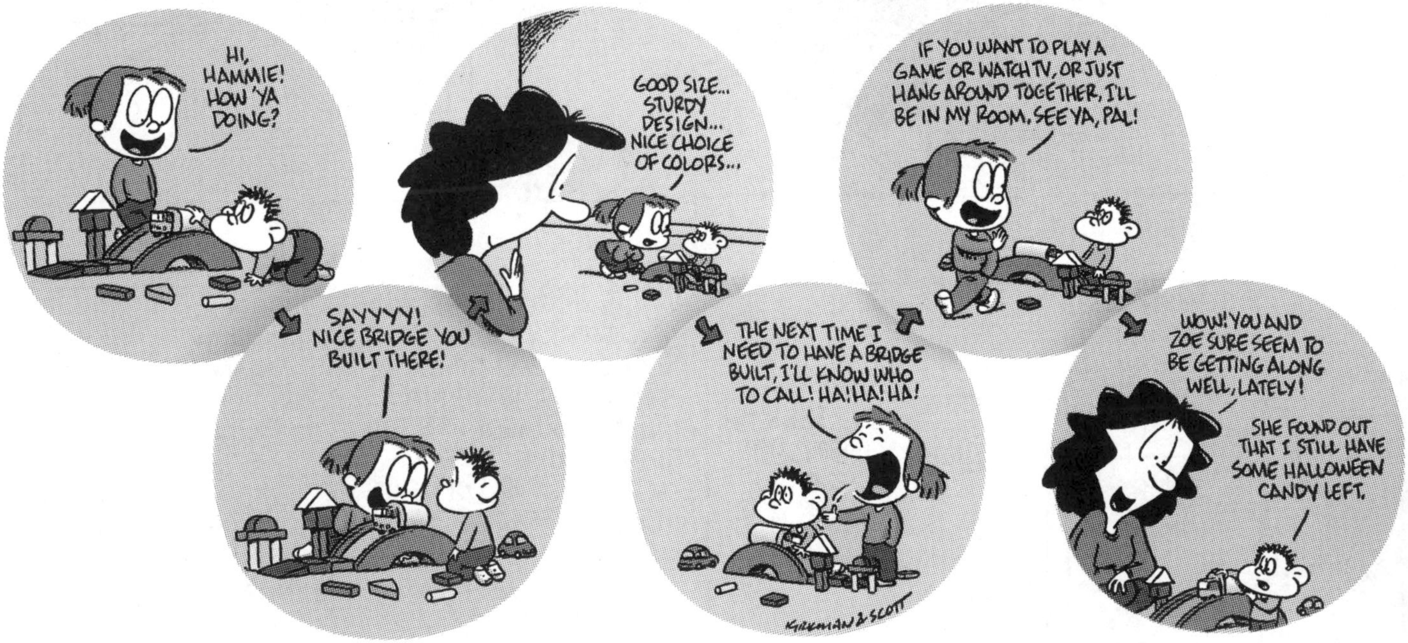
HI, HAMMIE! HOW 'YA DOING?
SAYYYY! NICE BRIDGE YOU BUILT THERE!
GOOD SIZE... STURDY DESIGN... NICE CHOICE OF COLORS...
THE NEXT TIME I NEED TO HAVE A BRIDGE BUILT, I'LL KNOW WHO TO CALL! HA! HA! HA!
IF YOU WANT TO PLAY A GAME OR WATCH TV, OR JUST HANG AROUND TOGETHER, I'LL BE IN MY ROOM. SEE YA, PAL!
WOW! YOU AND ZOE SURE SEEM TO BE GETTING ALONG WELL, LATELY!
SHE FOUND OUT THAT I STILL HAVE SOME HALLOWEEN CANDY LEFT.
KIRKMAN & SCOTT

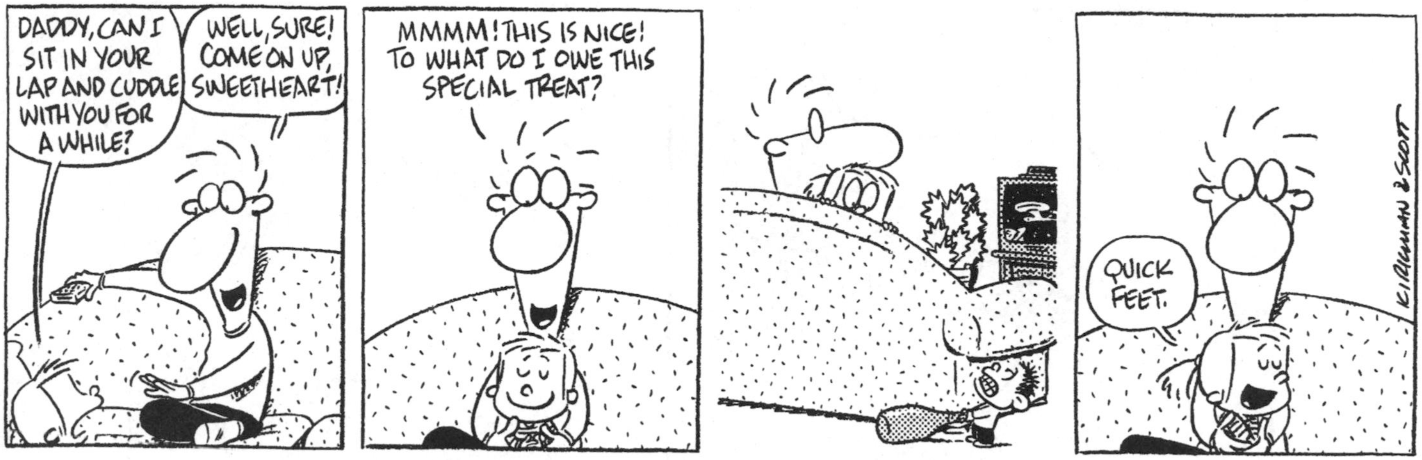
DADDY, CAN I SIT IN YOUR LAP AND CUDDLE WITH YOU FOR A WHILE?
WELL, SURE! COME ON UP, SWEETHEART!
MMMM! THIS IS NICE! TO WHAT DO I OWE THIS SPECIAL TREAT?
QUICK FEET.
KIRKMAN & SCOTT

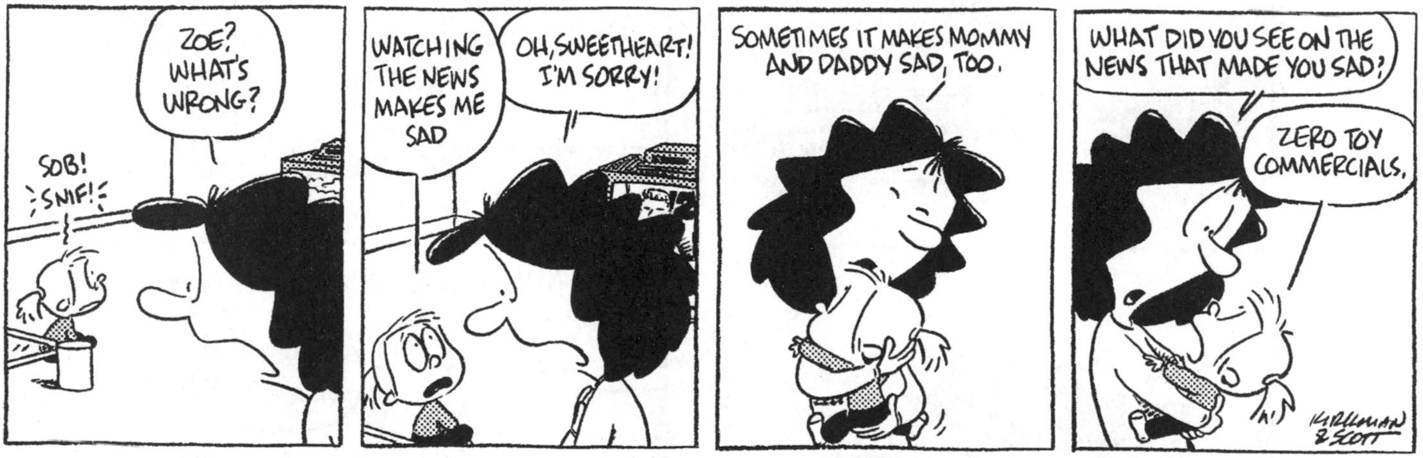
SOB! SNIF!
ZOE? WHAT'S WRONG?
WATCHING THE NEWS MAKES ME SAD
OH, SWEETHEART! I'M SORRY!
SOMETIMES IT MAKES MOMMY AND DADDY SAD, TOO.
WHAT DID YOU SEE ON THE NEWS THAT MADE YOU SAD?
ZERO TOY COMMERCIALS.
KIRKMAN & SCOTT

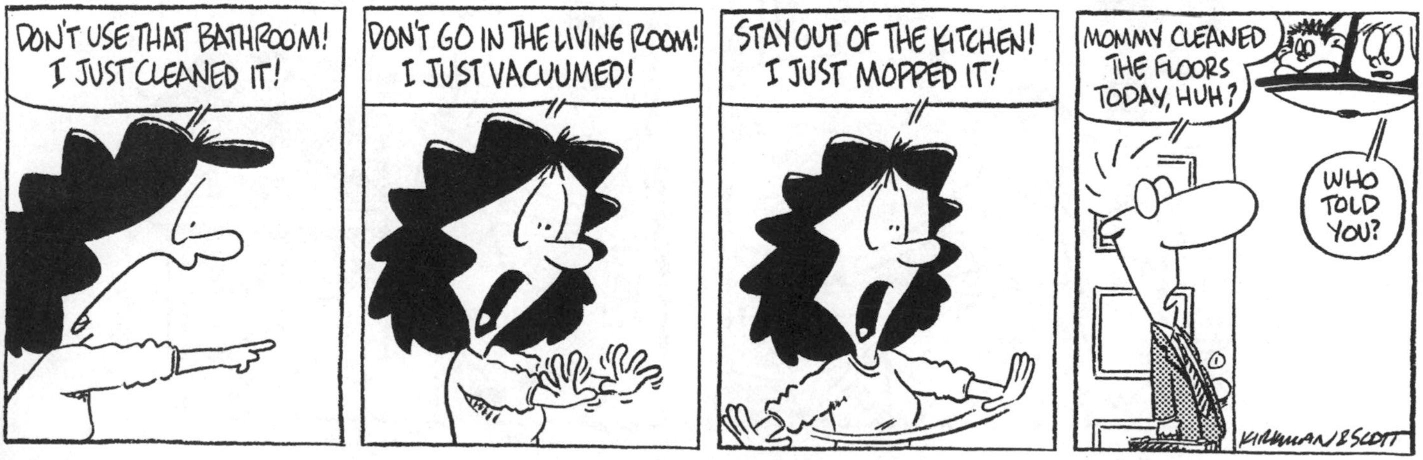
DON'T USE THAT BATHROOM! I JUST CLEANED IT!
DON'T GO IN THE LIVING ROOM! I JUST VACUUMED!
STAY OUT OF THE KITCHEN! I JUST MOPPED IT!
MOMMY CLEANED THE FLOORS TODAY, HUH?
WHO TOLD YOU?
KIRKMAN & SCOTT

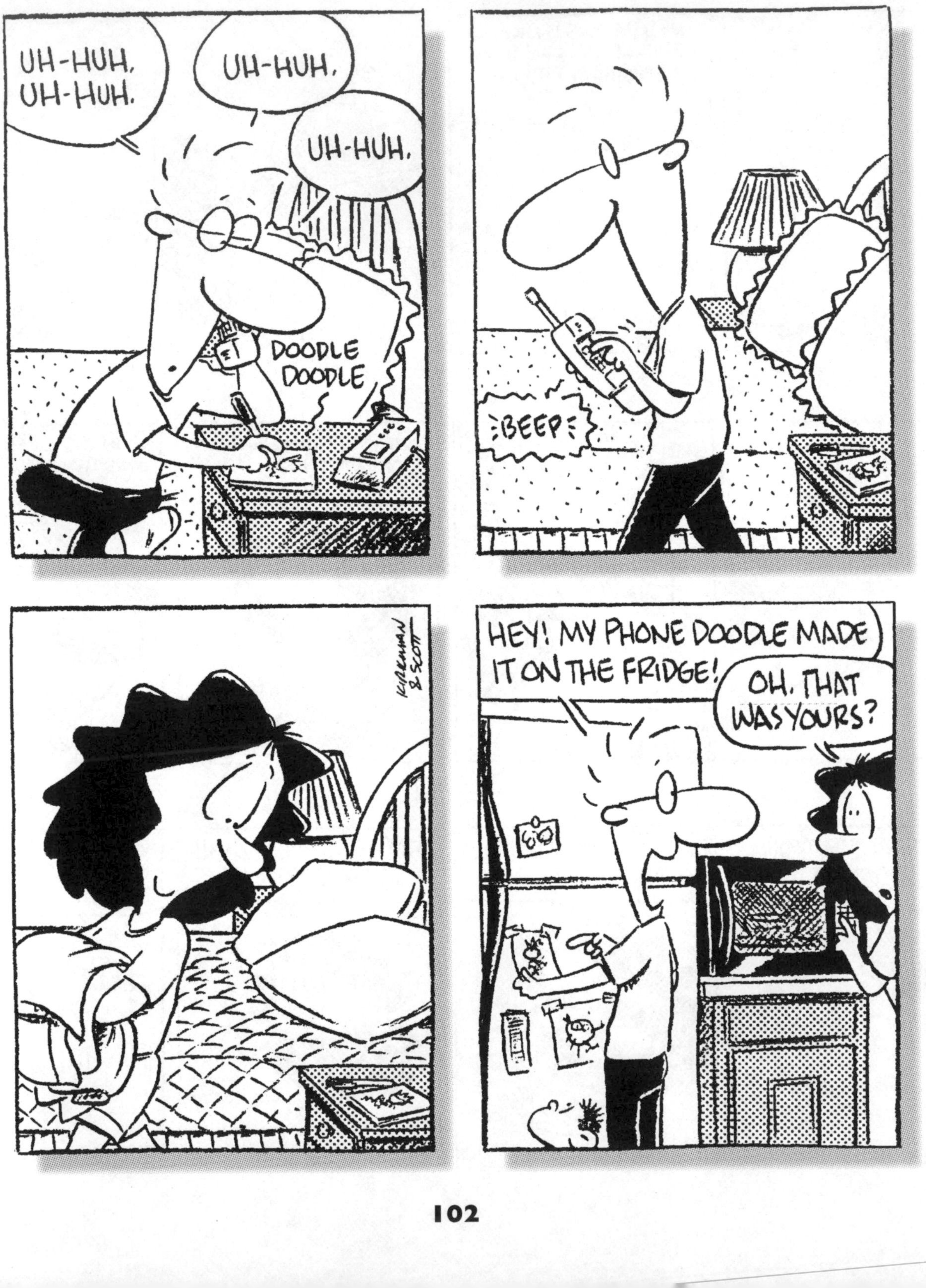
UH-HUH, UH-HUH.
UH-HUH,
UH-HUH,
DOODLE DOODLE
BEEP
KIRKMAN & SCOTT
HEY! MY PHONE DOODLE MADE IT ON THE FRIDGE!
OH. THAT WAS YOURS?

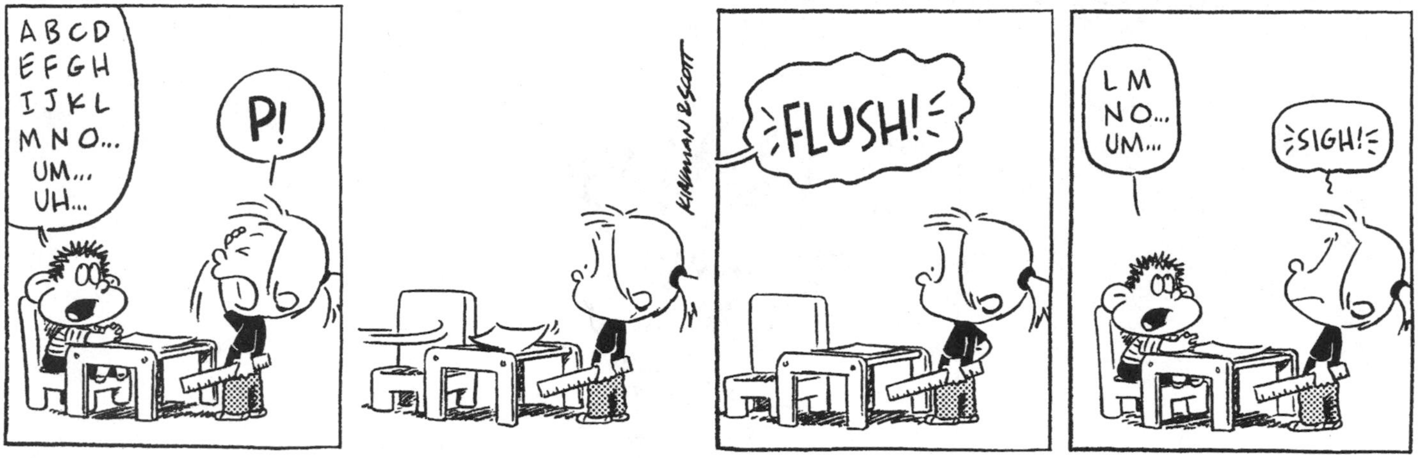
A B C D
E F G H
I J K L
M N O...
UM...
UH...
P!
KIRKMAN & SCOTT
FLUSH!
L M
N O...
UM...
SIGH!

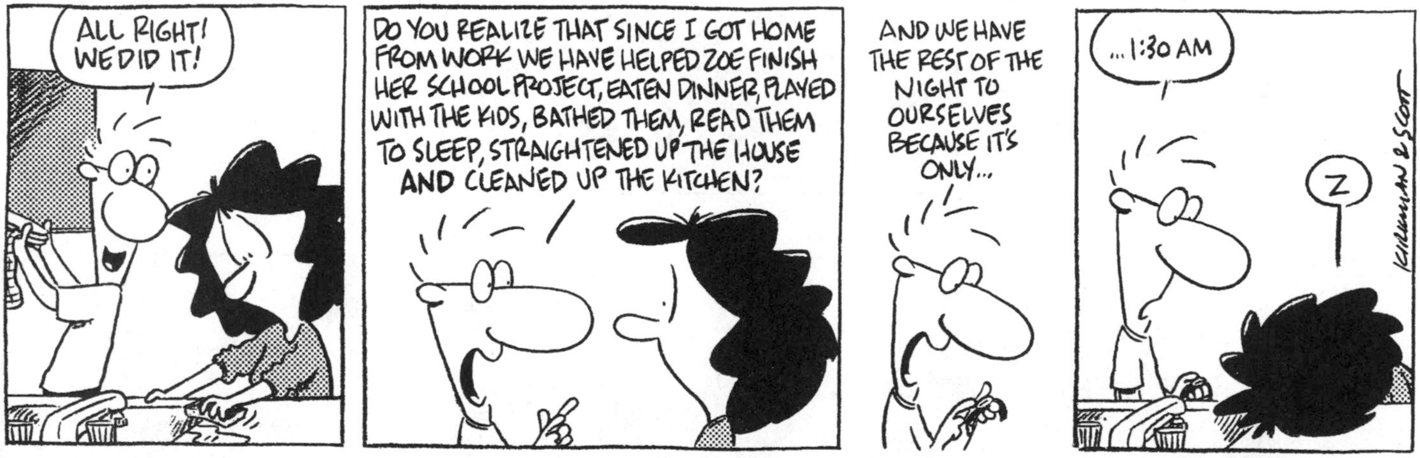
ALL RIGHT! WE DID IT!
DO YOU REALIZE THAT SINCE I GOT HOME FROM WORK WE HAVE HELPED ZOE FINISH HER SCHOOL PROJECT, EATEN DINNER, PLAYED WITH THE KIDS, BATHED THEM, READ THEM TO SLEEP, STRAIGHTENED UP THE HOUSE AND CLEANED UP THE KITCHEN?
AND WE HAVE THE REST OF THE NIGHT TO OURSELVES BECAUSE IT'S ONLY...
...1:30 AM
Z
KIRKMAN & SCOTT

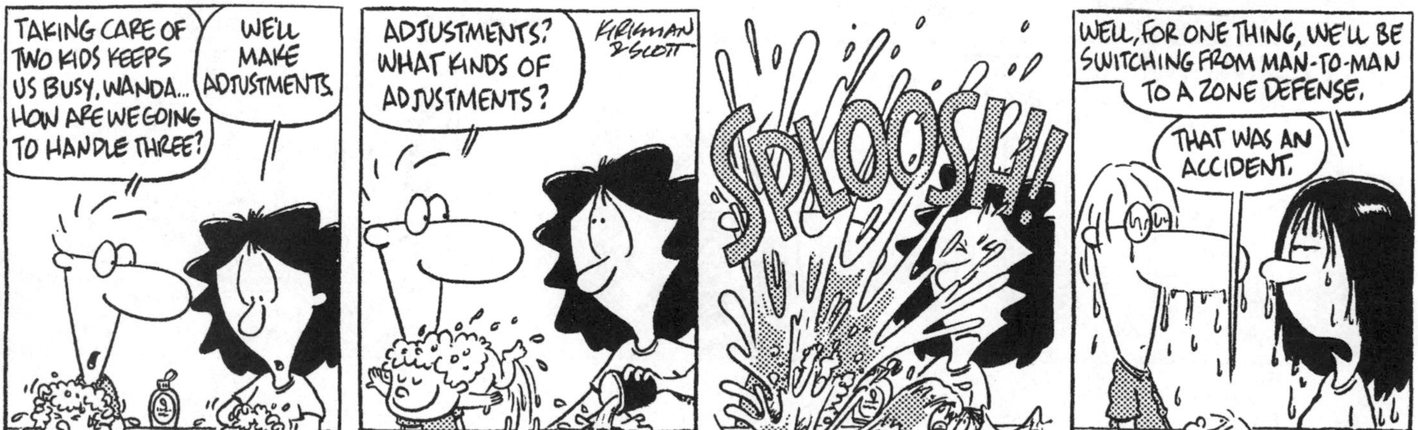
TAKING CARE OF TWO KIDS KEEPS US BUSY, WANDA... HOW ARE WE GOING TO HANDLE THREE?
WE'LL MAKE ADJUSTMENTS.
ADJUSTMENTS? WHAT KINDS OF ADJUSTMENTS?
KIRKMAN & SCOTT
SPLOOSH!
WELL, FOR ONE THING, WE'LL BE SWITCHING FROM MAN-TO-MAN TO A ZONE DEFENSE.
THAT WAS AN ACCIDENT.

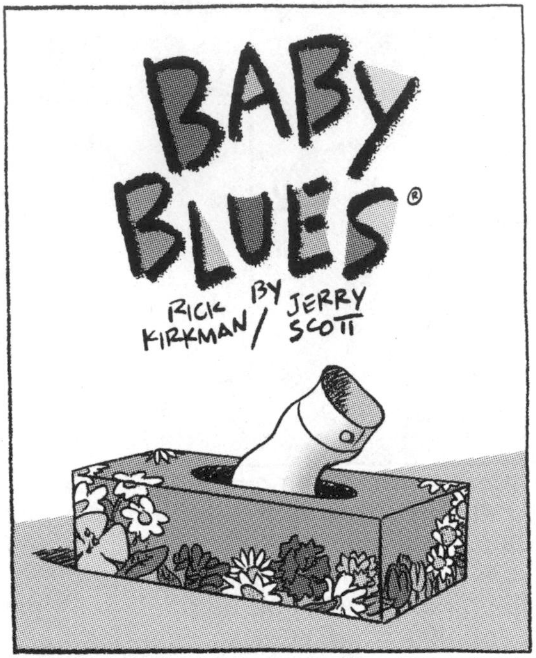
BABY BLUES®
BY RICK KIRKMAN / JERRY SCOTT

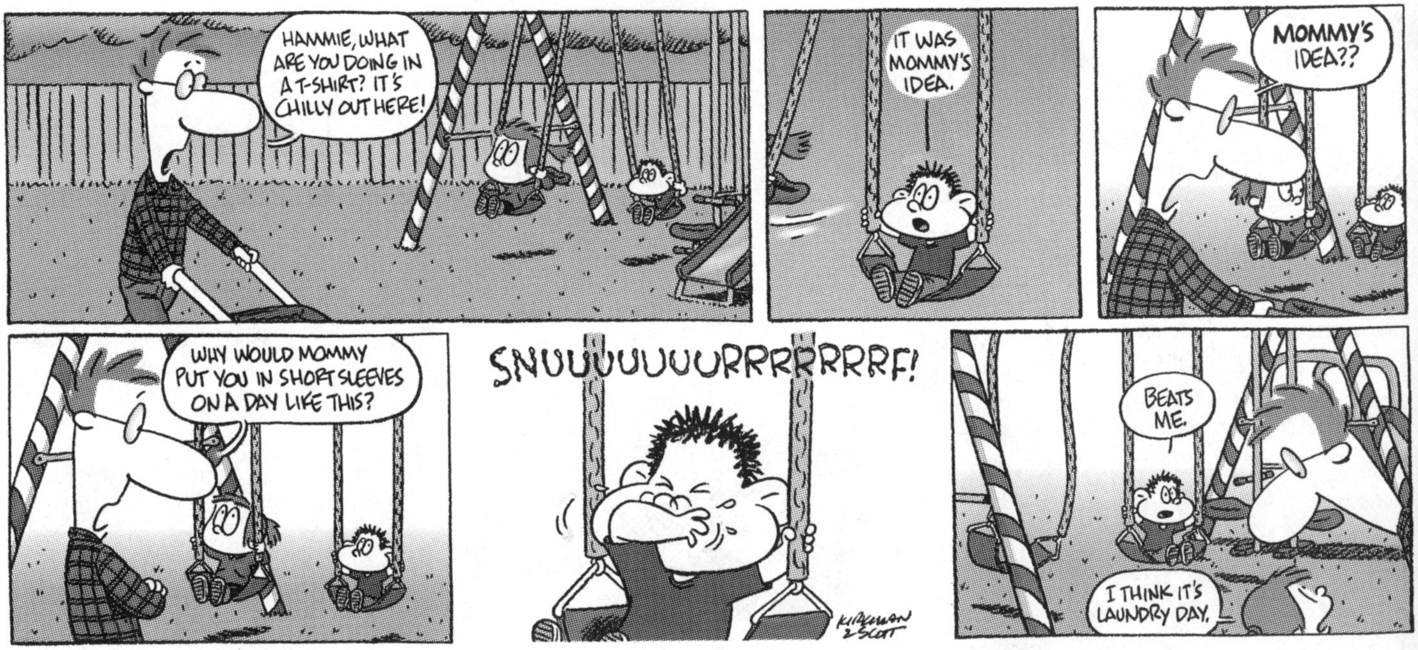
HAMMIE, WHAT ARE YOU DOING IN A T-SHIRT? IT'S CHILLY OUT HERE!
IT WAS MOMMY'S IDEA.
MOMMY'S IDEA??
WHY WOULD MOMMY PUT YOU IN SHORT SLEEVES ON A DAY LIKE THIS?
SNUUUUUUUURRRRRRRF!
KIRKMAN & SCOTT
BEATS ME.
I THINK IT'S LAUNDRY DAY.

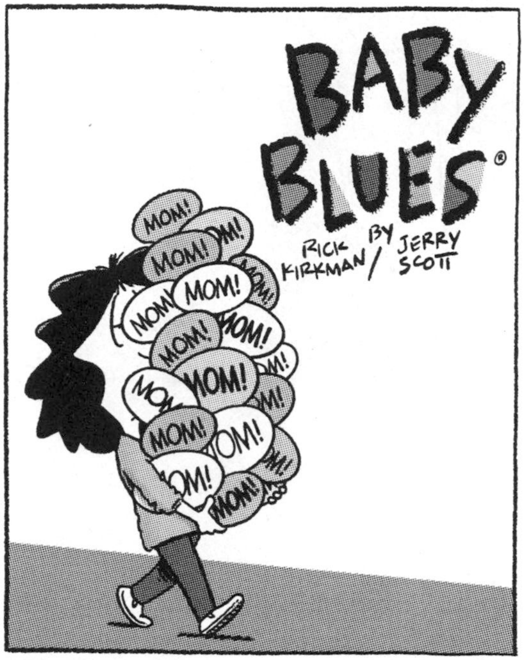
BABY BLUES®
BY RICK KIRKMAN / JERRY SCOTT
MOM!
MOM!
MOM!
MOM!

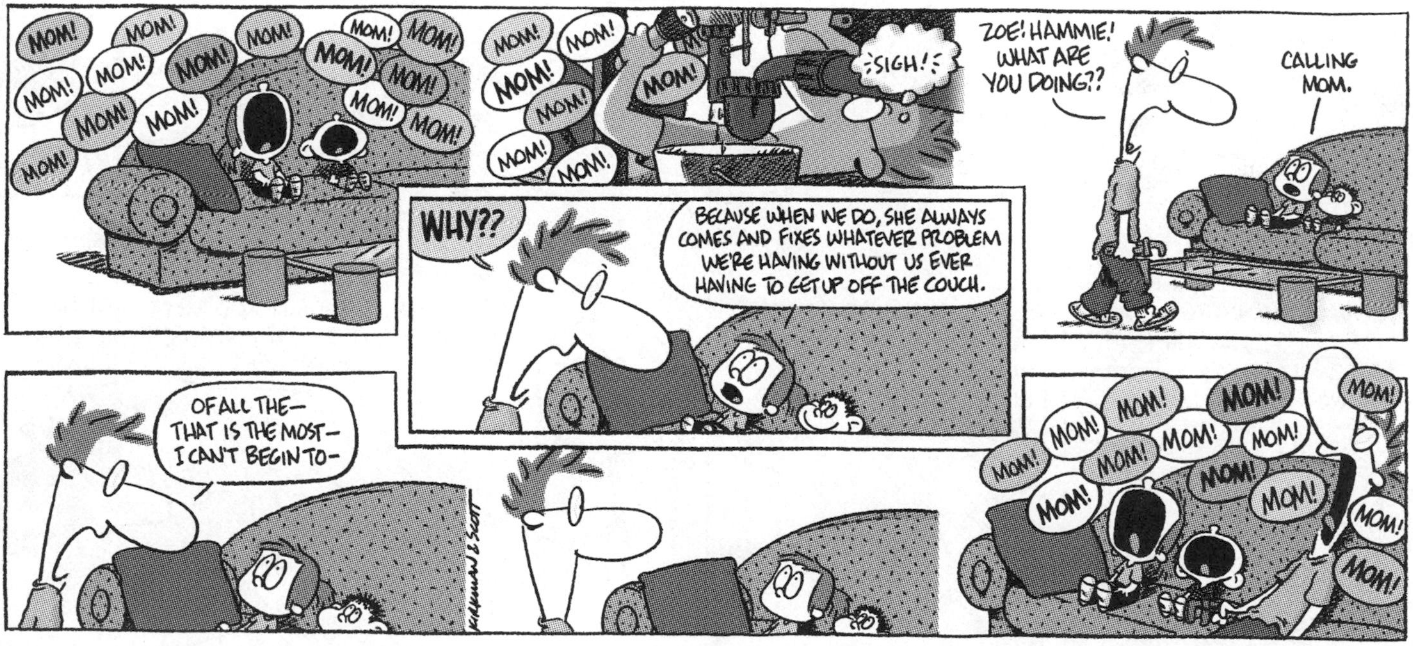
MOM!
MOM!
MOM!
MOM!
SIGH!
ZOE! HAMMIE! WHAT ARE YOU DOING??
CALLING MOM.
WHY??
BECAUSE WHEN WE DO, SHE ALWAYS COMES AND FIXES WHATEVER PROBLEM WE'RE HAVING WITHOUT US EVER HAVING TO GET UP OFF THE COUCH.
OF ALL THE— THAT IS THE MOST— I CAN'T BEGIN TO—
KIRKMAN & SCOTT
MOM!
MOM!
MOM!

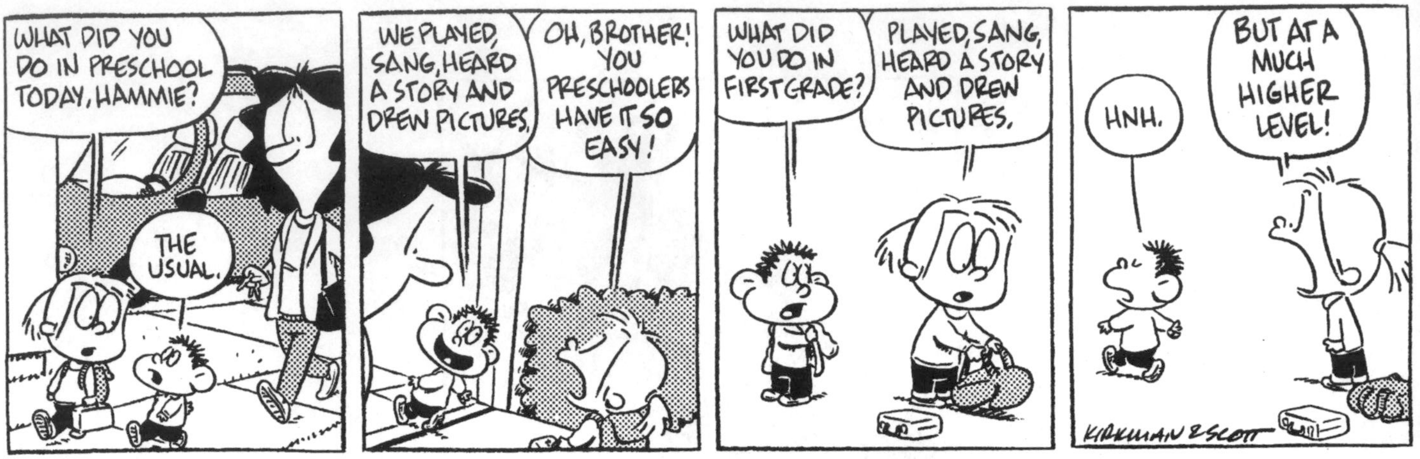
WHAT DID YOU DO IN PRESCHOOL TODAY, HAMMIE?
THE USUAL.
WE PLAYED, SANG, HEARD A STORY AND DREW PICTURES.
OH, BROTHER! YOU PRESCHOOLERS HAVE IT SO EASY!
WHAT DID YOU DO IN FIRST GRADE?
PLAYED, SANG, HEARD A STORY AND DREW PICTURES.
HNH.
BUT AT A MUCH HIGHER LEVEL!
KIRKMAN & SCOTT

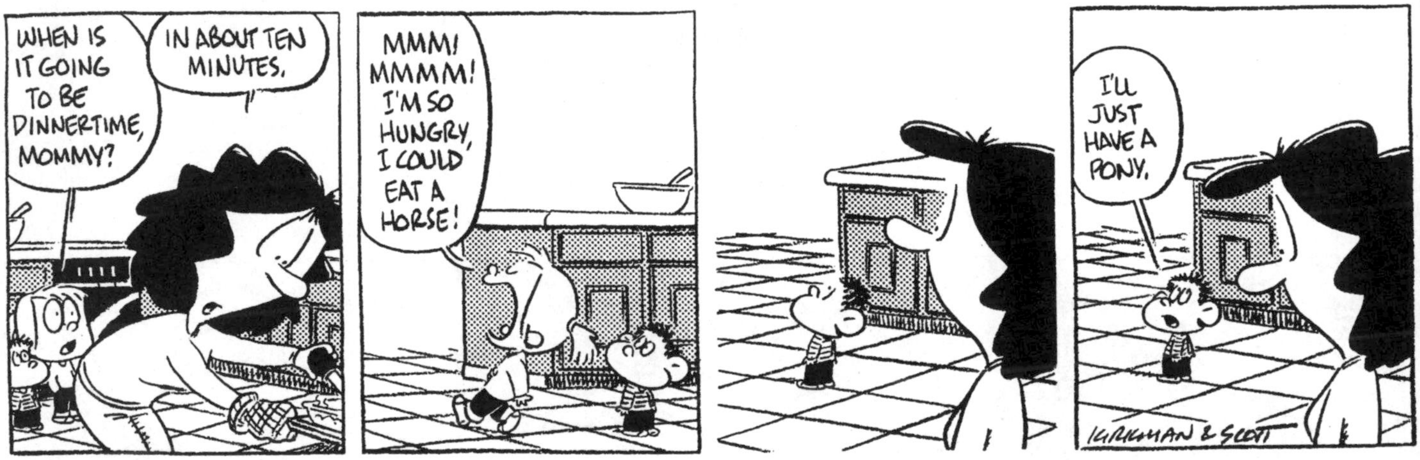
WHEN IS IT GOING TO BE DINNERTIME, MOMMY?
IN ABOUT TEN MINUTES.
MMM! MMMM! I'M SO HUNGRY, I COULD EAT A HORSE!
I'LL JUST HAVE A PONY.
KIRKMAN & SCOTT

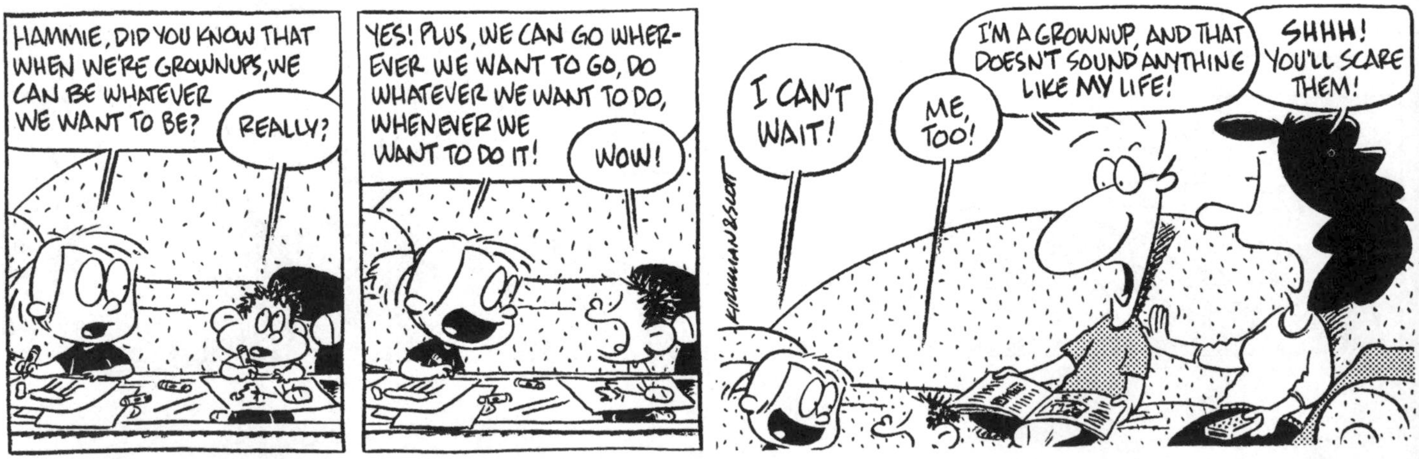
HAMMIE, DID YOU KNOW THAT WHEN WE'RE GROWNUPS, WE CAN BE WHATEVER WE WANT TO BE?
REALLY?
YES! PLUS, WE CAN GO WHEREVER WE WANT TO GO, DO WHATEVER WE WANT TO DO, WHENEVER WE WANT TO DO IT!
WOW!
KIRKMAN & SCOTT
I CAN'T WAIT!
ME, TOO!
I'M A GROWNUP, AND THAT DOESN'T SOUND ANYTHING LIKE MY LIFE!
SHHH! YOU'LL SCARE THEM!

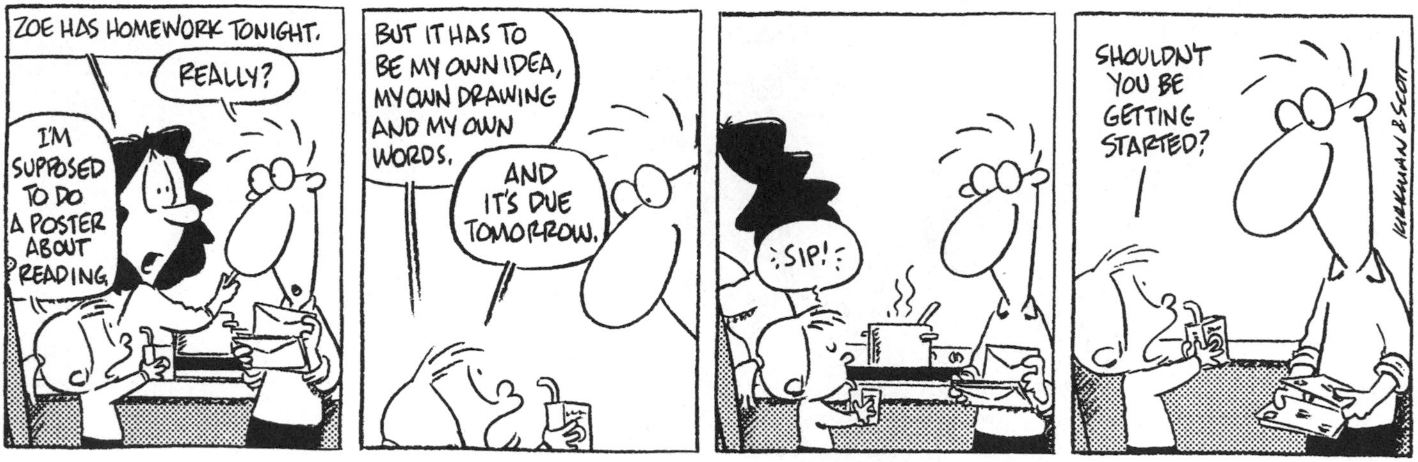
ZOE HAS HOMEWORK TONIGHT.
REALLY?
I'M SUPPOSED TO DO A POSTER ABOUT READING.
BUT IT HAS TO BE MY OWN IDEA, MY OWN DRAWING AND MY OWN WORDS.
AND IT'S DUE TOMORROW.
SIP!
SHOULDN'T YOU BE GETTING STARTED?
KIRKMAN & SCOTT

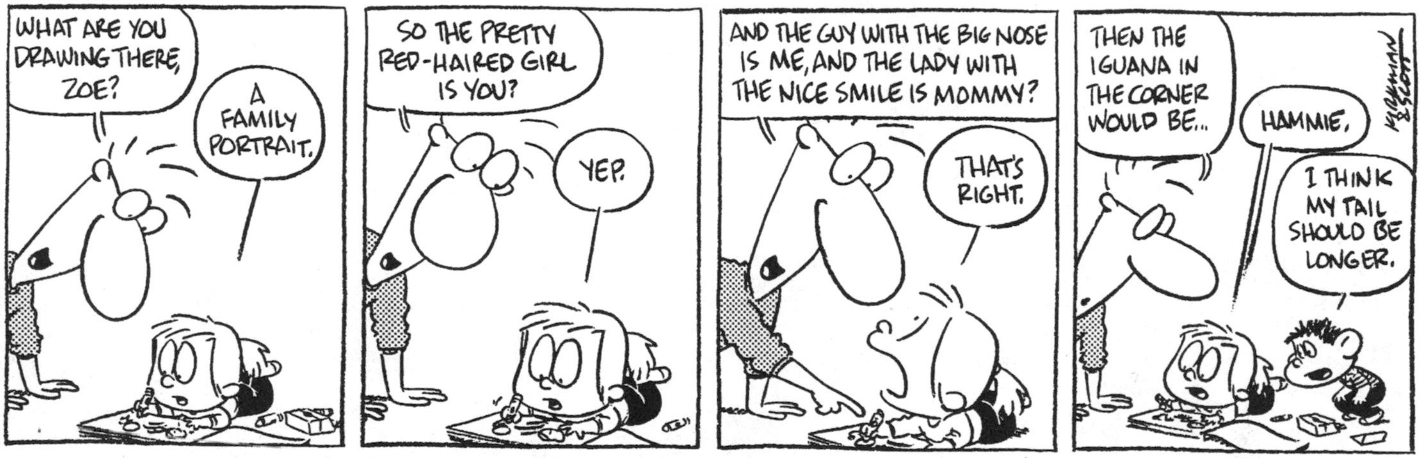
WHAT ARE YOU DRAWING THERE, ZOE?
A FAMILY PORTRAIT.
SO THE PRETTY RED-HAIRED GIRL IS YOU?
YEP.
AND THE GUY WITH THE BIG NOSE IS ME, AND THE LADY WITH THE NICE SMILE IS MOMMY?
THAT'S RIGHT.
THEN THE IGUANA IN THE CORNER WOULD BE...
HAMMIE.
I THINK MY TAIL SHOULD BE LONGER.
KIRKMAN & SCOTT

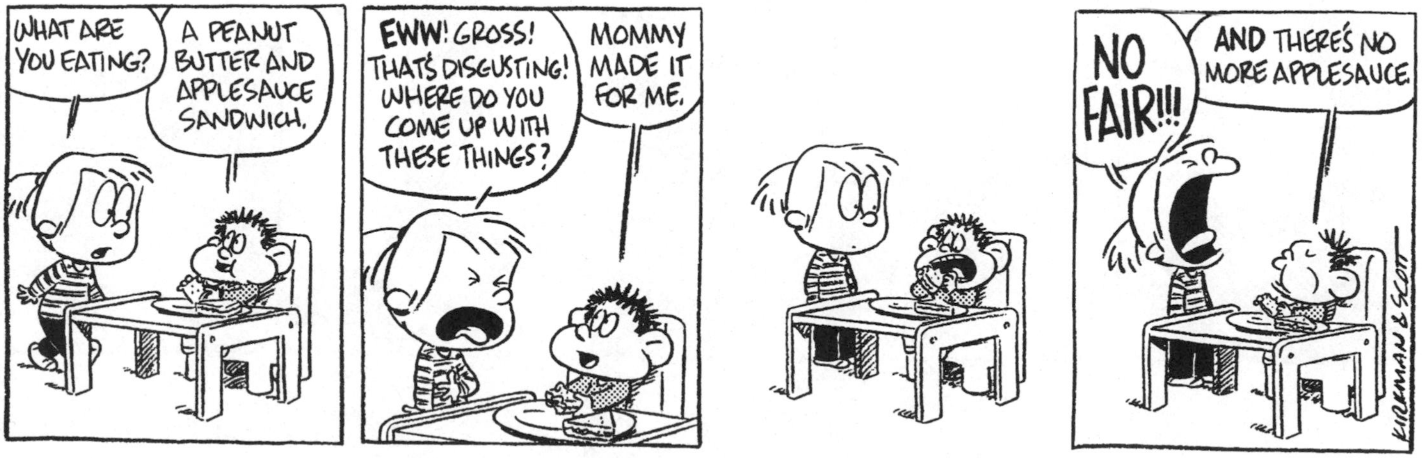
WHAT ARE YOU EATING?
A PEANUT BUTTER AND APPLESAUCE SANDWICH.
EWW! GROSS! THAT'S DISGUSTING! WHERE DO YOU COME UP WITH THESE THINGS?
MOMMY MADE IT FOR ME.
NO FAIR!!!
AND THERE'S NO MORE APPLESAUCE.
KIRKMAN & SCOTT

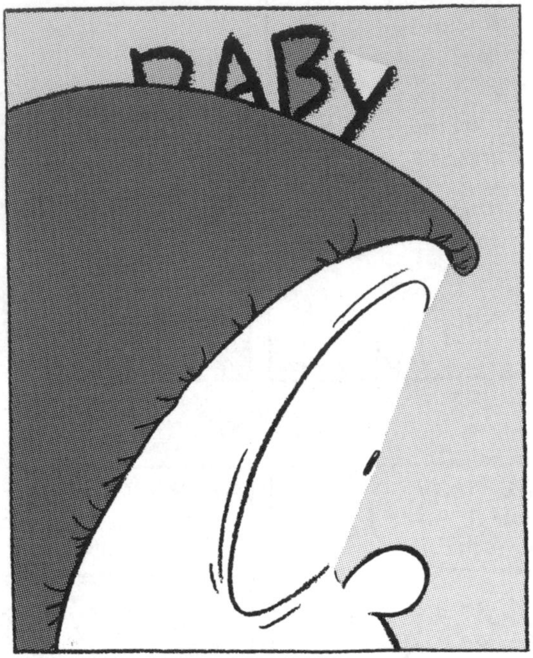
BABY

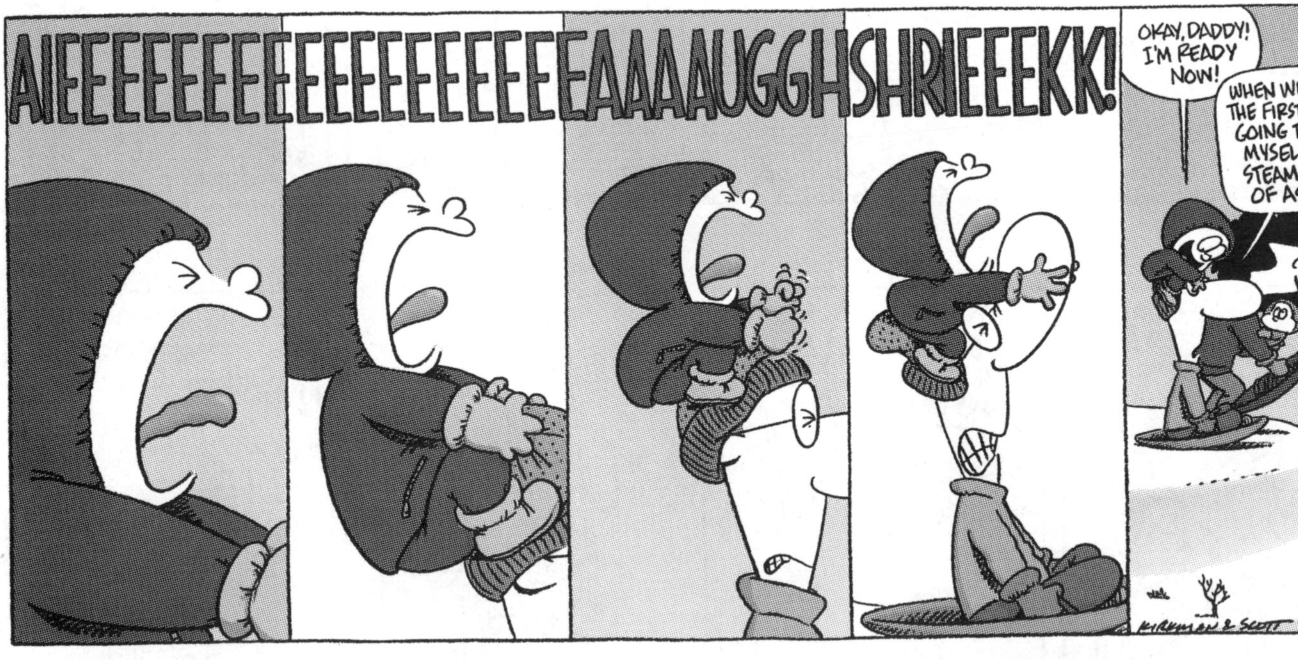
AIEEEEEEEEEEEEEEEEEEEEAAAAUGGHSHRIEEEKK!
OKAY, DADDY! I'M READY NOW!
WHEN WE GET HOME, THE FIRST THING I'M GOING TO DO IS FIX MYSELF A NICE, STEAMING CUP OF ASPIRIN.
KIRKMAN & SCOTT

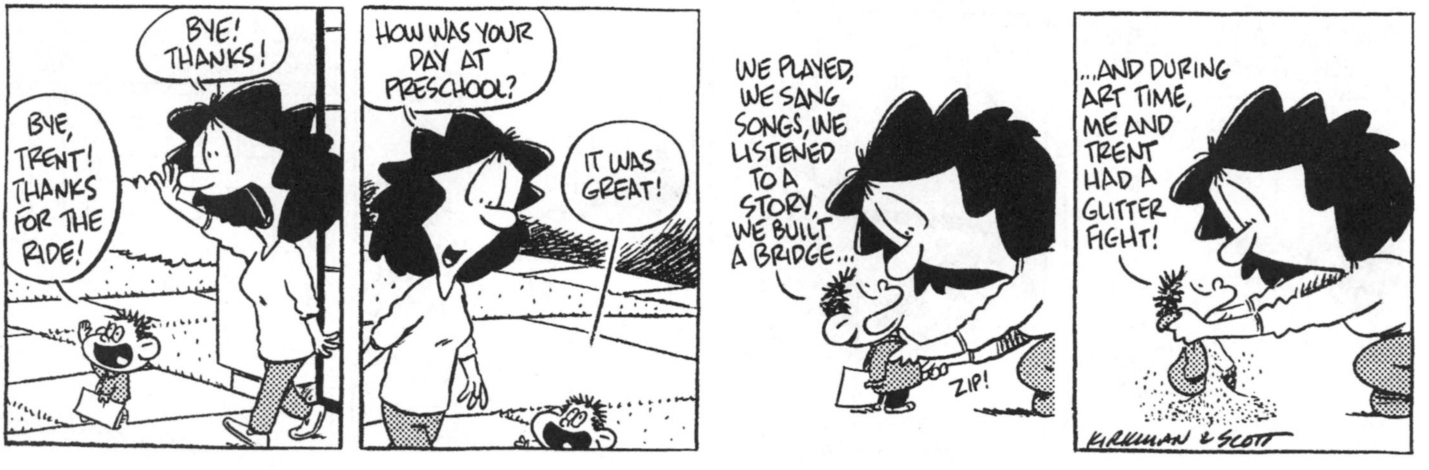
BYE, TRENT! THANKS FOR THE RIDE!
BYE! THANKS!
HOW WAS YOUR DAY AT PRESCHOOL?
IT WAS GREAT!
WE PLAYED, WE SANG SONGS, WE LISTENED TO A STORY, WE BUILT A BRIDGE...
ZIP!
...AND DURING ART TIME, ME AND TRENT HAD A GLITTER FIGHT!
KIRKMAN & SCOTT

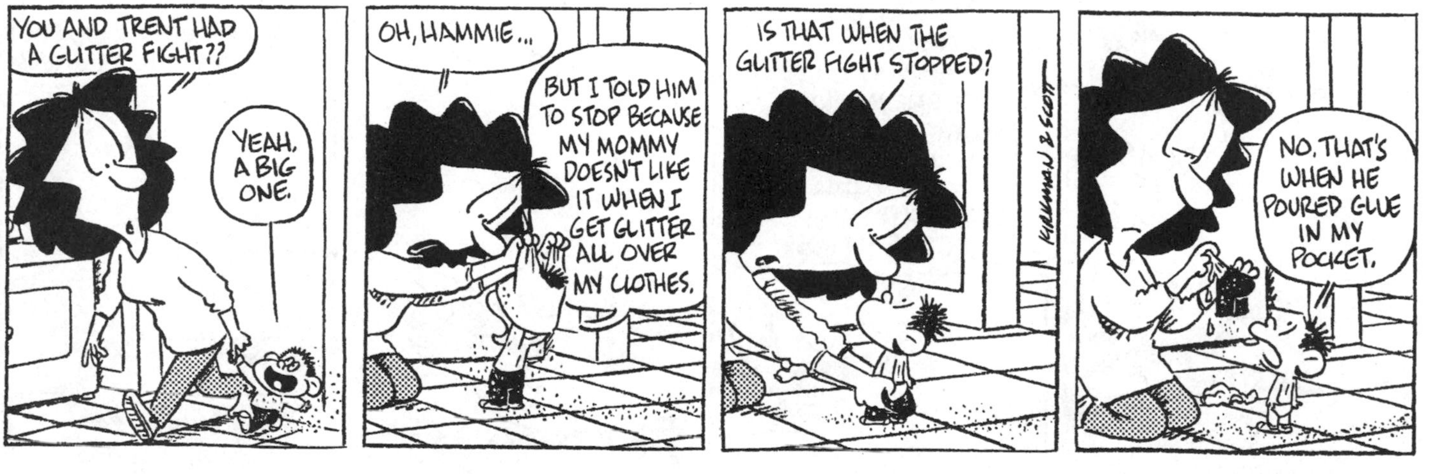
YOU AND TRENT HAD A GLITTER FIGHT??
YEAH. A BIG ONE.
OH, HAMMIE...
BUT I TOLD HIM TO STOP BECAUSE MY MOMMY DOESN'T LIKE IT WHEN I GET GLITTER ALL OVER MY CLOTHES.
IS THAT WHEN THE GLITTER FIGHT STOPPED?
KIRKMAN & SCOTT
NO. THAT'S WHEN HE POURED GLUE IN MY POCKET.

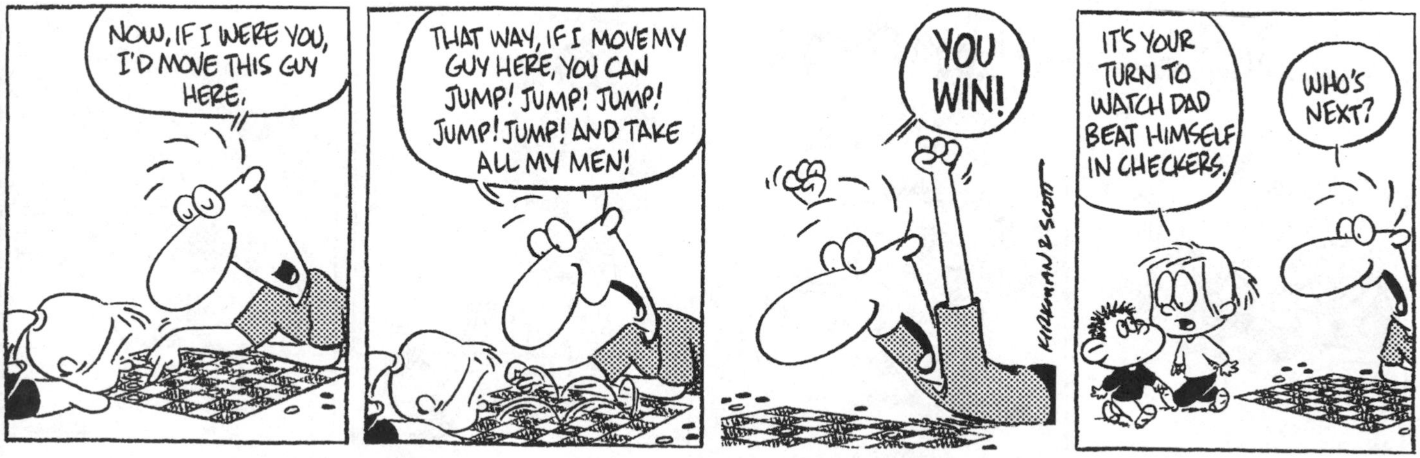
NOW, IF I WERE YOU, I'D MOVE THIS GUY HERE.
THAT WAY, IF I MOVE MY GUY HERE, YOU CAN JUMP! JUMP! JUMP! JUMP! JUMP! AND TAKE ALL MY MEN!
YOU WIN!
KIRKMAN & SCOTT
IT'S YOUR TURN TO WATCH DAD BEAT HIMSELF IN CHECKERS.
WHO'S NEXT?

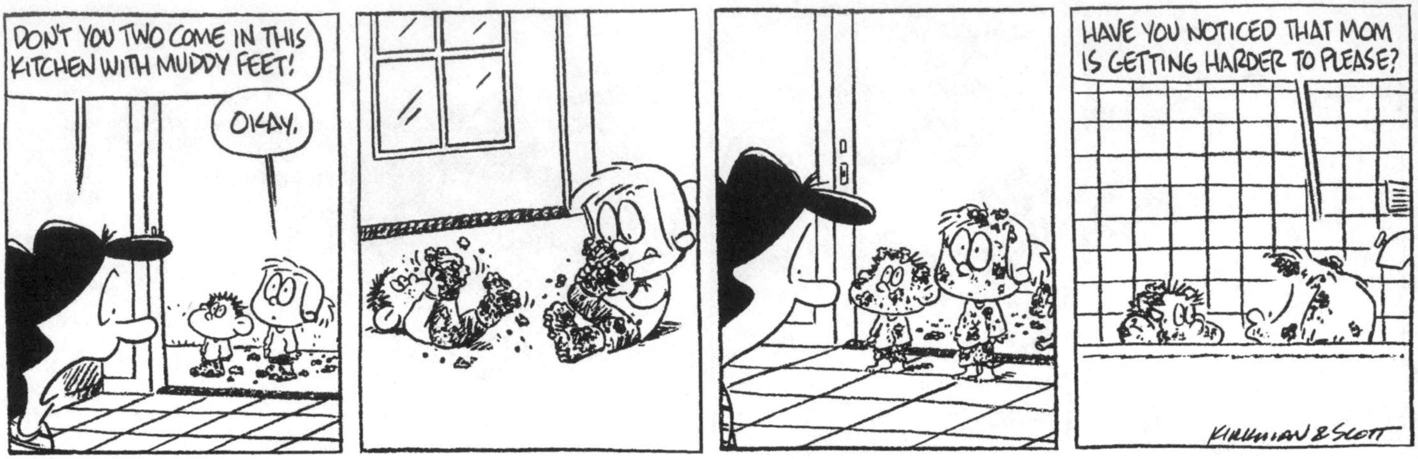
DON'T YOU TWO COME IN THIS KITCHEN WITH MUDDY FEET!
OKAY.
HAVE YOU NOTICED THAT MOM IS GETTING HARDER TO PLEASE?
KIRKMAN & SCOTT

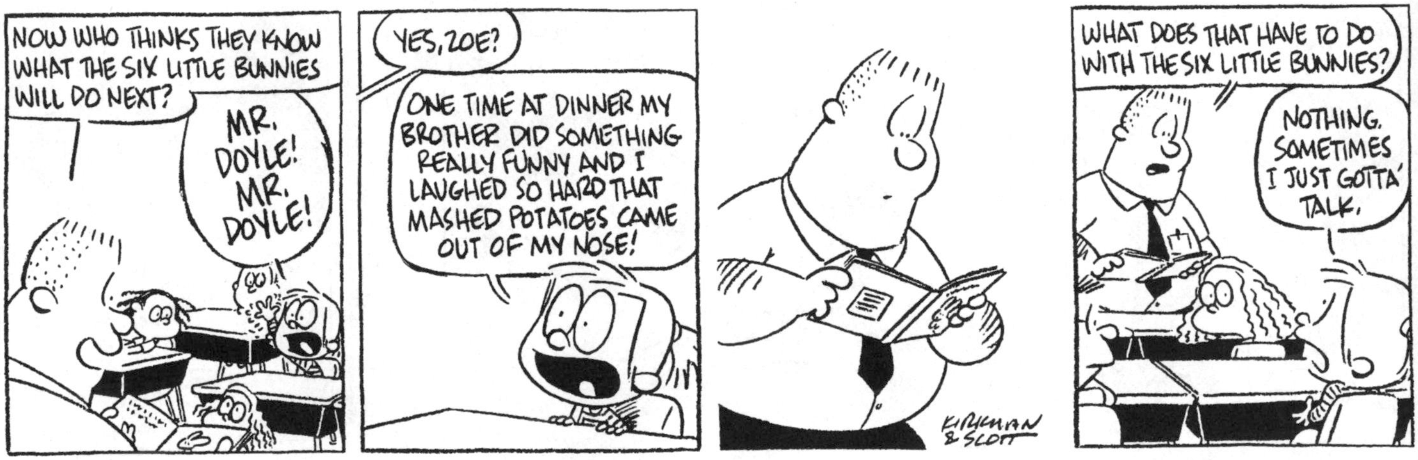
NOW WHO THINKS THEY KNOW WHAT THE SIX LITTLE BUNNIES WILL DO NEXT?
MR. DOYLE! MR. DOYLE!
YES, ZOE?
ONE TIME AT DINNER MY BROTHER DID SOMETHING REALLY FUNNY AND I LAUGHED SO HARD THAT MASHED POTATOES CAME OUT OF MY NOSE!
KIRKMAN & SCOTT
WHAT DOES THAT HAVE TO DO WITH THE SIX LITTLE BUNNIES?
NOTHING. SOMETIMES I JUST GOTTA' TALK.

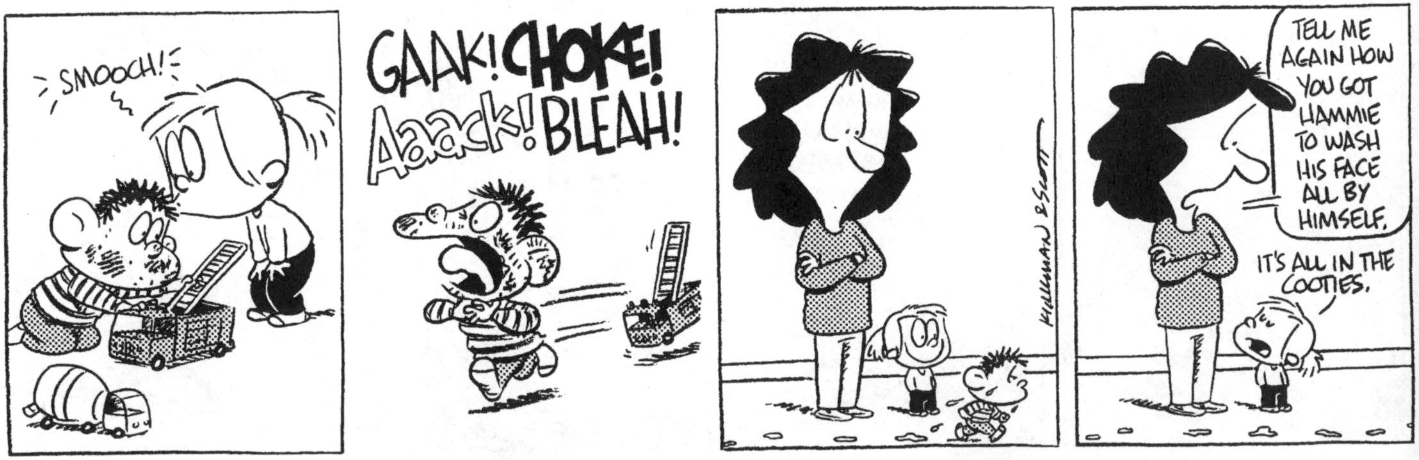
SMOOCH!
GAAK! CHOKE! Aaack! BLEAH!
KIRKMAN & SCOTT
TELL ME AGAIN HOW YOU GOT HAMMIE TO WASH HIS FACE ALL BY HIMSELF.
IT'S ALL IN THE COOTIES.

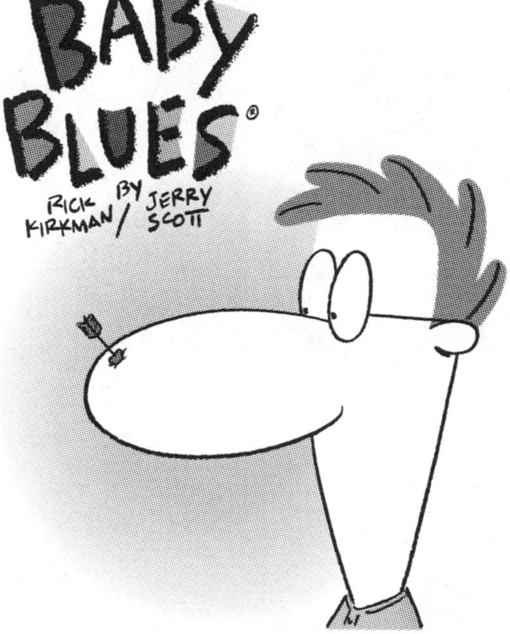
BABY BLUES®
BY RICK KIRKMAN / JERRY SCOTT

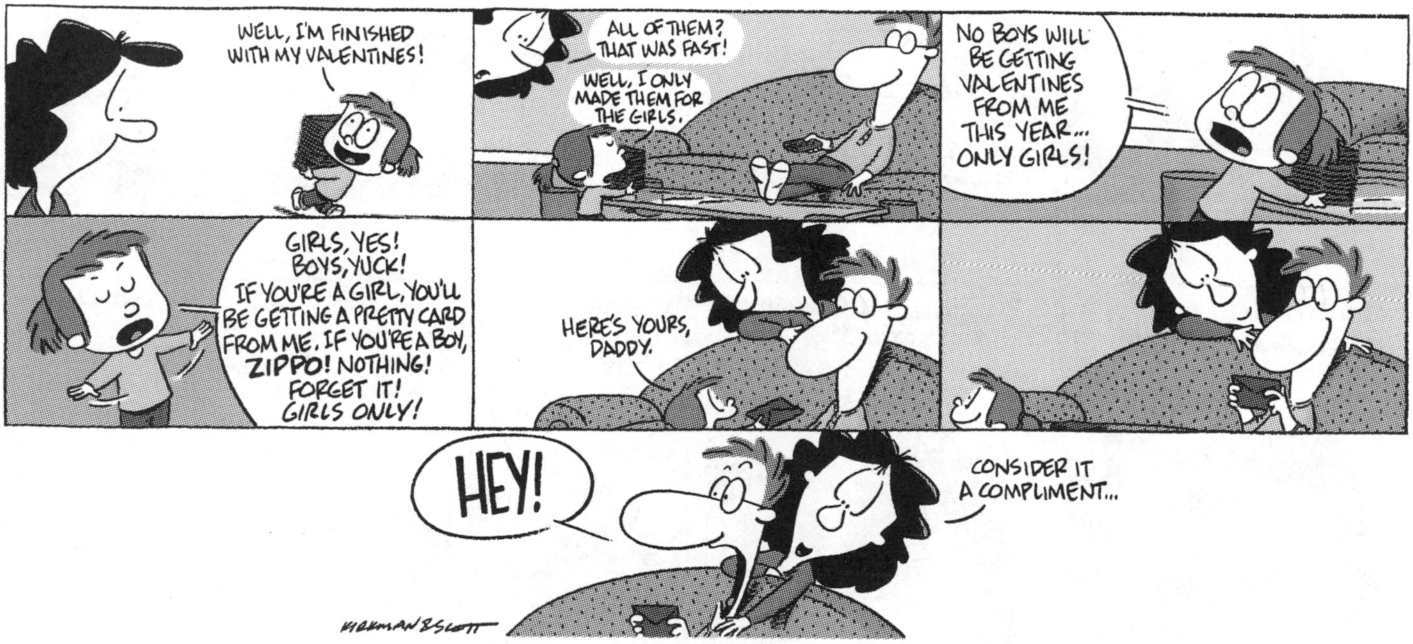
WELL, I'M FINISHED WITH MY VALENTINES!
ALL OF THEM? THAT WAS FAST!
WELL, I ONLY MADE THEM FOR THE GIRLS.
NO BOYS WILL BE GETTING VALENTINES FROM ME THIS YEAR... ONLY GIRLS!
GIRLS, YES! BOYS, YUCK! IF YOU'RE A GIRL, YOU'LL BE GETTING A PRETTY CARD FROM ME. IF YOU'RE A BOY, ZIPPO! NOTHING! FORGET IT! GIRLS ONLY!
HERE'S YOURS, DADDY.
HEY!
CONSIDER IT A COMPLIMENT...
KIRKMAN & SCOTT

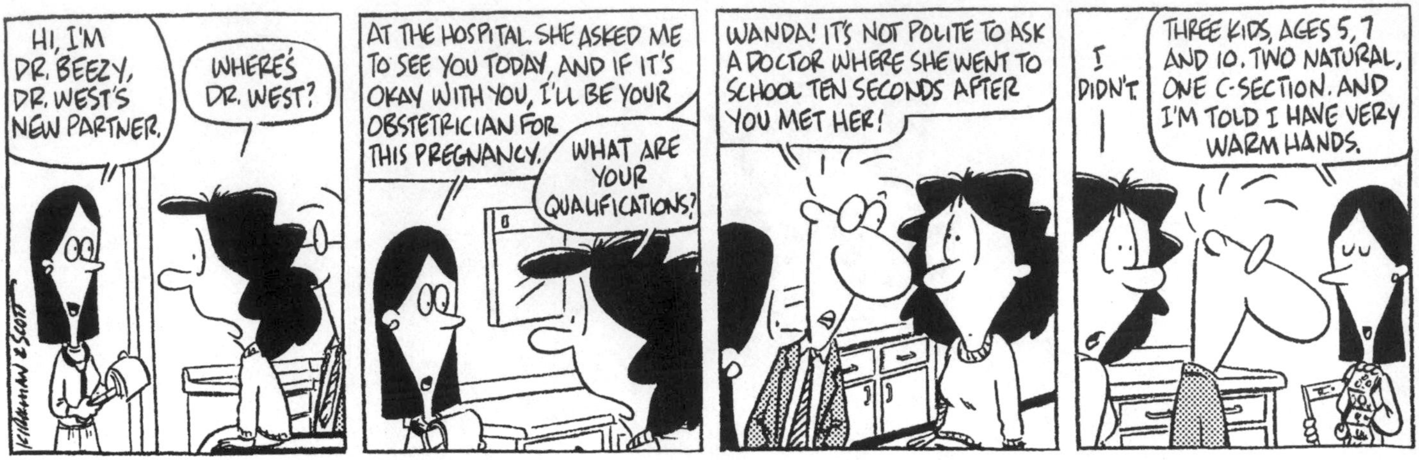
HI, I'M DR. BEEZY, DR. WEST'S NEW PARTNER.
WHERE'S DR. WEST?
AT THE HOSPITAL. SHE ASKED ME TO SEE YOU TODAY, AND IF IT'S OKAY WITH YOU, I'LL BE YOUR OBSTETRICIAN FOR THIS PREGNANCY.
WHAT ARE YOUR QUALIFICATIONS?
WANDA! IT'S NOT POLITE TO ASK A DOCTOR WHERE SHE WENT TO SCHOOL TEN SECONDS AFTER YOU MET HER!
I DIDN'T.
THREE KIDS, AGES 5, 7 AND 10. TWO NATURAL, ONE C-SECTION. AND I'M TOLD I HAVE VERY WARM HANDS.
KIRKMAN & SCOTT

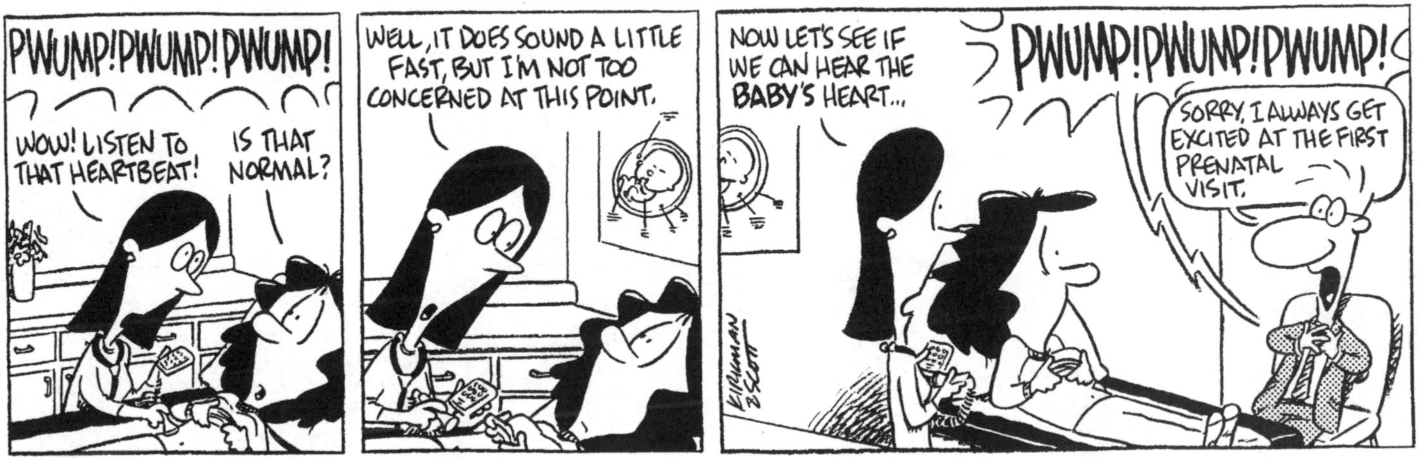
PWUMP! PWUMP! PWUMP!
WOW! LISTEN TO THAT HEARTBEAT!
IS THAT NORMAL?
WELL, IT DOES SOUND A LITTLE FAST, BUT I'M NOT TOO CONCERNED AT THIS POINT.
NOW LET'S SEE IF WE CAN HEAR THE BABY'S HEART...
PWUMP! PWUMP! PWUMP!
SORRY. I ALWAYS GET EXCITED AT THE FIRST PRENATAL VISIT.
KIRKMAN & SCOTT

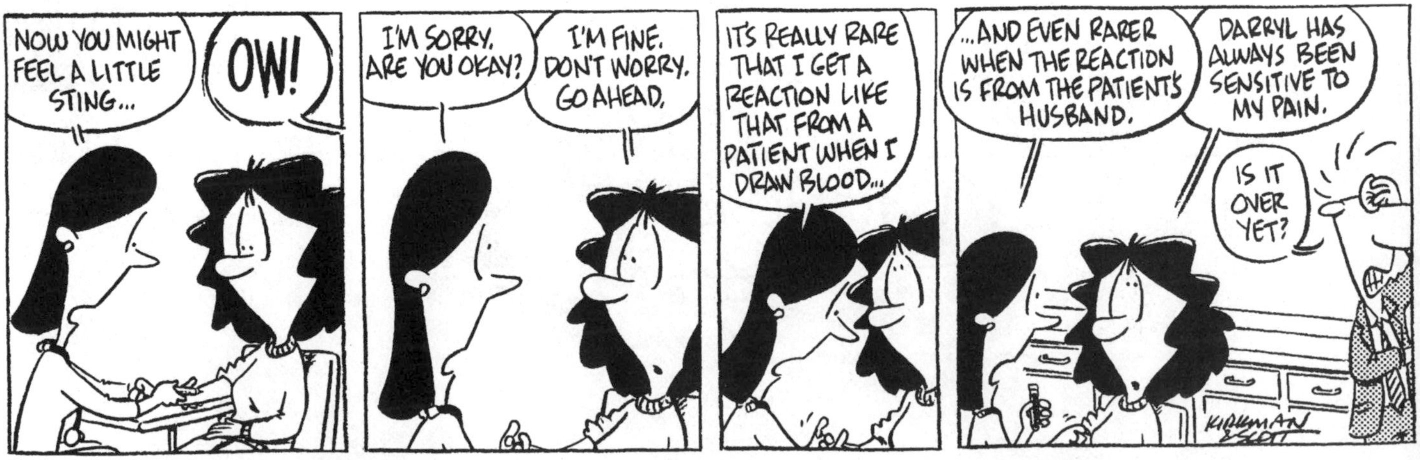
NOW YOU MIGHT FEEL A LITTLE STING...
OW!
I'M SORRY. ARE YOU OKAY?
I'M FINE. DON'T WORRY. GO AHEAD.
IT'S REALLY RARE THAT I GET A REACTION LIKE THAT FROM A PATIENT WHEN I DRAW BLOOD...
...AND EVEN RARER WHEN THE REACTION IS FROM THE PATIENT'S HUSBAND.
DARRYL HAS ALWAYS BEEN SENSITIVE TO MY PAIN.
IS IT OVER YET?
KIRKMAN & SCOTT

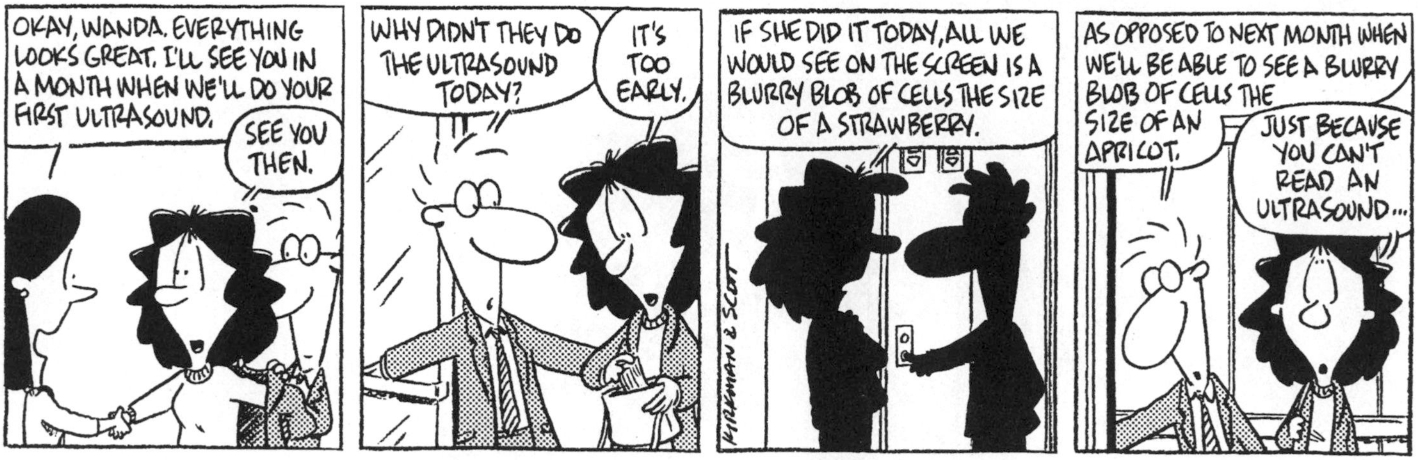
OKAY, WANDA. EVERYTHING LOOKS GREAT. I'LL SEE YOU IN A MONTH WHEN WE'LL DO YOUR FIRST ULTRASOUND.
SEE YOU THEN.
WHY DIDN'T THEY DO THE ULTRASOUND TODAY?
IT'S TOO EARLY.
IF SHE DID IT TODAY, ALL WE WOULD SEE ON THE SCREEN IS A BLURRY BLOB OF CELLS THE SIZE OF A STRAWBERRY.
KIRKMAN & SCOTT
AS OPPOSED TO NEXT MONTH WHEN WE'LL BE ABLE TO SEE A BLURRY BLOB OF CELLS THE SIZE OF AN APRICOT.
JUST BECAUSE YOU CAN'T READ AN ULTRASOUND...

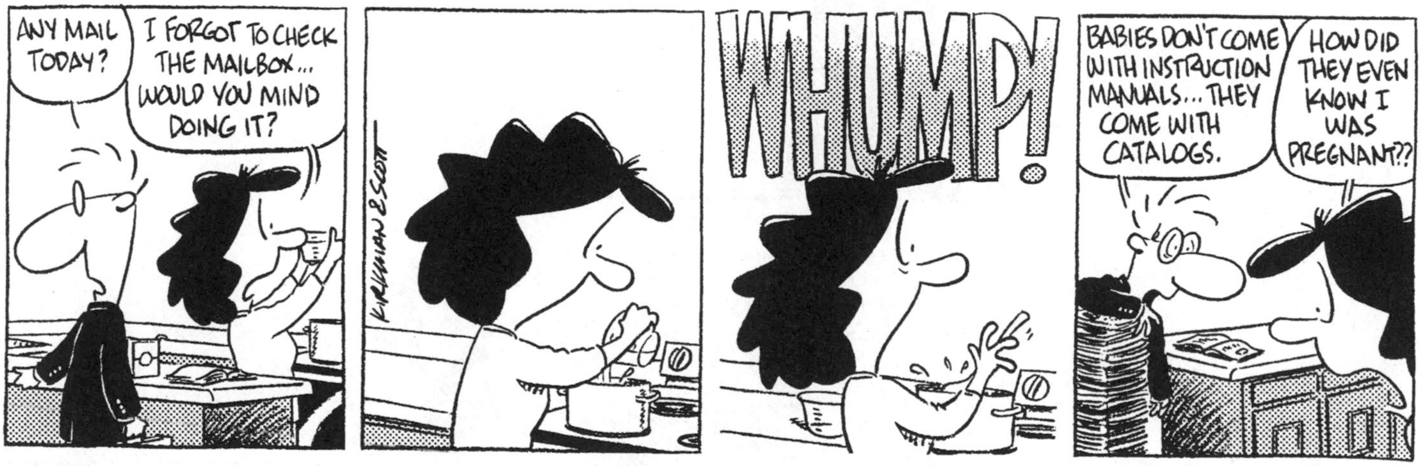
ANY MAIL TODAY?
I FORGOT TO CHECK THE MAILBOX... WOULD YOU MIND DOING IT?
KIRKMAN & SCOTT
WHUMP!
BABIES DON'T COME WITH INSTRUCTION MANUALS... THEY COME WITH CATALOGS.
HOW DID THEY EVEN KNOW I WAS PREGNANT??

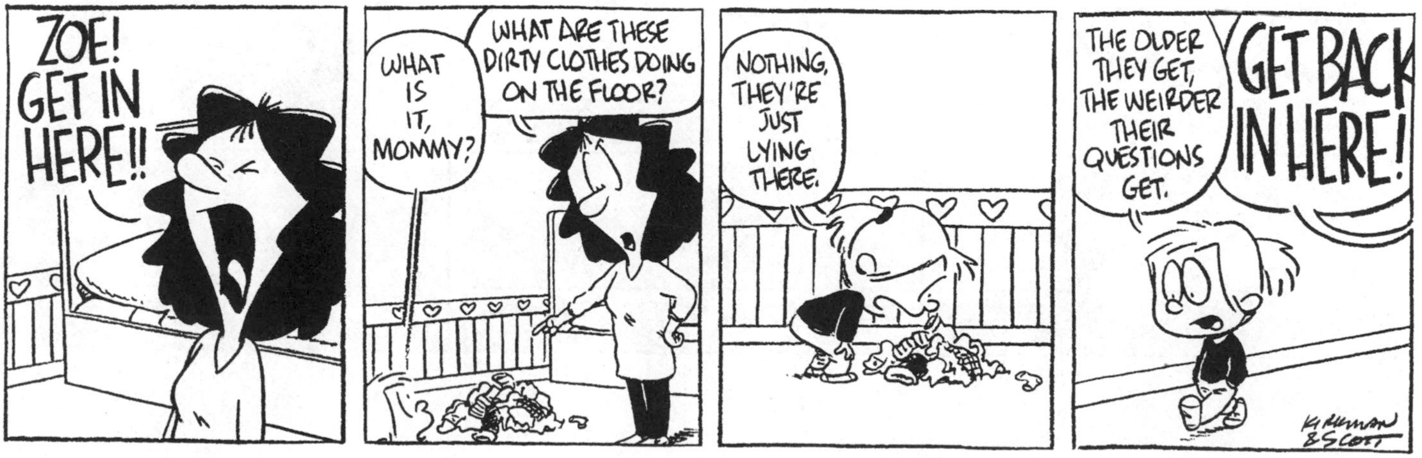
ZOE! GET IN HERE!!
WHAT IS IT, MOMMY?
WHAT ARE THESE DIRTY CLOTHES DOING ON THE FLOOR?
NOTHING, THEY'RE JUST LYING THERE.
THE OLDER THEY GET, THE WEIRDER THEIR QUESTIONS GET.
GET BACK IN HERE!
KIRKMAN & SCOTT

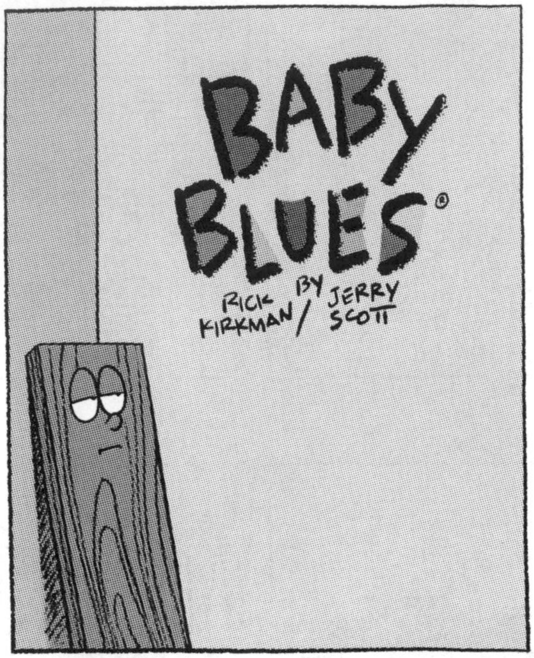
BABY BLUES®
BY RICK KIRKMAN / JERRY SCOTT

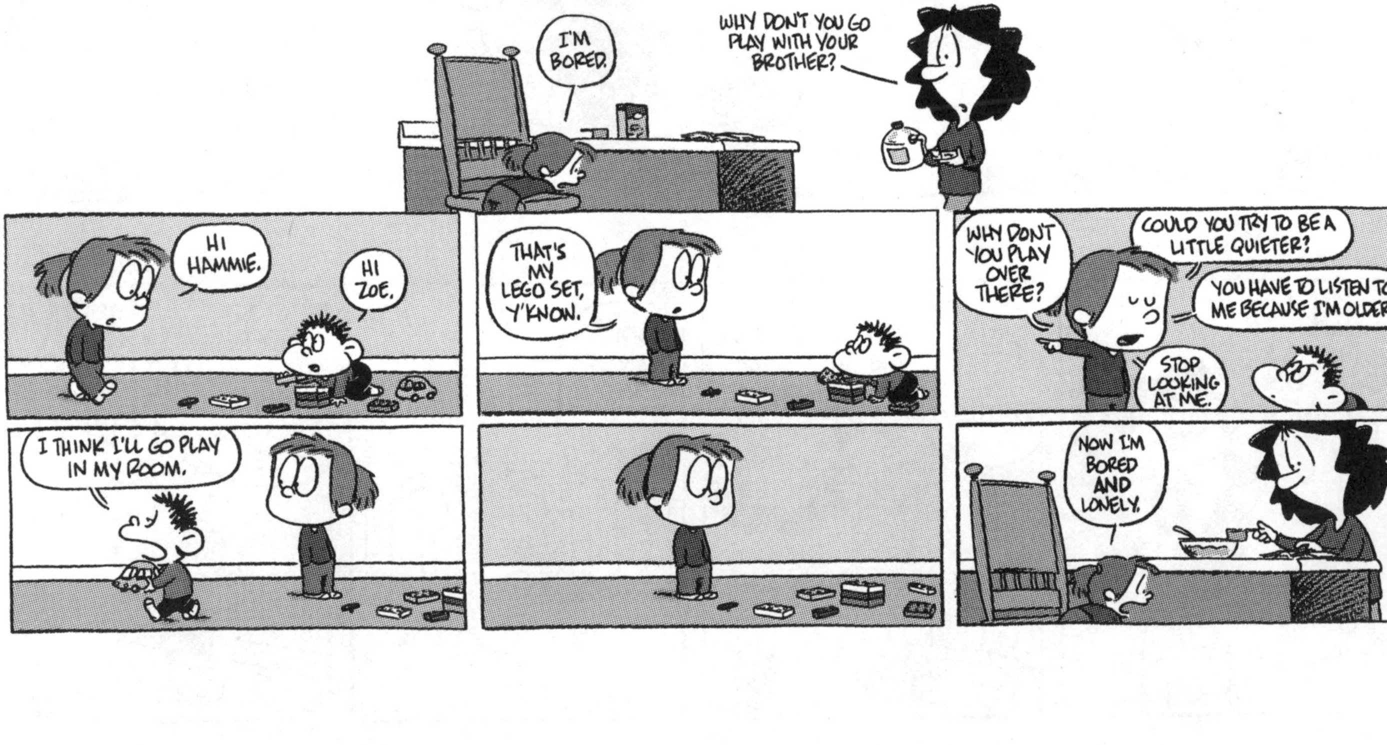
I'M BORED.
WHY DON'T YOU GO PLAY WITH YOUR BROTHER?
HI HAMMIE.
HI ZOE.
THAT'S MY LEGO SET, Y'KNOW.
WHY DON'T YOU PLAY OVER THERE?
COULD YOU TRY TO BE A LITTLE QUIETER?
YOU HAVE TO LISTEN TO ME BECAUSE I'M OLDER.
STOP LOOKING AT ME.
I THINK I'LL GO PLAY IN MY ROOM.
NOW I'M BORED AND LONELY.

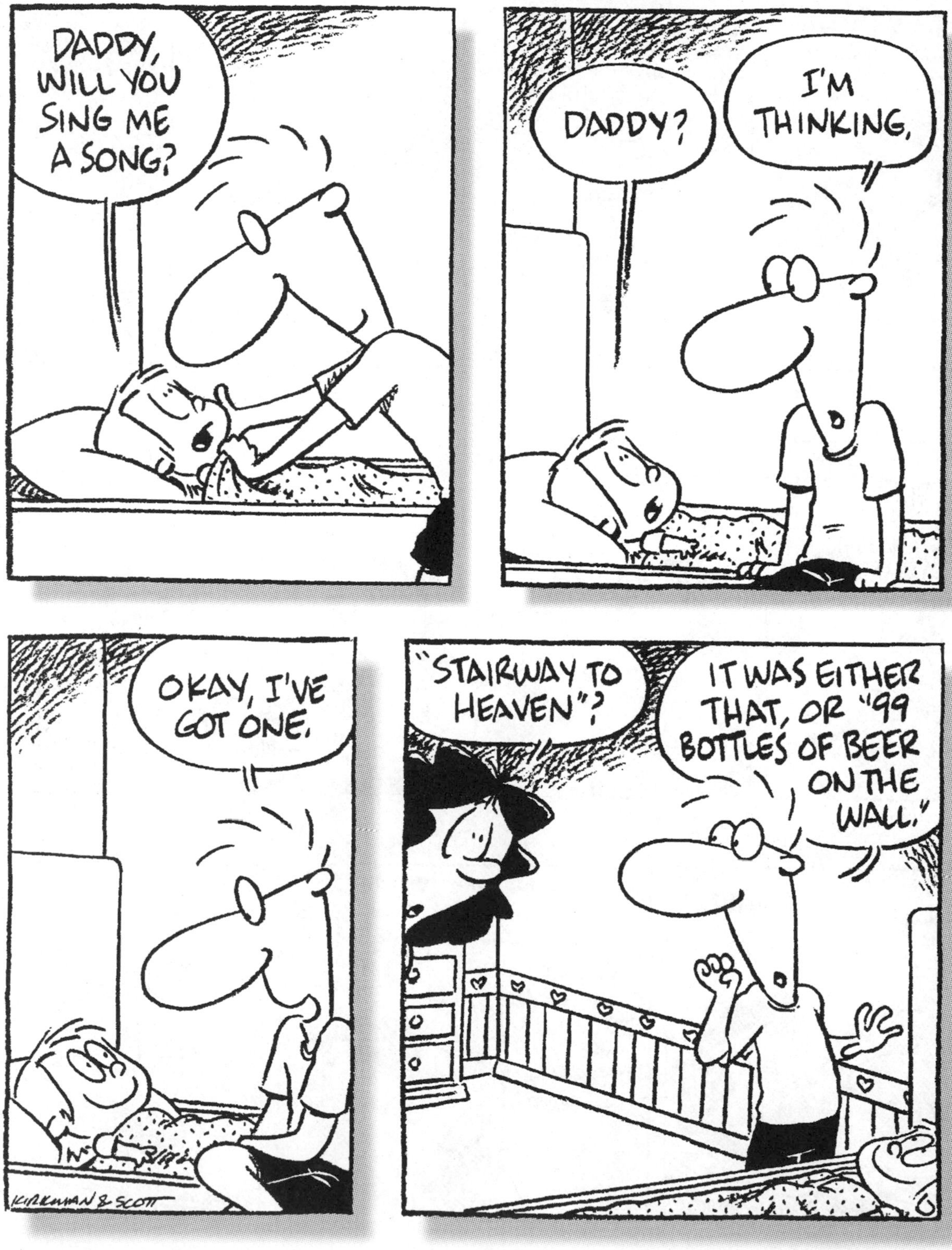
DADDY, WILL YOU SING ME A SONG?
DADDY?
I'M THINKING.
OKAY, I'VE GOT ONE.
"STAIRWAY TO HEAVEN"?
IT WAS EITHER THAT, OR "99 BOTTLES OF BEER ON THE WALL."
KIRKMAN & SCOTT

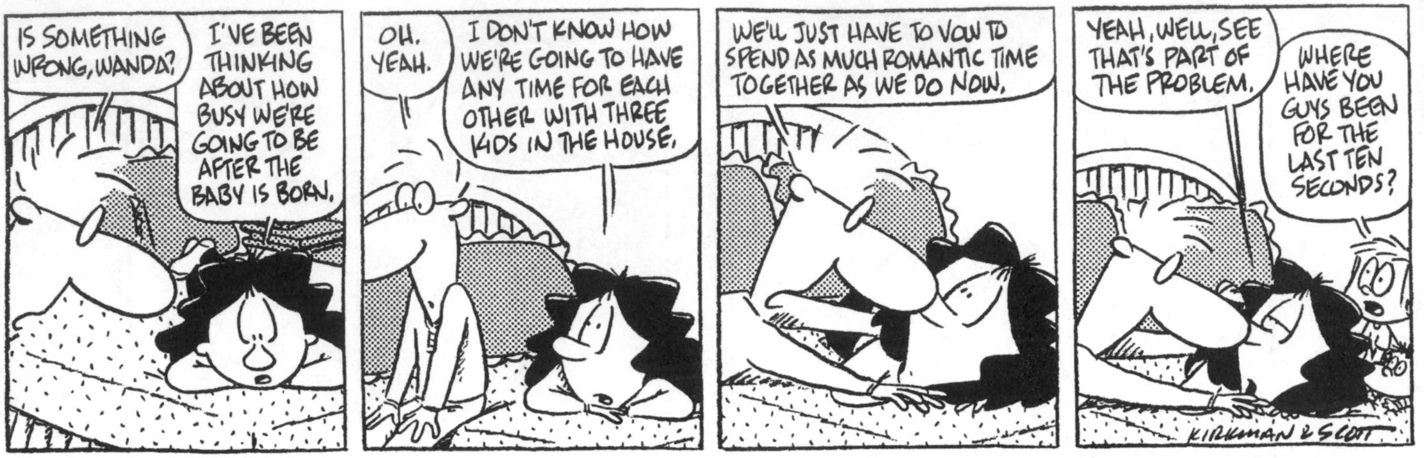
IS SOMETHING WRONG, WANDA?
I'VE BEEN THINKING ABOUT HOW BUSY WE'RE GOING TO BE AFTER THE BABY IS BORN.
OH. YEAH.
I DON'T KNOW HOW WE'RE GOING TO HAVE ANY TIME FOR EACH OTHER WITH THREE KIDS IN THE HOUSE.
WE'LL JUST HAVE TO VOW TO SPEND AS MUCH ROMANTIC TIME TOGETHER AS WE DO NOW.
YEAH, WELL, SEE THAT'S PART OF THE PROBLEM.
WHERE HAVE YOU GUYS BEEN FOR THE LAST TEN SECONDS?
KIRKMAN & SCOTT

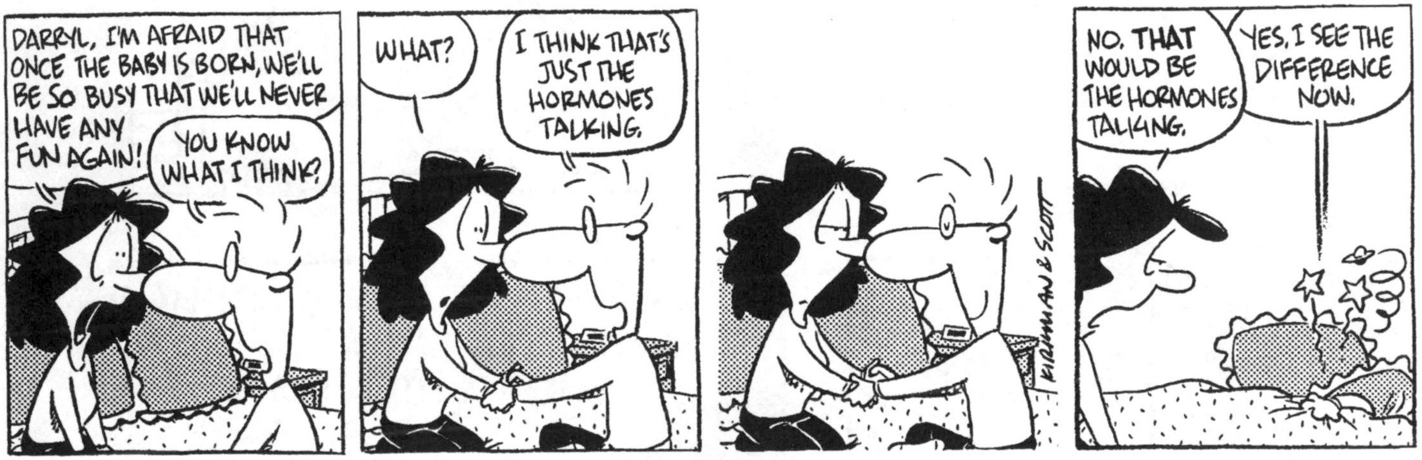
DARRYL, I'M AFRAID THAT ONCE THE BABY IS BORN, WE'LL BE SO BUSY THAT WE'LL NEVER HAVE ANY FUN AGAIN!
YOU KNOW WHAT I THINK?
WHAT?
I THINK THAT'S JUST THE HORMONES TALKING.
KIRKMAN & SCOTT
NO. THAT WOULD BE THE HORMONES TALKING.
YES. I SEE THE DIFFERENCE NOW.

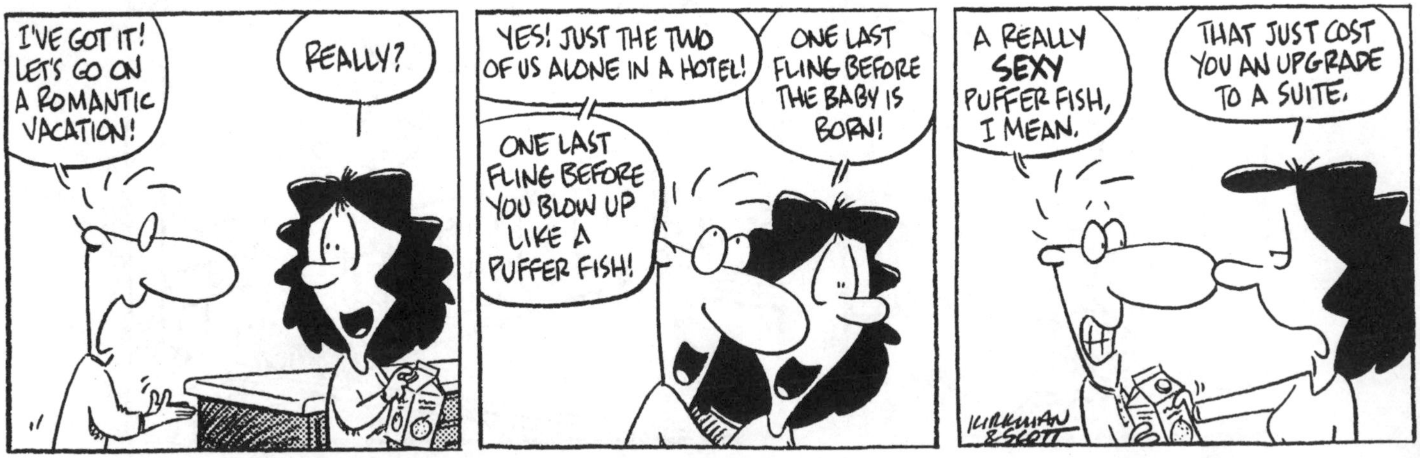
I'VE GOT IT! LET'S GO ON A ROMANTIC VACATION!
REALLY?
YES! JUST THE TWO OF US ALONE IN A HOTEL!
ONE LAST FLING BEFORE THE BABY IS BORN!
ONE LAST FLING BEFORE YOU BLOW UP LIKE A PUFFER FISH!
A REALLY SEXY PUFFER FISH, I MEAN.
THAT JUST COST YOU AN UPGRADE TO A SUITE.
KIRKMAN & SCOTT

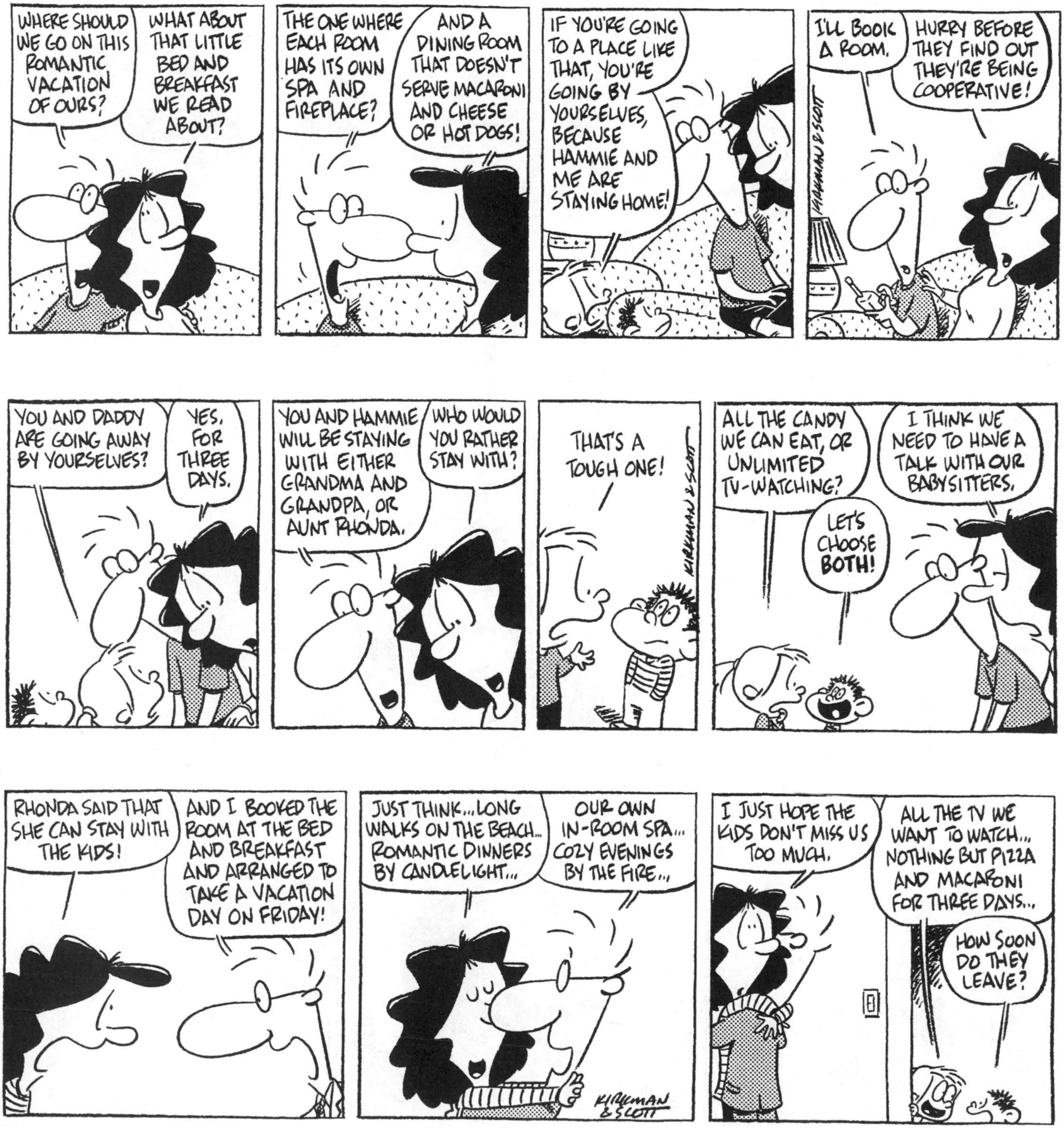
WHERE SHOULD WE GO ON THIS ROMANTIC VACATION OF OURS?
WHAT ABOUT THAT LITTLE BED AND BREAKFAST WE READ ABOUT?
THE ONE WHERE EACH ROOM HAS ITS OWN SPA AND FIREPLACE?
AND A DINING ROOM THAT DOESN'T SERVE MACARONI AND CHEESE OR HOT DOGS!
IF YOU'RE GOING TO A PLACE LIKE THAT, YOU'RE GOING BY YOURSELVES, BECAUSE HAMMIE AND ME ARE STAYING HOME!
I'LL BOOK A ROOM.
HURRY BEFORE THEY FIND OUT THEY'RE BEING COOPERATIVE!
KIRKMAN & SCOTT
YOU AND DADDY ARE GOING AWAY BY YOURSELVES?
YES. FOR THREE DAYS.
YOU AND HAMMIE WILL BE STAYING WITH EITHER GRANDMA AND GRANDPA, OR AUNT RHONDA.
WHO WOULD YOU RATHER STAY WITH?
THAT'S A TOUGH ONE!
KIRKMAN & SCOTT
ALL THE CANDY WE CAN EAT, OR UNLIMITED TV-WATCHING?
LET'S CHOOSE **BOTH!**
I THINK WE NEED TO HAVE A TALK WITH OUR BABYSITTERS.
RHONDA SAID THAT SHE CAN STAY WITH THE KIDS!
AND I BOOKED THE ROOM AT THE BED AND BREAKFAST AND ARRANGED TO TAKE A VACATION DAY ON FRIDAY!
JUST THINK...LONG WALKS ON THE BEACH... ROMANTIC DINNERS BY CANDLELIGHT...
OUR OWN IN-ROOM SPA... COZY EVENINGS BY THE FIRE...
KIRKMAN & SCOTT
I JUST HOPE THE KIDS DON'T MISS US TOO MUCH.
ALL THE TV WE WANT TO WATCH... NOTHING BUT PIZZA AND MACARONI FOR THREE DAYS...
HOW SOON DO THEY LEAVE?

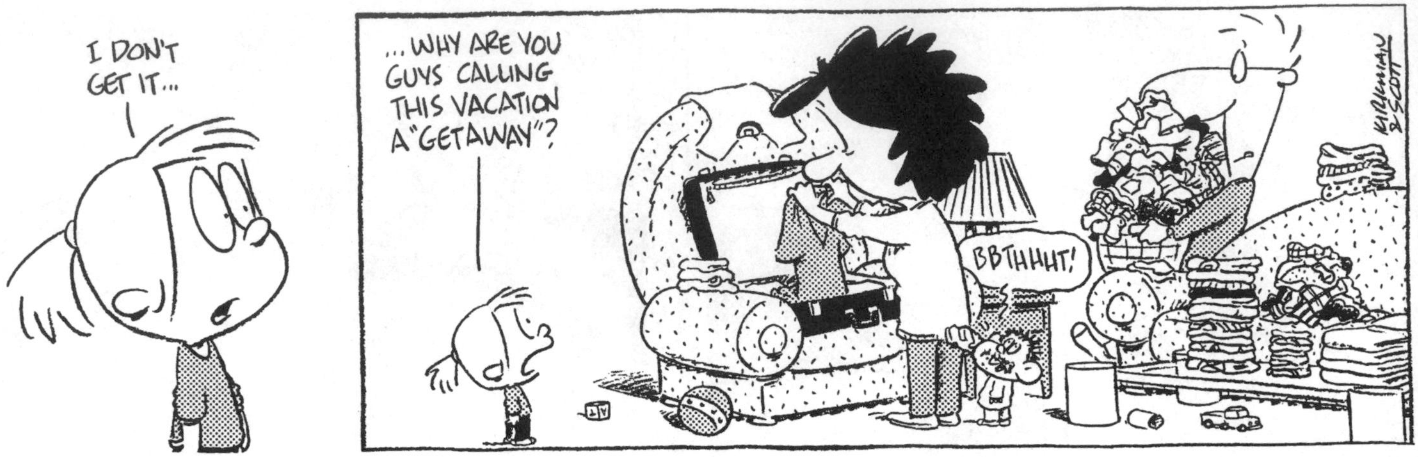
I DON'T GET IT...
...WHY ARE YOU GUYS CALLING THIS VACATION A "GETAWAY"?
BBTHHHT!
KIRKMAN & SCOTT

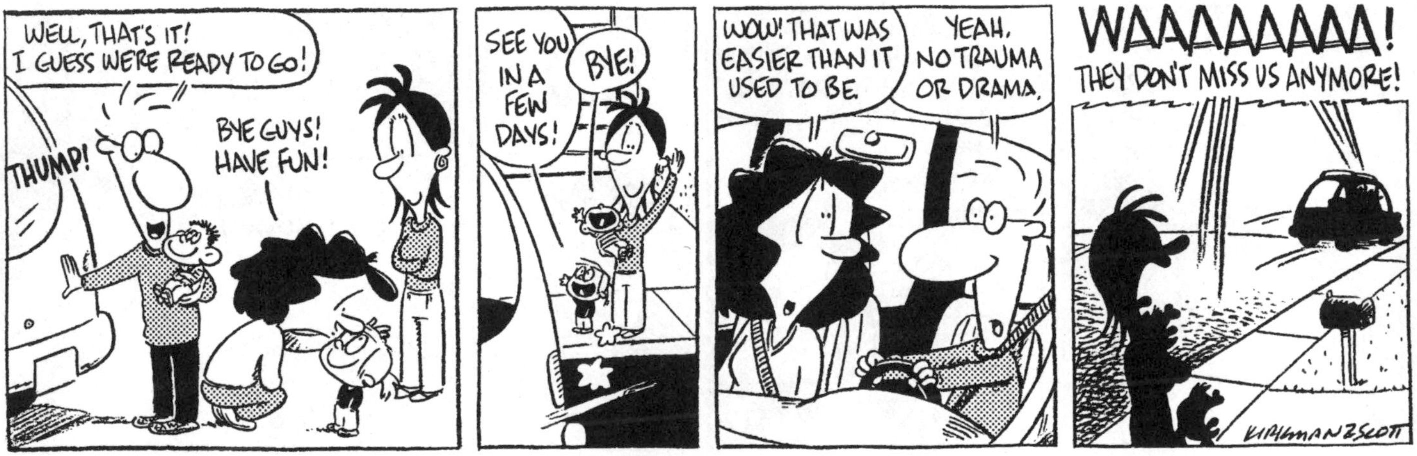
WELL, THAT'S IT! I GUESS WE'RE READY TO GO!
THUMP!
BYE GUYS! HAVE FUN!
SEE YOU IN A FEW DAYS!
BYE!
WOW! THAT WAS EASIER THAN IT USED TO BE.
YEAH. NO TRAUMA OR DRAMA.
WAAAAAAAA!
THEY DON'T MISS US ANYMORE!
KIRKMAN & SCOTT

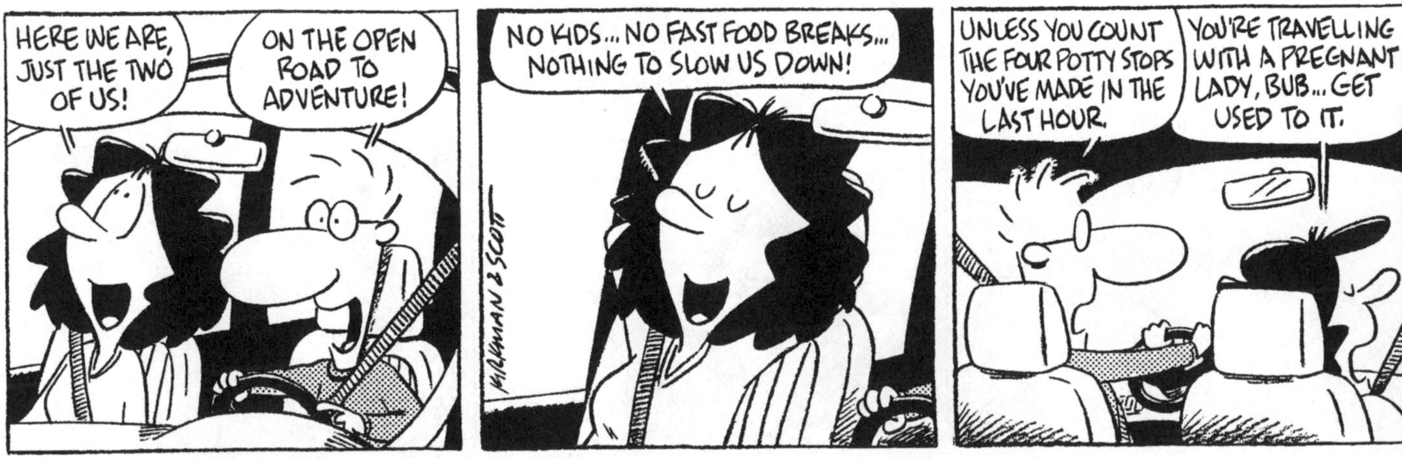
HERE WE ARE, JUST THE TWO OF US!
ON THE OPEN ROAD TO ADVENTURE!
KIRKMAN & SCOTT
NO KIDS... NO FAST FOOD BREAKS... NOTHING TO SLOW US DOWN!
UNLESS YOU COUNT THE FOUR POTTY STOPS YOU'VE MADE IN THE LAST HOUR.
YOU'RE TRAVELLING WITH A PREGNANT LADY, BUB... GET USED TO IT.

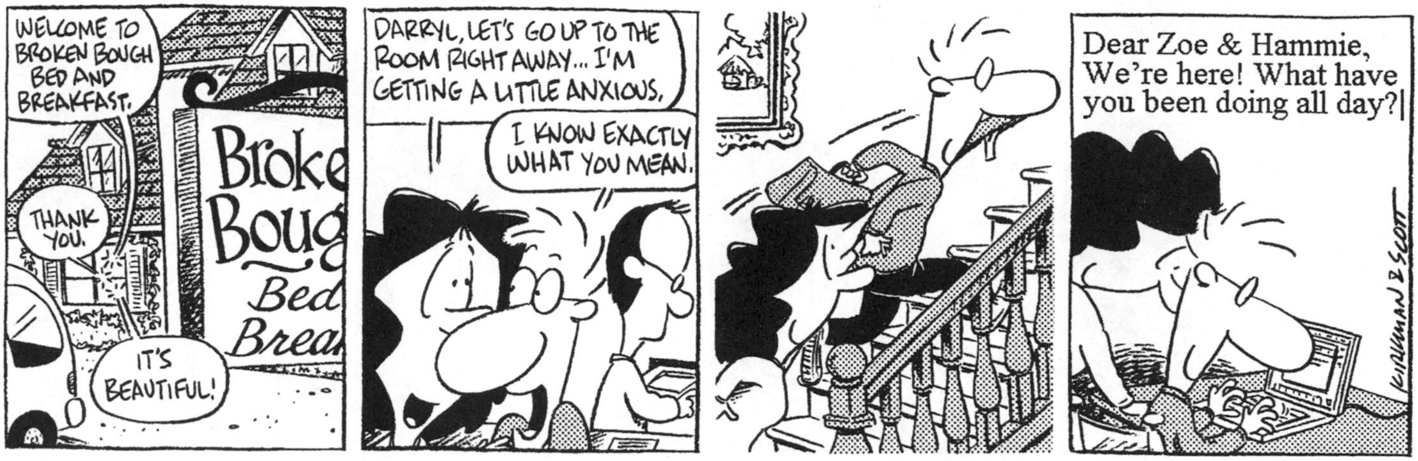
WELCOME TO BROKEN BOUGH BED AND BREAKFAST.
THANK YOU.
IT'S BEAUTIFUL!
Broke
Boug
Bed
Brea
DARRYL, LET'S GO UP TO THE ROOM RIGHT AWAY... I'M GETTING A LITTLE ANXIOUS.
I KNOW EXACTLY WHAT YOU MEAN.
Dear Zoe & Hammie,
We're here! What have you been doing all day?|
KIRKMAN & SCOTT

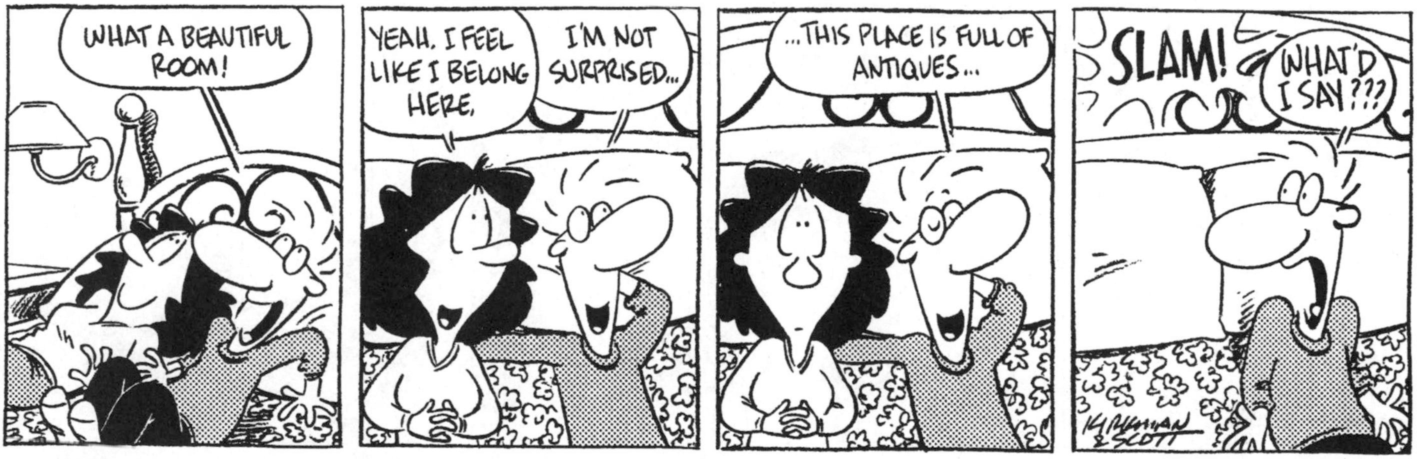
WHAT A BEAUTIFUL ROOM!
YEAH. I FEEL LIKE I BELONG HERE.
I'M NOT SURPRISED...
...THIS PLACE IS FULL OF ANTIQUES...
SLAM!
WHAT'D I SAY???
KIRKMAN & SCOTT

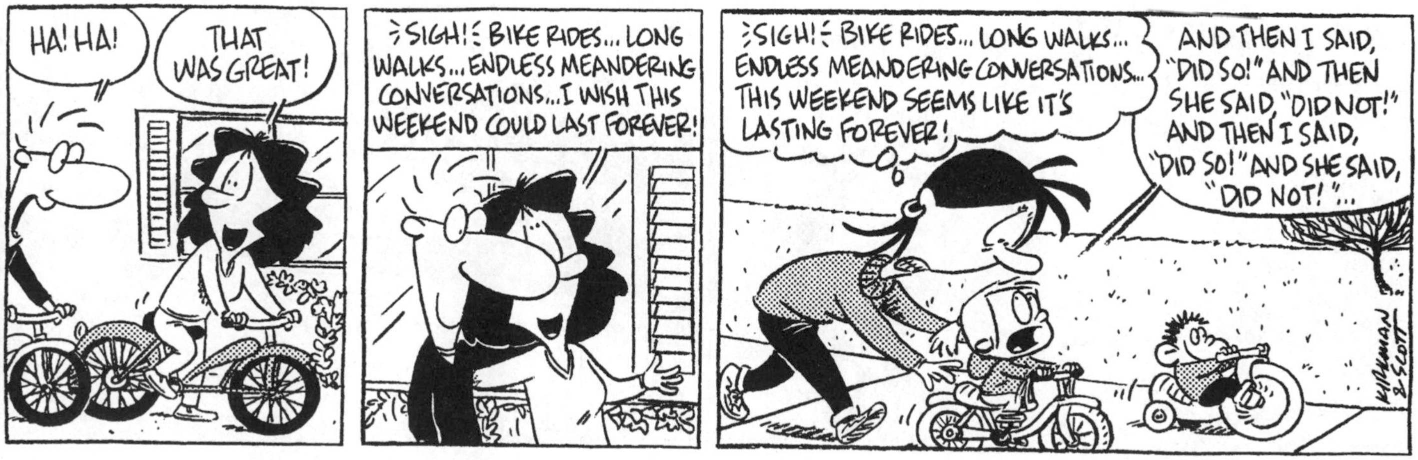
HA! HA!
THAT WAS GREAT!
SIGH! BIKE RIDES... LONG WALKS... ENDLESS MEANDERING CONVERSATIONS... I WISH THIS WEEKEND COULD LAST FOREVER!
SIGH! BIKE RIDES... LONG WALKS... ENDLESS MEANDERING CONVERSATIONS... THIS WEEKEND SEEMS LIKE IT'S LASTING FOREVER!
AND THEN I SAID, "DID SO!" AND THEN SHE SAID, "DID NOT!" AND THEN I SAID, "DID SO!" AND SHE SAID, "DID NOT!"...
KIRKMAN & SCOTT

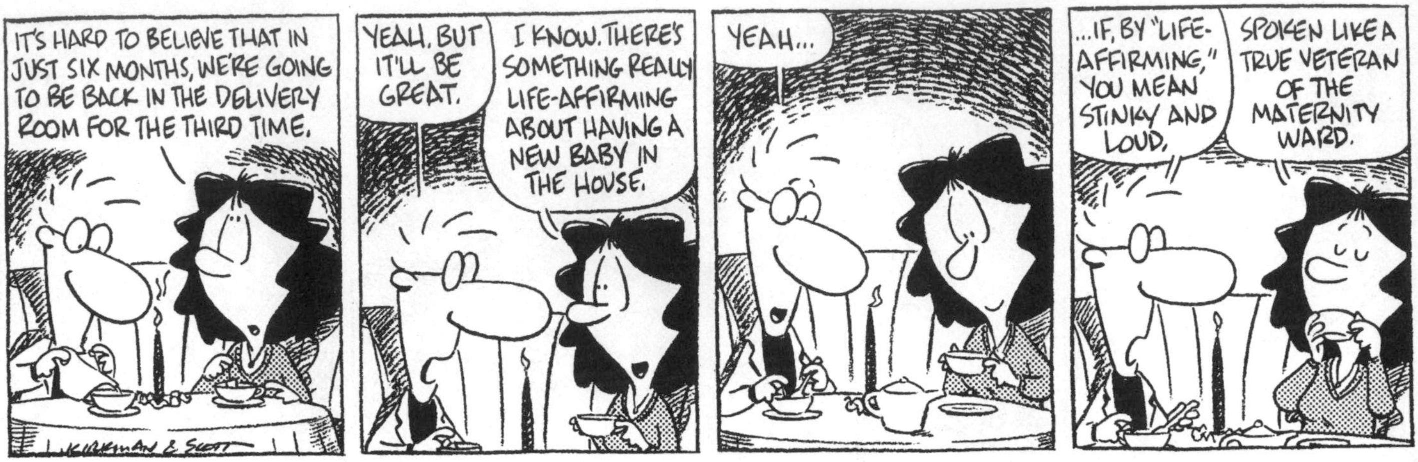
IT'S HARD TO BELIEVE THAT IN JUST SIX MONTHS, WE'RE GOING TO BE BACK IN THE DELIVERY ROOM FOR THE THIRD TIME.
KIRKMAN & SCOTT
YEAH. BUT IT'LL BE GREAT.
I KNOW. THERE'S SOMETHING REALLY LIFE-AFFIRMING ABOUT HAVING A NEW BABY IN THE HOUSE.
YEAH...
...IF, BY "LIFE-AFFIRMING," YOU MEAN STINKY AND LOUD.
SPOKEN LIKE A TRUE VETERAN OF THE MATERNITY WARD.

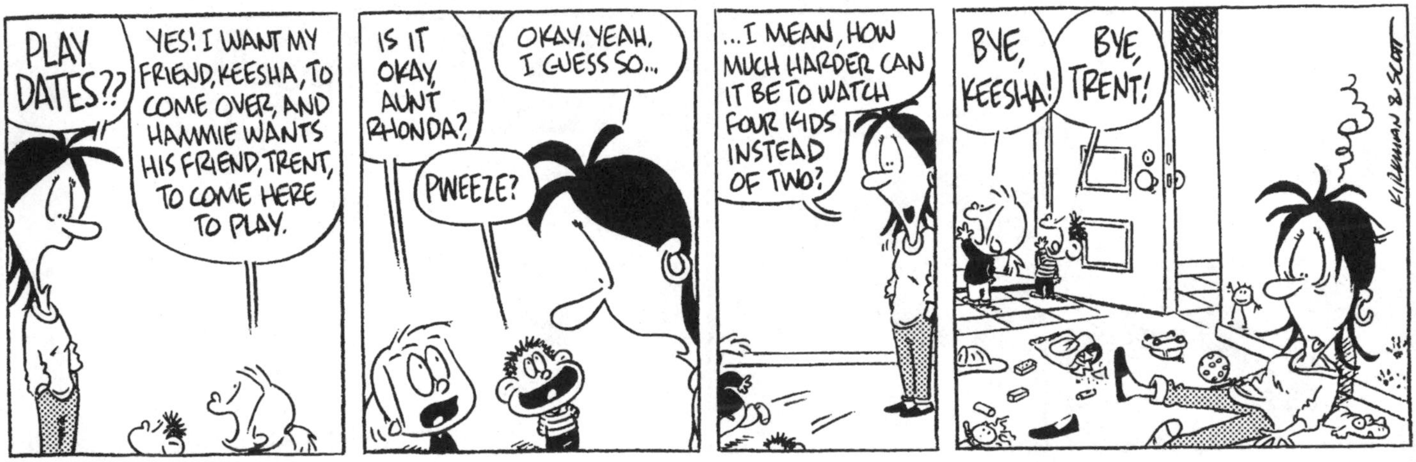
PLAY DATES??
YES! I WANT MY FRIEND, KEESHA, TO COME OVER, AND HAMMIE WANTS HIS FRIEND, TRENT, TO COME HERE TO PLAY.
IS IT OKAY, AUNT RHONDA?
PWEEZE?
OKAY. YEAH. I GUESS SO...
...I MEAN, HOW MUCH HARDER CAN IT BE TO WATCH FOUR KIDS INSTEAD OF TWO?
BYE, KEESHA!
BYE, TRENT!
KIRKMAN & SCOTT

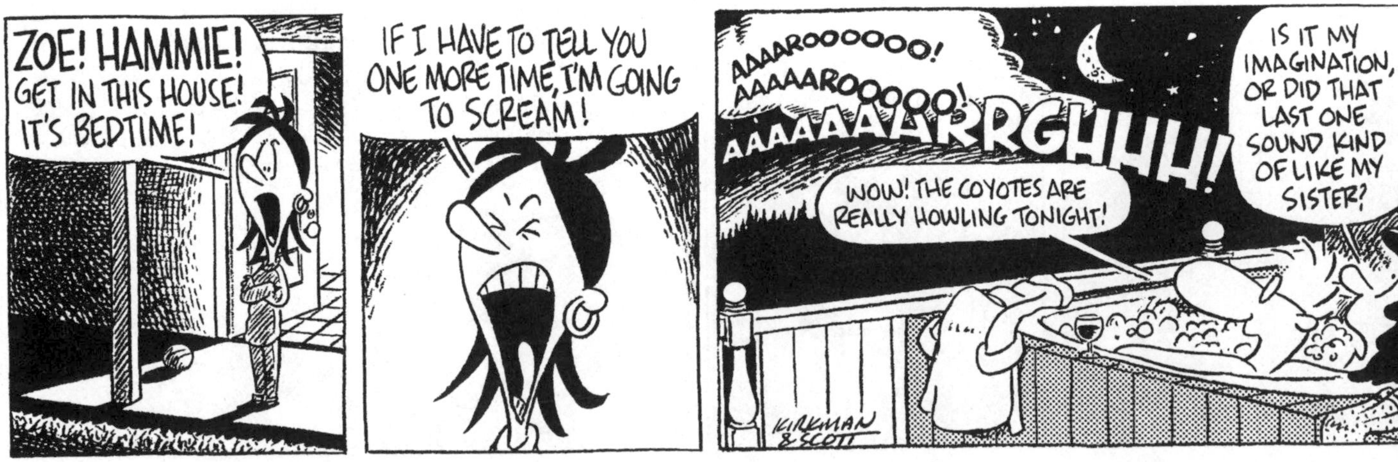
ZOE! HAMMIE! GET IN THIS HOUSE! IT'S BEDTIME!
IF I HAVE TO TELL YOU ONE MORE TIME, I'M GOING TO SCREAM!
AAAAROOOOOOO!
AAAAAROOOOOO!
AAAAAAAARRGHHHH!
IS IT MY IMAGINATION, OR DID THAT LAST ONE SOUND KIND OF LIKE MY SISTER?
WOW! THE COYOTES ARE REALLY HOWLING TONIGHT!
KIRKMAN & SCOTT

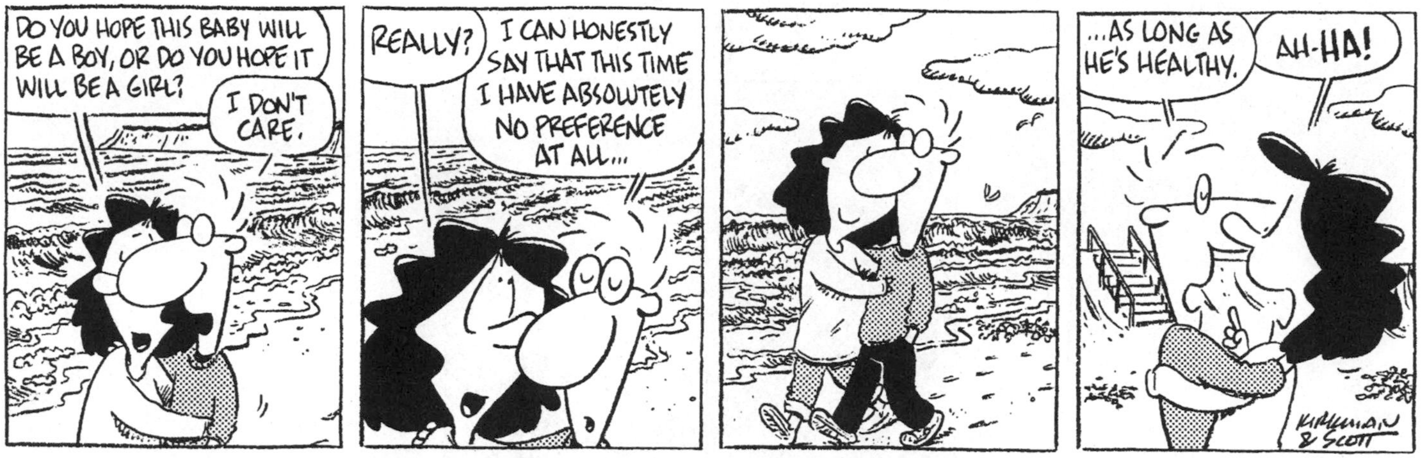
DO YOU HOPE THIS BABY WILL BE A BOY, OR DO YOU HOPE IT WILL BE A GIRL?
I DON'T CARE.
REALLY?
I CAN HONESTLY SAY THAT THIS TIME I HAVE ABSOLUTELY NO PREFERENCE AT ALL...
...AS LONG AS HE'S HEALTHY.
AH-HA!
KIRKMAN & SCOTT

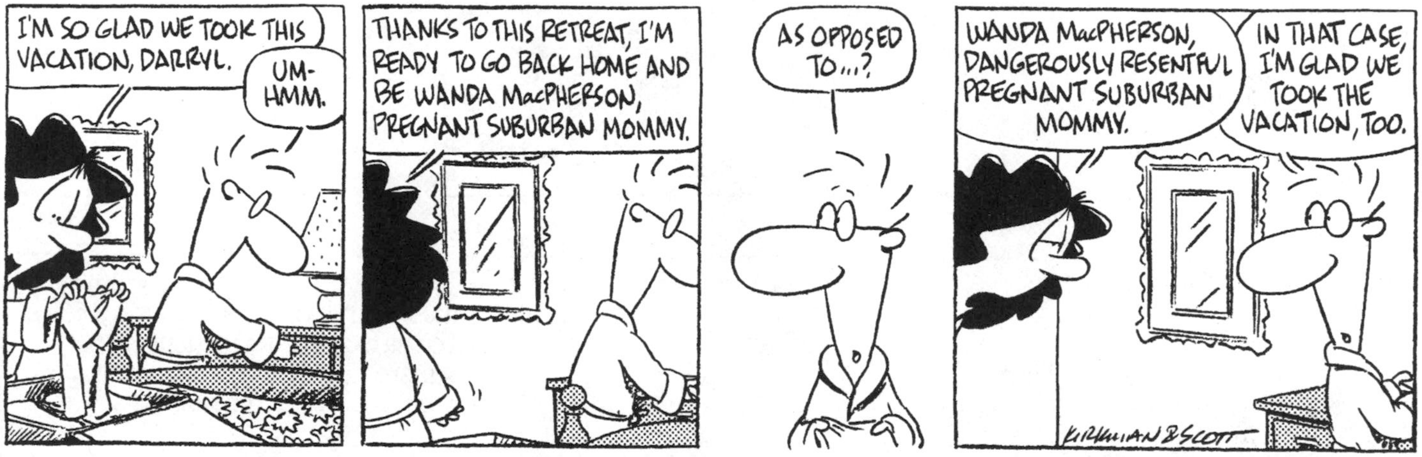
I'M SO GLAD WE TOOK THIS VACATION, DARRYL.
UM-HMM.
THANKS TO THIS RETREAT, I'M READY TO GO BACK HOME AND BE WANDA MacPHERSON, PREGNANT SUBURBAN MOMMY.
AS OPPOSED TO...?
WANDA MacPHERSON, DANGEROUSLY RESENTFUL PREGNANT SUBURBAN MOMMY.
IN THAT CASE, I'M GLAD WE TOOK THE VACATION, TOO.
KIRKMAN & SCOTT

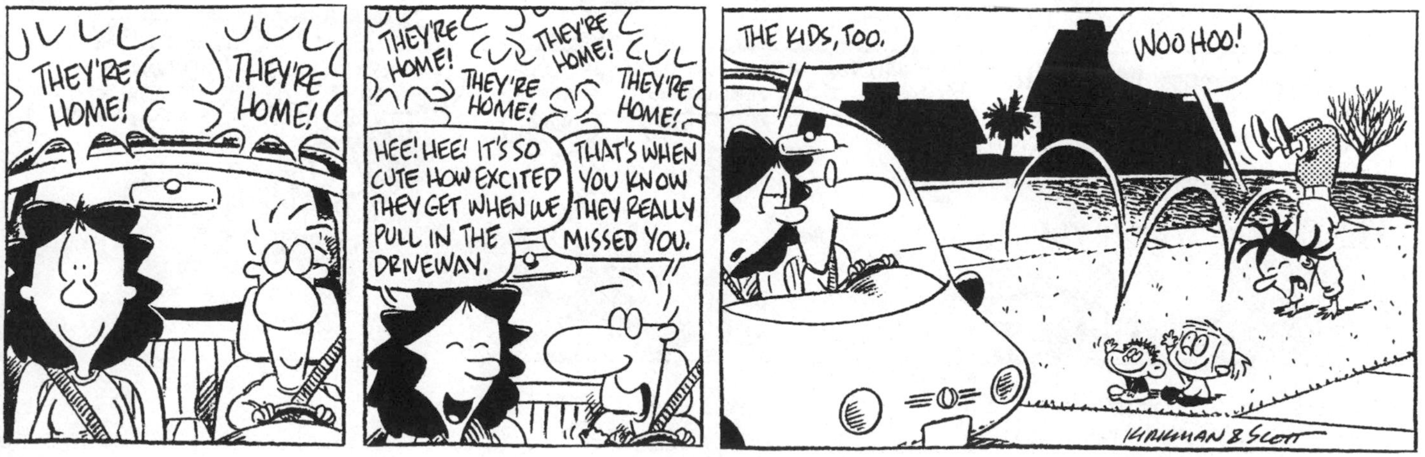
THEY'RE HOME!
THEY'RE HOME!
THEY'RE HOME!
THEY'RE HOME!
THEY'RE HOME!
THEY'RE HOME!
HEE! HEE! IT'S SO CUTE HOW EXCITED THEY GET WHEN WE PULL IN THE DRIVEWAY.
THAT'S WHEN YOU KNOW THEY REALLY MISSED YOU.
THE KIDS, TOO.
WOO HOO!
KIRKMAN & SCOTT

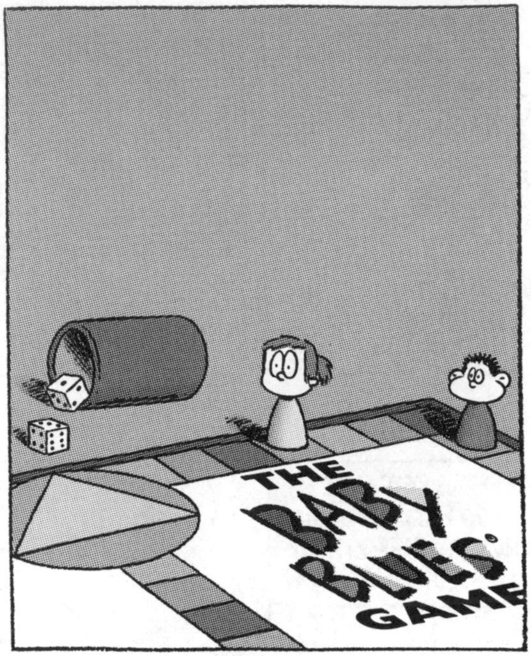
THE BABY BLUES GAME

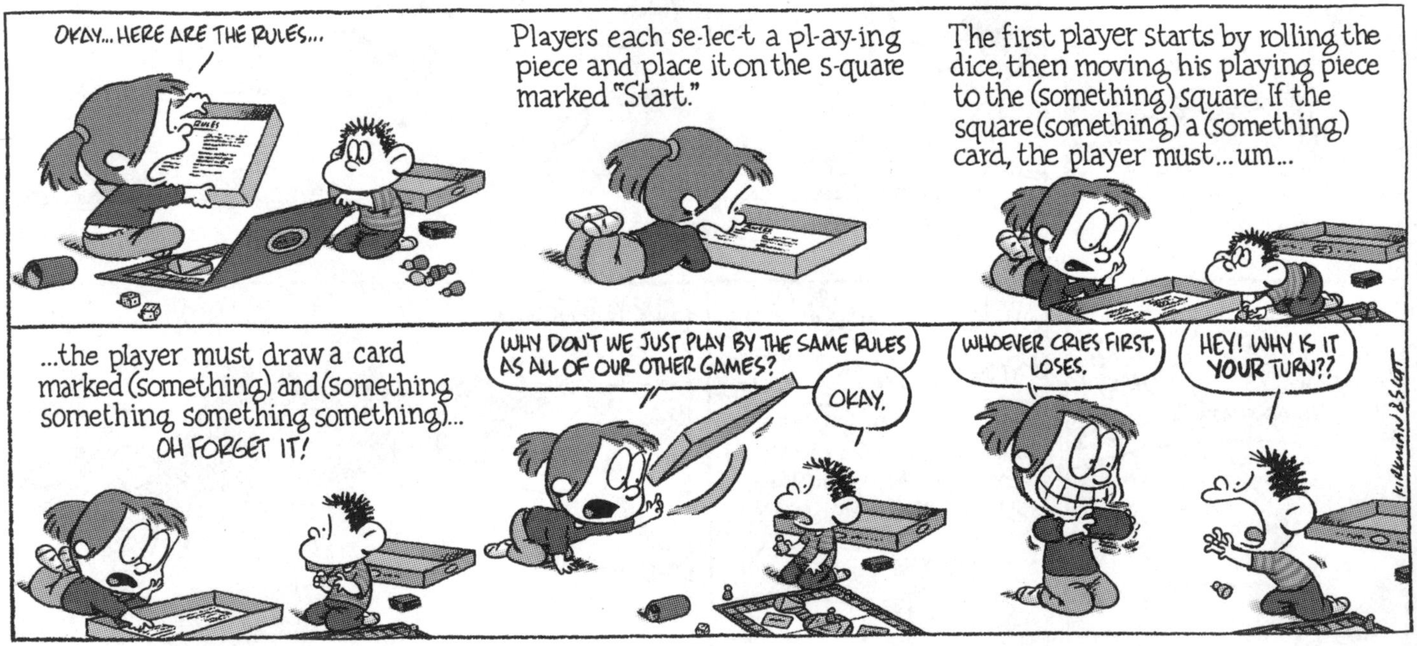
OKAY... HERE ARE THE RULES...
Players each se-lec-t a pl-ay-ing piece and place it on the s-quare marked "Start."
The first player starts by rolling the dice, then moving his playing piece to the (something) square. If the square (something) a (something) card, the player must... um...
...the player must draw a card marked (something) and (something something something something)...
OH FORGET IT!
WHY DON'T WE JUST PLAY BY THE SAME RULES AS ALL OF OUR OTHER GAMES?
OKAY.
WHOEVER CRIES FIRST, LOSES.
HEY! WHY IS IT YOUR TURN??

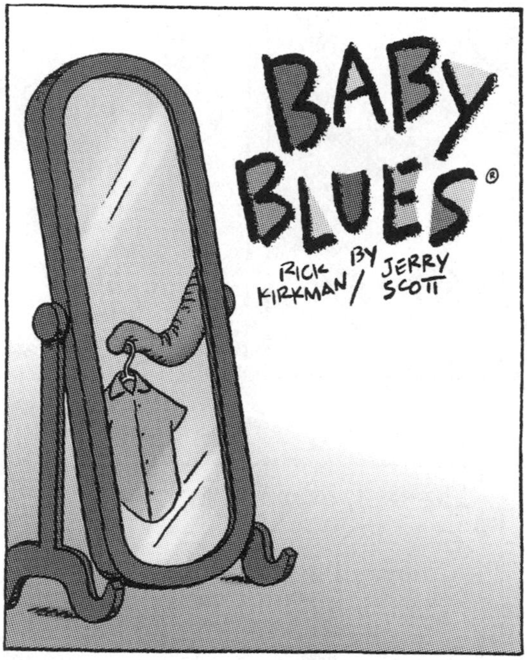
BABY BLUES®
BY RICK KIRKMAN / JERRY SCOTT

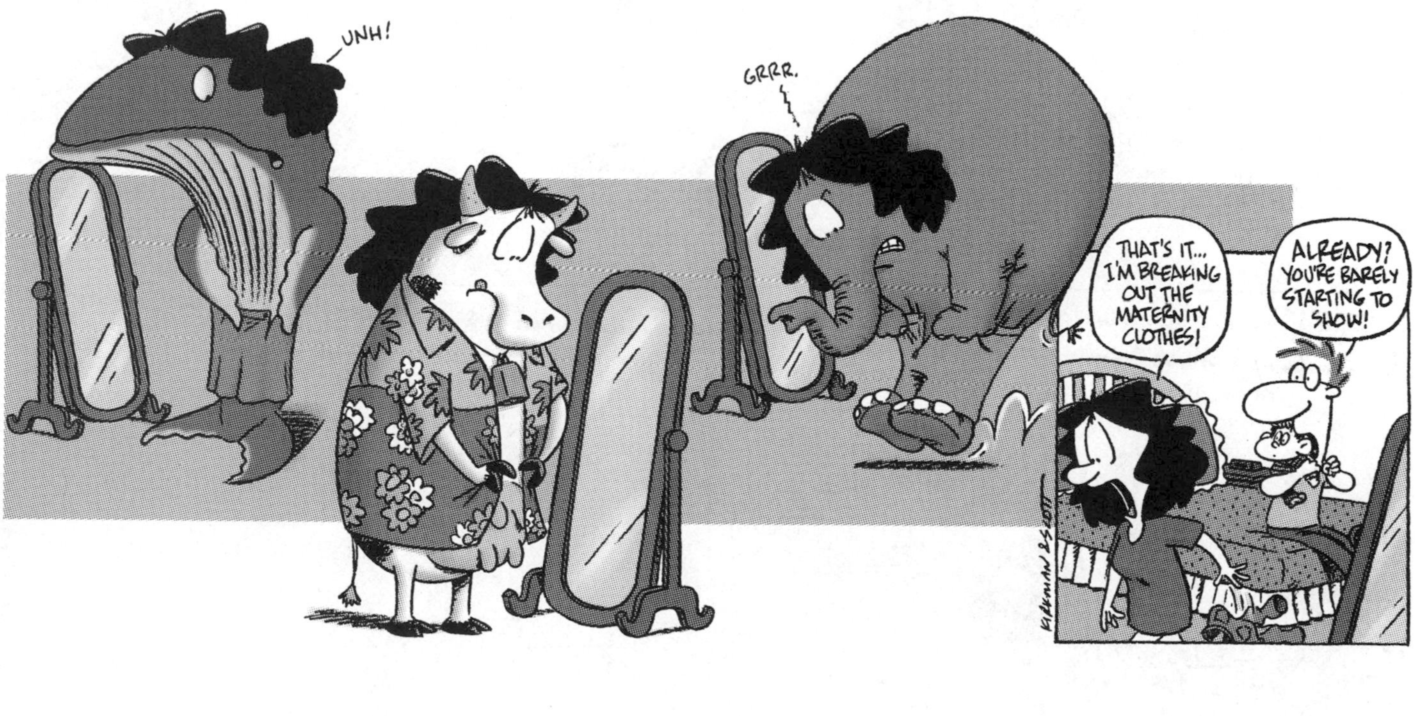
UNH!
GRRR.
THAT'S IT... I'M BREAKING OUT THE MATERNITY CLOTHES!
ALREADY? YOU'RE BARELY STARTING TO SHOW!
KIRKMAN & SCOTT

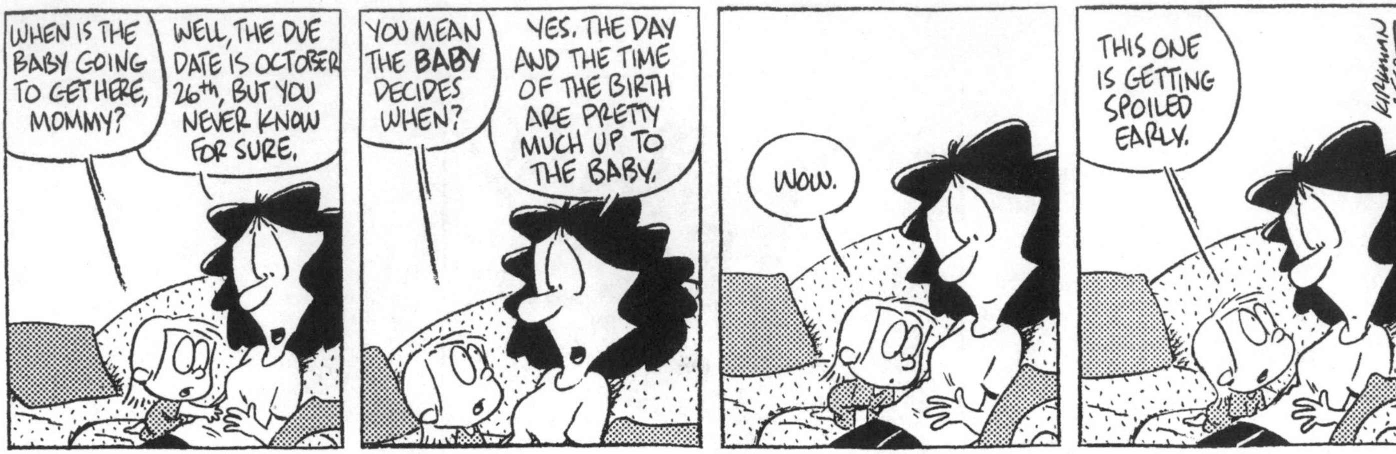
WHEN IS THE BABY GOING TO GET HERE, MOMMY?
WELL, THE DUE DATE IS OCTOBER 26th, BUT YOU NEVER KNOW FOR SURE.
YOU MEAN THE BABY DECIDES WHEN?
YES. THE DAY AND THE TIME OF THE BIRTH ARE PRETTY MUCH UP TO THE BABY.
WOW.
THIS ONE IS GETTING SPOILED EARLY.
KIRKMAN & SCOTT

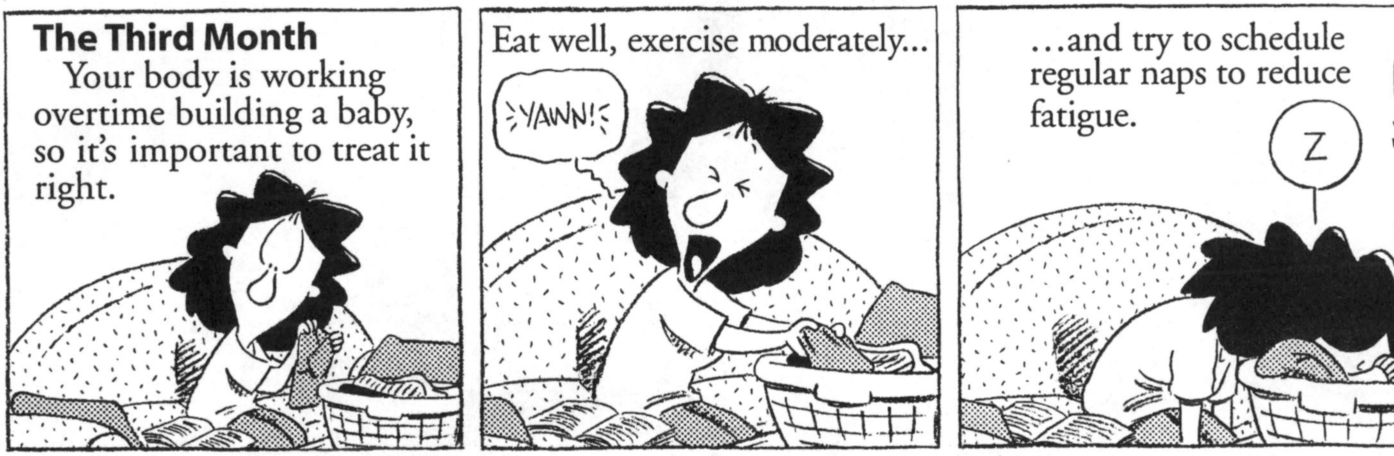
The Third Month
Your body is working overtime building a baby, so it's important to treat it right.
Eat well, exercise moderately...
YAWN!
...and try to schedule regular naps to reduce fatigue.
Z
KIRKMAN & SCOTT

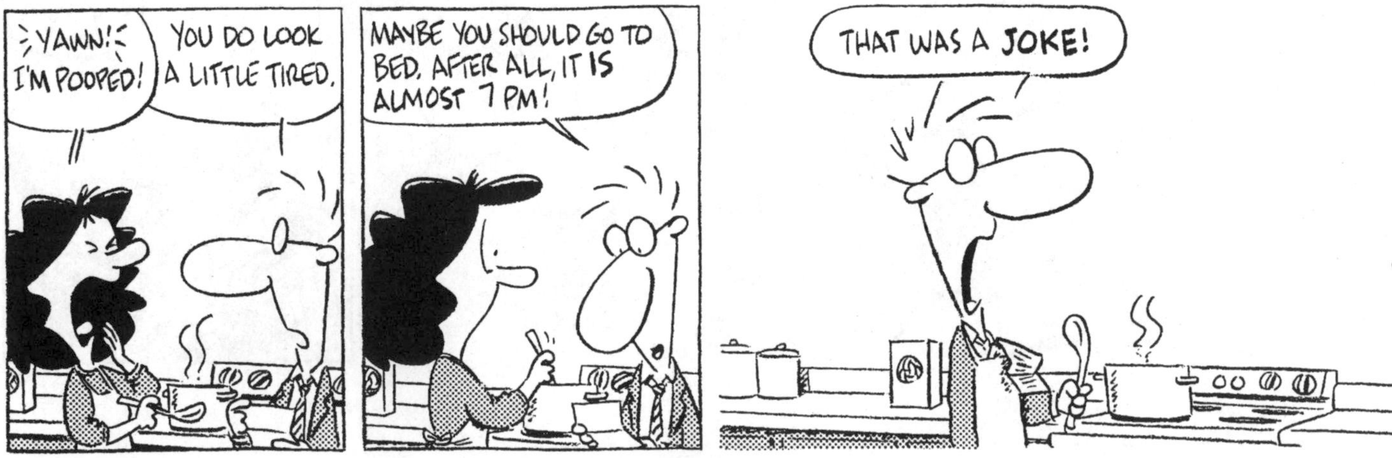
YAWN! I'M POOPED!
YOU DO LOOK A LITTLE TIRED.
MAYBE YOU SHOULD GO TO BED. AFTER ALL, IT IS ALMOST 7 PM!
THAT WAS A JOKE!
KIRKMAN & SCOTT

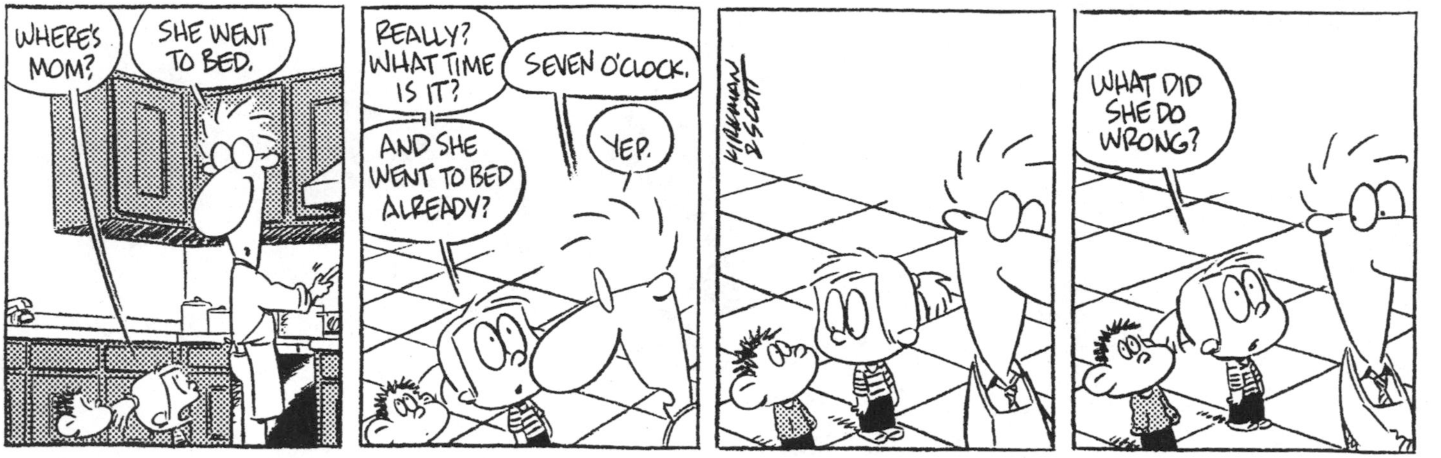
WHERE'S MOM?
SHE WENT TO BED.
REALLY? WHAT TIME IS IT?
SEVEN O'CLOCK.
AND SHE WENT TO BED ALREADY?
YEP.
KIRKMAN & SCOTT
WHAT DID SHE DO WRONG?

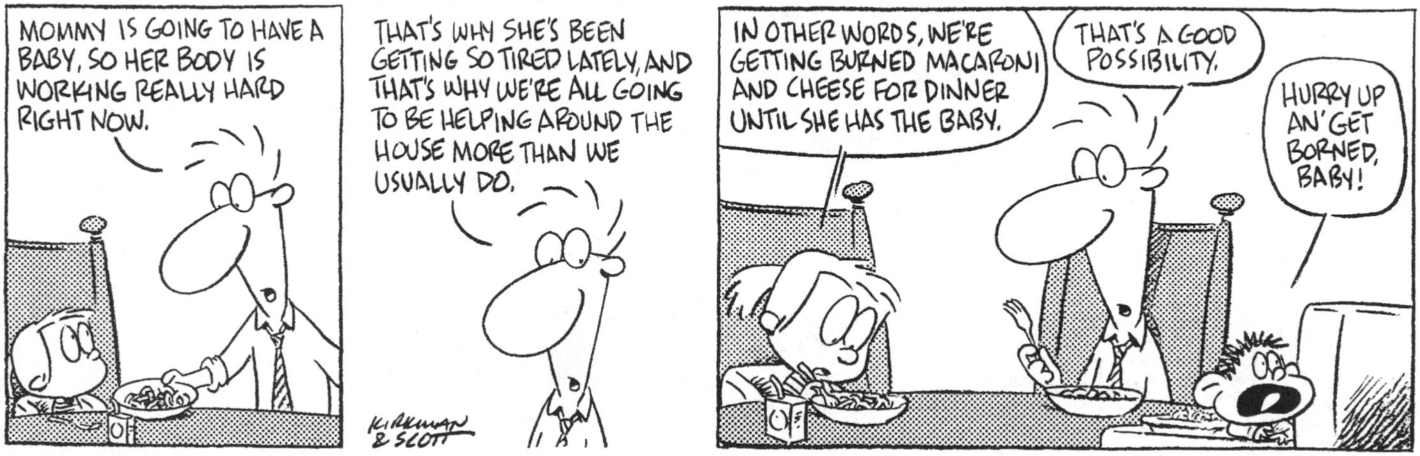
MOMMY IS GOING TO HAVE A BABY, SO HER BODY IS WORKING REALLY HARD RIGHT NOW.
THAT'S WHY SHE'S BEEN GETTING SO TIRED LATELY, AND THAT'S WHY WE'RE ALL GOING TO BE HELPING AROUND THE HOUSE MORE THAN WE USUALLY DO.
KIRKMAN & SCOTT
IN OTHER WORDS, WE'RE GETTING BURNED MACARONI AND CHEESE FOR DINNER UNTIL SHE HAS THE BABY.
THAT'S A GOOD POSSIBILITY.
HURRY UP AN' GET BORNED, BABY!

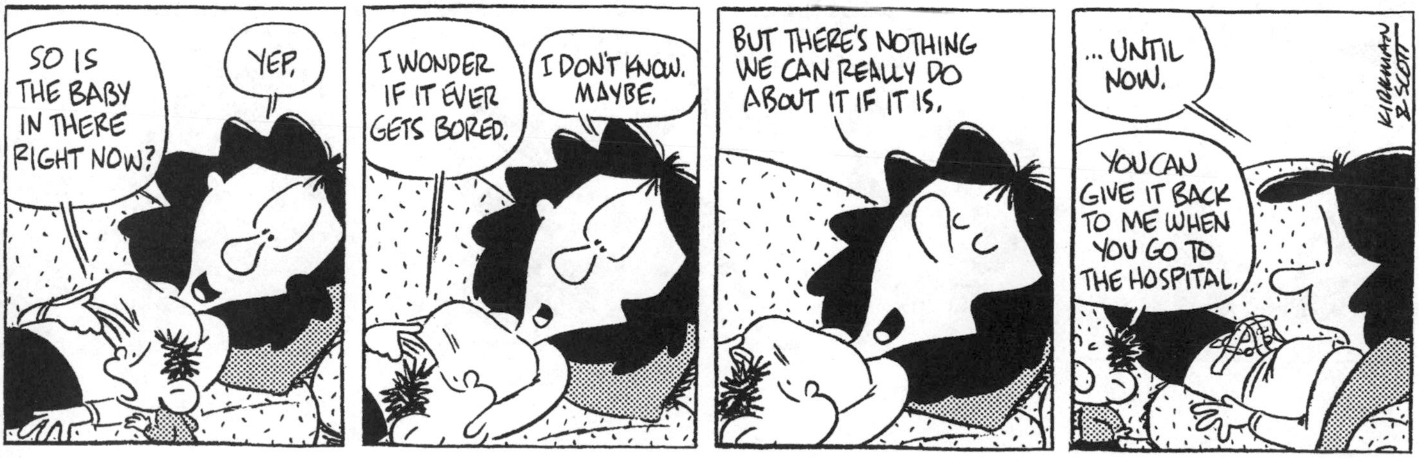
SO IS THE BABY IN THERE RIGHT NOW?
YEP.
I WONDER IF IT EVER GETS BORED.
I DON'T KNOW. MAYBE.
BUT THERE'S NOTHING WE CAN REALLY DO ABOUT IT IF IT IS.
... UNTIL NOW.
YOU CAN GIVE IT BACK TO ME WHEN YOU GO TO THE HOSPITAL.
KIRKMAN & SCOTT

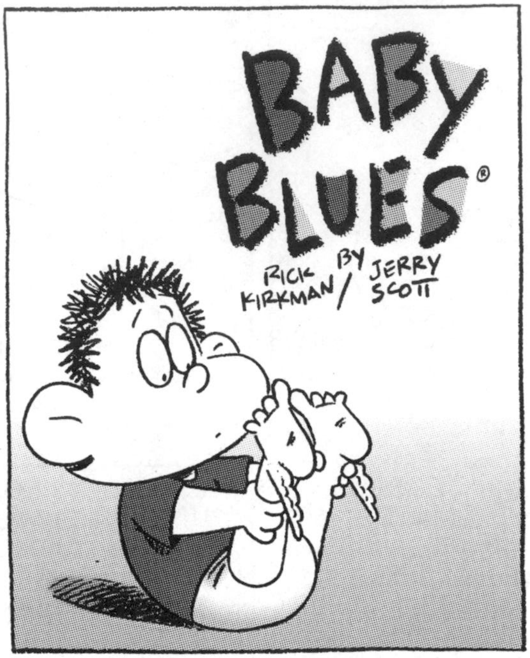
BABY BLUES®
BY RICK KIRKMAN / JERRY SCOTT

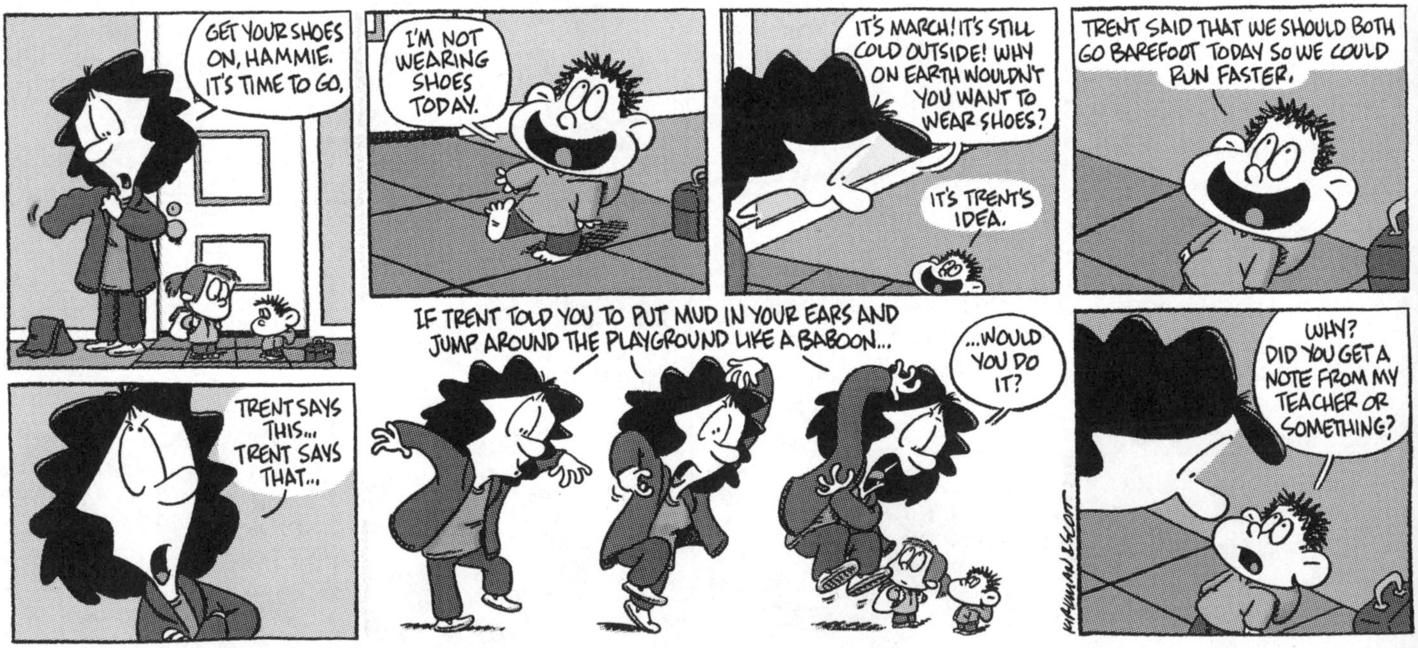
GET YOUR SHOES ON, HAMMIE. IT'S TIME TO GO.
I'M NOT WEARING SHOES TODAY.
IT'S MARCH! IT'S STILL COLD OUTSIDE! WHY ON EARTH WOULDN'T YOU WANT TO WEAR SHOES?
IT'S TRENT'S IDEA.
TRENT SAID THAT WE SHOULD BOTH GO BAREFOOT TODAY SO WE COULD RUN FASTER.
TRENT SAYS THIS... TRENT SAYS THAT...
IF TRENT TOLD YOU TO PUT MUD IN YOUR EARS AND JUMP AROUND THE PLAYGROUND LIKE A BABOON...
...WOULD YOU DO IT?
WHY? DID YOU GET A NOTE FROM MY TEACHER OR SOMETHING?
KIRKMAN & SCOTT

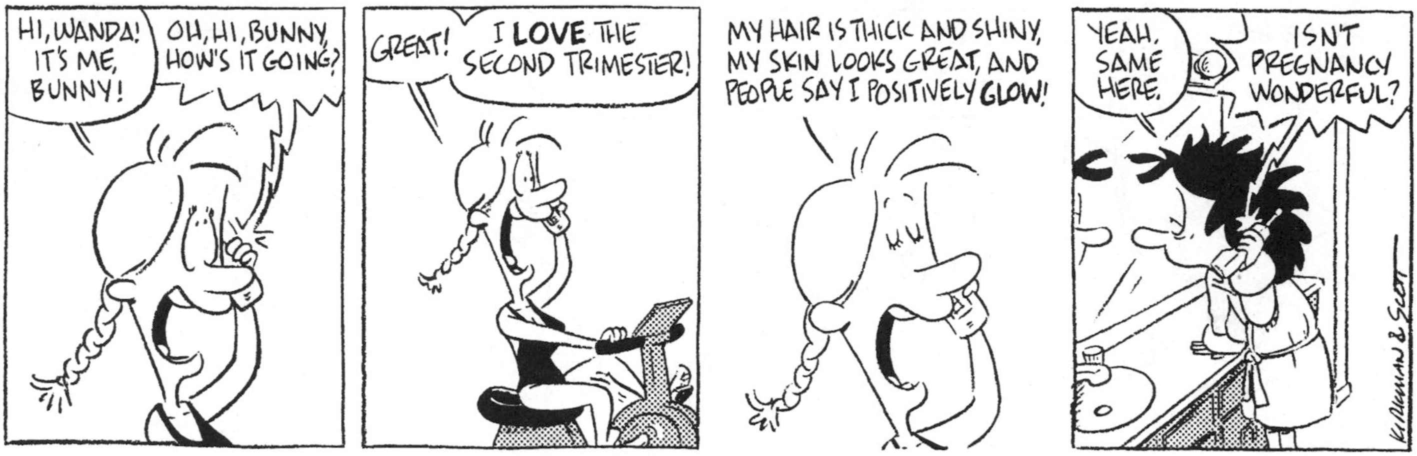
HI, WANDA! IT'S ME, BUNNY!
OH, HI, BUNNY, HOW'S IT GOING?
GREAT!
I LOVE THE SECOND TRIMESTER!
MY HAIR IS THICK AND SHINY, MY SKIN LOOKS GREAT, AND PEOPLE SAY I POSITIVELY GLOW!
YEAH, SAME HERE.
ISN'T PREGNANCY WONDERFUL?
KIRKMAN & SCOTT

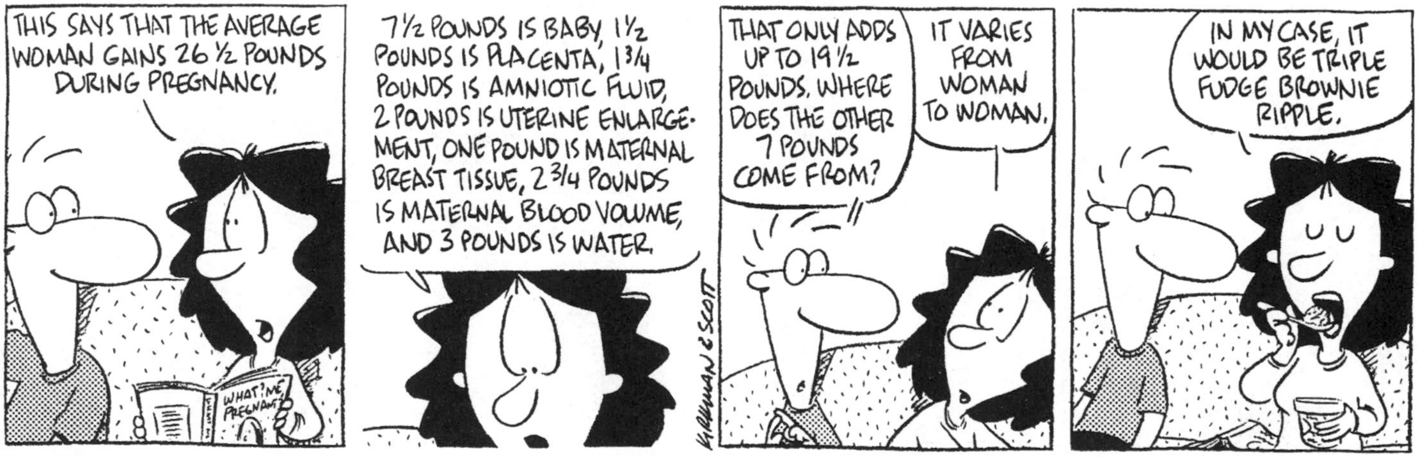
THIS SAYS THAT THE AVERAGE WOMAN GAINS 26 ½ POUNDS DURING PREGNANCY.
WHAT? ME PREGNANT?
7½ POUNDS IS BABY, 1½ POUNDS IS PLACENTA, 1¾ POUNDS IS AMNIOTIC FLUID, 2 POUNDS IS UTERINE ENLARGEMENT, ONE POUND IS MATERNAL BREAST TISSUE, 2¾ POUNDS IS MATERNAL BLOOD VOLUME, AND 3 POUNDS IS WATER.
KIRKMAN & SCOTT
THAT ONLY ADDS UP TO 19 ½ POUNDS. WHERE DOES THE OTHER 7 POUNDS COME FROM?
IT VARIES FROM WOMAN TO WOMAN.
IN MY CASE, IT WOULD BE TRIPLE FUDGE BROWNIE RIPPLE.

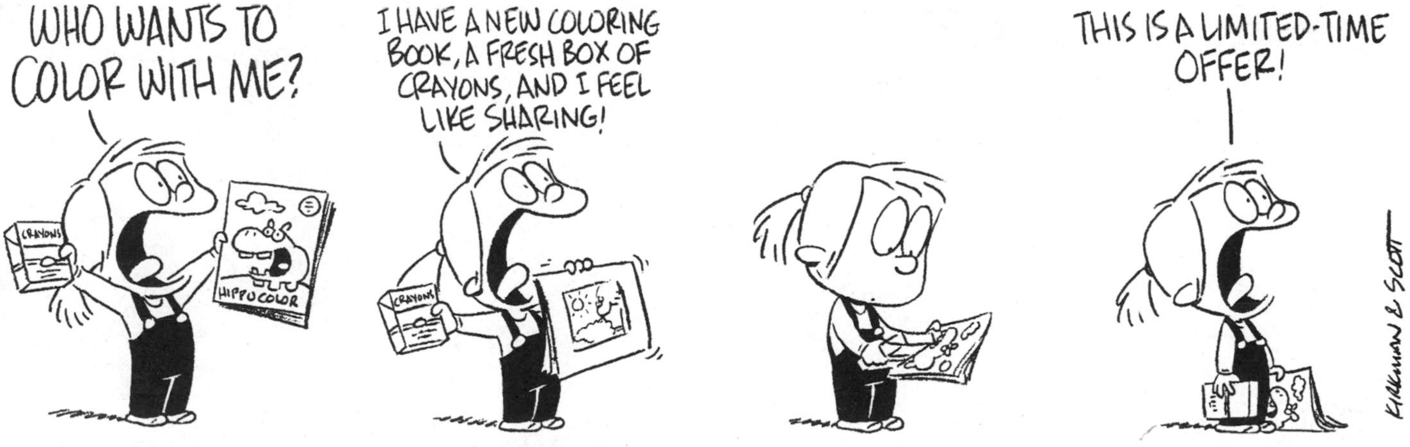
WHO WANTS TO COLOR WITH ME?
CRAYONS
HIPPO COLOR
I HAVE A NEW COLORING BOOK, A FRESH BOX OF CRAYONS, AND I FEEL LIKE SHARING!
CRAYONS
THIS IS A LIMITED-TIME OFFER!
KIRKMAN & SCOTT

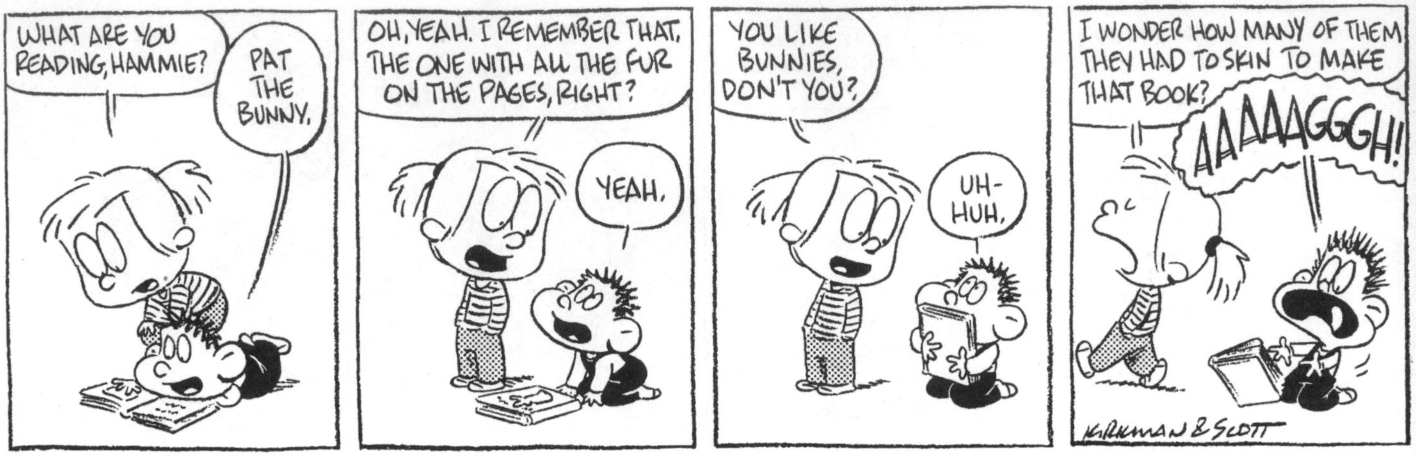
WHAT ARE YOU READING, HAMMIE?
PAT THE BUNNY.
OH, YEAH. I REMEMBER THAT. THE ONE WITH ALL THE FUR ON THE PAGES, RIGHT?
YEAH.
YOU LIKE BUNNIES, DON'T YOU?
UH-HUH.
I WONDER HOW MANY OF THEM THEY HAD TO SKIN TO MAKE THAT BOOK?
AAAAAGGGH!
KIRKMAN & SCOTT

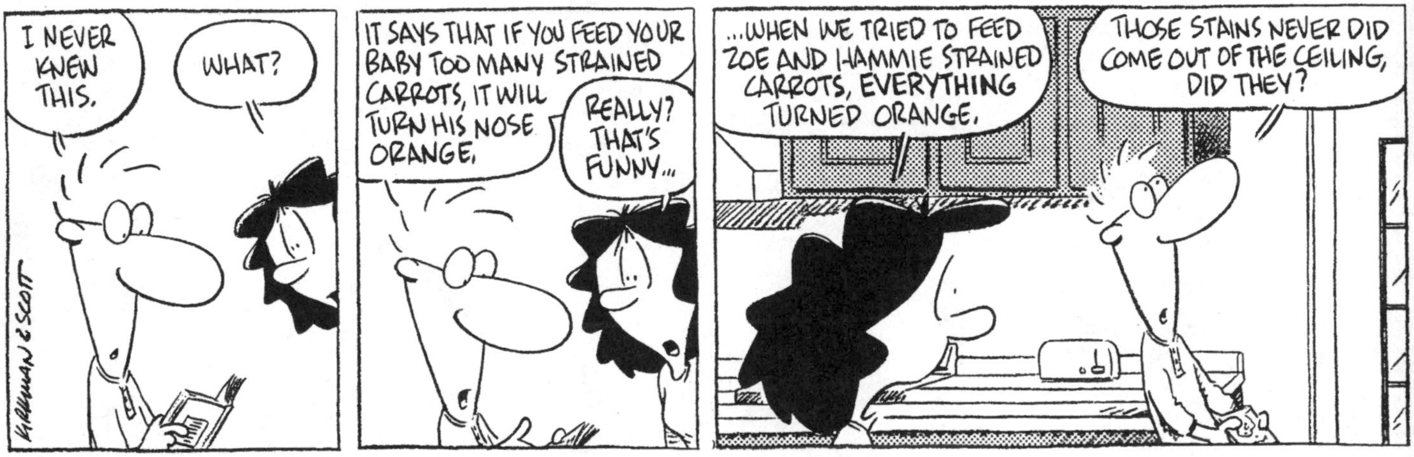
I NEVER KNEW THIS.
WHAT?
KIRKMAN & SCOTT
IT SAYS THAT IF YOU FEED YOUR BABY TOO MANY STRAINED CARROTS, IT WILL TURN HIS NOSE ORANGE.
REALLY? THAT'S FUNNY...
...WHEN WE TRIED TO FEED ZOE AND HAMMIE STRAINED CARROTS, EVERYTHING TURNED ORANGE.
THOSE STAINS NEVER DID COME OUT OF THE CEILING, DID THEY?

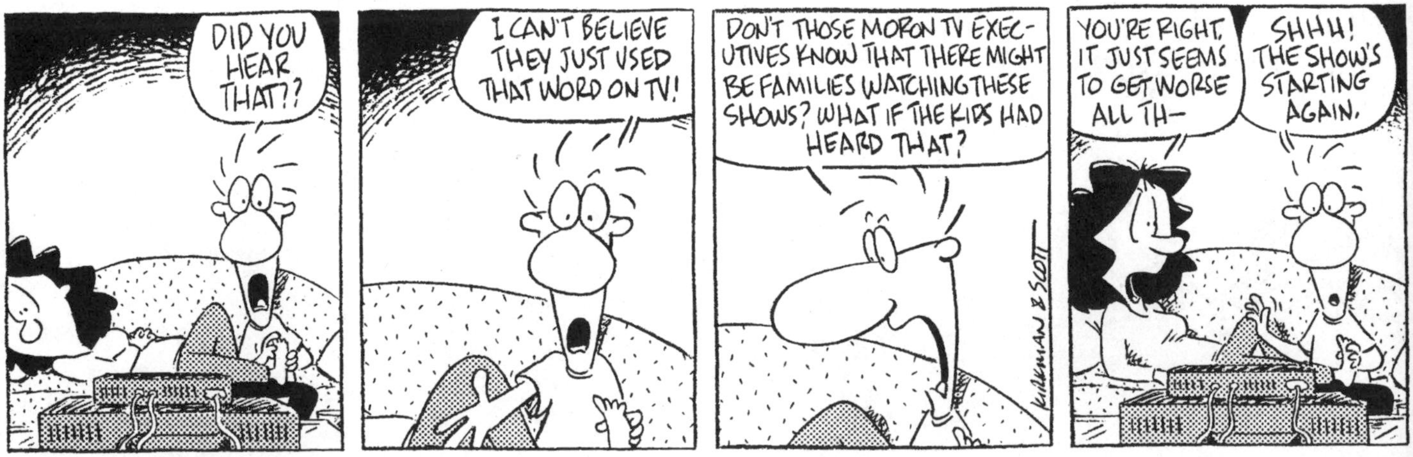
DID YOU HEAR THAT??
I CAN'T BELIEVE THEY JUST USED THAT WORD ON TV!
DON'T THOSE MORON TV EXECUTIVES KNOW THAT THERE MIGHT BE FAMILIES WATCHING THESE SHOWS? WHAT IF THE KIDS HAD HEARD THAT?
KIRKMAN & SCOTT
YOU'RE RIGHT. IT JUST SEEMS TO GET WORSE ALL TH—
SHHH! THE SHOW'S STARTING AGAIN.

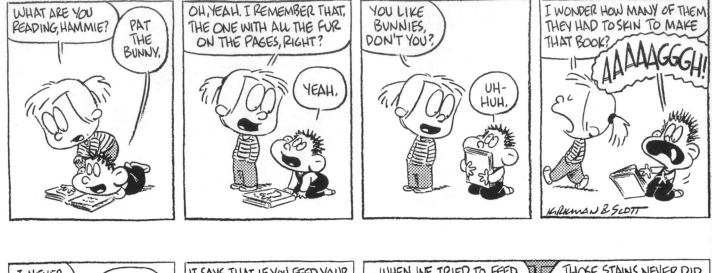